I0592275

Thomas Ellwood, Joseph Wyeth

The history of the life of Thomas Ellwood

Or, an account of his birth, education. With divers observations on his life and manners when a youth: and how he came to be convinced of the truth; with his many sufferings and services for the same. Third Edition

Thomas Ellwood, Joseph Wyeth

The history of the life of Thomas Ellwood
Or, an account of his birth, education. With divers observations on his life and manners when a youth: and how he came to be convinced of the truth; with his many sufferings and services for the same. Third Edition

ISBN/EAN: 9783337775254

Printed in Europe, USA, Canada, Australia, Japan

Cover: Foto ©ninafisch / pixelio.de

THE HISTORY OF THE LIFE OF Thomas Ellwood:

OR,

An Account of his BIRTH, EDUCATION, &c. with divers Obſervations on his Life and Manners when a Youth: And how he came to be convinced of the TRUTH; with his many Sufferings and Services for the ſame.

ALSO,

Several other remarkable Paſſages and Occurrences.

Written by his own Hand.

To which is added,

A SUPPLEMENT by *J. W.*

Heb, xi. 2. *By Faith the Elders obtained a good Report.*

The THIRD EDITION.

LONDON:

Printed and Sold by LUKE HINDE, at the Bible in *George-yard*, *Lombard-ſtreet*, 1765.

THE

PREFACE.

Gather up the Fragments that remain, that nothing be lost; John 6. 12. was the Direction of our Saviour to His Disciples, after He had fed the Multitude. Which may well and usefully be applied, to the collecting and preserving the Accounts of the *Lives of good Men*: Men, who in their Day have been eminently useful in those Stations of Life wherein God, by His good Providence, hath placed them. And this preserving, by Publication, is the rather to be done, when themselves do leave behind them, in writing, an Account of their Lives, and of the signal Mercies of God to them therein: For from such Accounts may best be gathered, by the Reader, the Man's particular State, Exercise and Growth in the Work of Restoration, out of the Fall and Degeneracy; and, in the reading thereof, be not only excited to bless the Name of the Lord, on his Behalf, but also gain some Direction from the Path so fairly tract out, and Ground of *Hope*; that by being *faithful*, they may likewise attain to the same good *Experience*.

There is not with me any Doubt, but something of this kind may be the Lot of many, into whose Hands this *Treatise* may happen to come; for that they will herein meet with Variety of *Exercises*, and the *Providences* of God therein, all related with great Strength and Plainness of Speech: Our deceased Friend *Thomas Ellwood*, having been a Man whom God had endued with *singular Abilities*, both as a Man, and as a *Christian*; which is evident, not

not only from this ſhort Account of his *Life*, which was written by himſelf, and by the *Supplement* added hereunto; but more largely from his many uſeful Labours and Services in the many Books which he writ in the Defence of *Truth*, and the *Friends* thereof: For which *Service*, he was in a particular manner qualified by *ſpiritual Wiſdom* and *Chriſtian Obedience*; to which, in him, was added great Strength and Depth of *Judgment*, wherein he could diſcern the Spirits of others, and was very much the Maſter of his own, as did appear to ſuch who knew him, not only by the Soundneſs of his *Reaſoning*, and the Seaſonableneſs of his *Words*; but alſo by his great and exemplary *Modeſty*, in that he was not haſty to propoſe, nor rudely tenacious to inſiſt on what he had propoſed, if any thing, though not well expreſt, yet well intended, was offered by any one much weaker, nay, though but by a *Babe* in *Christ*.

His *Countenance* was manly and chearful; his *Deportment* grave, yet affable and courteous, even to the meanest Person; his Conversation innocent, pleasant and instructive, yet severe against any thing that was beyond the Liberty of *Truth*. These, with his other Qualifications of *Body* and *Mind*, did render him both very acceptable and very useful, as a *Friend*, as a *Neighbour*, and as a *Member* and *Elder* in the *Church of Christ*; and the more, for that his Time was chiefly imployed in being serviceable in one or other of these *Capacities*.

I might here particularly mention the several *Labours* of our *deceased Friend*, according to their respective Times, and the Nature of their several Subjects; but much of this being already done in the ensuing

ensuing Pages, I chuse to remit the *Reader* thither; by which possibly he may be excited to the Perusal of them, and shall only say concerning them, *That the judicious Reader will easily observe, that his Method and Stile do denote him to have been a Scholar: And yet not farther so, than the Simplicity and Purity of the* Truth, *whereof he made Profession, would permit him.*

I was with our Friend *Thomas Ellwood* the greater Part of his *Sickness*: In which he was also very frequently visited by our Friend *George Bowles*, who was his Neighbour; to whom therefore I refer, for the Account which he may give of his *Sickness* and *dying Words*.

As it was my good Lot to be well acquainted with him (though only in the latter Years of his Life) and know that he did neither use nor encourage the bestowing elaborate

Encomiums upon Perſons deceaſed: So neither ſhall I add further concerning him, than to ſay with the *Apoſtle* concerning the Faithful,
Heb. 11. 4. *That he was righteous, God teſtifying of his Gifts; and by it being dead, yet ſpeaketh.*

London, the 12th of the ſecond Month, 1714.

J. W.

George

George Bowles *his* TESTIMONY *concerning* THOMAS ELLWOOD.

Dear Friends,

IT *is in my Heart briefly, on this Occasion, to commemorate the* tender Dealings *of the Lord with His People in this latter Age of the World, when it hath pleased Him, in Love to poor lost Man, graciously to appear, by the breaking forth of His* glorious Gospel-day. *And by the secret divine Reaches of the Hand of God, which hath been felt and seen in the Light of it, many have been drawn in their Spirits to seek after the Lord, and to enquire after the Knowledge of the Way of* Life *and* Salvation; *and blessed be His holy Name, who was graciously pleased, by the Inshinings of this* divine Light *in the Hearts of many, to expel the* Darkness *and rend the* Vail. *And then was the Arm of His mighty Power made bare, for the gathering many Thousands to the saving* Knowledge of Himself. *And in that Day was the Lord pleased, according to His Promise, to* pour forth of His Spirit upon Sons and upon Daughters; *yea, upon* Servants *and upon* Handmaids, *and many were made to prophesy; and being qualified by the holy Spirit which they received, and were baptized by it into His Name, became willing, and were freely given up in Obedience to the Lord, and in Bowels of tender Love to the Souls of Mankind, in His Power to preach the Gospel of Life and Salvation to those to whom they were sent, and many were*

turned

turned from Darkneſs to Light, and from the Power of Satan unto God, *by their Miniſtry: Amongſt whom our dear deceaſed Friend and Brother*, THOMAS ELLWOOD, *was one, whoſe Conſcience was reached and awakened by the powerful Miniſtry of dear* Edward Burrough, *as I have heard him relate (and as by the following Sheets will more plainly appear.) And of that Day and Time, and the worthy Inſtrument by whoſe Miniſtry he was convinced, and turned unto God, and made ſenſible of the* divine Principle *of* Life *and Light in his own Heart, have I heard him ſpeak with great Regard; and alſo of the Sufferings which did attend him, after he received the* Truth, *in his Father's Family, for the* Truth's *Sake; and how the Lord preſerved him in that Time, under the various Exerciſes which he paſſed through for* Truth's *Teſtimony; which for Chriſt's Sake he was conſcientiouſly concerned to ſtand in, according to that Plainneſs and Simplicity which* Truth *then led, and ſtill continues to lead the ſincere Diſciples of Chriſt into, by which they were diſtinguiſhed from the World; and, for the Sake thereof, they were deſpiſed of Men, and hated of the World. Such was the plain Language of* Thou *to one, and refuſing the* Hat-Honour; *for which, dear* T. Ellwood *ſuffered not a little in that Day, as, by the following Account of his Life more fully appears. And it were well if all, who come up in a Profeſſion of the bleſſed* Truth *in this Time, were faithful in theſe, and in the other Branches of its Teſtimony. And let all conſider, that the neglecting thereof, is, in a Degree, a making void the Sufferings of the*

Faithful

Faithful (and ſtrengthening the Hands of evil Doers) who for the Sake of their Teſtimony, loved not their Lives to the Death; *but underwent cruel* Mockings, Buffetings, Stonings, Whippings, Stockings, Revilings, Impriſonments, *and* Spoiling of Goods; *rejoicing in the Lord, that they were counted worthy to ſuffer, either leſs or more, for His Name Sake. In reſpect of which, this my dear* Friend *was a good Example, he being a Man of a ſteady* Mind, *and very patient in* Suffering, *as well as faithful in his Teſtimony for* Truth, *and took joyfully the Spoiling of his* Goods, *wherein he was tried but a few Years before his Death. He was often concerned in Defence of* Truth's *Teſtimony, both againſt our profeſſed* Adverſaries, *and alſo againſt the* libertine Spirit *which appeared in ſome, profeſſing the ſame* Truth *with us, who oppoſed themſelves againſt that good Order and Diſcipline which the* Truth *led* Friends *into. All which will abundantly appear from the Books themſelves, which are in print, which he writ upon* various Occaſions, *and upon* divers Subjects; *and let not his great Labour and Induſtry be forgotten, in his writing thoſe Two Hiſtorical Volumes, relating to the* Old *and* New Teſtament: *A Work truly great, and is, and may be of great Uſe and Service. By all which his many Labours, it may be perceived by the wary and inlightned* Reader, *that the Lord had endowed him with an excellent Gift, and qualified him for the Service of* Truth, *His* Church *and* People; *in which he imployed the Talent which the bountiful Lord had given him, to the Honour of the great Giver, and to the Com-*

fort

fort and Edification of the Churh of Chriſt: But more eſpecially were his Services known to the Brethren *in this County of* Bucks; *moſt of which are fallen aſleep, and but few remaining here, who knew him in his Beginning, or his firſt Services for the Lord, His Church and People; amongſt whom he was a zealous Aſſerter of that excellent Diſcipline the Lord had opened in, and led His People to, for the preſerving His Church as a Garden encloſed: For which Cauſe, how did many of thoſe* Libertines *ſet themſelves fiercely againſt him, and ſhot their Arrows at him; but the Lord defended him, and covered his Head in the* Day of Battle, and his Bow abode in Strength, and his Bough ſpread over the Wall, and continued freſh and green: *But a Blaſt from the Lord came upon their evil Work; and how have they melted away? And how is their Strength failed, and their Work brought to naught? But the Bleſſing of the Lord is with His People, even with the Faithful, to this Day, whom He hath preſerved as a peculiar Treaſure to Himſelf: Bleſſed be His holy Name for evermore. And furthermore, it may be truly ſaid of this our dear Friend, that as the Lord fitted him for His Service, ſo was he eminently ſerviceable in His Hand, in the Church of Chriſt; particularly in theſe Parts, of which there are many living Witneſſes, in this and the adjacent Counties, of his great Labour of Love, having ſerved the Church freely, with great Diligence and Faithfulneſs: The true Senſe of which, toucheth me and others, with the deeper Senſe of the great Loſs the Church hath by his Removal; but being alſo ſenſible through the*

the Lord's Goodneſs, that our Loſs *is his* eternal Gain, *I feel in my Heart an humble Submiſſion to the Will of Him, who doth whatſoever pleaſeth Him, both in Heaven and in Earth; and who ſhall ſay unto him,* What doeſt Thou? *And it is the tender Breathing of my Spirit to the God and Father of our Lord Jeſus Chriſt, that He would be graciouſly pleaſed, in Pity and Compaſſion to His poor People, to raiſe up, fit and furniſh more faithful Servants for His Work and Service, and make them zealous for His Name and Truth upon the Earth, that the Place of this my* dear Friend, *and other faithful Servants of the Lord and His People, of late removed from amongſt us in theſe Parts, may be ſupplied; and that the Spouſe of Chriſt may, amidſt all her Tribulations, Afflictions and ſore Exerciſes, be made to praiſe the Lord, and bleſs His holy Name, who taketh away one, and raiſeth up another, and bleſſeth His Children with His Goodneſs, according to His Promiſe made of old by the holy Prophet,* Iſa. xliv. ver. 3. *ſaying,* I will pour my Spirit upon thy Seed, and my Bleſſing upon thine Off-ſpring. *And thus hath the Lord preſerved* Zion *from Age to Age: And I doubt not, but am fully perſwaded, that He will ſtill bleſs His People, and preſerve* Zion, *and deliver her from all her Enemies.*

And my dear Friends, Brethren, *and* Siſters, *although it be matter of Sorrow to us, to part with our dear* Friends, *eſpecially ſuch as have been made ſerviceable in their Day, and have faithfully ſerved the Lord and His People in their Generation, as it may (I hope without juſt Occaſion of Offence*

Offence to any) be ſaid of dear T. Ellwood, *that he was a Man who ſerved the Lord in* Faithfulneſs, *and His People with* Chearfulneſs, *and his Neighbours with* Uprightneſs *and* Integrity: *And therefore both they and we have the greater Loſs; yet may we not ſorrow unſeaſonably, as thoſe which ſorrow without Hope, but believing that the Lord hath taken him to Himſelf in Mercy (though it may be in Judgment to ſome who were unworthy) let us all learn Reſignation to His bleſſed Will, and ſay with holy* Job, The Lord giveth, and the Lord taketh away: Bleſſed be the Name of the Lord. *And* dear Friends, *I may farther ſignify unto you, that it being my Lot to be with this our dear Friend (of whom I am ſpeaking) almoſt every Day of his laſt Ilneſs, I did obſerve in him, to my great Comfort and Satisfaction, a quiet compoſed Frame of Mind and Spirit, and Reſignation to the Will of God. When I came firſt to him, which was ſoon after I heard of his being taken ill, which was the 24th of the ſecond Month, I found him very much diſabled by the* Diſtemper, *which was thought to be a* Palſy, *that had ſeized him, eſpecially on his right Side, ſo that he could not ſtand alone, nor help himſelf, but a little with his left Hand; and his Speech was alſo very much interrupted, inſomuch that it was with great Difficulty, for the moſt part, that he expreſſed himſelf ſo as to be underſtood: Some Time after I came to him, there being alſo other* Friends *with him, we ſate down together under a weighty Exerciſe of Spirit, waiting upon the Lord in deep Silence, with our Eye to Him; it pleaſed the Lord eminently*

nently to appear amongst us, and to fill our Hearts with the refreshing Streams of His divine Love, and to open the Mouth of one of us in Prayer and Supplication; and the Lord was graciously pleased abundantly to replenish our Spirits, to our mutual Comfort, in a living Sense of divine Goodness; and this our dear Friend, *expressed himself in great Tenderness and Brokenness of Spirit, on this wise,* I am sensibly comforted and refreshed in this Visit. *And that Afternoon, he, fixing his Eyes upon me, with great Earnestness of Spirit expressed, as well as he could at that Time, a great Concern that was upon his Mind for* Truth, *and the* Friends *of it, in divers Particulars; especially, in relation to our own* Monthly *and* Quarterly-meetings, *the* Writings *of both which, had been under his Care for more than forty Years: After which, he was much eased in his Spirit, and so continued to the last, so far as I perceived; often saying, when asked how he did?* I am easy, I am quiet. *And he was often very tender in his Spirit, expressing his Resignation to the Will of God, whether in Life or Death, saying,* If the Lord hath no more Work for me to do, I am content and resigned to His Will; and my hearty Farewel to all my Brethren. *And at another Time, nearer his End, he said to us present, in much Brokenness of Heart,* I am full of Joy and Peace, my Spirit is filled with Joy; *or to this Effect: For by reason that his Speech was so weakned, several Things could not be so well collected, which he at Times spake, in a tender Sense of the Lord's Goodness; the Sense of which* deeply affected some of us who were with him. And my Heart is sorrowfully affected at this Time, in a Sense of the great Loss which the Church of Christ (in these Parts especially) hath by his Removal: But in this I am comforted, in a living Sense of the Lord's Mercy and Goodness towards him, in carrying him through his Affliction in great Patience and Quietness; under which he was sweetly refreshed by the Streams of divine Love, and his Cup was often made to overflow: And we, who were present, being touched with a Sense thereof, were comforted therein, being in a Travail of Spirit for him, and did in our Measures truly sympathize with him under his Affliction. And I am fully satisfied, he laid down his Head in Peace with the Lord, and is gathered to his everlasting Rest. He departed this Life the 1st of the third Month, 1713, about the second Hour in the Morning, in the seventy fourth Year of his Age. He received the Truth in the Year 1659, and lived in Fellowship with the Friends of it about fifty three Years. And I think it may be truly said of him, that as he lived so he died, the Servant of the LORD and His People, and hath left a sweet Savour behind him, and his Memory is blessed with the Righteous for ever. Amen.

The eighth Month,
1713.

GEORGE BOWLES.

A

A Testimony from the Monthly-meeting at *Hunger-hill*, the 7th of the fourth Month, 1713, concerning our dear and well-beloved Friend and Brother in the Truth, Thomas Ellwood, deceased.

THAT *the Dead which* die in the Lord, *are blessed of Him, we have great Assurance of, from* John *the* Divine *his writing to the* seven Churches, *Rev.* xiv. 13. *Where he tells them, that he* heard a Voice from Heaven, saying, write, Blessed are the Dead which die in the Lord, from henceforth: Yea, saith the Spirit, that they may rest from their Labours, and their Works do follow them. *Of which Number, we have no Cause to doubt, but this our dear Friend is one; who was eminently serviceable in the Church of Christ. A Man to whom the Lord had given a large Capacity beyond many, and furnished him with an excellent Gift; whereby he was qualified for those Services in the Church, in the Performance of which he did shine as a* Star, *which received its Luster and Brightness from the glorious* Sun of Righteousness. *He was wise, but humble; condescending to the Weak, and ready to help where he saw and felt Sincerity; but sharp to that which he apprehended to be insincere and deceitful; for which Cause, he was not acceptable to Hypocrites and disorderly Walkers: Yet he was a Man of a very acceptable and agreeable Conversation, as well as sober and religious, both in the Church and in the World, being of a free and affable Temper and Disposition, far from Affectation; but of a courteous Behaviour and graceful Carriage to all, and very serviceable to and amongst his Neighbours: He was very near and dear to many of us, who were most intimately acquainted with him, and his Memorial is sweet to us: His Services in our* Meetings, *and in the* Quarterly-meeting *for the*

County of Bucks, *were very great, and of many Years Continuance; in which he shewed great Diligence, being of a ready Mind, willing to serve the Church, according to that Ability which the Lord had given him; and his Heart and House was open to his* Friends, *and the* Monthly-meeting *was kept there more than Forty Years, and remains there to this Day. Our Loss is great by his Removal: But in this we are satisfied, that it is his everlasting Gain; being gathered, as we have good Cause to believe, to his eternal Rest. The Knowledge we had of him, and the good Account which we have received of him, in the Time of his last Ilness, by those who were most constantly with him, and of his quiet and peaceable Departure, doth sensibly engage our Hearts to acquiesce in the Will of the Lord; and therein we have Peace and Comfort. He departed this Life, the* 1st *of the third Month* 1713, *and was honourably buried in* Friends *Burying-place at New* Jourdans, *in the Parish of* Giles-Chalfont, *in the County of* Bucks, *the* 4*th Day of the same Month.*

Signed by the Appointment of the Monthly-meeting, by us,

George Bowles,
William Grimsdall,
James Smith,
Daniel Wharley,
Daniel Roberts,
Abraham Barber,
Thomas Olliffe.

A TESTIMONY from the Womens-meeting, concerning THOMAS ELLWOOD.

A *Concern is upon our Spirits, to write somewhat concerning our dear deceased Friend and Elder,* Thomas Ellwood, *who was highly valued by us, for that Wisdom and Counsel which were with him; and being of a free and affable Temper, ready to assist those which stood in need thereof, encouraged many to apply to him for Advice, under the divers Circumstances and various Exercises which this uncertain World affords; which we have found to be for our Good, as we followed it. He was an early Comer to* Meetings, *seldom hindered by Weather (though he lived three Miles distant) when* bodily Weakness *did not hinder of late Years, being oft indisposed as to his* Health. *The* Monthly-meeting *was held at his House about forty Years, and he always look'd very kind and courteous on* Friends *when they came there, and took Care and Notice of the* meanest, *who came in* Sincerity. *He was zealous for* good Order, *and against such, who, being in an* apostatized Spirit, opposed it; *and may well be numbered amongst the* Worthies, *whose Names are upon Record for their* Valour; *so is this our* Friend *worthy to be, who never turned his Back on such who* opposed *the* Truth; *but stood his* Ground, *as his* printed Sheets *on such Occasions do shew. As also his other* Works *of several kinds, do manifest how great* Endowments *God had bestowed on him, (yet we, who knew him in his Conversation, are engaged to set forth how kind and condescending he was to the* weakest Capacity, *and would help out when they wanted a* Word) *that Generations to come may learn how good it is to* forsake All, *and* follow Christ Jesus, *as this our* Friend *did, and the* Account *of his* Life, *following, shews; who not only* gives Wisdom, *but* teacheth Humility *also.*

He was greatly respected by his Neighbours, for his Services amongst them; his Heart and Doors were open to the Poor, *both* sick *and* lame, *who wanted* Help, *and had it freely, taking Care to provide Things useful for such* Occasions, (*blest also with good* Success) *often saying,* He mattered not what Cost he was at, to do Good. *Such lament their* Loss: *What then may we do, who miss him in an* higher Station, *in his great Service in the* Church of Christ, *but even desire to be resigned to the* Will of the Lord? *who preserved him through all his* Hardships, *to a* Dominion *over* false Brethren, *and is now out of their Reach, and of* Temptation *too*; *on whose Head the* Blessing, *ask'd for* Joseph, *rests*; *who as a fruitful* Bough *his* Branch *spreads over the* Wall *of* Opposition, *and* his Bow abode in Strength; the Hands of whose Arms were made strong, by the Help of the mighty God of *Jacob*, *to whom be the* Glory *for what He hath wrought in our Day, whose own Works* praise Him *for evermore. And the Tears of* Sorrow *that we shed, for the Loss of this our deceased* Friend, *let them be remembred to bow our Spirits, each of us, into a* godly Care, *that we may come up according to our several* Capacities, *to follow the Lord* faithfully, *in a* godly Zeal *for His* Honour; *and so come to lay down our Heads in* Joy *and* Peace, *as this our* Friend *expressed he did.*

This eminent Servant of Christ, was early convinced of the Way of Truth, *wherein he continued to the finishing of his Days*; *for the Sake of which, he soon became a* Sufferer; *not only by* Imprisonment, *for* worshipping God *in the Assemblies of His People, but also, from his* Father, *by whom he was made as an* Outcast, *for no other Cause, but for his faithful* Testimony *in taking up the* Cross *to the* World's Behaviour *and* Language: *Whereupon he was invited by his much valued Friend* Isaac Penington, *to his House, where he abode several Years, until he* Married. *He was a Blessing in, as well as a great Comfort and Help to that* Family; *and by his*

his wise Conduct therein, gained much Esteem, *not only from the* Elders, *but the* Youth, *whom he instructed in* Learning; *and though most of them are by* Death *removed, yet One still remains, who from certain and experimental Knowledge, can commemorate his* Worth; *being engaged thereto, from a Sense of the* Benefit *of his good and wholsome* Advice, *given at* sundry Times *and on* divers Occasions. *Which Friendship continued firm to the last.*

His natural Capacity *was large, and his* Understanding, *in the* Things of God, *very deep; which excellent Qualifications meeting in one, rendred him useful beyond many to his* Country, *as well as very serviceable in the* Church; *by both which he is, and will be greatly missed. But he is gone to his Grave in a full Age, and* gathered as a Shock of Corn in its Season, having done his Day's-work faithfully: *So that Saying may be verified in him,* The END crowns all.

His Sickness was sudden, which soon deprived him of the Use of his Limbs; *yet he retained the Faculties of his inward and outward* Senses *clear all along; and notwithstanding at times, his Pains were great, his exemplary* Patience, *and composed Resignation, was remarkable apparent to those that visited and attended him; so that their Sorrow in parting with so dear a Friend, was intermixed with Comfort in beholding the heavenly Frame of Mind wherewith he was adorned.*

Thus after all his Labours, he entred into everlasting Rest, *and left many behind* weeping, *though not without Hope, that they shall again meet at the* general Assembly of Saints, *where the Redeemed shall sing* Praises *to their blessed* Redeemer, *whose Right it is to reign for ever.*

We have this farther to add, namely, *That our Esteem of him was great, because of that real Worth that was in him, through the Operation of the mighty Power of the Lord that separated him from the* Love of the World: *So that he chose (with* Moses*) rather to* suffer Affliction with the People of God, than to enjoy the Pleasures

of

of Sin for a Season, *and it pleased the Lord to fit him with Wisom and Counsel, so that he was made able to give Judgment in difficult Cases, wherein many of us have particularly received Benefit, and therefore have Cause to lament the Loss we have by his Removal. And oh! say our Souls, That the Lord would raise up many more in his Room, to the Praise and Honour of the good* Husbandman. *And it is our Desire that we, who are yet behind, may be made able so to steer our Course through this troublesome World, that when our End comes, we may lay down our Heads in Peace with the Lord, and leave a good Savour behind us, as this our Friend hath done.*

This is written in true Love and Respect to the Memory of our deceased Friend, *as it pleased the Lord to move upon our Hearts, And being read and approved in our* Womens-meeting *at* Hungerhill, *the 4th of the eleventh Month* 1713, *was subscribed in Behalf of the said Meeting by us,*

MARY BAKER,
MARY WHARLEY,
MARY LARCUM.

Concerniug

Concerning our dear Friend THOMAS ELLWOOD, of *Hunger-hill.*

HE *was much esteemed amongst good Men: Good Men, in their Day and Station upon the Earth, represent Him who made all Things good in the Beginning, who said,* Gen. i. 3. Let there be Light, and there was Light. *And also said,* ver. 26. Let us make Man in our Image, after our Likeness. *Oh, high Favour!* So God created Man in His own Image, in the Image of God created He him; Male and Female created He them, *ver.* 27, *and blessed them, and gave them Dominion under Himself; for He was chief Commander then; and so He is witnessed to be now, where His heavenly Image is come into again, and Men live in it, as did this our* dear Friend, *who did Good in his* Day *and* Generation: Counsel *was with him, to give to such as needed, and did apply to him: He was of a* tender Spirit, *and had Dominion over* Passion, *over* Pride, *and over* Covetousness: *So he was comfortable to, and in his* Family. *He was amiable in the* Church of Christ, *and a* Doer of Good *amongst his* Neighbours. *And being an* Elder *amongst, and with the* Elders, *he hath not only obtained a* good Report, *but also the* Blessing *in the* promised Seed, *which* bruises the Serpent's Head. *He was* valiant *in suffering for his Testimony which he held in the* Truth; *and may not I say,* unwearied *in his* Labours *for the setting forth the* Fame *and* Excellency *of it: Whereby we see what the* Truth *makes Men to be, who do come under the Conduct and Power of it; even as* fixed Stars *in the* Firmament *of His* divine Power, *who has caused the* Morning *of His* heavenly *and* glorious Gospel-day to break forth; *and as with the* Day that springs from high, *in* tender Mercy *hath He* visited many Souls. *And early did this our* worthy deceased Friend *embrace it, as it appears by his Testimony concerning that eminent and blessed Messenger and Minister of the Gospel,* George Fox.

And

And now, he having endured the Times of Proving, and the Days of Tribulation and Suffering, together with the Perils and Slights, and Undervaluings of false Brethren, *against whose ungodly Work he was engaged to stand as a noble Warrior, in the Defence of, and for the glorious Gospel of Christ: Not admiring Mens Persons, but the Work of the Gospel-power. And although he was endowed with Parts and Accomplishments above many, he was humble and grave; not Self-seeking, but esteeming the Power of Truth, though it did appear through mean Instruments. He was honourable, and honoured, for that he sought not his own Honour, but the Honour of Truth; not only by his Sufferings for it, and Labours in it, but also, in standing firmly against the loose libertine Ones, who would have thrust in amongst the Lambs and Flock of Christ, in an unclean adulterating Spirit, from the Life of the true Shepherd, and heavenly Husband, Christ Jesus: But to the tender hearted, and sincere minded, he was strengthening and comfortable. I knew him when I was but young, and I can truly say, my Heart has often been affected, on his Behalf, with Thankfulness to the Lord, who made him as a strong Pillar, in His spiritual House, with many more of His dear Servants and Children, who shall no more go out. His Memory is in my Heart esteemed beyond what I can write. Oh surely!* The Righteous shall be had in everlasting Remembrance, *Psal.* cxii. 6. And they that be wise, shall shine as the Brightness of the Firmament: And they that turn many to Righteousness, as the Stars for ever and ever, *Dan.* xii. 3.

Hunger-hill, the 5th of the seventh Month, 1713.

ELIZ. RICHARDSON.

RICHARD VIVERS his Teſtimony concerning THOMAS ELLWOOD.

HE *was a Man of great Wiſdom and Underſtanding, and the Lord, the Giver of it, being pleaſed to viſit him in his early Days, made Choice of him, and by the Sanctification of His holy Spirit, fitted and prepared him for His* Work *and* Service, *whereunto he was called. And altho' he did not often appear as a* Miniſter, *yet in thoſe Meetings ſet apart for the Affairs of* Truth, *he often appeared in great* Wiſdom, *having an extraordinary Talent given of the Lord for that* Work, *more than many other Brethren; and faithful he was in waiting for Inſtruction from God, to improve the ſame to His* Glory, *and the* Churches Advantage; *for nothing was more deſirable to him, than to be employed in the* Lord's Service: *So it pleaſed the* Almighty *to furniſh him with* Underſtanding *and Strength, faithfully to do his Day's-work. And now He hath taken him to Himſelf, where his Soul is at Reſt; and altho' our Loſs be his Gain, therein I with many more are greatly comforted, for I can truly ſay, I loved him, in the* Truth, *from the firſt of my Acquaintance with him, and ſo it remained to the End of his Courſe, being near forty Years ſince we knew each other: And whenever we converſed together, our Diſcourſe was chiefly concerning* heavenly Things, *and the* Affairs *of the* Church; *and I always thought my Time well ſpent with him, although Opportunity would not ſerve for ſo much of it as I deſired, had it been the Will of God.*

And this I can ſay, according to my Obſervation, He was a Man true *to his* Friend, *and deliberate in the Choice of his* Acquaintance, *to whom he ſhewed real Love and Sincerity of Heart. And he was one of a ſteady and ſound* Judgment, *as to the Things of God*; *often deſiring, that thoſe who came amongſt us, eſpecially Children of believing Parents, might not ſettle down only in a* Form *of* Godlineſs, *without the* Power *(at which Door the* Apoſtacy *entred) but that they might be raiſed up to walk in that, wherein the* Saints *Fellowſhip doth ſtand, which is the* Light of our Lord Jeſus Chriſt, *enlightening* every Man that cometh into the World: *And then the ancient* Teſtimony of Truth *will be more and more raiſed up in their Hearts, and they being preſerved of the Lord in it, it will more be maintained in its ſeveral Branches, as in former Days. Bleſſed be the Name of the Lord, who hath a People in theſe latter Ages of the World, to whom He hath given* Power *to ſtand for His* Truth, whilſt on Earth, *and to be* tender *of the* Honour of His Name; *of the Number of whom, this our* deceaſed Friend *and* Brother *was*; *who, altho'* dead, *yet his Memory* liveth, *and will be preſerved amongſt the* Righteous *in* Generations yet to come.

Banbury the 30th of the Eleventh Month 1714. } RICHARD VIVERS.

THE

THE HISTORY OF THE LIFE OF Thomas Ellwood.

ALTHOUGH my Station not being ſo eminent either in the Church of Chriſt, or in the World, as others who have moved in higher Orbs, may not afford ſuch conſiderable Remarks as theirs; yet, inaſmuch as in the Courſe of my Travels through this Vale of Tears, I have paſſed through various, and ſome uncommon Exerciſes, which the Lord hath been graciouſly pleaſed to ſupport me under, and conduct me through; I hold it a matter excuſable at leaſt, if not commendable, to give the World ſome little Account of my Life, that in recounting the many Deliverances and Preſervations, which the Lord hath vouchſafed to work for me, both I, by a grateful Acknowledgment thereof, and Return of Thanksgivings unto Him therefor, may in some measure set forth His abundant Goodness to me; and others, whose Lot it may be to tread the same Path, and fall into the same or like Exercises, may be encouraged to persevere in the Way of Holiness, and, with full Assurance of Mind, to trust in the Lord, whatsoever Trials may befall them.

1639. To begin therefore with mine own Beginning. I was born in the Year of our Lord 1639, about the Beginning of the eighth Month, (so far as I have been able to inform myself) for the Parish Register, which relates to the Time (not of Birth, but) of Baptism, as they call it, is not to be relied on.

The Place of my Birth was a little Country-town called *Crowell*, situate in the upper Side of *Oxfordshire*, three Miles East-ward from *Thame* the nearest Market-town.

My Father's Name was *Walter Ellwood*; and my Mother's Maiden-name was *Elizabeth Potman*; both well descended, but of declining Families. So that what my Father possessed (which was a pretty Estate in Lands, and more as I have heard in Monies) he received, as he had done his Name *Walter*, from his Grandfather *Walter Gray*, whose Daughter and only Child was his Mother.

1641. In my very Infancy, when I was but about two Years old, I was carried to *London*. For the Civil War, between King and Parliament breaking then forth, my Father, who favoured the

the Parliament-ſide, though he took not Arms, 1641.
not holding himſelf ſafe at his Country Habitation, which lay too near ſome Garriſons of the King's, betook himſelf to *London*, that City then holding for the Parliament.

There was I bred up, though not without much Difficulty, the City-Air not agreeing with my tender Conſtitution, and there continued until *Oxford* was ſurrendred, and the War in Appearance ended.

In this Time, my Parents contracted an Acquaintance and intimate Friendſhip with the Lady *Springett*, who being then the Widow of Sir *William Springett*, who died in the Parliament Service, was afterwards the Wife of *Iſaac Penington*, eldeſt Son of Alderman *Penington* of *London*. And this Friendſhip devolving from the Parents to the Children, I became an early and particular Play-fellow to her Daughter *Gulielma*; being admitted, as ſuch, to ride with her in her little Coach, drawn by her Footman about *Lincoln's-Inn-Fields*.

I mention this in this Place, becauſe the Continuation of that Acquaintance and Friendſhip, having been an occaſional Means of my being afterwards brought to the Knowledge of the bleſſed TRUTH, I ſhall have frequent Cauſe, in the Courſe of the following Diſcourſe, to make honourable Mention of that Family, to which I am under ſo many and great Obligations.

Soon after the Surrender of *Oxford*, my Fa- 1646.
ther returned to his Eſtate at *Crowell*; which

1646. by that Time he might have Need enough to look after, having ſpent, I ſuppoſe, the greateſt Part of the Monies which had been left him by his Grandfather, in maintaining himſelf and his Family at an high Rate in *London.*

My elder Brother (for I had one Brother and two Siſters, all elder than myſelf) was, while we lived in *London*, boarded at a private School, in the Houſe of one *Francis Atkinſon*, at a Place called *Hadley* near *Barnet* in *Hertfordſhire*, where he had made ſome good Proficiency in the *Latin* and *French* Tongues. But after we had left the City, and were reſettled in the Country, he was taken from that private School, and ſent to the Free-ſchool at *Thame* in *Oxfordſhire.*

Thither alſo was I ſent, as ſoon as my tender Age would permit; for I was indeed but young when I went, and yet ſeemed younger than I was, by reaſon of my low and little Stature. For it was held, for ſome Years a doubtful Point, whether I ſhould not have proved a Dwarf. But after I was arrived to the fifteenth Year of my Age, or thereabouts, I began to ſhoot up, and gave not over growing till I had attained the middle Size and Stature of Men.

At this School, which at that Time was in good Reputation, I profited apace, having then a natural Propenſity to Learning; ſo that at the firſt reading over of my Leſſon, I commonly made myſelf Maſter of it: And yet, which is ſtrange to think of, few Boys in the

School

School wore out more Birch than I. For tho' I was never, that I remember, whipt upon the Score of not having my Leſſon ready, or of not ſaying it well; yet being a little buſy Boy, full of Spirit, of a working Head and active Hand, I could not eaſily conſorm myſelf to the grave and ſober Rules, and, as I then thought, ſevere Orders of the School; but was often playing one waggiſh Prank or other among my Fellow-ſcholars, which ſubjected me to Correction, ſo that I have come under the Diſcipline of the Rod twice in a Forenoon; which yet brake no Bones.

Had I been continued at this School, and in due Time preferred to an higher, I might in likelihood have been a Scholar; for I was obſerved to have a Genius apt to learn. But my Father having, ſo ſoon as the Republican Government began to ſettle, accepted the Office of a Juſtice of the Peace (which was no way beneficial, but meerly honorary, and every way expenſive) and put himſelf into a Port and Courſe of Living agreeable thereunto; and having alſo removed my Brother from *Thame* School to *Merton* College in *Oxford*, and entred him there in the higheſt and moſt chargeable Condition of a *Fellow-Commoner*, he found it needful to retrench his Expences elſewhere; the Hurt of which fell upon me. For he thereupon took me from School, to ſave the Charge of maintaining me there; which was ſomewhat like plucking green Fruit from the Tree, and laying it by before it was come to its due Ripeneſs, which will thenceforth ſhrink and wither, and looſe that little Juice and Reliſh which it began to have.

Even ſo it fared with me. For being taken home when I was but young, and before I was well ſettled in my Studies, (though I had made a good Progreſs in the *Latin* Tongue, and was entred in the *Greek)* being left too much to myſelf, to ply or play with my Books, or without them, as I pleaſed, I ſoon ſhook Hands with my Books, by ſhaking my Books out of my Hands, and laying them, by degrees, quite aſide, and addicted myſelf to ſuch youthful Sports and Pleaſures as the Place afforded, and my Condition could reach unto.

By this Means, in a little Time, I began to loſe that little Learning I had acquired at School; and, by a continued Diſuſe of my Books, became at length ſo utterly a Stranger to Learning, that I could not have read, far leſs have underſtood, a Sentence in *Latin*. Which I was ſo ſenſible of, that I warily avoided reading to others, even in an *Engliſh* Book, leſt, if I ſhould meet with a *Latin* Word, I ſhould ſhame myſelf by miſpronouncing it.

Thus I went on, taking my Swing in ſuch vain Courſes as were accounted harmleſs Recreations; entertaining my Companions and familiar Acquaintance, with pleaſant Diſcourſes in our Converſations, by the meer Force of Mother-wit and natural Parts, without the Help of ſchool Cultivation; and was accounted good Company too.

But

But I always ſorted myſelf with Perſons of Ingenuity, Temperance and Sobriety; for I loathed Scurrilities in Converſation, and had a natural Averſion to immoderate Drinking. So that in the Time of my greateſt Vanity, I was preſerved from Prophaneneſs, and the groſſer Evils of the World; which render'd me acceptable to Perſons of the beſt Note in that Country then. I often waited on the Lord *Wenman*, at his Houſe *Thame-Park*, about two Miles from *Crowell* where I lived; to whoſe Favour I held myſelf intituled in a two-fold Reſpect, both as my Mother was nearly related to his Lady, and as he had been pleaſed to beſtow his Name upon me, when he made large Promiſes for me at the Font. He was a Perſon of great Honour and Virtue, and always gave me a kind Reception at his Table, how often ſoever I came. And I have Cauſe to think, I ſhould have received from this Lord ſome advantageous Preferment in this World, as ſoon as he had found me capable of it (though betwixt him and my Father there was not then ſo good an Underſtanding as might have been wiſh'd) had I not been, in a little Time after, called into the Service of the beſt and higheſt Lord; and thereby loſt the Favour of all my Friends, Relations and Acquaintance of this World. To the Account of which moſt happy Exchange I haſten, and therefore willingly paſs over many Particularities of my youthful Life. Yet one Paſſage I am willing to mention, for the Effect it had upon me afterwards, which was thus:

My

1657. My Father being then in the Commission of the Peace, and going to a Petty Sessions at *Watlington*, I waited on him thither. And when we came near the Town, the Coachman seeing a nearer and easier Way (than the common Road) through a Corn-field, and that it was wide enough for the Wheels to run, without endamaging the Corn, turned down there. Which being observed by an Husbandman, who was at plow not far off, he ran to us, and stopping the Coach, poured forth a Mouthful of Complaints, in none of the best Language, for driving over the Corn. My Father mildly answered him, *That if there was an Offence committed, he must rather impute it to his Servant, than himself; since he neither directed him to drive that Way, nor knew which Way he drove.* Yet added, *that he was going to such an Inn at the Town; whither if he came, he would make him full Satisfaction for whatsoever Damage he had sustained thereby.* And so on we went, the Man venting his Discontent, as he went back, in angry Accents. At the Town, upon Enquiry, we understood that it was a Way often used, and without Damage, being broad enough; but that it was not the common Road, which yet lay not far from it, and was also good enough; wherefore my Father bid his Man drive home that Way.

It was late in the Evening when we returned, and very dark; and this quarrelsome Man, who had troubled himself and us in the Morning,

ing, having gotten another lusty Fellow, like himself, to assist him, way-lay'd us in the Night, expecting we would return the same Way we came. But when they found we did not, but took the common Way, they angry that they were disappointed, and loth to lose their Purpose, (which was to put an Abuse upon us) coasted over to us in the dark, and laying hold on the Horses Bridles, stopt them from going on. My Father asking his Man, what the Reason was that he went not on, was answered, *That there were two Men at the Horses Heads, who held them back, and would not suffer them to go forward.* Whereupon my Father opening the Boot, stept out, and I followed close at his Heels. Going up to the Place where the Men stood, he demanded of them the Reason of this Assault. They said, *We were upon the Corn.* We knew, by the Routs, we were not on the Corn, but in the common Way, and told them so. But they told us, *They were resolved they would not let us go on any farther, but would make us go back again.* My Father endeavoured, by gentle Reasoning, to perswade them to forbear, and not run themselves farther into the Danger of the Law, which they were run too far into already; but they rather derided him for it. Seeing therefore fair Means would not work upon them, he spake more roughly to them, charging them to deliver their Clubs (for each of them had a great Club in his Hand, somewhat like those which are called *Quarter-Staves.*) They thereupon, laughing, told him,

1657.

They

1657. *They did not bring them thither for that End.* Thereupon my Father, turning his Head to me, ſaid, TOM, *diſarm them.*

I ſtood ready at his Elbow, waiting only for the Word of Command. For being naturally of a bold Spirit, full then of youthful Heat, and that too heightned by the Senſe I had, not only of the Abuſe, but inſolent Behaviour of thoſe rude Fellows; my Blood began to boil, and my Fingers itch'd, as the Saying is, to be dealing with them. Wherefore ſtepping boldly forward, to lay hold on the Staff of him that was neareſt to me, I ſaid, *Sirrah, deliver your Weapon.* He thereupon raiſed his Club, which was big enough to have knockt down an Ox, intending no doubt to have knockt me down with it, as probably he would have done, had I not, in the Twinkling of an Eye, whipt out my Rapier and made a Paſs upon him. I could not have failed running of him through up to the Hilt, had he ſtood his Ground; but the ſuddain and unexpected Sight of my bright Blade, gliſtering in the dark Night, did ſo amaze and terrify the Man, that ſlipping aſide, he avoided my Thruſt; and letting his Staff ſink, betook himſelf to his Heels for Safety, which his Companion ſeeing, fled alſo. I followed the former as faſt as I could, but *Timor addidit Alas*, Fear gave him Wings, and made him ſwiftly fly; ſo that although I was accounted very nimble, yet the farther we ran, the more Ground he gain'd on me, ſo that I could not overtake him; which made me think he

took

took Shelter under ſome Buſh, which he knew where to find, though I did not. Mean while the Coachman, who had ſufficiently the Outſide of a Man, excus'd himſelf from intermedling, under Pretence that he durſt not leave his Horſes, and ſo left me to ſhift for myſelf. And I was gone ſo far beyond my Knowledge, that I underſtood not which Way I was to go, till by hollowing, and being hollowed to again, I was directed where to find my Company.

We had eaſy Means to have found out who theſe Men were (the principal of them having been in the Day-time at the Inn, and both quarrelled with the Coachman, and threatned to be even with him when he went back;) but ſince they came off no better in their Attempt, my Father thought it better not to know them, than to oblige himſelf to a Proſecution of them.

At that Time, and for a good while after, I had no Regret upon my Mind for what I had done, and deſigned to have done, in this Caſe; but went on, in a ſort of Bravery, reſolving to kill, if I could, any Man that ſhould make the like Attempt, or put any Affront upon us; and for that Reaſon, ſeldom went afterwards upon thoſe publick Services, without a loaded Piſtol in my Pocket. But when it pleaſed the Lord, in His infinite Goodneſs, to call me out of the Spirit and Ways of the World, and give me the Knowledge of His ſaving Truth, whereby the Actions of my fore-paſt Life were ſet in Order before me; a ſort of Horror ſeized on me, when I conſidered how near I had been to

1657. the ſtaining of my Hands with human Blood. And whenſoever afterwards I went that Way, and indeed as often ſince as the Matter has come into my Remembrance, my Soul has bleſſed the Lord for my Deliverance, and Thankſgivings and Praiſes have ariſen in my Heart (as now, at the relating of it, they do) to Him who preſerved and with-held me from ſhedding Man's Blood. Which is the Reaſon, for which I have given this Account of that Action, that others may be warned by it.

1658. About this Time my dear and honoured Mother, who was indeed a Woman of ſingular Worth and Virtue, departed this Life, having a little before heard of the Death of her eldeſt Son; who (falling under the Diſpleaſure of my Father, for refuſing to reſign his Intereſt in an Eſtate which my Father ſold, and thereupon deſiring that he might have Leave to travel, in hopes that Time and Abſence might work a Reconciliation) went into *Ireland* with a Perſon powerful there in thoſe Times, by whoſe Means he was quickly preferred to a Place of Truſt and Profit, but lived not long to enjoy it.

I mentioned before, that during my Father's Abode in *London*, in the Time of the Civil Wars, he contracted a Friendſhip with the Lady *Springett*, then a Widow, and afterwards married to *Iſaac Penington*, Eſq; to continue which, he ſometimes viſited them at their Country Lodgings, as at *Datchet*, and at *Cauſham* Lodge near *Reading*. And having heard, that they were come to live upon their own Eſtate at *Chalfont*

in

in *Buckinghamſhire*, about fifteen Miles from Crowell, he went one Day to viſit them there, and to return at Night, taking me with him. 1659.

But very much ſurprized we were, when, being come thither, we firſt heard, then found, they were become *Quakers*; a People we had no Knowledge of, and a Name we had, till then, ſcarce heard of.

So great a Change from a free, debonair and courtly ſort of Behaviour, which we formerly had found them in, to ſo ſtrict a Gravity as they now received us with, did not a little amuſe us, and diſappoint our Expectation of ſuch a pleaſant Viſit as we uſed to have, and had now promiſed ourſelves. Nor could my Father have any Opportunity, by a private Conference with them, to underſtand the Ground or Occaſion of this Change, there being ſome other Strangers with them (related to *Iſaac Penington*) who came that Morning from *London* to viſit them alſo.

For my part I ſought, and at length found Means to caſt myſelf into the Company of the Daughter, whom I found gathering ſome Flowers in the Garden, attended by her Maid who was alſo a *Quaker*. But when I addreſſed myſelf to her after my accuſtomed Manner, with Intention to engage her in ſome Diſcourſe, which might introduce Converſation, on the Foot of our former Acquaintance; though ſhe treated me with a courteous Mein, yet, as young as ſhe was, the Gravity of her Look and Behaviour ſtruck ſuch an Awe upon me, that

1659. that I found myſelf not ſo much Maſter of myſelf, as to purſue any further Converſe with her. Wherefore aſking Pardon for my Boldneſs, in having intruded myſelf into her private Walks, I withdrew, not without ſome Diſorder (as I thought at leaſt) of Mind.

We ſtaid Dinner, which was very handſome, and lacked nothing to recommend it to me, but the want of Mirth and pleaſant Diſcourſe, which we could neither have with them, nor, by reaſon of them, with one another amongſt ourſelves; the Weightineſs that was upon their Spirits and Countenances, keeping down the Lightneſs that would have been up in us. We ſtaid notwithſtanding till the reſt of the Company took Leave of them, and then we alſo, doing the ſame, returned, not greatly ſatisfied with our Journey, nor knowing what in particular to find Fault with.

Yet this good Effect that Viſit had upon my Father, who was then in the Commiſſion for the Peace, that it diſpoſed him to a more favourable Opinion of, and Carriage towards thoſe People when they came in his Way; as not long after one of them did. For a young Man, who lived in *Buckinghamſhire*, came on a Firſt-day to the Church (ſo called) at a Town called *Chinner*, a Mile from *Crowell*, having it ſeems, a Preſſure on his Mind to ſay ſomething to the Miniſter of that Pariſh. He being an Acquaintance of mine, drew me ſometimes to hear him, as it did then. The young Man ſtood in the Iſle before the Pulpit, all the Time of the Sermon,

Sermon, not ſpeaking a Word till the Sermon and Prayer after it was ended; and then ſpake a few Words to the Prieſt. Of which, all that I could hear was, That *the Prayer of the Wicked is Abomination to the Lord*; and *that God heareth not Sinners.* 1659.

Somewhat more, I think, he did ſay, which I could not diſtinctly hear for the Noiſe the People made; and more probably he would have ſaid, had he not been interrupted by the Officers who took him into Cuſtody, and led him out in order to carry him before my Father.

When I underſtood that, I haſtened home, that I might give my Father a fair Account of the Matter before they came. I told him the young Man behaved himſelf quietly and peaceably, ſpake not a Word till the Miniſter had quite done his Service; and that what he then ſpake was but ſhort, and was delivered without Paſſion or ill Language. This I knew would furniſh my Father with a fair Ground, whereon to diſcharge the Man if he would.

And accordingly when they came, and made an high Complaint againſt the Man (who ſaid little for himſelf) my Father having examined the Officers who brought him, *what the Words that he ſpake were?* (which they did not well agree in) and *at what Time he ſpake them?* (which they all agreed to be after the Miniſter had done) and then, *whether he gave the Miniſter any reviling Language, or endeavoured to raiſe a Tumult among the People?*

 (which

1659. (which they could not charge him with ;) not finding that he had broken the Law, he counſelled the young Man to be careful that he did not make or occaſion any publick Diſturbances ; and ſo diſmiſſed him. Which I was glad of.

Some Time after this, my Father having gotten ſome further Account of the People called *Quakers*, and being deſirous to be informed concerning their Principles, made another Viſit to *Iſaac Penington* and his Wife, at their Houſe called the *Grange* in *Peter's Chalſont*, and took both my Siſters and me with him.

It was in the tenth Month, in the Year 1659, that we went thither, where we found a very kind Reception, and tarried ſome Days ; one Day at leaſt the longer, for that, while we were there, a Meeting was appointed at a Place about a Mile from thence, to which we were invited to go, and willingly went.

It was held in a Farm-houſe called *The Grove*, which having formerly been a Gentleman's Seat, had a very large Hall, and that well filled.

To this Meeting came *Edward Burrough*, beſides other Preachers, as *Thomas Curtis* and *James Nailor* ; but none ſpake there at that Time but *Edward Burrough*. Next to whom (as it were under him) it was my Lot to ſit on a Stool by the Side of a long Table on which he ſate, and I drank in his Words with Deſire ; for they not only anſwered my Underſtanding, but warmed my Heart with a cer-

tain

tain Heat, which I had not till then felt from 1659.
the Miniſtry of any Man.

When the Meeting was ended, our Friends took us home with them again; and after Supper, the Evenings being long, the Servants of the Family, who were *Quakers*, were called in, and we all ſate down in Silence. But long we had not ſo ſate before *Edward Burrough* began to ſpeak among us. And although he ſpake not long, yet what he ſaid did touch, as I ſuppoſe, my Father's (religious) Copy-hold, as the Phraſe is. And he having been from his Youth a Profeſſor (though not join'd in that which is call'd *cloſe Communion* with any one Sort) and valuing himſelf upon the Knowledge he eſteemed himſelf to have, in the various Notions of each Profeſſion, thought he had now a fair Opportunity to diſplay his Knowledge, and thereupon began to make Objections againſt what had been delivered.

The Subject of the Diſcourſe was, *The univerſal free Grace of God to all Mankind.* To which he oppoſed the *Calviniſtical* Tenet of *particular* and *perſonal Predeſtination.* In Defence of which indefenſible Notion, he found himſelf more at a Loſs than he expected. *Edward Burrough* ſaid not much to him upon it, though what he ſaid was cloſe and cogent. But *James Nailor* interpoſing, handled the Subject with ſo much Perſpicuity and clear Demonſtration, that his Reaſoning ſeemed to be irreſiſtible; and ſo I ſuppoſe my Father found it, which made him willing to drop the Diſcourſe.

 As

1659. As for *Edward Burrough*, he was a briſk young Man, of a ready Tongue, and might have been, for ought I then knew, a Scholar, which made me the leſs to admire his Way of Reaſoning. But what dropt from *James Nailor* had the greater Force upon me, becauſe he look'd but like a plain ſimple Country-man, having the Appearance of an Huſbandman or a Shepherd.

As my Father was not able to maintain the Argument on his Side; ſo neither did they ſeem willing to drive it on to an Extremity on their Side. But treating him in a ſoft and gentle Manner, did after a while let fall the Diſcourſe, and then we withdrew to our reſpective Chambers.

The next Morning we prepared to return home (that is, my Father, my younger Siſter, and myſelf; for my elder Siſter was gone before by the Stage Coach to *London)* and when, having taken our Leaves of our Friends, we went forth; they, with *Edward Burrough*, accompanying us to the Gate, he there directed his Speech in a few Words to each of us ſeverally, according to the Senſe he had of our ſeveral Conditions. And when we were gone off, and they gone in again, they aſking him what he thought of us? he anſwered them, (as they afterwards told me) to this Effect; *As for the old Man, he is ſettled on his Lees*; *and the young Woman is light and airy*; *but the young Man is reach'd, and may do well if he don't loſe it.* And ſurely that which he ſaid to me, or

rather

rather that Spirit in which he ſpake it, took 1659.
ſuch faſt hold on me, that I felt Sadneſs and Trouble come over me, though I did not diſtinctly underſtand what I was troubled for. I knew not what I ailed, but I knew I ailed ſomething more than ordinary, and my Heart was very heavy.

I found it was not ſo with my Father and Siſter; for as I rode after the Coach, I could hear them talk pleaſantly one to the other, but they could not diſcern how it was with me, becauſe I, riding on Horſback, kept much out of Sight.

By that Time we got home it was Night. And the next Day, being the Firſt-day of the Week, I went in the Afternoon to hear the Miniſter of *Chinner*; and this was the laſt Time I ever went to hear any of that Function. After the Sermon I went with him to his Houſe, and in a Freedom of Diſcourſe (which, from a certain Intimacy that was between us, I commonly uſed with him) told him where I had been, what Company I had met with there, and what Obſervations I had made to myſelf thereupon. He ſeemed to underſtand as little of them as I had done before, and civilly abſtained from caſting any unhandſome Reflections on them.

I had a Deſire to go to another Meeting of the *Quakers*, and bid my Father's Man enquire, if there was any in the Country thereabouts? He thereupon told me, he had heard at *Iſaac*

1659. *Penington's*, that there was to be a Meeting at *High-Wiccomb* on *Thursday* next.

Thither therefore I went, though it was ſeven Miles from me. And that I might be rather thought to go out a Courſing, than to a Meeting, I let my Greyhound run by my Horſe-ſide.

When I came there, and had ſet up my Horſe at an Inn, I was at a Loſs how to find the Houſe where the Meeting was to be. I knew it not, and was aſhamed to aſk after it. Wherefore having order'd the Horſtler to take Care of my Dog, I went into the Street and ſtood at the Inn-gate, muſing with myſelf what Courſe to take. But I had not ſtood long, e're I ſaw an Horſeman riding along the Street, whom I remember'd I had ſeen before at *Iſaac Penington's*, and he put up his Horſe at the ſame Inn. Him therefore I reſolved to follow, ſuppoſing he was going to the Meeting, as indeed he was.

Being come to the Houſe, which proved to be *John Raunce's*, I ſaw the People ſitting together in an outer Room; wherefore I ſtept in and ſate down on the firſt void Seat, the End of a Bench juſt within the Door, having my Sword by my Side and black Cloaths on, which drew ſome Eyes upon me. It was not long e're one ſtood up and ſpake, whom I was afterwards well acquainted with, his Name was *Samuel Thornton*; and what he ſpake was very ſuitable and of good Service to me, for it it reached home as if it had been directed to me. 1659.

As ſoon as ever the Meeting was ended, and the People began to riſe, I being next the Door ſtept out quickly, and haſtning to my Inn took Horſe immediately homewards; and (ſo far as I remember) my having being gone was not taken Notice of by my Father.

This latter Meeting was like the clinching of a Nail; confirming, and faſtening in my Mind, thoſe good Principles which had ſunk into me at the former. My Underſtanding began to open, and I felt ſome Stirrings in my Breaſt, tending to the Work of a new Creation in me. The general Trouble and Confuſion of Mind, which had for ſome Days lain heavy upon me, and preſſed me down, without a diſtinct Diſcovery of the particular Cauſe for which it came, began now to wear off, and ſome Glimmerings of Light began to break forth in me, which let me ſee my inward State and Condition towards God. The Light, which before had ſhone in my Darkneſs, and the Darkneſs could not comprehend it, began now to ſhine out of Darkneſs, and in ſome meaſure diſcovered to me, what it was that had before clouded me, and brought that Sadneſs and Trouble upon me. And now I ſaw, that although I had been, in a great degree, preſerved from the common Immoralities and groſs Pollutions of the World, yet the Spirit of the World had hitherto ruled in me, and led me into Pride, Flattery, Vanity and Super-

1659. fluity; all which was naught. I found there were many Plants growing in me, which were not of the *heavenly Father's planting*; and that all these, of whatever sort or kind they were, or how specious soever they might appear, must be plucked up.

Now was all my former Life ripped up, and my Sins, by degrees, were set in Order before me. And though they looked not with so black a Hue and so deep a Dye, as those of the lewdest Sort of People did, yet I found that all Sin (even that which had the fairest or finest Shew, as well as that which was more course and foul) brought Guilt, and *with* and *for Guilt*, Condemnation on the Soul that sinned. This I felt, and was greatly bowed down under the Sense thereof.

Now also did I receive a new Law, (an *inward Law* superadded to the *outward) the Law of the Spirit of Life in Christ Jesus*, which wrought in me against all Evil, not only *in Deed*, and *in Word*, but even *in Thought* also; so that every Thing was brought to Judgment, and Judgment passed upon all. So that I could not any longer go on in my former Ways and Course of Life, for when I did, Judgment took hold upon me for it.

Thus the Lord was graciously pleased to deal with me, in somewhat like manner as He had dealt with His People *Israel* of old (when they had transgressed His righteous LAW) whom, by His Prophet He called back, required *to put away the Evil of their Doings*; bidding

bidding them, first, *Cease to do Evil*; then, *Learn to do well*; before He would admit them to *reason with Him*; and before He would impart to them the *Effects of His free Mercy*, Isa. i. 16, 17.

I was now required by this inward and spiritual Law *(the Law of the Spirit of Life in Christ Jesus)* to *put away the Evil of my Doings*, and to *cease to do Evil.* And what, in Particulars, the *Evil* was which I was required to *put away*, and to *cease from*, that Measure of the divine LIGHT, which was now manifested in me, discovered to me; and what the Light made manifest to be *Evil*, Judgment passed upon.

So that here began to be a Way cast up before me, for me to walk in; a direct and plain Way; so plain, that *a way-faring Man*, how weak and simple soever *(though a Fool* to the Wisdom, and in the Judgment of the World) *could not err*, while he continued to walk in it; the Error *coming in* by his *going out of* it. And this Way with respect to me, I saw was that Measure of *divine Light* which was manifested in me, by which the *Evil of my Doings* which I was to put away and to cease from, was discovered to me.

By this *divine Light* then I saw, that though I had not the Evil of the *common Uncleanness, Debauchery, Profaneness*, and *Pollutions of the World* to *put away*, because I had, through the great *Goodness of GOD*, and a *civil Education*, been preserved out of those *grosser Evils*;

yet

1659. yet I had many other Evils to *put away*, and to *ceaſe from*; ſome of which were not by the World (*which lies in Wickedneſs*, 1 John v. 19.) accounted *Evils*; but by the *Light of Chriſt* were made manifeſt to me to be *Evils*, and as ſuch condemned in me.

As particularly, thoſe *Fruits* and *Effects* of *PRIDE*, that diſcover themſelves in the *Vanity* and *Superfluity* of APPAREL; which I, as far as my Ability would extend to, took alas, too much Delight in. This *Evil of my Doings* I was required to *put away* and *ceaſe from*; and Judgment lay upon me till I did ſo. Wherefore in Obedience to the *inward Law* (which agreed with the *outward*, 1 *Tim.* ii. 9. 1 *Pet.* iii. 3. 1 *Tim.* vi. 8. *Jam.* i. 21.) I took off from my Apparel thoſe unneceſſary Trimmings of *Lace*, *Ribbands* and *uſeleſs Buttons*, which had no real Service, but were ſet on only for that which was, by Miſtake, called *Ornament*. And I ceaſed to wear *Rings*.

Again, the giving of *flattering Titles* to Men, between whom and me there was not any Relation, to which ſuch Titles could be pretended to belong. This was an *Evil* I had been much addicted to, and was accounted a ready Artiſt in; therefore this *Evil* alſo was I required to *put away* and *ceaſe from*. So that thenceforward I durſt not ſay *Sir*, *Maſter*, *My Lord*, *Madam* (or *My Dame*) or ſay *Your Servant*, to any one to whom I did not ſtand in the real Relation of a Servant; which I had never done to any.

Again,

Again, *Reſpect of Perſons*, in uncovering the 1659.
Head, and *bowing* the *Knee* or *Body* in *Saluta-
tions*, was a Practice I had been much in the Uſe of. And this being one of the *vain Cuſtoms* of the World, introduced by the Spirit of the World, inſtead of the true *Honour*, which this is a falſe Repreſentation of, and uſed in Deceit, as a Token of *Reſpect*, by Perſons one to another, who bear no *real Reſpect* one to another. And beſides, this being a *Type* and proper *Emblem* of that *divine Honour* which all ought to pay to Almighty *GOD*, and which all, of all Sorts, who take upon them the *Chriſtian* Name, appear in when they offer their Prayers to Him, and therefore ſhould not be given to Men. I found this to be one of thoſe *Evils* which I had been too long doing, therefore I was now required to put it away, and ceaſe from it.

Again, *the corrupt and unſound Form of ſpeaking in the Plural Number to a ſingle Perſon, YOU to One*, inſtead of *THOU*, contrary to the *pure, plain*, and *ſingle Language* of TRUTH, *THOU* to *One*, and *YOU* to more than *One*, which had always been uſed by *GOD* to Men, and Men to *GOD*, as well as one to another, from the oldeſt Record of Time, till corrupt Men, for corrupt Ends, in later and corrupt Times, to flatter, fawn, and work upon the corrupt Nature in Men, brought in that falſe and ſenſeleſs Way of ſpeaking *YOU* to *One*; which hath ſince corrupted the modern Languages, and hath grealy debaſed the Spirits, and depraved the Manners of Men. This *evil*

Cuſtom

1659. *Custom* I had been as forward in as others, and this I was now called out of, and required to cease from.

These, and many more *evil Customs*, which had sprung up in the Night of Darkness, and general Apostacy from the TRUTH, and true RELIGION, were now by the Inshining of this pure Ray of *divine Light* in my Conscience, gradually discovered to me to be what I ought to cease from, shun, and stand a Witness against.

But so subtilly, and withal so powerfully did the Enemy work upon the weak Part in me, as to perswade me that in these Things, I ought to make a Difference between my Father and all other Men; and that therefore, though I did disuse these Tokens of Respect to others, yet I ought still to use them towards him, as he was my Father. And so far did this Wile of his prevail upon me, through a Fear lest I should do amiss, in withdrawing any Sort of Respect or Honour from my Father, which was due unto him, that being thereby beguiled, I continued for a while to demean myself in the same manner towards him, with respect both to *Language* and *Gesture*, as I had always done before. And so long as I did so (standing *bare* before him, and giving him the accustomed Language) he did not express, whatever he thought, any Dislike of me.

But as to myself, and the Work begun in me, I found it was not enough for me to *cease to do Evil*; though that was a good and a great Step. I had another Lesson before me, which was

was, *to learn to do well*; which I could by no 1659.
means do, till I had given up, with full Purpose of Mind, to *ceaſe from doing Evil.* And when I had done that, the Enemy took Advantage of my Weakneſs to miſlead me again.

For whereas I ought to have waited in the Light, for Direction and Guidance into and in the Way of *Well-doing*, and not to have moved till the *divine Spirit* (a Manifeſtation of which the Lord has been pleaſed to give unto me, for me to profit with, or by) the Enemy transforming himſelf into the Appearance of an Angel of Light, offered himſelf in that Appearance, to be my Guide and Leader into the Performance of *religious Exerciſes.* And I, not then knowing the Wiles of Satan, and being eager to be doing ſome acceptable Service to God, too readily yielded myſelf to the Conduct of my Enemy, inſtead of my Friend.

He thereupon humouring the Warmth and Zeal of my Spirit, put me upon religious Performances in my *own Will*, in my *own Time*, and in my *own Strength*; which in themſelves were good, and would have been profitable unto me, and acceptable unto the Lord, if they had been performed in *His Will*, in *His Time*, and in the Ability which *He gives.* But being wrought in the Will of Man, and at the prompting of the *evil One*, no wonder that it did me Hurt inſtead of Good.

I read abundantly in the BIBLE, and would ſet myſelf Taſks in reading; enjoyning myſelf to read ſo many Chapters, ſometimes an whole Book,

1659. Book, or long Epiſtle, at a Time. And I thought that Time well ſpent, though I was not much the wiſer for what I had read, reading it too curſorily, and without the true Guide, the *Holy Spirit*, which alone could open the Underſtanding, and give the true Senſe of what was read.

I prayed often, and drew out my Prayers to a great Length; and appointed unto myſelf certain ſet Times to pray at, and a certain Number of Prayers to ſay in a Day; yet knew not, mean while, what *true Prayer* was. Which ſtands not in Words, though the Words which are uttered in the *Movings* of the *Holy Spirit*, are very available; but in the breathing of the Soul to the heavenly Father, through the Operation of the *Holy Spirit*, who maketh *Interceſſion* ſometimes in Words, and ſometimes with Sighs and Groans only, which the Lord vouchſafes to hear and anſwer.

This *Will-worſhip*, which all is, that is performed in the Will of Man, and not in the Movings of the *Holy Spirit*, was a great Hurt to me, and Hinderance of my ſpiritual Growth in the Way of Truth. But my heavenly Father, who knew the Sincerity of my Soul to Him, and the hearty Deſire I had to ſerve Him, had Compaſſion on me; and in due Time was graciouſly pleaſed to illuminate my Underſtanding farther, and to open in me an Eye to diſcern the *falſe Spirit*, and its Way of working, from the *true*; and to reject the former, and cleave to the latter.

But

But though the Enemy had by his Subtilty, gain'd ſuch Advantages over me, yet I went on notwithſtanding, and firmly perſiſted in my godly Reſolution of ceaſing from, and denying thoſe Things which I was now convinced in my Conſcience were evil. And on this Account a great Trial came quickly on me. For the general Quarter-Seſſions for the Peace coming on, my Father, willing to excuſe himſelf from a dirty Journey, commanded me to get up betimes and go to *Oxford*, and deliver in the Recognizances he had taken; and bring him an Account what Juſtices were on the Bench, and what principal Pleas were before 'em; which he knew I knew how to do, having often attended him on thoſe Services. 1659.

I, who knew how it ſtood with me better than he did, felt a Weight come over me as ſoon as he had ſpoke the Word. For I preſently ſaw it would bring a very great Exerciſe upon me. But having never reſiſted his Will in any Thing that was lawful, as this was, I attempted not to make any Excuſe, but ordering an Horſe to be ready for me early in the Morning, I went to Bed, having great Struglings in my Breaſt.

For the Enemy came in upon me like a Flood, and ſet many Difficulties before me, ſwelling them up to the higheſt Pitch, by repreſenting them as Mountains which I ſhould never be able to get over; and, alas! that *Faith* which could remove ſuch Mountains, and caſt

them

1659. them into the Sea, was but very ſmall and weak in me.

He caſt into my Mind, not only how I ſhould behave myſelf in Court, and diſpatch the Buſineſs I was ſent about; but how I ſhould demean myſelf towards my Acquaintance, of which I had many in that City, with whom I was wont to be jolly; whereas now I could not put off my Hat, nor bow to any of them, nor give them their honorary Titles (as they are called) nor uſe the corrupt Language of *You* to any one of them, but muſt keep to the plain and true Language of *Thou* and *Thee*.

Much of this Nature revolved in my Mind, thrown in by the Enemy to diſcourage and caſt me down. And I had none to have Recourſe to for Counſel or Help, but the Lord alone. To whom therefore I poured forth my Supplications, with earneſt Cries and Breathings of Soul, that HE, in whom all Power was, would enable me to go through this great Exerciſe, and keep me faithful to Himſelf therein. And after ſome Time, He was pleaſed to compoſe my Mind to Stilneſs, and I went to Reſt.

Early next Morning I got up, and found my Spirit pretty calm and quiet, yet not without a Fear upon me, leſt I ſhould ſlip and let fall the Teſtimony which I had to bear. And as I rode, a frequent Cry ran through me to the Lord, on this wiſe; *O my God, preſerve me faithful, whatever befals me! Suffer me not to be drawn*

drawn into Evil, how much Scorn and Contempt ſoever may be caſt upon me!

Thus was my Spirit exerciſed on the Way almoſt continually. , And when I was come within a Mile or two of the City, whom ſhould I meet upon the Way, coming from thence, but *Edward Burrough!* I rode in a Mountier-cap (a Dreſs more uſed then than now) and ſo did he; and becauſe the Weather was exceeding ſharp, we both had drawn our Caps down, to ſhelter our Faces from the Cold, and by that means neither of us knew the other, but paſſed by without taking Notice one of the other, till a few Days after meeting again, and obſerving each others Dreſs, we recollected where we had ſo lately met. Then thought I with my ſelf, O! *how glad ſhould I have been of a Word of Encouragement and Counſel from him, when I was under that weighty Exerciſe of Mind!* But the Lord ſaw it was not good for me; that my Reliance might be wholly upon Him, and not on Man.

When I had ſet up my Horſe, I went directly to the Hall where the Seſſions were held, where I had been but a very little while, before a Knot of my old Acquaintances eſpying me, came to me. One of theſe was a Scholar in his Gown; another a Surgeon of that City (both my School-fellows and Fellow-boarders at *Thame* School) and the third, a Country Gentleman, with whom I had long been very familiar.

When they were come up to me, they all ſaluted me after the uſual Manner, putting off

1659. their Hats and bowing, and ſaying, *Your humble Servant, Sir*; expecting, no doubt, the like from me. But when they ſaw me ſtand ſtill, not moving my Cap, nor bowing my Knee in way of *Congee* to them, they were amazed, and looked firſt one upon another, then upon me, and then one upon another again for a while, without a Word ſpeaking.

At length the Surgeon, a briſk young Man, who ſtood neareſt to me, clapping his Hand in a familiar way upon my Shoulder, and ſmiling on me, ſaid, *What!* TOM, *a* Quaker! To which I readily and cheerfully anſwered, *Yes, a* Quaker. And as the Words paſſed out of my Mouth, I felt Joy ſpring in my Heart; for I rejoiced that I had not been drawn out by them, into a Compliance with them, and that I had Strength and Boldneſs given me, to confeſs myſelf to be one of that deſpiſed People.

They ſtaid not long with me, nor ſaid any more, that I remember, to me; but looking ſomewhat confuſedly one upon another, after a while took their Leave of me, going off in the ſame ceremonious Manner as they came on.

After they were gone, I walked a while about the Hall, and went up nearer to the Court, to obſerve both what Juſtices were on the Bench, and what Buſineſs they had before them. And I went in Fear, not of what they could or would have done to me, if they ſhould have taken Notice of me, but leſt I ſhould be ſurprized, and drawn unwarily into that which I was to keep out of.

It

It was not long before the Court adjourned to go to Dinner, and that Time I took to go to the Clerk of the Peace at his House, whom I was well acquainted with. So soon as I came into the Room where he was, he came and met me, and saluted me after his Manner; for he had a great Respect for my Father, and a kind Regard for me. And tho' he was at first somewhat startled at my Carriage and Language, yet he treated me very civilly, whithout any Reflection or Shew of Lightness. I delivered him the Recognizances which my Father had sent, and having done the Business I came upon, withdrew, and went to my Inn to refresh myself, and then to return home. 1659.

But when I was ready to take Horse, looking out into the Street, I saw two or three Justices standing just in the Way where I was to ride. This brought a fresh Concern upon me. I knew if they saw me, they would know me; and I concluded if they knew me, they would stop me to enquire after my Father; and I doubted how I should come off with them.

This Doubting brought Weakness on me, and that Weakness led to Contrivance, how I might avoid this Trial. I knew the City pretty well, and remembred there was a Back-way, which though somewhat about, would bring me out of Town, without passing by those Justices; yet loth I was to go that Way. Wherefore I staid a pretty Time, in hopes they would have parted Company, or removed to some other Place out of my Way. But when

1659 I had waited till I was uneasy for losing so much Time, having entred into Reasonings with Flesh and Blood, the Weakness prevailed over me, and away I went the Back-way; which brought Trouble and Grief upon my Spirit for having shunned the Cross.

But the Lord looked on me with a tender Eye, and seeing my Heart was right to Him, and that what I had done was meerly through Weakness and Fear of falling, and that I was sensible of my Failing therein, and sorry for it, He was graciously pleased to pass it by, and speak Peace to me again. So that before I got home, as when I went in the Morning, my Heart was full of breathing Prayer to the Lord, that He would vouchsafe to be with me, and uphold and carry me through that Day's Exercise; so now at my Return in the Evening, my Heart was full of thankful Acknowledgments, and Praises unto Him for His great Goodness and Favour to me, in having thus far preserved, and kept me from falling into any Thing that might have brought Dishonour to His holy Name, which I had now taken on me.

But notwithstanding that it was thus with me, and that I found Peace and Acceptance with the Lord in some good degree, according to my Obedience to the Convictions I had received by His *holy Spirit* in me; yet was not the Vail so done away, or fully rent, but that there still remained a Cloud upon my Understanding, with respect to my Carriage towards my Father. And that Notion which the Enemy had

had brought into my Mind, that *I ought to put* 1659.
ſuch a Difference between him and all others, as that, on the Account of paternal Relation, I ſhould ſtill deport myſelf towards him, both in Geſture and Language, as I had always heretofore done; did yet prevail with me. So that when I came home, I went to my Father bare-headed as I uſed to do, and gave him a particular Account of the Buſineſs he had given me in Command, in ſuch manner, that he obſerving no Alteration in my Carriage towards him, found no Cauſe to take Offence at me.

I had felt for ſome Time before, an earneſt Deſire of Mind to go again to *Iſaac Penington*'s. And I began to queſtion whether, when my Father ſhould come (as I concluded e're long he would) to underſtand I enclined to ſettle among the People called *Quakers*, he would permit me the Command of his Horſes as before. Wherefore, in the Morning when I went to *Oxford*, I gave Direction to a Servant of his, to go that Day to a Gentleman of my Acquaintance, who I knew had a riding Nag to put off either by Sale, or to be kept for his Work, and deſire him, in my Name, to ſend him to me; which he did, and I found him in the Stable when I came home.

On this Nag I deſigned to ride next Day to *Iſaac Penington*'s; and in order thereunto, aroſe betimes and got myſelf ready for the Journey. But becauſe I would pay all due Reſpects to my Father, and not go without his Conſent, or Knowledge at the leaſt, I ſent one up to him

E 3 (for

1659. (for he was not yet ſtirring) to acquaint him, that I had a Purpoſe to go to *Iſaac Penington*'s; and deſired to know if he pleaſed to command me any Service to them. He ſent me Word, *He would ſpeak with me before I went, and would have me come up to him*; which I did, and ſtood by his Bed-ſide.

Then in a mild and gentle Tone he ſaid, *I underſtand you have a Mind to go to Mr.* Penington'*s.* I anſwered, I have ſo. *Why*, ſaid he, *I wonder why you ſhould. You were there, you know, but a few Days ago, and unleſs you had Buſineſs with them, don't you think it will look odly?* I ſaid, I thought not. *I doubt*, ſaid he, *You'll tire them with your Company, and make them think they ſhall be troubled with you.* If, replied I, I find any Thing of that, I'll make the ſhorter Stay. *But*, ſaid he, *can you propoſe any ſort of Buſineſs with them, more than a meer Viſit?* Yes, ſaid I, I propoſe to myſelf not only to ſee them, but to have ſome Diſcourſe with them. *Why*, ſaid he, in a Tone a little harſher, *I hope you don't encline to be of their Way.* Truly, anſwered I, I like them and their Way very well, ſo far as I yet underſtand it; and I am willing to go to them, that I may underſtand it better.

Thereupon he began to reckon up a Bead-roll of Faults againſt the *Quakers*; telling me *They were a rude unmannerly People, that would not give civil Reſpect or Honour to their Superiors, no not to Magiſtrates; that they held many dangerous Principles; that they were an immodeſt, ſhameleſs People; and that one of them ſtript himself stark naked, and went in that unseemly manner about the Streets, at Fairs, and on Market-days in great Towns.* 1659.

To all the other Charges, I answered only, That perhaps they might be either misreported or misunderstood, as the best of People had sometimes been. But to the last Charge, of *going naked*, a particular Answer, by way of Instance, was just then brought into my Mind, and put into my Mouth, which I had not thought of before; and that was the Example of *Isaiah*, who went *Naked* among the People for a long Time, *(Isa.* xx. 4.) *Aye*, said my Father, *but you must consider that he was a Prophet of the Lord, and had an express Command from God to* go so. Yes, Sir, replied I, I do consider that; but I consider also, that the *Jews* among whom he lived, did not own him for a Prophet, nor believe that he had such a Command from God. And, added I, how know we but that this *Quaker* may be a Prophet too, and might be commanded to do as he did, for some Reason which we understand not?

This put my Father to a stand; so that letting fall his Charges against the *Quakers*, he only said, *I would wish you not to go so soon, but take a little Time to consider of it*; *you may visit Mr.* Penington *hereafter.* Nay, Sir, replied I, pray don't hinder my going now, for I have so strong a Desire to go, that I do not well know how to forbear. And as I spake those Words, I withdrew gently to the Chamber-door, and then hastning down Stairs, went immediately

1659. to the Stable, where finding my Horse ready bridled, I forthwith mounted and went off, lest I should receive a Countermand.

This Discourse with my Father had cast me somewhat back in my Journey, and it being fifteen long Miles thither, the Ways bad, and my Nag but small, it was in the Afternoon that I got thither. And understanding by the Servant that took my Horse, that there was then a Meeting in the House (as there was Weekly on that Day, which was the Fourth-day of the Week, though I till then understood it not) I hastened in; and knowing the Rooms, went directly to the little Parlour, where I found a few Friends sitting together in Silence, and I sate down among them well satisfied, though without Words.

When the Meeting was ended, and those of the Company, who were Strangers, withdrawn, I addressed myself to *Isaac Penington* and his Wife, who received me courteously; but not knowing what Exercise I had been in and yet was under, nor having heard any Thing of me, since I had been there before in another Garb, were not forward at first to lay sudden Hands on me; which I observed, and did not dislike. But as they came to see a Change in me, not in Habit only, but in Gesture, Speech and Carriage, and which was more, in Countenance also, (for the Exercise I had passed through, and yet was under, had imprinted a visible Character of Gravity upon my Face;) they were exceeding kind and tender towards me.

There

There was then in the Family a Friend, whoſe Name was *Anne Curtis*, the Wife of *Thomas Curtis* of *Reading*, who was come upon a Viſit to them, and particularly to ſee *Mary Penington*'s Daughter *Guli*, who had been ill of the Small-pox ſince I had been there before. Betwixt *Mary Penington* and this Friend, I obſerved ſome private Diſcourſe and Whiſperings, and I had an Apprehenſion that it was upon ſomething that concerned me. Wherefore I took the Freedom to aſk *Mary Penington*, If my coming thither had occaſioned any Inconvenience in the Family? She aſked me, *If I had had the Small-pox?* I told her no. She then told me, *Her Daughter had newly had them, and though ſhe was well recovered of them, ſhe had not as yet been down amongſt them; but intended to have come down, and ſate with them in the Parlour that Evening; yet would rather forbear till another Time, than endanger me.* And that *that was the Matter they had been diſcourſing of.* I aſſured her, that I had always been, and then more eſpecially, was free from any Apprehenſion of Danger in that reſpect; and therefore intreated, that her Daughter might come down. And although they were ſomewhat unwilling to yield to it, in regard of me, yet my Importunity prevailed, and after Supper ſhe did come down and ſit with us; and tho' the Marks of the Diſtemper were freſh upon her, yet they made no Impreſſion upon me, *Faith* keeping out *Fear*. 1659.

We

1659. We ſpent much of the Evening in Retiredneſs of Mind, our Spirits being weightily gathered inward; ſo that not much Diſcourſe paſſed among us, neither they to me, nor I to them, offered any Occaſion. Yet I had good Satisfaction in that Stilneſs, feeling my Spirit drawn near to the Lord, and to them therein.

Before I went to Bed, they let me know, that there was to be a Meeting at *Wiccomb* next Day, and that ſome of the Family would go to it. I was very glad of it; for I greatly deſired to go to Meetings, and this fell very aptly, it being in my Way home. Next Morning *Iſaac Penington* himſelf went, having *Anne Curtis* with him, and I accompanied them.

At *Wiccomb* we met with *Edward Burrough*, who came from *Oxford* thither, that Day that I, going thither, met him on the Way; and having both our Montier-caps on, we recollected that we had met, and paſſed by each other on the Road unknown.

This was a Monthly-meeting, conſiſting of Friends chiefly, who gathered to it from ſeveral Parts of the Country thereabouts; ſo that it was pretty large, and was held in a fair Room in *Jeremiah Stevens*'s Houſe; the Room, where I had been at a Meeting before in *John Raunce*'s Houſe, being too little to receive us.

A very good Meeting was this in itſelf and to me. *Edward Burrough*'s Miniſtry came forth among us in Life and Power, and the Aſſembly was covered therewith. I alſo, according to my ſmall Capacity, had a Share therein.

therein. For I felt ſome of that divine Power working my Spirit into a great Tenderneſs, and not only confirming me in the Courſe I had already entred, and ſtrengthning me to go on therein; but rending alſo the Vail ſomewhat further, and clearing my Underſtanding in ſome other Things which I had not ſeen before. For the Lord was pleaſed to make His Diſcoveries to me by degrees, that the Sight of too great a Work, and too many Enemies to encounter with at once, might not diſcourage me and make me faint. 1659.

When the Meeting was ended, the Friends of the Town taking Notice, that I was the Man that had been at their Meeting the Week before, whom they then did not know, ſome of them came and ſpake lovingly to me, and would have had me ſtaid with them; but *Edward Burrough* going home with *Iſaac Penington*, he invited me to go back with him, which I willingly conſented to. For the Love I had more particularly to *Edward Burrough*, through whoſe Miniſtry I had received the firſt awakning Stroke, drew me to deſire his Company, and ſo away we rode together.

But I was ſomewhat diſappointed of my Expectation; for I hoped he would have given me both Opportunity and Encouragement to have opened myſelf to him, and to have poured forth my Complaints, Fears, Doubts and Queſtionings into his Boſom. But he, being ſenſible that I was truly reach'd, and that the Witneſs of GOD was raiſed, and the Work of GOD

rightly

1659. rightly begun in me; choſe to leave me to the *Guidance of the good Spirit in myſelf* (the *Counſellor* that could reſolve all Doubts) that I might not have any Dependance on Man. Wherefore, although he was naturally of an open and free Temper and Carriage, and was afterwards always very familiar and affectionately kind to me; yet at this Time he kept himſelf ſomewhat reſerved, and ſhewed only common Kindneſs to me.

Next Day we parted. He for *London*, I home, under a very great Weight and Exerciſe upon my Spirit. For I now ſaw, in and by the farther *Openings* of the DIVINE LIGHT in me, that the Enemy, by his falſe Reaſonings, had beguiled and miſled me, with reſpect to *my Carriage towards my Father*. For I now clearly ſaw, that the *Honour* due to *Parents*, did not conſiſt in *uncovering the Head*, and *bowing the Body* to them; but in a *ready Obedience to their lawful Commands*, and in *performing all needful Services unto them*. Wherefore, as I was greatly troubled for what I already had done in that Caſe, though it was through Ignorance; ſo I plainly felt I could no longer continue therein, without drawing on myſelf the Guilt of *wilful Diſobedience*; which I well knew, would draw after it *divine Diſpleaſure* and *Judgment*.

Hereupon the Enemy aſſaulted me afreſh, ſetting before me the *Danger* I ſhould run myſelf into, of provoking my Father to uſe Severity towards me; and perhaps to the caſting

me

me utterly off. But over this Temptation the 1659.
Lord, whom I cried unto, ſupported me, and gave me Faith to believe, that He would bear me through whatever might befal me on that Account. Wherefore I reſolved, in the Strength which He ſhould give me, to be faithful to His *Requirings*, whatever might come on it.

Thus labouring under various Exerciſes on the Way, I at length got home, expecting I ſhould have but a rough Reception from my Father. But when I came home, I underſtood my Father was from home. Wherefore I ſate down by the Fire in the Kitchen, keeping my Mind retired to the Lord, with Breathings of Spirit to Him, that I might be preſerved from falling.

After ſome Time I heard the Coach drive in, which put me into a little Fear, and a ſort of Shivering came over me. But by that Time he was alighted and come in, I had pretty well recovered myſelf; and as ſoon as I ſaw him, I roſe up, and advanced a Step or two towards him, with my Head covered, and ſaid, *Iſaac Penington* and his Wife remember their Loves to thee.

He made a Stop to hear what I ſaid, and obſerving that I did not ſtand bare, and that I uſed the Word [*Thee*] to him; he, with a ſtern Countenance, and Tone that ſpake high Diſpleaſure, only ſaid, *I ſhall talk with you, Sir, another Time*; and ſo haſtening from me went into the Parlour, and I ſaw him no more that Night.

Tho'

1659. Tho' I foresaw there was a Storm arising, the Apprehension of which was uneasy to me, yet the Peace which I felt in my own Breast, raised in me a Return of Thanksgivings to the Lord, for His gracious supporting Hand, which had thus far carried me through this Exercise; with humble Cries in Spirit to Him, that He would vouchsafe to stand by me in it to the End, and uphold me, that I might not fall.

My Spirit longed to be among Friends, and to be at some Meeting with them on the First-day, which now drew on, this being the Sixth-day Night. Wherefore I purposed to go to *Oxford* on the Morrow (which was the Seventh-day of the Week) having heard there was a Meeting there. Accordingly, having ordered my Horse to be made ready betimes, I got up in the Morning and made myself ready also. Yet before I would go, (that I might be as observant to my Father as possibly I could) I desired my Sister to go up to him in his Chamber, and acquaint him, that I had a Mind to go to *Oxford*; and desired to know, if he pleased to command me any Service there. He bid her tell me, *He would not have me go, till he had spoken with me.* And getting up immediately, he hastened down to me before he was quite dressed.

As soon as he saw me standing with my Hat on, his Passion transporting him, he fell upon me with both his Fists; and having by that Means somewhat vented his Anger, he plucked off my Hat and threw it away. Then step-

ping

ping haſtily out to the Stable, and ſeeing my borrowed Nag ſtand ready ſaddled and bridled, he aſked his Man, *Whence that Horſe came?* who telling him, he fetcht it from *Mr.* ——— ſuch an One's: *Then ride him preſently back*, ſaid my Father, *and tell* Mr.——— *I deſire he will never lend my Son an Horſe again, unleſs he brings a Note from me.*

The poor Fellow, who loved me well, would fain have made Excuſes and Delays; but my Father was poſitive in his Command, and ſo urgent, that he would not let him ſtay ſo much as to take his Breakfaſt (though he had five Miles to ride) nor would he himſelf ſtir from the Stable, till he had ſeen the Man mounted and gone.

Then coming in, he went up into his Chamber, to make himſelf more fully ready, thinking he had me ſafe enough now my Horſe was gone; for I took ſo much Delight in riding, that I ſeldom went on Foot.

But while he was dreſſing himſelf in his Chamber, I (who underſtood what had been done) changing my Boots for Shoes, took another Hat, and acquainting my Siſter, who loved me very well, and whom I could confide in, whither I meant to go, went out privately and walked away to *Wiccomb*, having ſeven long Miles thither, which yet ſeem'd little and eaſy to me, from the Deſire I had to be among Friends.

As thus I travelled all alone, under a Load of Grief, from the Senſe I had of the Oppoſition and

1659. and Hardſhip I was to expect from my Father; the Enemy took Advantage to aſſault me again, caſting a Doubt into my Mind, *Whether I had done well, in thus coming away from my Father, without his Leave or Knowledge?*

I was quiet and peaceable in my Spirit before this Queſtion was darted into me; but after that, Diſturbance and Trouble ſeized upon me, ſo that I was at a ſtand what to do; whether to go forward or backward? Fear of *offending* inclined me to go back; but Deſire *of the Meeting*, and to be with Friends, preſſed me to go forward.

I ſtood ſtill a while, to conſider and weigh, as well as I could, the Matter. I was ſenſibly ſatisfied, that I had not left my Father with any Intention of *Undutifulneſs* or *Diſreſpect* to him; but meerly in Obedience to that Drawing of Spirit, which I was perſwaded was of the LORD, to join with *His People in worſhipping Him*; and this made me eaſy.

But then the Enemy, to make me uneaſy again, objected, *But how could that Drawing be of the* LORD, *which drew me to diſobey my Father?*

I conſidered thereupon the Extent of *Paternal Power*; which I found was not wholly arbitrary and unlimited, but had Bounds ſet unto it. So that as in civil Matters, it was reſtrained to *Things lawful*; ſo in ſpiritual and religious Caſes, it had not a *compulſory Power* over *Conſcience*; which ought to be ſubject to the *heavenly Father*. And therefore, though *Obedience* to *Parents* be enjoined to *Children*; yet it is with this Limitation, [IN THE LORD:]

Children,

Children, obey your Parents in the Lord; for this is right, 1 Pet. vi. 1. 1659.

This turned the Scale for going forward, and ſo on I went. And yet I was not wholly free from ſome Fluctuations of Mind, from the Beſettings of the Enemy. Wherefore, altho' I knew that *outward Signs* did not properly belong to the Goſpel Diſpenſation; yet for my better Aſſurance, I did, in Fear and great Humility, beſeech the Lord, that He would be pleaſed ſo far to condeſcend to the Weakneſs of His Servant, as to give me a Sign, by which I might certainly know, whether my Way was right before Him or not?

The Sign which I aſked was, *That if I had done wrong in coming as I did, I might be rejected, or but coldly received at the Place I was going to; but if this mine Undertaking was right in His Sight, He would give me Favour with them I went to, ſo that they ſhould receive me with hearty Kindneſs and Demonſtrations of Love.* Accordingly, when I came to *John Rance*'s Houſe (which, being ſo much a Stranger to all, I choſe to go to, becauſe I underſtood the Meeting was commonly held there;) they received me with more than ordinary Kindneſs, eſpecially *Frances Rance*, *John Rance*'s then Wife, who was both a grave and motherly Woman, and had a hearty Love to Truth, and Tenderneſs towards all that in Sincerity ſought after it. And this ſo kind Reception, confirming me in the Belief that my Undertaking was *Approved of by the LORD*, gave great Satisfaction and Eaſe

F to

1659. to my Mind; and I was thankful to the Lord therefor.

Thus it fared with me there; but at home it fared otherwise with my Father. He supposing I had betaken myself to my Chamber, when he took my Hat from me, made no Enquiry after me till Evening came; and then sitting by the Fire, and considering that the Weather was very cold, he said to my Sister, who sate by him, *Go up to your Brother's Chamber, and call him down; it may be he will sit there else, in a sullen Fit, till he has caught Cold. Alas! Sir*, said she, *He is not in his Chamber, nor in the House neither.* At that my Father startling, said, *Why where is he then? I know not, Sir*, said she, *where he is; but I know that, when he saw you had sent away his Horse, he put on Shoes, and went out on Foot, and I have not seen him since. And indeed, Sir*, added she, *I don't wonder at his going away, considering how you used him.* This put my Father into a great Fright, doubting I was gone quite away; and so great a Passion of Grief seized on him, that he forbore not to weep, and to cry out aloud, so that the Family heard him, *Oh! my Son! I shall never see him more! For he is of so bold and resolute a Spirit, that he will run himself into Danger, and so may be thrown into some Goal or other, where he may lie and die before I can hear of him.* Then bidding her light him up to his Chamber, he went immediately to Bed, where he lay restless and groaning, and often bemoaning himself and me, for the greatest Part of the Night.

Next

Next Morning my Siſter ſent a Man (whom, 1659.
for his Love to me, ſhe knew ſhe could truſt) to give me this Account; and though by him ſhe ſent me alſo freſh Linen for my Uſe, in caſe I ſhould go farther, or ſtay out longer; yet ſhe deſired me to come home as ſoon as I could.

This Account was very uneaſy to me. I was much grieved that I had occaſioned ſo much Grief to my Father. And I would have returned that Evening after the Meeting, but the Friends would not permit it; for the Meeting would in likelihood end late, the Days being ſhort, and the Way was long and dirty. And beſides, *John Rance* told me, that he had ſomething on his Mind to ſpeak to my Father, and that if I would ſtay till the next Day, he would go down with me; hoping perhaps, that while my Father was under this Sorrow for me, he might work ſome good upon him. Hereupon, concluding to ſtay till the Morrow, I diſmiſs'd the Man with the Things he brought, bidding him tell my Siſter, *I intended* (God willing) *to return home To-morrow*; and charging him not to let any Body elſe know that he had ſeen me, or where he had been.

Next Morning *John Rance* and I ſet out, and when we were come to the End of the Town, we agreed that he ſhould go before and knock at the great Gate, and I would come a little after, and go in by the Back-way. He did ſo; and when a Servant came to open the Gate, he aſking if the Juſtice were at home, ſhe told

1659. him, *Yes*; and desiring him to come in and sit down in the Hall, went and acquainted her Master, that there was one who desired to speak with him. He, supposing it was one that came for Justice, went readily into the Hall to him. But he was not a little surprized when he found it was a *Quaker*. Yet not knowing on what Account he came, he staid to hear his Business. But when he found it was about me, he fell somewhat sharply on him.

In this Time I was come by the Back-way into the Kitchen, and hearing my Father's Voice so loud, I began to doubt Things wrought not well; but I was soon assured of that. For my Father having quickly enough of a *Quaker*'s Company, left *John Rance* in the Hall, and came into the Kitchen, where he was more surprized to find me.

The Sight of my Hat upon my Head, made him presently forget that I was that Son of his, whom he had so lately lamented as lost; and his Passion of Grief turning into Anger, he could not contain himself; but running upon me, with both his Hands, first violently snatcht off my Hat, and threw it away; then giving me some Buffets on my Head, he said, *Sirrah, get you up to your Chamber*.

I forthwith went; he following me at the Heels, and now and then giving me a Whirret on the Ear; which (the Way to my Chamber lying through the Hall where *John Rance* was) he, poor Man, might see and be sorry for (as I doubt not but he was) but could not help me.

This

This was ſure an unaccountable thing, That 1659.
my Father ſhould, but a Day before, expreſs
ſo high a Sorrow for me, as fearing he ſhould never ſee me any more; and yet now, ſo ſoon as he did ſee me, ſhould fly upon me with ſuch Violence, and that only becauſe I did not put off my Hat, which he knew I did not keep on in *Diſreſpect* to him, but upon a *religious Principle.* But as this *Hat-honour* (as it was accounted) was grown to be a great *Idol,* in thoſe Times more eſpecially, ſo the Lord was pleaſed to engage his Servants in a ſteady Teſtimony againſt it, what Suffering ſoever was brought upon them for it. And though ſome, who have been called into the Lord's Vineyard at latter Hours, and ſince the Heat of that Day hath been much over, may be apt to account this Teſtimony a *ſmall Thing* to ſuffer *ſo much* upon, as ſome have done, not only to *Beating,* but to *Fines,* and *long* and *hard Impriſonments*; yet they who, in thoſe Times, were faithfully exerciſed in and under it, durſt not deſpiſe the *Day of ſmall Things*; as knowing that he who ſhould do ſo, would not be thought worthy to be concerned in *higher Teſtimonies.*

I had now loſt one of my Hats, and I had but one more. That therefore I put on, but did not keep it long; for the next Time my Father ſaw it on my Head, he tore it violently from me, and laid it up with the other, I knew not where. Wherefore I put on my Mountier-cap, which was all I had left to wear on my Head, and it was but a very little while

1659. that I had that to wear; for as ſoon as my Father came where I was, I loſt that alſo. And now I was forced to go bare-headed, wherever I had Occaſion to go, within Doors and without.

This was in the Eleventh Month, called *January*, and the Weather ſharp; ſo that I, who had been bred up more tenderly, took ſo great a Cold in my Head, that my Face and Head were much ſwelled; and my Gums had on them Boils ſo ſore, that I could neither chew Meat, nor without Difficulty ſwallow Liquids. It held long, and I underwent much Pain, without much Pity, except from my poor Siſter, who did what ſhe could to give me Eaſe; and at length, by frequent Applications of Figs and ſtoned Raiſins toaſted, and laid to the Boils as hot as I could bear them, they ripened fit for lancing, and ſoon after ſunk; then I had Eaſe.

Now was I laid up, as a kind of Priſoner, for the reſt of this Winter, having no means to go forth among Friends, nor they Liberty to come to me. Wherefore I ſpent the Time much in my Chamber, in waiting on the LORD, and in reading, moſtly in the Bible.

But whenever I had Occaſion to ſpeak to my Father, though I had no Hat now to offend him, yet my Language did as much; for I durſt not ſay [You] to him; but Thou, or Thee, as the Occaſion required, and then would he be ſure to fall on me with his Fiſts.

At one of these Times, I remember, when he had beaten me in that Manner, he commanded me, as he commonly did at such Times, to *go to my Chamber*; which I did, and he followed me to the Bottom of the Stairs. Being come thither, he gave me a Parting-blow, and in a very angry Tone said, *Sirrah, if ever I hear you say* Thou *or* Thee *to me again, I'll strike your Teeth down your Throat.* I was greatly grieved to hear him say so. And feeling a Word rise in my Heart unto him, I turned again, and calmly said unto him, *Would it not be just, if God should serve thee so, when thou sayest* Thou *or* Thee *to Him?* Though his Hand was up, I saw it sink and his Countenance fall, and he turned away and left me standing there. But I notwithstanding went up into my Chamber, and cried unto the Lord, earnestly beseeching Him, that He would be pleased to open my Father's Eyes, that he might see whom he fought against, and for what; and that He would turn his Heart. 1659.

After this I had a pretty time of Rest and Quiet from these Disturbances; my Father not saying any Thing to me, nor giving me Occasion to say any Thing to him. But I was still under a kind of Confinement, unless I would have run about the Country bare-headed like a Mad-man; which I did not see it was my Place to do. For I found that, although to be abroad and at Liberty among my Friends, would have been more pleasant to me; yet Home was at present my proper Place, a

1659. School in which I was to learn with *Patience* to *bear the Cross*, and I willingly submitted to it.

But after some Time a fresh Storm, more fierce and sharp than any before, arose and fell upon me; the Occasion whereof was this: My Father, having been in his younger Years, more especially while he lived in *London*, a constant Hearer of those who are called *Puritan* Preachers, had stored up a pretty Stock of *Scripture Knowledge*, did sometimes (not constantly, nor very often) cause his Family to come together on a First-day in the Evening, and expound a Chapter to them, and pray. His Family now, as well as his Estate, was lessen'd; for my Mother was dead, my Brother gone, and my elder Sister at *London*; and having put off his Husbandry, he had put off with it most of his Servants, so that he had now but one Man and one Maid-servant. It so fell out, that on a First-day Night he bid my Sister, who sate with him in the Parlour, *Call in the Servants to Prayer.*

Whether this was done as a Trial upon me or no, I know not; but a Trial it proved to me: For they, loving me very well, and disliking my Father's Carriage to me, made no haste to go in, but staid a second Summons. This so offended him, that when at length they did go in, he instead of going to *Prayer*, examined them, *Why they came not in when they were first called?* and the Answer they gave him being such as rather heightned, than abated

his

his Displeasure, he, with an angry Tone, said, 1659.
Call in that Fellow (meaning me, who was left alone in the Kitchen) *for he is the Cause of all this.* They, as they were backward to go in themselves, so were not forward to call me in, fearing the Effect of my Father's Displeasure would fall upon me, as it soon did; for I hearing what was said, and not staying for the Call, went in of myself. And as soon as I was come in, my Father discharged his Displeasure on me, in very sharp and bitter Expressions; which drew from me (in the Grief of my Heart, to see him so transported with Passion) these few Words; *They that can pray with such a Spirit let 'em; for my part I cannot.* With that my Father flew upon me with both his Fists, and not thinking that sufficient, stept hastily to the Place where his Cane stood, and catching that up, laid me on, I thought, with all his Strength. And, I being bare-headed, I thought his Blows must needs have broken my Skull, had I not laid mine Arm over my Head to defend it.

His Man seeing this, and not able to contain himself, stept in between us, and laying hold on the Cane, by Strength of Hand held it so fast, that though he attempted not to take it away, yet he with-held my Father from striking with it; which did but enrage him the more. I disliked this in the Man, and bid him *let go the Cane, and be gone*; which he immediately did, and turning to be gone, had a Blow

1659. Blow on the Shoulders for his Pains, which yet did not much hurt him.

But now my Sister, fearing lest my Father should fall upon me again, besought him to forbear; adding, *Indeed Sir, if you strike him any more, I will throw open the Casement and cry Murther; for I am afraid you will kill my Brother.* This stopt his Hand; and after some threatning Speeches, he commanded me to *Get to my Chamber*, which I did; as I always did whenever he bid me.

Thither, soon after, my Sister followed me to see my Arm and dress it, for it was indeed very much bruised and swelled between the Wrist and the Elbow; and in some Places the Skin was broken and beaten off. But though it was very sore, and I felt for some Time much Pain in it, yet I had Peace and Quietness in my Mind, being more grieved for my Father than for myself, who I knew had hurt himself more than me.

This was, so far as I remember, the last Time that ever my Father called his Family to *Prayer*. And this was also the last Time that he ever fell, so severely at least, upon me.

Soon after this, my elder Sister, who in all the Time of these Exercises of mine, had been at *London*, returned home; much troubled to find me a *Quaker*, a Name of Reproach and great Contempt then; and she, being at *London*, had received, I suppose, the worst Character of them. Yet, though she disliked the

People,

People, her affectionate Regard to me, made 1659.
her rather pity than despise me; and the more, when she understood what hard Usage I had met with.

The rest of this Winter I spent in a lonesome solitary Life, having none to converse with, none to unbosom myself unto, none to ask Counsel of, none to seek Relief from, but the LORD alone; who yet was more than All. And yet the Company and Society of faithful and judicious Friends, would, I thought, have been very welcome, as well as helpful to me in my spiritual Travel; in which I thought I made but a slow Progress, my Soul breathing after further Attainments: The Sense of which drew from me the following Lines;

> The Winter Tree
> Resembles me,
> Whose Sap lies in its Root:
> The Spring draws nigh;
> As it, so I
> Shall bud, I hope, and shoot.

At length it pleased the Lord to move *Isaac* 1660.
Penington and his Wife to make a Visit to my Father, and see how it fared with me: And very welcome they were to me, whatever they were to him; to whom I doubt not but they would have been more welcome, had it not been for me.

They tarried with us all Night, and much Discourse they had with my Father both about the

1660. the Principles of TRUTH in general, and me in particular; which I was not privy to. But one Thing, I remember, I afterwards heard of, which was this:

When my Father and we were at their Houſe ſome Months before, *Mary Penington*, in ſome Diſcourſe between them, had told him how hardly her Huſband's Father (Alderman *Penington)* had dealt with him about his Hat; which my Father (little then thinking that it would, and ſo ſoon too, be his own Caſe) did very much cenſure the Alderman for; wondring that ſo wiſe a Man as he was, ſhould take Notice of ſuch a trivial Thing as the *putting of*, or *keeping on a Hat*; and he ſpared not to blame him liberally for it.

This gave her a Handle to take hold of him by. And having had an ancient Acquaintance with him, and he having always had an high Opinion of and Reſpect for her; ſhe, who was a Woman of great Wiſdom, of ready Speech, and of a well-reſolved Spirit, did preſs ſo cloſe upon him with this Home-argument, that he was utterly to ſeek, and at a loſs how to defend himſelf.

After Dinner next Day, when they were ready to take Coach to return home, ſhe deſired my Father that, ſince my Company was ſo little acceptable to him, he would give me Leave to go and ſpend ſome Time with them, where I ſhould be ſure to be welcome.

He was very unwilling I ſhould go, and made many Objections againſt it; all which

ſhe

ſhe anſwered and removed ſo clearly, that 1660.
not finding what Excuſe further to alledge, he
at length left it to me; and I ſoon turned the
Scale for going.

We were come to the Coach-ſide before this was concluded on, and I was ready to ſtep in; when one of my Siſters privately put my Father in Mind, that I had never a Hat on. That ſomewhat ſtartled him; for he did not think it fit I ſhould go from home (and that ſo far, and to ſtay abroad) without a Hat. Wherefore he whiſpered to her, to *fetch me a Hat*, and he entertained them with ſome Diſcourſe in the mean Time. But as ſoon as he ſaw the Hat coming, he would not ſtay till it came, leſt I ſhould put it on before him; but breaking off his Diſcourſe abruptly, took his Leave of them, and haſtened in before the Hat was brought to me.

I had not one Penny of Money about me, nor any, indeed, elſewhere. For my Father, ſo ſoon as he ſaw that I would be a *Quaker*, took from me both what Money I had, and every Thing elſe of Value, or that would have made Money, as ſome Plate Buttons, Rings, &c. pretending that he would keep them for me, till I came to myſelf again, leſt I in the mean time ſhould deſtroy them.

But as I had no Money, ſo being among my Friends, I had no need of any, nor ever honed after it; though once upon a particular Occaſion I had like to have wanted it. The Caſe was thus:

I had

1660. I had been at *Reading*, and ſet out from thence on the Firſt-day of the Week in the Morning, intending to reach (as, in point of Time I well might) to *Iſaac Penington*'s, where the Meeting was to be that Day; but when I came to *Maidenhead*, a thorough-fair Town on the Way, I was ſtopt by the Watch for riding on that Day.

The Watchman laying hold on the Bridle, told me *I muſt go with him to the Conſtable*; and accordingly I, making no Reſiſtance, ſuffered him to lead my Horſe to the Conſtable's Door. When we were come there, the Conſtable told me, *I muſt go before the Warden*, who was the chief Officer of that Town, and bid the Watchman bring me on, himſelf walking before.

Being come to the Warden's Door, the Conſtable knockt, and deſired to ſpeak with Mr. Warden. He thereupon quickly coming to the Door, the Conſtable ſaid, *Sir, I have brought a Man here to you, whom the Watch took riding through the Town.* The Warden was a budge old Man; and I looked ſomewhat big too, having a good Gelding under me, and a good Riding-coat on my Back, both which my Friend *Iſaac Penington* had kindly accommodated me with for that Journey.

The Warden therefore taking me to be (as the Saying is) *Somebody*, put off his Hat and made a low Congee to me; but when he ſaw that I ſate ſtill, and neither bowed to him, nor moved my Hat, he gave a Start, and ſaid to the

the Constable, *You said you had brought a Man, but he don't behave himself like a Man.* 1660.

I sate still upon my Horse, and said not a Word, but kept my Mind retired to the Lord, waiting to see what this would come to.

The Warden then began to examine me, asking me *Whence I came?* and *Whither I was going?* I told him I came from *Reading*, and was going to *Chalfont*. He asked me, *Why I did travel on that Day?* I told him, I did not know that it would give any Offence barely to ride or walk on that Day, so long as I did not carry or drive any Carriage, or Horses laden with Burthens. *Why*, said he, *if your Business was urgent, did you not take a Pass from the Mayor of* Reading? Because, replied I, I did not know, nor think I should have needed one. *Well*, said he, *I will not talk with you now, because it is Time to go to Church; but I will examine you further anon.* And turning to the Constable, *Have him*, said he, *to an Inn, and bring him before me after Dinner.*

The naming of an Inn put me in Mind, that such publick Houses were Places of Expence, and I knew I had no Money to defray it. Wherefore I said to the Warden, Before thou sendest me to an Inn, which may occasion some Expence, I think it needful to acquaint thee, that I have no Money.

At that the Warden startled again; and turning quick upon me, said, *How! no Money! How can that be? You don't look like a Man that has no Money.* However I look, said I, I tell thee

1660. thee the Truth, that I have no Money; and I tell it to forewarn thee, that thou mayst not bring any Charge upon the Town. *I wonder,* said he, *what Art you have got, that you can travel without Money; you can do more, I assure you, than I can.*

I making no Answer, he went on and said, *Well, well! but if you have no Money, you have a good Horse under you, and we can distrain him for the Charge.* But, said I, the Horse is not mine. *No!* said he, *But you have a good Coat on your Back, and that, I hope, is your own.* No, said I, but it is not; for I borrowed both the Horse and the Coat.

With that the Warden holding up his Hands and smiling, said, *Bless me! I never met with such a Man as you are before! What! were you set out by the Parish?* Then turning to the Constable, he said, *Have him to the* Greyhound, *and bid the People be civil to him.* Accordingly to the *Greyhound* I was led, my Horse set up, and I put into a large Room; and some Account, I suppose, given of me to the People of the House.

This was new Work to me, and what the Issue of it would be, I could not foresee; but being left there alone, I sate down and retired in Spirit to the Lord, in whom alone my Strength and Safety was, and beg'd Support of Him; even that He would be pleased to give me Wisdom and Words to answer the Warden, when I should come to be examined again before him.

After

After ſome Time, having Pen, Ink and Paper about me, I ſet myſelf to write what I thought might be proper, if Occaſion ſerved, to give the Warden. And while I was writing, the Maſter of the Houſe being come home from his Worſhip, ſent the Tapſter to me, to invite me to dine with him. I bid him tell his Maſter, that I had not any Money to pay for my Dinner. He ſent the Man again to tell me, *I ſhould be welcome to dine with him, though I had no Money.* I deſired him to tell his Maſter, that I was very ſenſible of his Civility and Kindneſs, in ſo courteouſly inviting me to his Table; but I had not Freedom to eat of his Meat, unleſs I could have paid for it. So he went on with his Dinner, and I with my writing. 1660.

But before I had finiſhed what was on my Mind to write, the Conſtable came again, bringing with him his fellow Conſtable. This was a briſk, genteel young Man, a Shopkeeper in the Town, whoſe Name was *Cherry.* They ſaluted me civilly, and told me they were come to have me before the Warden. This put an End to my writing; which I put into my Pocket, and went along with them.

Being come to the Warden's, he aſked me again the ſame Queſtions he had aſked me before; to which I gave him the like Anſwers. Then he told me the Penalty I had incurred; which, he ſaid, was *either to pay ſo much Money, or lie ſo many Hours in the Stocks*; and aſked me, *which I would chuſe?* I reply'd, I ſhall not chuſe either. And ſaid I, I have told

1660. thee already that I have no Money; though if I had, I could not so far acknowledge myself an Offender, as to pay any. But as to lying in the Stocks, I am in thy Power, to do unto me what it shall please the Lord to suffer thee.

When he heard that, he paused a while, and then told me, *He considered that I was but a young Man, and might not, perhaps, understand the Danger I had brought myself into, and therefore he would not use the Severity of the Law upon me; but in hopes that I would be wiser hereafter, he would pass by this Offence and discharge me.*

Then putting on a Countenance of the greatest Gravity, he said to me; *But, young Man, I would have you know, that you have not only broken the Law of the Land, but the Law of God also; and therefore you ought to ask Him Forgiveness, for you have highly offended Him.* That, said I, I would most willingly do, if I were sensible that, in this Case, I had offended Him by breaking any Law of His. *Why*, said he, *do you question that?* Yes truly, said I; for I do not know that any Law of God doth forbid me to ride on this Day.

No! said he, *that's strange! Where, I wonder, were you bred? You can read; can't you?* Yes said I, that I can. *Don't you read then*, said he, *the Commandment*; Remember the Sabbath-day to keep it holy. Six Days shalt thou labour, and do all thy Work; but the Seventh-day is the Sabbath of the Lord thy God; in it thou shalt not do any Work. Yes, replyed I, I have both read it often, and remember it very well.

well. But that Command was given to the *Jews*, not to *Christians*; and this is not that Day, for that was the Seventh-day, but this is the first. *How!* said he, *do you know the Days of the Week no better? you had need then be better taught.* 1660.

Here the younger Constable, whose Name was *Cherry*, interposing, said, *Mr.* Warden, *the Gentleman is in the right as to that; for this is the First-day of the Week, and not the seventh.*

This the old Warden took in dudgeon; and looking severely on the Constable, said, *What! do you take upon you to teach me! I'll have you know, I will not be taught by you. As you please for that, Sir,* said the Constable, *but I am sure you are mistaken in this Point; for* Saturday, *I know, is the* Seventh-day, *and you know Yesterday was* Saturday.

This made the Warden hot and testy, and put him almost out of all Patience, so that I fear'd it would have come to a downright Quarrel betwixt them; for both were confident, and neither would yield. And so earnestly were they engaged in the Contest, that there was no room for me to put in a Word between them.

At length the old Man, having talk'd himself out of Wind, stood still a while as it were to take Breath, and then bethinking himself of me, he turn'd to me and said, *You are discharged, and may take your Liberty to go about your Occasions.* But, said I, I desire my Horse may be discharged too, else I know not how to go. *Ay, ay,* said he, *you shall have your Horse*; and

1660. turning to the other Conſtable who had not offended him, he ſaid, *Go, ſee that his Horſe be delivered to him.*

Away thereupon went I with that Conſtable, leaving the old Warden and the young Conſtable to compoſe their Difference as they could. Being come to the Inn, the Conſtable called for my Horſe to be brought out. Which done, I immediately mounted and began to ſet forward. But the Hoſtler, not knowing the Condition of my Pocket, ſaid modeſtly to me, *Sir, don't you forget to pay for your Horſe's ſtanding?* No truly, ſaid I, I don't forget it, but I have no Money to pay it with, and ſo I told the Warden before. *Well, hold you your Tongue,* ſaid the Conſtable to the Hoſtler, *I'll ſee you paid.* Then opening the Gate they let me out, the Conſtable wiſhing me a good Journey, and through the Town I rode without further Moleſtation; though it was as much Sabbath, I thought, when I went out, as it was when I came in.

A ſecret Joy aroſe in me as I rode on the Way, for that I had been preſerved from doing or ſaying any Thing, which might give the Adverſaries of TRUTH Advantage againſt it, or the Friends of it; and Praiſes ſprang in my thankful Heart to the Lord, my Preſerver.

It added alſo not a little to my Joy, that I felt the Lord near unto me, by His Witneſs in my Heart, to check and warn me; and my Spirit was ſo far ſubjected to Him, as readily to

take

take Warning, and ſtop at His Check; an Inſtance of both, that very Morning I had. 1660.

For as I rode between *Reading* and *Maidenhead*, I ſaw lying in my Way the Scabbard of an Hanger, which, having loſt its Hook, had ſlipt off, I ſuppoſe, and dropt from the Side of the Wearer; and it had in it a Pair of Knives, whoſe Hafts being inlaid with Silver, ſeemed to be of ſome Value. I alighted and took it up, and clapping it between my Thigh and the Saddle, rode on a little Way; but I quickly found it too heavy for me, and the Reprover in me ſoon began to check. The Word aroſe in me, *What haſt thou to do with that? Doth it belong to thee?* I felt I had done amiſs in taking it; wherefore I turned back to the Place where it lay, and laid it down where I found it. And when afterwards I was ſtopt and ſeized on at *Maidenhead*, I ſaw there was a Providence in not bringing it with me; which, if it ſhould have been found (as it needs muſt) under my Coat when I came to be unhorſed, might have raiſed ſome evil Suſpicion or ſiniſter Thoughts concerning me.

The Stop I met with at *Maidenhead* had ſpent me ſo much Time, that when I came to *Iſaac Penington*'s, the Meeting there was half over; which gave them Occaſion, after Meeting, to enquire of me, *If any Thing had befallen me on the Way, which had cauſed me to come ſo late?* Whereupon I related to them what Exerciſe I had met with, and how the Lord had helped me through it: Which when

 they

1660. they had heard, they rejoiced with me, and for my Sake.

Great was the Love, and manifold the Kindneſſes, which I received from theſe my worthy Friends, *Iſaac* and *Mary Penington*, while I abode in their Family. They were indeed as affectionate Parents, and tender Nurſes to me, in this Time of my *religious Childhood*. For beſides their weighty and ſeaſonable Counſels, and exemplary Converſations, they furniſhed me with Means to go to the other Meetings of Friends in that Country, when the Meeting was not in their own Houſe. And indeed, the Time I ſtaid with them was ſo well ſpent, that it not only yielded great Satisfaction to my Mind; but turned, in good meaſure, to my ſpiritual Advantage in the TRUTH.

But that I might not, on the one hand, bear too hard upon my Friends; nor on the other hand, forget the Houſe of Thraldom; after I had ſtaid with them ſome ſix or ſeven Weeks (from the Time called *Eaſter*, to the Time called *Whitſuntide)* I took my Leave of them to depart home, intending to walk to *Wiccomb* in one Day, and from thence home in another.

That Day that I came home I did not ſee my Father, nor until Noon the next Day, when I went into the Parlour where he was, to take my uſual Place at Dinner.

As ſoon as I came in, I obſerved by my Father's Countenance, that my Hat was ſtill an Offence to him; but when I was ſitten down, and before I had eaten any Thing, he made me

underſtand

understand it more fully, by saying to me, but 1660.
in a milder Tone than he had formerly used
to speak to me in, *If you cannot content yourself to come to Dinner without your Hive on your Head* (so he called my Hat) *pray rise, and go take your Dinner somewhere else.*

Upon those Words I arose from the Table, and leaving the Room, went into the Kitchen, where I staid till the Servants went to Dinner, and then sate down very contentedly with them. Yet I suppose my Father might intend that I should have gone into some other Room, and there have eaten by myself. But I chose rather to eat with the Servants; and did so from thenceforward, so long as he and I lived together. And from this Time he rather chose, as I thought, to avoid seeing me, than to renew the Quarrel about my Hat.

My Sisters, mean while observing my Wariness in Words and Behaviour, and being satisfied, I suppose, that I acted upon a *Principle of Religion* and *Conscience*, carried themselves very kindly to me, and did what they could to mitigate my Father's Displeasure against me. So that I now enjoyed much more Quiet at home, and took more Liberty to go abroad amongst my Friends, than I had done, or could do before. And having informed myself, where any Meetings of Friends were holden, within a reasonable Distance from me, I resorted to them.

At first I went to a Town called *Haddenham* in *Buckinghamshire*, five Miles from my Fa-

 ther's,

1660. ther's, where, at the House of one *Belson*, a few who were called *Quakers* did meet sometimes on a First-day of the Week; but I found little Satisfaction there. Afterwards, upon further Enquiry, I understood there was a settled Meeting at a little Village called *Meadle*, about four long Miles from me, in the House of one *John White*, which is continued there still; and to that thenceforward I constantly went, while I abode in that Country and was able. Many a sore Day's Travel have I had thither and back again; being commonly in the Winter-time (how fair soever the Weather was over head) wet up to the Ancles at least; yet through the Goodness of the Lord to me, I was preserved in Health.

A little Meeting also there was, on the Fourth-day of the Week, at a Town called *Bledlow* (two Miles from me) in the House of one *Thomas Saunders*, who professed the Truth; but his Wife, whose Name was *Damaris*, did *possess* it (she being a Woman of great Sincerity and lively Sense) and to that Meeting also I usually went.

But though I took this Liberty for the Service of GOD, that I might worship Him in the Assemblies of His People, yet did I not use it upon other Occasions; but spent my Time, on other Days for the most part in my Chamber, in Retiredness of Mind, waiting on the LORD. And the LORD was graciously pleased to visit me, by His quickening *Spirit* and *Life*; so that I came to feel the *Operation of His*

Power

Power in my Heart, working out that which 1660.
was contrary to His Will, and giving me, in
measure, Dominion over it.

And as my Spirit was kept in a due Subjection to this *divine Power*, I grew into a nearer Acquaintance with the LORD; and the LORD vouchsafed to speak unto me in the Inward of my Soul, and to open my Understanding in His Fear, to receive *Counsel* from Him; so that I not only at some Times heard His Voice, but could distinguish His Voice from the Voice of the Enemy.

As thus I daily waited on the LORD, a weighty and unusual Exercise came upon me, which bowed my Spirit very low before the LORD. I had seen, in the *Light of the* LORD, the horrible Guilt of those deceitful *Priests*, of divers Sorts and Denominations, who made a *Trade* of PREACHING, and for *filthy Lucre-sake* held the People *always learning*; yet so taught them, as that, by their *Teaching* and *Ministry*, they were never able *to come to the Knowledge* (much less to the Acknowledgement) *of the Truth*: For as they themselves hated the *Light*, because their own *Deeds were evil*; so by *reviling*, *reproaching*, and *blaspheming* the TRUE LIGHT, (*wherewith every Man that cometh into the World is enlightned*, John i. 9.) they begat in the People a Dis-esteem of the *Light*; and laboured, as much as in them lay, to keep their Hearers in the *Darkness*, that they might not be turned to the *Light* in *themselves*, lest by the *Light* they should discover the *Wicked-*
ness

1660. *ness* of these their *deceitful Teachers*, and turn from them.

Against this Practice of these *false Teachers*, the Zeal of the LORD had flamed in my Breast for some Time; and now the Burthen of the Word of the LORD against them fell heavy upon me, with Command to proclaim His Controversy against them.

Fain would I have been excused from this Service, which I judged too heavy for me: Wherefore I besought the Lord to take this Weight from off me, who was, in every respect, but young, and lay it upon some other of His Servants, of whom He had many, who were much more able and fit for it. But the Lord would not be intreated, but continued the Burden upon me with greater Weight; requiring *Obedience* from me, and promising to assist me therein. Whereupon I arose from my Bed, and in the Fear and Dread of the Lord, committed to Writing what He, in the Motion of His *divine Spirit*, dictated to me to write. When I had done it, though the Sharpness of the Message therein delivered, was hard to my Nature to be the Publisher of; yet I found Acceptance with the Lord, in my Obedience to His Will, and His Peace filled my Heart. As soon as I could, I communicated to my Friends what I had written; and it was printed in the Year 1660, in one Sheet of Paper, under the Title of *An Alarm to the* PRIESTS; or, *a Message from Heaven to forewarn them*, &c.

Some

Some Time after the publiſhing of this Paper, 1660.
having Occaſion to go to *London*, I went to viſit *George Fox* the younger, who, with another Friend, was then a Priſoner in a Meſſenger's Hands. I had never ſeen him, nor he me before; yet this Paper lying on the Table before him, he pointing to it, aſked me, *If I was the Perſon that writ it?* I told him, I was. *It's much*, ſaid the other Friend, *that they bear it. It is*, replied he, *their Portion; and they muſt bear it.*

While I was then in *London*, I went to a little Meeting of Friends, which was then held in the Houſe of one *Humphry Bache* a Goldſmith, at the Sign of the *Snail* in *Tower-ſtreet*. It was then a very troubleſome Time, not from the Government, but from the Rabble of Boys and rude People, who upon the Turn of the Times (at the Return of the King) took Liberty to be very abuſive.

When the Meeting ended, a pretty Number of theſe unruly Folk were got together at the Door, ready to receive the Friends as they came forth, not only with evil Words, but with Blows; which I ſaw they beſtowed freely on ſome of them that were gone out before me, and expected I ſhould have my Share of when I came amongſt them. But quite contrary to my Expectation, when I came out, they ſaid one to another, *Let him alone; don't meddle with him; he is no* Quaker *I'll warrant you.*

This ſtruck me, and was worſe to me than if they had laid their Fiſts on me, as they did on

1660. on others. I was troubled to think what the Matter was, or what these rude People saw in me, that made them not take me for a *Quaker*. And upon a close Examination of myself, with respect to my Habit and Deportment, I could not find any Thing to place it on, but that I had then on my Head a large Montier-cap of black Velvet, the Skirt of which being turned up in Folds, looked (it seems) somewhat above the then common Garb of a *Quaker*; and this put me out of Conceit with my Cap.

I came, at this Time, to *London* from *Isaac Penington*'s, and thither I went again in my way home; and while I staid there, amongst other Friends who came thither, *Thomas Loe* of *Oxford* was one. A faithful and diligent Labourer he was in the Work of the Lord, and an excellent ministerial Gift he had. And I, in my Zeal for Truth, being very desirous that my Neighbours might have the Opportunity of hearing the Gospel, the glad Tidings of Salvation, livingly and powerfully preached among them, entered into Communication with him about it; offering to procure some convenient Place, in the Town where I lived, for a Meeting to be held, and to invite my Neighbours to it, if he could give me any Ground to expect his Company at it. He told me, *he was not at his own Command, but at the Lord's; and he knew not how He might dispose of him; but wish'd me, if I found when I was come home, that the Thing continued with Weight upon my Mind, and that I could get a fit Place for a Meeting, I would*

would advertize him of it by a few Lines, direct-ed to him in Oxford, *whither he was then going, and he might then let me know how his Freedom ſtood in that Matter.* 1660.

When therefore I was come home, and had treated with a Neighbour for a Place to have a Meeting in, I wrote to my Friend *Thomas Loe*, to acquaint him that I had procured a Place for a Meeting, and would invite Company to it, if he would fix the Time, and give me ſome Ground to hope that he would be at it.

This Letter I ſent by a Neighbour to *Thame*, to be given to a *Dyer* of *Oxford*, who conſtantly kept *Thame* Market, with whom I was pretty well acquainted, having ſometimes formerly uſed him, not only in his Way of Trade, but to carry Letters between my Brother and me, when he was a Student in that Univerſity, for which he was always paid; and had been ſo careful in the Delivery, that our Letters had always gone ſafe until now. But this Time (Providence ſo ordering, or at leaſt for my Trial permitting it) this Letter of mine, inſtead of being delivered according to its Direction, was ſeized and carried, as I was told, to the Lord *Faulkland*, who was then called Lord-Lieutenant of that County.

The Occaſion of this Stopping of Letters at that Time, was that mad Prank of thoſe infatuated *Fifth-monarchy-men*, who from their Meeting-houſe in *Coleman-ſtreet*, *London*, breaking forth in Arms, under the Command of

their

1660. their Chieftain *Venner*, made an Insurrection in the City, on Pretence of setting up the *Kingdom of Jesus*; who it is said, they expected would come down from Heaven to be their Leader. So little understood they the *Nature of His Kingdom*; though He Himself had declared, *it was not of this World.*

The King, a little before his Arrival in *England*, had, by his *Declaration* from *Breda*, given Assurance of Liberty to *tender Consciences*; and that no Man should be disquieted, or called in Question for *Difference of Opinion* in Matters of *Religion*, who do not disturb the *Peace of the Kingdom:* Upon this Assurance, Dissenters of all Sorts relied, and held themselves secure. But now, by this frantick Action of a few hot-brain'd Men, the King was, by some, holden discharged from this his ROYAL WORD and PROMISE, in his foregoing *Declaration* publickly given. And hereupon Letters were intercepted and broken open, for Discovery of suspected Plots and Designs against the Government; and not only Dissenters Meetings, of all Sorts, without Distinction were disturbed, but very many were imprisoned in most Parts throughout the Nation; and great Search there was, in all Countries, for suspected Persons, who, if not found at Meetings, were fetch'd in from their own Houses.

The Lord-Lieutenant (so called) of *Oxford-shire* had on this Occasion taken *Thomas Loe*, and many other of our Friends, at a Meeting, and sent them Prisoners to *Oxford* Castle, just before

before my Letter was brought to his Hand, 1660.
wherein I had invited *Thomas Loe* to a Meeting; and he, putting the worst Construction upon it, as if I (a poor simple Lad) had intended a *seditious Meeting*, in order to raise *Rebellion*, ordered two of the Deputy-Lieutenants, who lived nearest to me, to send a Party of Horse to fetch me in.

Accordingly, while I (wholly ignorant of what had passed at *Oxford*) was in daily Expectation of an agreeable Answer to my Letter; came a Party of Horse one Morning to my Father's Gate, and asked for me.

It so fell out, that my Father was at that Time from home, I think in *London*; whereupon he that commanded the Party alighted, and came in. My eldest Sister, hearing the Noise of Soldiers, came hastily up into my Chamber, and told me there were Soldiers below who enquired for me. I forthwith went down to them, and found the Commander was a *Barber* of *Thame*, and one who had always been my *Barber* till I was a *Quaker*. His Name was *Whately*, a bold brisk Fellow.

I asked him, what his Business was with me? He told me, *I must go with him*. I demanded to see his Warrant: He laid his Hand on his Sword and said, *That was his Warrant*. I told him, Though that was not a legal Warrant, yet I would not dispute it; but was ready to bear Injuries. He told me, *He could not help it; he was commanded to bring me forthwith before the Deputy-Lieutenants*; and therefore

1660. therefore desired me *to order an Horse to be got ready*, because *he was in haste.* I let him know, I had no Horse of my own, and would not meddle with any of my Father's Horses, in his Absence especially; and that therefore, if he would have me with him, he must carry me as he could.

He thereupon taking my Sister aside, told her *he found I was resolute*, and *his Orders were peremptory*; wherefore he desired, *that she would give Order for an Horse to be made ready for me; for otherwise he should be forced to mount me behind a Trooper, which would be very unsuitable for me, and which he was very unwilling to do.* She thereupon ordered an Horse to be got ready, upon which, when I had taken Leave of my Sisters, I mounted and went off, not knowing whither he intended to carry me.

He had Orders, it seems, to take some others also in a neighbouring Village, whose Names he had, but their Houses he did not know. Wherefore, as we rode, he asked me, *If I knew such and such Men* (whom he named) and *where they lived*; and when he understood that I knew them, he *desired me to shew him their Houses.* No, said I, I scorn to be an Informer against my Neighbours, to bring them into Trouble. He thereupon riding to and fro, found by Enquiry most of their Houses; but, as it happened, found none of them at home, at which I was glad.

At length he brought me to the House of one called Esquire *Clark* of *Weston* by *Thame*, who

who being afterwards Knighted, was called Sir *John Clark*; a jolly Man, too much addicted to Drinking in *soberer* Times, but was now grown more *licentious* that way, as the Times did now more favour *Debauchery*. He and I had known one another for some Years, though not very intimately, having met sometimes at the Lord *Wenman*'s Table. 1660.

This *Clark* was one of the Deputy-Lieutenants, whom I was to be brought before. And he had gotten another thither, to join with him in tendering me the Oaths, whom I knew only by Name and Character; he was called Esquire *Knowls* of *Grays* by *Henley*, and reputed a Man of better Morals than the other.

I was brought into the Hall, and kept there. And as *Quakers* were not so common then, as they now are (and indeed even yet, the more is the pity, they are not common in that Part of the Country) I was made a Spectacle and Gazing-stock to the Family, and by divers I was diversly set upon. Some spake to me courteously, with Appearance of Compassion; others ruggedly, with evident Tokens of Wrath and Scorn. But though I gave them the Hearing of what they said, which I could not well avoid, yet I said little to them; but keeping my Mind as well retired as I could, I breathed to the Lord for Help and Strength from Him, to bear me up and carry me through this Trial, that I might not sink under it, or be prevailed on by any Means, fair or foul, to do any Thing that might dishonour or displease my GOD.

 At

1660. At length came forth the Juſtices themſelves, (for ſo they were, as well as Lieutenants) and after they had ſaluted me, they diſcourſed with me pretty familiarly: And though *Clark* would ſometimes be a little jocular and waggiſh (which was ſomewhat natural to him) yet *Knowls* treated me very civilly, not ſeeming to take any Offence at my not ſtanding bare before him. And when a young Prieſt, who, as I underſtood was Chaplain in the Family, took upon him pragmatically to reprove me for ſtanding with my Hat on before the Magiſtrates, and ſnatch'd my Cap from off my Head, *Knowls* in a pleaſant manner corrected him, telling him *he miſtook himſelf, in taking a Cap for a Hat* (for mine was a Mountier-cap) and bid him *give it me again*; which he (though unwillingly) doing, I forthwith put it on my Head again, and thenceforward none meddled with me about it.

Then they began to examine me, putting divers Queſtions to me, relating to the preſent Diſturbances in the Nation, occaſioned by the late fooliſh Inſurrection of thoſe frantick *Fifth-monarchy-men*. To all which I readily anſwered, according to the Simplicity of my Heart, and Innocency of my Hands; for I had neither done nor thought any Evil againſt the Government.

But they endeavoured to affright me with Threats of Danger; telling me (with *Innuendo's)* that for all my Pretence of Innocency, there was high Matter againſt me, which, if I would

I would ſtand out, would be brought forth, and 1660.
that under my own Hand. I knew not what they meant by this; but I knew my Innocency, and kept to it.

At length, when they ſaw I regarded not their Threats in general, they aſked me, *If I knew one* Thomas Loe, *and had written of late to him.* I then remembred my Letter, which till then I had not thought of, and thereupon frankly told them, That I did both know *Thomas Loe*, and had lately written to him; but that as I knew I had written no Hurt, ſo I did not fear any Danger from that Letter. They ſhook their Heads, and ſaid, *It was dangerous to write Letters to appoint Meetings in ſuch troubleſome Times.*

They added, *That by appointing a Meeting, and endeavouring to gather a Concourſe of People together, in ſuch a Juncture eſpecially as this was, I had rendered myſelf a dangerous Perſon. And therefore they could do no leſs, than tender me the Oaths of* Allegiance *and* Supremacy; *which therefore they required me to take.*

I told them, If I could take any Oath at all, I would take the Oath of *Allegiance*; for I owed Allegiance to the King. But I durſt not take any Oath, becauſe my Lord and Maſter Jesus Christ, had commanded me not to *ſwear at all*; and if I brake His Command, I ſhould thereby both diſhonour and diſpleaſe Him.

Hereupon they undertook to reaſon with me, and uſed many Words to perſwade me, That *that Command of Chriſt related only to common and*

1660. *prophane Swearing, not to Swearing before a Magistrate.* I heard them and ſaw the Weakneſs of their Arguings, but did not return them any Anſwer; for I found my preſent Buſineſs was not to diſpute, but to ſuffer; and that it was not ſafe for me, in this my weak and Childiſh State eſpecially, to enter into Reaſonings with ſharp, quick, witty and learned Men, leſt I might thereby hurt both the Cauſe of Truth, which I was to bear Witneſs to, and myſelf: Therefore I choſe rather to be a Fool, and let them triumph over me, than by my Weakneſs give them Advantage to triumph over the Truth. And my Spirit being cloſely exerciſed in a deep Travail towards the Lord, I earneſtly begged of Him, that He would be pleaſed to keep me faithful to the Teſtimony He had committed to me, and not ſuffer me to be taken in any of the Snares which the Enemy laid for me. And, bleſſed be His holy Name, He heard my Cries, and preſerved me out of them.

When the Juſtices ſaw they could not bow me to their Wills, they told me *they muſt ſend me to Priſon.* I told them, I was contented to ſuffer whatſoever the Lord ſhould ſuffer them to inflict upon me. Whereupon they withdrew into the Parlour, to conſult together what to do with me; leaving me mean while to be gazed on in the Hall.

After a pretty long Stay, they came forth to me again with great Shew of Kindneſs, telling me, They were *very unwilling to ſend me to Goal,*

but

but would be as favourable to me as possibly they could; and that, if I would take the Oaths, they would pass by all the other Matter, which they had against me. I told them, I knew they could not justly have any Thing against me, for I had neither done, nor intended any Thing against the Government, or against them. And as to the Oaths, I assured them, that my refusing them was meerly Matter of Conscience to me, and that I durst not take any Oath whatsoever, if it were to save my Life.

When they heard this, they left me again, and went and signed a *Mittimus* to send me to Prison at *Oxford* and charged one of the Troopers that brought me thither, who was one of the newly raised Militia-troop, to convey me safe to *Oxford*. But before we departed, they called the Trooper aside, and gave him private Instructions, what he should do with me; which I knew nothing of till I came thither, but expected I should go directly to the Castle.

It was almost dark when we took Horse, and we had about nine or ten Miles to ride, the Weather thick and cold (for it was about the Beginning of the twelfth Month) and I had no Boots, being snatch'd away from home on a sudden, which made me not care to ride very fast: And my Guard, who was a Tradesman in *Thame*, having Confidence in me, that I would not give him the Slip, jogged on without heeding how I followed him.

1660. When I was gone about a Mile on the Way, I overtook my Father's Man, who, without my Knowledge, had followed me at a Diſtance to *Weſton*, and waited there abroad in the Stables, till he underſtood by ſome of the Servants, that I was to go to *Oxford*; and then ran before, reſolving not to leave me till he ſaw what they would do with me.

I would have had him return home, but he deſired me not to ſend him back, but let him run on till I came to *Oxford*. I conſidered that it was a Token of the Fellow's affectionate Kindneſs to me, and that poſſibly I might ſend my Horſe home by him; and thereupon ſtopping my Horſe, I bid him, if he would go on, get up behind me. He modeſtly refuſed, telling me, *He could run as faſt I rid.* But when I had told him, if he would not ride, he ſhould not go forward; he, rather than leave me, leap'd up behind me, and on we went.

But he was not willing I ſhould have gone at all. He had a great Cudgel in his Hand, and a ſtrong Arm to uſe it; and being a ſtout Fellow, he had a great mind to fight the Trooper and reſcue me. Wherefore he deſired me to turn my Horſe and ride off. And if the Trooper offered to purſue, leave him to deal with him.

I check'd him ſharply for that, and charged him to be quiet, and not think hardly of the poor Trooper, who could do no other nor leſs than he did; and who, though he had an ill

Journey

Journey in going with me, carried himſelf civilly to me. I told him alſo, that I had no need to fly, for I had done nothing that would bring Guilt or Fear upon me; neither did I go with an ill Will; and this quieted the Man. So on we went; but were ſo far caſt behind the Trooper, that we had loſt both Sight and Hearing of him, and I was fain to mend my Pace to get up to him again. 1660.

We came pretty late into *Oxford* on the Seventh-day of the Week, which was the Market-day; and contrary to my Expectation (which was to have been carried to the Caſtle) my Trooper ſtop'd in the *High-Street*, and calling at a Shop, aſked for the Maſter of the Houſe; who coming to the Door, he delivered to him the *Mittimus*, and with it a Letter from the Deputy-Lieutenants (or one of them) which when he had read, he aſked *where the Priſoner was.* Whereupon the Soldier pointing to me, he deſired me to alight and come in; which when I did, he received me civilly.

The Trooper, being diſcharged of his Priſoner, marched back, and my Father's Man, ſeeing me ſettled in better Quarters than he expected, mounted my Horſe and went off with him.

I did not preſently underſtand the Quality of my Keeper; but I found him a genteel, courteous Man, by Trade a *Linen-draper*; and, as I afterwards underſtood, he was the City-Marſhall, had a Command in the County

1660. Troop, and was a Person of good Repute in the Place; his Name was ——— *Galloway*.

Whether I was committed to him out of Regard to my Father, that I might not be thrust into a common Goal; or out of a politick Design, to keep me from the Conversation of my Friends, in hopes that I might be drawn to abandon this Profession, which I had but lately taken up; I do not know. But this I know, that though I wanted no civil Treatment, nor kind Accommodations where I was, yet after once I understood, that many Friends were Prisoners in the Castle, and amongst the rest, *Thomas Loe*, I had much rather have been among them there, with all the Inconveniencies they underwent, than where I was with the best Entertainment. But this was my present Lot; and therefore with this I endeavoured to be content.

It was quickly known in the City, that a *Quaker* was brought in Prisoner and committed to the Marshall. Whereupon, the Men Friends being generally Prisoners already in the Castle, some of the Women Friends came to enquire after me and to visit me; as *Silas Norton*'s Wife, and *Thomas Loe*'s Wife, who were Sisters, and another Woman Friend who lived in the same Street where I was, whose Husband was not a *Quaker*, but kindly affected towards them; a *Baker* by Trade, and his Name, as I remember, ——— *Ryland*.

By some of these an Account was soon given to the Friends, who were Prisoners in the

Castle,

Castle, of my being taken up and brought Prisoner to the Marshall's. Whereupon it pleased the Lord to move on the Heart of my dear Friend *Thomas Loe*, to salute me with a very tender and affectionate Letter in the following Terms: 1660.

My beloved FRIEND,

IN *the Truth and Love of the Lord Jesus, by which Life and Salvation is revealed in the Saints, is my dear Love unto thee, and in much Tenderness do I salute thee. And dear Heart, a Time of Trial God hath permitted to come upon us, to try our Faith and Love to Him; and this will work for the Good of them, that through Patience endure to the End. And I believe* GOD *will be glorified through our Sufferings, and His Name will be exalted in the Patience and Long-suffering of His Chosen. When I heard that thou wast called into this Trial, with the Servants of the Most High, to give thy Testimony to the Truth of what we have believed, it came into my Heart to write unto thee, and to greet thee with the Embraces of the Power of an endless Life; where our Faith stands, and Unity is felt with the Saints for ever. Well, my dear Friend, let us live in the pure Counsel of the Lord, and dwell in His Strength, which gives us Power and Sufficiency to endure all Things, for His Name's-sake; and then our Crown and Reward will be with the Lord for ever, and the Blessings of His heavenly Kingdom will be our Portion.*

Oh,

1660. *Oh, dear Heart, let us give up all freely into the Will of God, that God may be glorified by us, and we comforted together in the Lord Jesus; which is the Desire of my Soul, who am*

Thy dear and loving Friend in the eternal Truth,

THOMAS LOE.

We are more than Forty here, who suffer innocently for the Testimony of a good Conscience; because we cannot Swear, and break Christ's Commands: And we are all well; and the Blessing, and Presence of God is with us. Friends here salute thee. Farewel.
The Power and the Wisdom of the Lord God be with thee, Amen.

Greatly was my Spirit refreshed, and my Heart gladded, at the reading of this consolating Letter from my Friend; and my Soul blessed the Lord for His Love and tender Goodness to me, in moving His Servant to write thus unto me.

But I had Cause soon after to double, and redouble my thankful Acknowledgment to the Lord my God, who put it into the Heart of my dear Friend *Isaac Penington* also, to visit me with some encouraging Lines from *Aylesbury* Goal, where he was then a Prisoner; and from whence (having heard that I was carried Prisoner to *Oxford)* he thus saluted me:

Dear

Dear THOMAS,

GReat hath been the Lord's Goodness to thee, in calling thee out of that Path of Vanity and Death, wherein thou wast running towards Destruction; to give thee a living Name, and an Inheritance of Life among His People; which certainly will be the End of thy Faith in Him, and Obedience to Him. And let it not be a light Thing in thine Eyes, that He now accounteth thee worthy to suffer among His choice Lambs, that He might make thy Crown weightier, and thy Inheritance the fuller. O that that Eye and Heart may be kept open in thee, which knoweth the Value of these Things! And that thou mayst be kept close to the Feeling of the Life, that thou mayst be fresh in thy Spirit in the midst of thy Sufferings, and mayst reap the Benefit of them; finding that pared off thereby, which hindereth the Bubblings of the everlasting Springs, and maketh unfit for the breaking forth and Enjoyment of the pure Power! This is the brief Salutation of my dear Love to thee, which desireth thy Strength and Settlement in the Power, and the utter weakning of thee as to Self. My dear Love is to thee, with dear Thomas Goodyare, *and the rest of imprisoned Friends. I remain*

Thine in the Truth, to which, the Lord my God preserve thee single and faithful.

From *Aylesbury* Goal, the 14th of the twelfth Month, 1660.

I. PENINGTON.

Though

Though these epistolary Visits in the Love of God, were very comfortable and confirming to me, and my Heart was thankful to the Lord for them; yet I honed after personal Conversation with Friends, and it was hard, I thought, that there should be so many faithful Servants of God so near me, yet I should not be permitted to come at them, to enjoy their Company, and reap both the Pleasure and Benefit of their sweet Society.

For although my Marshall-keeper was very kind to me, and allowed me the Liberty of his House, yet he was not willing I should be seen abroad; the rather perhaps, because he understood I had been pretty well known in that City. Yet once the friendly *Baker* got him to let me step over to his House; and once (and but once) I prevailed with him, to let me visit my Friends in the Castle; but it was with these Conditions, That I should not go forth till it was dark; That I would muffle myself up in my Cloak; and that I would not stay out late. All which I punctually observed.

When I came thither, though there were many Friends Prisoners, I scarce knew one of them by Face, except *Thomas Loe*, whom I had once seen at *Isaac Penington*'s: Nor did any of them know me, though they had generally heard, that such a young Man as I, was convinced of the Truth and come among Friends.

Our Salutation to each other was very grave and solemn; nor did we entertain one another with much Talk, or with common Discourses;

but

but moſt of the little Time I had with them, was ſpent in a ſilent Retiredneſs of Spirit, waiting upon the Lord. Yet, before we parted, we imparted one to another ſome of the Exerciſes we had gone through; and they ſeeming willing to underſtand the Ground and Manner of my Commitment, I gave them a brief Account thereof, letting *Thomas Loe* more particularly know, that I had directed a Letter to him, which, having fallen into the Hand of the Lord-Lieutenant, was (ſo far as I could learn) the immediate Cauſe of my being taken up.

Having ſtaid with them as long as my limitted Time would permit (which I thought was but very ſhort) that I might keep Touch with my Keeper, and come home in due Time, I took Leave of my Friends there, and with mutual Embraces parting, returned to my (in ſome ſenſe more eaſy, but in others leſs eaſy) Priſon, where after this, I ſtaid not long before I was brought back to my Father's Houſe.

For after my Father was come home, who, as I obſerved before, was from home when I was taken, he applied himſelf to thoſe Juſtices that had committed me, and not having diſobliged them when he was in Office, eaſily obtained to have me ſent home; which between him and them was thus contrived.

There was about this Time a general Muſter and Training of the militia Forces at *Oxford*; whither, on that Occaſion, came the Lord-Lieutenant, and the Deputy-Lieutenants of the

County

1661. County, of which Number, they who committed me were two.

When they had been a while together, and the Marſhall with them, he ſtept ſuddenly in, and in haſte told me, *I muſt get ready quickly to go out of Town*, and that *a Soldier would come by and by to go with me.* This ſaid, he haſtned to them again, not giving me any Intimation how I was to go, or whither.

I needed not much Time to get ready in; but I was uneaſy in thinking what the Friends of the Town would think of this my ſudden and private Removal; and I feared leſt any Report ſhould be raiſed, that I had purchaſed my Liberty by an unfaithful Compliance. Wherefore I was in Care how to ſpeak with ſome Friend about it; and that friendly *Baker*, whoſe Wife was a Friend, living on the other Side of the Street at a little Diſtance, I went out at a back Door, intending to ſtep over the Way to their Houſe, and return immediately.

It ſo fell out, that ſome of the Lieutenants (of whom Eſquire *Clark*, who committed me, was one) were ſtanding in a Balcony at a great Inn or Tavern, juſt over the Place where I was to go by; and he ſpying me, called out to the Soldiers, who ſtood thick below in the Street, to ſtop me. They, being generally Gentlemens Servants, and many of them knowing me, did civilly forbear to lay hold on me, but calling modeſtly after me, ſaid, *Stay, Sir, ſtay; pray come back.* I heard, but was not willing to hear, therefore rather mended my Pace, that I

might

might have got within the Door. But he calling earnestly after me, and charging them to stop me, some of them were fain to run, and laying hold on me before I could open the Door, brought me back to my Place again. 1661.

Being thus disappointed, I took a Pen and Ink and wrote a few Lines, which I sealed up, and gave to the Apprentice in the Shop, who had carried himself handsomely to me, and desired him to deliver it to that Friend who was their Neighbour, which he promised to do.

By that Time I had done this, came the Soldier that was appointed to conduct me out of Town. I knew the Man, for he lived within a Mile of me, being through Poverty reduced to keep an Ale-house; but he had lived in better fashion, having kept an Inn at *Thame*, and by that means knew how to behave himself civilly, and did so to me.

He told me, he was ordered to wait on me to *Whately*, and to tarry there at such an Inn, till Esquire *Clark* came thither, who would then take me home with him in his Coach. Accordingly to *Whately* we walked (which is from *Oxford* some four or five Miles) and long we had not been there, before *Clark* and a great Company of rude Men came in.

He alighted, and staid a while to eat and drink (though he came but from *Oxford*) and invited me to eat with him; but I, though I had need enough, refused it, for indeed their Conversation was a Burthen to my Life, and made me often think of, and pity good *Lot*.

He

He ſeem'd at that Time to be in a ſort of mixt Temper, between Pleaſantneſs and Sourneſs. He would ſometimes joke (which was natural to him) and caſt out a jeſting Flirt at me; but he would rail maliciouſly againſt the *Quakers*. *If*, ſaid he to me, *the King would authorize me to do it*, *I would not leave a* Quaker *alive in* England, *except you*. *I would make no more*, added he, *to ſet my Piſtol to their Ears, and ſhoot them through the Head*, *than I would to kill a Dog*. I told him, I was ſorry he had ſo ill an Opinion of the *Quakers*, but I was glad he had no Cauſe for it, and I hoped he would be of a better Mind.

I had in my Hand a little Walking-ſtick with a Head on it, which he commended, and took out of my Hand to look on it; but I ſaw his Intention was to ſearch it, whether it had a Tuck in it, for he tried to have drawn the Head; but when he found it was faſt, he returned it to me.

He told me, *I ſhould ride with him to his Houſe in his Coach*, which was nothing pleaſant to me; for I had rather have gone on Foot (as bad as the Ways were) that I might have been out of his Company. Wherefore I took no Notice of any Kindneſs in the Offer, but only anſwered, *I was at his Diſpoſal*, *not mine own*.

But when we were ready to go, the Marſhall came to me, and told me, *If I pleaſed I ſhould ride his Horſe*, *and he would go in the Coach with Mr.* Clark. I was glad of the Offer, and only told him, he ſhould take out his Piſtols then,

for

for I would not ride with them. He took them out, and laid them in the Coach by him, and away we went. 1661.

It was a very fine Beast that I was set on, by much the best in the Company. But tho' she was very tall, yet the Ways being very foul, I found it needful, as soon as I was out of Town, to alight and take up the Stirrups. Mean while, they driving hard on, I was so far behind, that being at length missed by the Company, a Soldier was sent back to look after me.

As soon as I had fitted my Stirrups and was remounted, I gave the Rein to my Mare, which being courageous and nimble, and impatient of Delay, made great Speed to recover the Company. And in a narrow Passage, the Soldier, who was my *Barber* that had fetch'd me from home, and I met upon so brisk a Gallop, that we had enough to do on either Side, to take up our Horses and avoid a Brush.

When we were come to *Weston* where Esquire *Clark* lived, he took the Marshall and some others with him into the Parlour; but I was left in the Hall, to be exposed a second Time for the Family to gaze on.

At length himself came out to me, leading in his Hand a beloved Daughter of his, a young Woman of about eighteen Years of Age, who wanted nothing to have made her comely, but Gravity. An airy Piece she was; and very merry she made herself at me. When she had throughly viewed me, he, putting her a little

1661. forward towards me, ſaid, *Here*, Tom, *will you kiſs her?* I was grieved and aſhamed at this frothy Lightneſs, and I ſuppoſe he perceived it; whereupon he drew nearer, as if he would have whiſpered, and then ſaid, *Will you lie with her?* At which I, with a diſdainful Look, turning away, he ſaid, *I think it would be better for you, than to be a* Quaker; and ſo little Conſideration and Regard to Modeſty had ſhe, that ſhe added, *I think ſo too.*

This was all by Candle-light. And when they had made themſelves as much Sport with me as they would, the Marſhall took his Leave of them, and mounting me on a Horſe of *Clark*'s, had me home to my Father's that Night.

Next Morning, before the Marſhall went away, my Father and he conſulted together how to intangle me. I felt there were Snares laid, but I did not know in what Manner or to what End, till the Marſhall was ready to go. And then, coming where I was to take his Leave of me, he deſired me to take Notice, *That altho' he had brought me home to my Father's Houſe again, yet I was not diſcharged from my Impriſonment, but was his Priſoner ſtill; and that he had committed me to the Care of my Father, to ſee me forth-coming whenever I ſhould be called for. And therefore he expected I ſhould in all Things obſerve my Father's Orders; and not go at any Time from the Houſe without his Leave.*

Now

Now I plainly saw the Snare, and to what End it was laid. And I asked him, if this Device was not contrived to keep me from going to Meetings? He said, *I must not go to Meetings.* Whereupon I desired him to take Notice, That I would not own myself a Prisoner to any Man while I continued here. That if he had Power to detain me Prisoner, he might take me back again with him if he would, and I should not refuse to go with him. But I bid him assure himself, that while I was at home, I would take my Liberty both to go to Meetings and to visit Friends. He smiled and said, *If I would be resolute, he could not help it*; and so took his Leave of me, 1661.

By this I perceived that the Plot was of my Father's laying, to have brought me under such an Engagement, as should have tied me from going to Meetings; and thereupon I expected I should have a new Exercise from my Father.

It was the constant manner of my Father, to have all the Keys of the Out-doors of his House (which were four, and those linkt upon a Chain) brought up into his Chamber every Night, and fetch'd out from thence in the Morning; so that none could come in or go out, in the Night, without his Knowledge.

I knowing this, suspected that if I got not out before my Father came down, I should be stopped from going out at all that Day. Wherefore (the Passage from my Chamber lying by his Chamber-door) I went down softly without my Shoes, and as soon as the Maid had opened

1661 the Door, I went out (though too early) and walk'd towards the Meeting at *Meadle*, four long Miles off.

I expected to have been talked with about it when I came home, but heard nothing of it, my Father resolving to watch me better next Time.

This I was aware of; and therefore on the next First-day I got up early, went down softly, and hid myself in a Back-room before the Maid was stirring.

When she was up, she went into my Father's Chamber for the Keys; but he bid her leave them till he was up, and he would bring them down himself; which he did, and tarried in the Kitchen, through which he expected I would go.

The manner was, That when the common Doors were opened, the Keys were hung upon a Pin in the Hall. While therefore my Father staid in the Kitchen expecting my coming, I stepping gently out of the Room where I was, reached the Keys, and opening another Door (not often used) slipped out and so got away.

I thought I had gone off undiscovered. But whether my Father saw me through a Window, or by what other means he knew of my going, I know not; but I had gone but a little Way, before I saw him coming after me.

The Sight of him put me to a Stand in my Mind, whether I should go on or stop. Had it been in any other Case than that of going to a Meeting, I could not in any wise have gone a

Step further. But I considered, that the Intent of my Father's endeavouring to ſtop me, was to hinder me from obeying the Call of my heavenly Father, and to ſtop me from going to worſhip Him in the Aſſembly of His People; upon this I found it my Duty to go on, and obſerving that my Father gained Ground upon me, I ſomewhat mended my Pace.

This he obſerving, mended his Pace alſo, and at length ran. Whereupon I ran alſo; and a fair Courſe we had through a large Meadow of his, which lay behind his Houſe and out of Sight of the Town. He was not, I ſuppoſe, then above fifty Years of Age, and being light of Body and nimble of Foot, he held me to it for a while. But afterwards ſlacking his Pace to take Breath, and obſerving that I had gotten Ground of him, he turned back and went home; and (as I afterwards underſtood) telling my Siſters how I had ſerved him, he ſaid, *Nay, if he will take ſo much Pains to go, let him go if he will.* And from that Time forward he never attempted to ſtop me, but left me to my Liberty, to go when and whither I would; yet kept me at the uſual Diſtance, avoiding the Sight of me as much as he could, as not able to bear the Sight of my Hat on, nor willing to contend with me again about it.

Nor was it long after this, before I was left not only to myſelf, but in a manner by myſelf. For the Time appointed for the Coronation of the King (which was the 23d of the ſecond Month, called *April*) drawing on, my Father

1661. taking my two Sisters with him, went up to *London* some Time before, that they might be there in Readiness, and put themselves into a Condition to see that so great a Solemnity, leaving no body in the House but myself and a couple of Servants. And though this was intended only for a Visit on that Occasion, yet it proved the Breaking of the Family; for he bestowed both his Daughters there in Marriage, and took Lodgings for himself, so that afterwards they never returned to settle at *Crowell.*

Being now at Liberty, I walked over to *Aylesbury*, with some other Friends, to visit my dear Friend *Isaac Penington*, who was still a Prisoner there. With him I found dear *John Whitehead*, and between sixty and seventy more, being well nigh all the Men Friends that were then in the County of *Bucks*; many of them were taken out of their Houses by armed Men, and sent to Prison (as I had been) for refusing to Swear. Most of these were thrust into an old Room behind the Goal, which had anciently been a Malt-house, but was now so decayed, that it was scarce fit for a Dog-house. And so open it lay, that the Prisoners might have gone out at pleasure. But these were purposely put there, in Confidence that they would not go out, that there might be Room in the Prison for others, of other Professions and Names, whom the Goaler did not trust there.

While this Imprisonment lasted, which was for some Months, I went afterwards thither sometimes to visit my suffering Brethren; and

because

becauſe it was a pretty long Way (ſome eight or nine Miles) too far to be walked forward and backward in one Day, I ſometimes ſtaid a Day or two there, and lay in the Malt-houſe among my Friends, with whom I delighted to be.

After this Impriſonment was over, I went ſometimes to *Iſaac Penington*'s Houſe at *Chalfont*, to viſit that Family and the Friends thereabouts. There was then a Meeting, for the moſt part, twice a Week in his Houſe; but one Firſt-day in four, there was a more general Meeting (which was thence called the *Monthly-Meeting)* to which reſorted moſt of the Friends of other adjacent Meetings; and to that I uſually went, and ſometimes made ſome Stay there.

Here I came acquainted with a Friend of *London*, whoſe Name was *Richard Greenaway*, by Trade a *Taylor*, a very honeſt Man, and one who had received a Gift for the Miniſtry.

He, having been formerly in other Profeſſions of Religion, had then been acquainted with one *John Ovy* of *Watlington* in *Oxfordſhire*, (a Man of ſome Note among the Profeſſors there) and underſtanding, upon Enquiry, that I knew him, he had ſome Diſcourſe with me about him. The Reſult whereof was, that he, having an Intention then ſhortly to viſit ſome Meetings of Friends in this County, and the adjoining Parts of *Oxfordſhire* and *Berkſhire*, invited me to meet him (upon Notice given) and to bear him Company in that Journey;

1661. and in the Way bring him to *John Ovy*'s House, with whom I was well acquainted; which I did.

We were kindly received, the Man and his Wife being very glad to see both their old Friend *Richard Greenaway* and me also, whom they had been very well acquainted with formerly, but had never seen me since I was a *Quaker*.

Here we tarried that Night, and in the Evening had a little Meeting there with some few of *John Ovy*'s People, amongst whom *Richard Greenaway* declared the TRUTH; which they attentively heard and did not oppose, which at that time of Day we reckoned was pretty well; for many were apt to cavil.

This Visit gave *John Ovy* an Opportunity to enquire of me after *Isaac Penington*, whose Writings (those which he had written before he came among Friends) he had read, and had a great Esteem of; and he express'd a Desire to see him, that he might have some Discourse with him, if he knew how. Whereupon I told him, that if he would take the Pains to go to his House, I would bear him Company thither, introduce him, and engage he should have a kind Reception.

This pleased him much; and he embracing the Offer, I undertook to give him Notice of a suitable Time; which (after I had gone this little Journey with my Friend *Richard Greenaway*, and was returned) I did, making Choice of the *Monthly-meeting* to go to.

We

We met by Appointment at *Stoken-Church*, 1661.
with our Staves in our Hands like a couple of Pilgrims, intending to walk on Foot; and having taken ſome Refreſhment and Reſt at *Wiccomb*, went on cheerfully in the Afternoon, entertaining each other with grave and religious Diſcourſe, which made the Walk the eaſier, and ſo reached thither in good Time, on the Seventh-day of the Week.

I gave my Friends an Account who this Perſon was, whom I had brought to viſit them, and the Ground of his Viſit. He had been a Profeſſor of Religion, from his Childhood to his old Age (for he was now both grey-headed, and elderly) and was a Teacher at this Time, and had long been ſo amongſt a People, whether *Independants* or *Baptiſts*, I do not well remember. And ſo well thought of he was, for his Zeal and Honeſty, that in thoſe late profeſſing Times, he was thruſt into the *Commiſſion of the Peace*, and thereby lifted up upon the Bench; which neither became him, nor he it. For he wanted indeed moſt of the Qualifications requiſite for a Juſtice of the Peace; an Eſtate to defray the Charge of the Office, and to bear him up in a Courſe of living above Contempt; a competent Knowledge in the Laws, and a Preſence of Mind or Body, or both, to keep Offenders in ſome Awe; in all which he was deficient. For he was but a *Fell-monger* by Trade, accuſtomed to ride upon his Pack of Skins; and had very little Eſtate; as little Knowledge in the Law; and of but a

mean

1661. mean Presence and Appearance to look on. But as my Father I suppose, was the Means of getting him put into the Commission, so he, I know, did what he could to countenance him in it, and help him through it at every Turn, till that Turn came (at the King's Return) which turned them both out together.

My Friends received me in affectionate Kindness, and my Companion with courteous Civility. The Evening was spent in common, but grave Conversation; for it was not a proper Season for private Discourse, both as we were somewhat weary with our Walk, and there were other Companies of Friends come into the Family, to be at the Meeting next Day.

But in the Morning I took *John Ovy* into a private Walk, in a pleasant Grove near the House, whither *Isaac Penington* came to us; and there, in Discourse, both answered all his Questions, Objections and Doubts, and opened to him the Principles of TRUTH, to his both Admiration and present Satisfaction. Which done, we went in to take some Refreshment before the Meeting began.

Of those Friends who were come over Night, in order to be at the Meeting, there was *Isaac*'s Brother *William Penington*, a Merchant of *London*; and with him a Friend (whose Name I have forgotten) a *Grocer* of *Colchester* in *Essex*; and there was also our Friend *George Whitehead*, whom I had not, that I remember, seen before.

The

The Nation had been in a Ferment ever since that mad Action of the frantick *Fifth-monarchy-men*, and was not yet settled; but Storms, like Thunder-showers, flew here and there by Coast, so that we could not promise ourselves any Safety or Quiet in our Meetings. And though they had escaped Disturbance for some little Time before, yet so it fell out, that a Party of Horse were appointed to come and break up the Meeting that Day, though we knew nothing of it, till we heard and saw them. 1661.

The Meeting was scarce fully gathered when they came. But we that were in the Family, and many others, were settled in it in great Peace and Stilness, when on a sudden the prancing of the Horses gave Notice that Lightning was at hand.

We all sate still in our Places, except my Companion *John Ovy*, who sate next to me. But he being of a Profession that approved *Peter's* Advice to his Lord, *To save himself*, soon took the Alarm; and with the Nimbleness of a Stripling, cutting a Caper over the Form that stood before him, ran quickly out at a private Door (which he had before observed) which led through the Parlour into the Gardens, and from thence into an Orchard; where he hid himself in a Place so obscure, and withal so convenient for his Intelligence by Observation of what passed, that no one of the Family could scarce have found a likelier.

By

By that Time he was got into his Burrow, came the Soldiers in, being a Party of the County Troop, commanded by *Matthew Archdale* of *Wiccomb*. He behaved himſelf civilly, and ſaid, *He was commanded to break up the Meeting, and carry the Men before a Juſtice of the Peace*; *but*, he ſaid, *he would not take all*; and thereupon began to pick and chuſe, chiefly as his Eye guided him, for I ſuppoſe he knew very few.

He took *Iſaac Penington* and his Brother, *George Whitehead* and the Friend of *Colcheſter*, and me, with three or four more of the Country, who belonged to that Meeting.

He was not fond of the Work, and that made him take no more. *But he muſt take ſome*, he ſaid; and bid us provide to go with him before Sir *William Boyer* of *Denham*, who was a Juſtice of the Peace. *Iſaac Penington* being but weakly, rode; but the reſt of us walked thither, it being about four Miles.

When we came there, the Juſtice carried himſelf civilly to us all, courteouſly to *Iſaac Penington*, as being a Gentleman of his Neighbourhood, and there was nothing charged againſt us, but that we were met together without Word or Deed. Yet this being contrary to a late Proclamation (given forth upon the riſing of the *Fifth-monarchy-men*) whereby all Diſſenters Meetings were forbidden, the Juſtice could do no leſs than take Notice of us.

Wherefore he examined all of us (whom he did not perſonally know) aſking our Names,

and

and the Places of our respective Habitations. 1661.
But when he had them, and considered from what distant Parts of the Nation we came, he was amazed. For *George Whitehead* was of *Westmorland* in the North of *England*; the *Grocer* was of *Essex*; I was of *Oxfordshire*; and *William Penington* was of *London.*

Hereupon he told us, *That our Case look'd ill, and he was sorry for it: For how,* said he, *can it be imagined that so many could jump altogether at one Time and Place, from such remote Quarters and Parts of the Kingdom, if it was not by Combination and Appointment?*

He was answered, That we were so far from coming thither by Agreement or Appointment, that none of us knew of the others coming, and for the most of us, we had never seen one another before; and that therefore he might impute it to *Chance*, or, if he pleased, to *Providence.*

He urged upon us, *That an Insurrection had been lately made by armed Men, who pretended to be more religious than others; that that Insurrection had been plotted and contrived in their Meeting-house, where they assembled under Colour of worshipping GOD; that in their Meeting-house they hid their Arms, and armed themselves, and out of their Meeting-house issued forth in Arms, and killed many; so that the Government could not be safe, unless such Meetings were supprest.*

We reply'd, We hoped he would distinguish, and make a Difference between the *Guilty* and the *Innocent*; and between those who were

principled

1661. principled for *Fighting*, and those who were principled *against it*; which we were, and had been always known to be so. That our Meetings were publick, our Doors standing open to all Comers, of all Ages, Sexes and Perswasions; Men, Women and Children, and those that were not of our Religion, as well as those that were; and that it was next to Madness, for People to plot in such Meetings.

He told us, *We must find Sureties for our good Behaviour, and to answer our Contempt of the King's Proclamation at the next General Quarter-Sessions; or else he must commit us.*

We told him, That knowing our Innocency, and that we had not mis-behaved ourselves, nor did meet in Contempt of the King's Authority, but purely in Obedience to the LORD's Requirings, to worship Him, which we held ourselves in Duty bound to do, we could not consent to be bound, for that would imply Guilt, which we were free from.

Then, said he, *I must commit you*: And ordered his Clerk to make a *Mittimus*. And divers *Mittimusses* were made, but none of them would hold; for still, when they came to be read, we found such Flaws in them, as made him throw them aside and write more.

He had his Eye often upon me, for I was a young Man, and had at that Time a black Suit on. At length he bid me follow him, and went into a private Room and shut the Door upon me.

I knew

I knew not what he meant by this; but I cried in Spirit to the Lord, that He would be pleaſed to be a Mouth and Wiſdom to me, and keep me from being entangled in any Snare.

He aſked me many Queſtions concerning my Birth, my Education, my Acquaintance in *Oxfordſhire*; particularly *what Men of Note I knew there.* To all which I gave him brief, but plain and true Anſwers, naming ſeveral Families of the beſt Rank, in that Part of the Country where I dwelt.

He aſked me, *How long I had been of this Way*, and *how I came to be of it?* Which when I had given him ſome Account of, he began to perſwade me to leave it, and return to the right Way (the *Church*, as he called it.) I deſired him to ſpare his Pains in that Reſpect, and forbear any Diſcourſe of that kind, for that I was fully ſatisfied, the Way I was in was the right Way, and hoped the Lord would ſo preſerve me in it, that nothing ſhould be able to draw or drive me out of it. He ſeemed not pleaſed with that; and thereupon went out to the reſt of the Company, and I followed him, glad in my Heart that I had eſcaped ſo well, and praiſing God for my Deliverance.

When he had taken his Seat again at the upper End of a fair Hall, he told us, he was not willing to take the utmoſt Rigour of the Law againſt us, but would be as favourable to us as he could. And therefore he would diſcharge, he ſaid, Mr. *Penington* himſelf, becauſe he

1661. he was but at home in his own House. And he would discharge Mr. *Penington* of *London*; because he came but as a Relation to visit his Brother. And he would discharge the *Grocer* of *Colchester*, because he came to bear Mr. *Penington* of *London* Company, and to be acquainted with Mr. *Isaac Penington*, whom he had never seen before. And as for those others of us, who were of this Country, he would discharge them, for the present at least, because they being his Neighbours, he could send for them when he would. *But as for you,* said he to *George Whitehead* and me, *I can see no Business you had there*; *and therefore I intend to hold you to it, either to give Bail, or go to Goal.*

We told him we could not give Bail. *Then,* said he, *you must go to Goal*; and thereupon he began to write our *Mittimus*; which puzzled him again. For he had discharged so many, that he was at a Loss what to lay as the Ground of our Commitment, whose Case differed nothing in reality from theirs whom he had discharged.

At length, having made divers Draughts (which still *George Whitehead* shewed him the Defects of) he seemed to be weary of us; and rising up said unto us, *I consider that it is grown late in the Day, so that the Officer cannot carry you to* Aylesbury *to Night, and I suppose you will be willing to go back with Mr.* Penington; *therefore if you will promise to be forth-coming at his House To-morrow Morning, I will dismiss*

you

you for the preſent, and you ſhall hear from me again To-morrow. 1661.

We told him, we did intend, if he did not otherwiſe diſpoſe of us, to ſpend that Night with our Friend *Iſaac Penington*, and would (if the Lord gave us Leave) be there in the Morning, ready to anſwer his Requirings. Whereupon he diſmiſt us all, willing, as we thought, to be rid of us; for he ſeemed not to be of an ill Temper, nor deſirous to put us to Trouble if he could help it.

Back then we went to *Iſaac Penington*'s. But when we were come thither, O the Work we had with poor *John Ovy!* He was ſo dejected in Mind, ſo covered with Shame and Confuſion of Face for his Cowardlineſs, that we had enough to do to pacify him towards himſelf.

The Place he had found out to ſhelter himſelf in, was ſo commodiouſly contrived, that undiſcovered he could diſcern when the Soldiers went off with us, and underſtand when the Buſtle was over, and the Coaſt clear. Whereupon he adventured to peep out of his Hole, and in a while drew near, by degrees, to the Houſe again; and finding all Things quiet and ſtill, he adventured to ſtep within the Doors, and found the Friends, who were left behind, peaceably ſettled in the Meeting again.

The Sight of this ſmote him, and made him ſit down among them. And after the Meeting was ended, and the Friends departed to their ſeveral Homes, addreſſing himſelf to *Mary Penington.* (as the Miſtreſs of the Houſe)

1661. he could not enough magnify the Bravery and Courage of the Friends, nor sufficiently debase himself. He told her how long he had been a Professor, what Pains he had taken, what Hazards he had run, in his youthful Days, to get to Meetings; how, when the Ways were forelaid, and Passages stopt, he swam through Rivers to reach a Meeting; *And now*, said he, *that I am grown old in the Profession of Religion, and have long been an Instructor and Encourager of others; that I should thus shamefully fall short myself, is matter of Shame and Sorrow to me.*

Thus he bewailed himself to her. And when we came back, he renewed his Complaints of himself to us, with high Aggravations of his own Cowardice. Which gave Occasion to some of the Friends, tenderly to represent to him the Difference between *Profession* and *Possession*; *Form* and *Power*.

He was glad, he said, *on our Behalfs, that we came off so well, and escaped Imprisonment.*

But when he understood that *George Whitehead* and I were liable to an After-reckoning next Morning, he was troubled; and wish'd the Morning was come and gone, that we might be gone with it.

We spent the Evening in grave Conversation, and in religious Discourses, attributing the Deliverance, we hitherto had, to the LORD. And the next Morning when we were up and had eaten, we tarried some Time to see what the Justice would do further with us, and to discharge

discharge our Engagement to him; the rest of the Friends, who were before fully discharged, tarrying also with us to see the Event.

And when we had staid so long, that on all Hands it was concluded we might safely go, *George Whitehead* and I left a few Words in Writing, to be sent to the Justice, if he sent after us, importing that we had tarried till such an Hour, and not hearing from him, did now hold ourselves free to depart; yet so, as that if he should have Occasion to send for us again, upon Notice thereof we would return.

This done, we took our Leave of the Family, and one of another; they who were for *London* taking Horse, and I and my Companion, setting forth on Foot for *Oxfordshire*, went to *Wiccomb*, where we made a short Stay to rest and refresh ourselves, and from thence reached our respective Homes that Night.

After I had spent some Time at home, where, as I had no Restraint, so (my Sisters being gone) I had now no Society, I walked up to *Chalfont* again, and spent a few Days with my Friends there.

As soon as I came in, I was told, that my Father had been there that Day to see *Isaac Penington* and his Wife; but they being abroad at a Meeting, he returned to his Inn in the Town, where he intended to lodge that Night. After Supper, *Mary Penington* told me, she had a mind to go and see him at his Inn (the Woman of the House being a Friend of ours) and I went with her. He seem'd somewhat

1661. ſurprized to ſee me there, becauſe he thought I had been at home at his Houſe; but he took no Notice of my Hat, at leaſt ſhewed no Offence at it; for, as I afterwards underſtood, he had now an Intention to ſell his Eſtate, and thought he ſhould need my Concurrence therein; which made him now hold it neceſſary to admit me again into ſome degree of Favour. After we had tarried ſome little Time with him, ſhe riſing up to be gone, he waited on her home, and having ſpent about an Hour with us in the Family, I waited on him back to his Inn. On the Way, he invited me to come up to *London* to ſee my Siſters; the younger of whom was then newly married, and directed me where to find them; and alſo gave me Money to defray my Charges. Accordingly I went; yet ſtaid not long there, but returned to my Friend *Iſaac Penington*'s where I made a little Stay, and from thence went back to *Crowell*.

When I was ready to ſet forth, my Friend *Iſaac Penington* was ſo kind to ſend a Servant with a Brace of Geldings, to carry me as far as I thought fit to ride, and to bring the Horſes back. I, intending to go no farther that Day than to *Wiccomb*, rode no farther than to *Beaconsfield* Town's-end, having then but five Miles to walk. But here a new Exerciſe befel me, the manner of which was thus:

Before I had walked to the Middle of the Town, I was ſtopt and taken up by the Watch. I aſked the Watchman, What Authority he had to ſtop me, travelling peaceably

on

on the High-way? He told me he would ſhew 1661.
me his Authority; and in order thereunto, had me into an Houſe hard-by, where dwelt a *Scrivener* whoſe Name was *Pepys.* To him he gave the Order which he had received from the Conſtables, which directed him to take up all Rogues, Vagabonds and ſturdy Beggars. I aſked him, For which of theſe he ſtopped me; but he could not anſwer me.

I thereupon informed him, what a *Rogue* in Law is, *viz. One, who for ſome notorious Offence was burnt on the Shoulder*; and I told them, they might ſearch me if they pleaſed, and ſee if I was ſo branded. A *Vagabond*, I told them, was *One that had no Dwelling-houſe, nor certain Place of abode*; but I had, and was going to it; and I told them where it was. And for a *Beggar*, I bid them bring any one that could ſay, I had *begged* or *aſked Relief.*

This ſtopt the Fellow's Mouth, yet he would not let me go; but, being both weak-headed and ſtrong-willed, he left me there with the *Scrivener*, and went out to ſeek the Conſtable; and having found him, brought him thither. He was a young Man, by Trade a *Tanner*, ſomewhat better mannered than his Wardſman, but not of much better Judgment.

He took me with him to his Houſe. And having ſettled me there, went out to take Advice, as I ſuppoſed, what to do with me; leaving no Body in the Houſe to guard me,

1661. but his Wife, who had a young Child in her Arms.

She enquired of me, upon what Account I was taken up; and seeming to have some Pity for me, endeavoured to perswade me not to stay, but to go my way; offering to shew me a Back-way from their House, which would bring me into the Road again beyond the Town, so that none of the Town should see me, or know what was become of me. But I told her, I could not do so.

Then having sate a while in a muze, she asked me, *If there was not a Place of Scripture which said,* Peter *was at a Tanner's House?* I told her there was such a Scripture, and directed her where to find it.

After some Time, she laid her Child to sleep in the Cradle, and stept out on a sudden; but came not in again in a pretty while.

I was uneasy that I was left alone in the House, fearing lest, if any Thing should be missing, I might be suspected to have taken it; yet I durst not go out to stand in the Street, lest it should be thought I intended to slip away.

But besides that, I soon found Work to imploy myself in; for the Child quickly waking, fell to crying, and I was fain to rock the Cradle in my own Defence, that I might not be annoyed with a Noise, to me not more unpleasant than unusual. At length the Woman came in again, and finding me nursing the Child,

Child, gave me many Thanks, and ſeemed well pleaſed with my Company.

When Night came on, the Conſtable himſelf came in again, and told me, *Some of the Chief of the Town were met together, to conſider what was fit to do with me; and that I muſt go with him to them.* I went, and he brought me to a little naſty Hut, which they called a *Town-houſe* (adjoining to their Market-houſe) in which dwelt a poor old Woman whom they called *Mother Grime*, where alſo the Watch uſed by Turns, to come in and warm themſelves in the Night.

When I came in among them, they looked (ſome of them) ſomewhat ſourly on me, and aſk'd me ſome impertinent Queſtions; to which I gave them ſuitable Anſwers.

Then they conſulted one with another, how they ſhould diſpoſe of me that Night, till they could have me before ſome Juſtice of Peace to be examined. Some propoſed, *That I ſhould be had to ſome Inn, or other publick Houſe, and a Guard ſet on me there.* He that ſtarted this was probably an Inn-keeper, and conſulted his own Intereſt. Others objected againſt this, *That it would bring a Charge on the Town.* To avoid which, they were for having the Watch take Charge of me, and keep me walking about the Streets with them till Morning. Moſt Voices ſeemed to go this Way; till a third wiſhed them to conſider, *Whether they could anſwer the doing of that, and the Law would bear them out in it?* And this put them to a

1661. Stand. I heard all their Debates, but let them alone, and kept my Mind to the LORD.

While they thus bandied the Matter to and fro, one of the Company asked the rest, *If any of them knew who this young Man was, and whither he was going?* Whereupon the Constable (to whom I had given both my Name, and the Name of the Town where I dwelt) told them my Name was *Ellwood,* and that I lived at a Town called *Crowell* in *Oxfordshire.*

Old mother *Grime,* sitting by and hearing this, clap'd her Hand on her Knee, and cry'd out, *I know Mr.* Ellwood *of* Crowell *very well. For when I was a Maid I lived with his Grandfather there, when he was a young Man.* And thereupon she gave them such an Account of my Father, as made them look more regardfully on me; and so Mother *Grime*'s Testimony turned the Scale, and took me off from walking the Rounds with the Watch that Night.

The Constable hereupon bid them take no further Care, I should lie at his House that Night, and accordingly took me home with him, where I had as good Accommodation as the House did afford. Before I went to Bed, he told me, *That there was to be a Visitation, or Spiritual Court* (as he called it) *holden next Day at* Amersham, *about four Miles from* Beaconsfield, and that *I was to be carried thither.*

This was a new Thing to me, and it brought a fresh Exercise upon my Mind. But being given up, in the Will of God, to suffer what

He

He ſhould permit to be laid on me, I endea- 1661.
voured to keep my Mind quiet and ſtill.

In the Morning, as ſoon as I was up, my Spirit was exerciſed towards the Lord, in ſtrong Cries to Him, that He would ſtand by me, and preſerve me, and not ſuffer me to be taken in the Snare of the Wicked. While I was thus crying to the LORD, the other Conſtable came, and I was called down.

This was a budge Fellow, and talked high. He was a *Shoe-maker* by Trade, and his Name was *Clark*. He threat'ned me with the *Spiritual Court*. But when he ſaw I did not regard it, he ſtopt, and left the Matter to his Partner, who pretended more Kindneſs for me, and therefore went about to perſwade *Clark*, to let me go out at the Back-door, ſo ſlip away.

The Plot, I ſuppoſe, was ſo laid, that *Clark* ſhould ſeem averſe, but at length yield, which he did; but would have me take it for a Favour. But I was ſo far from taking it ſo, that I would not take it at all; but told them plainly, That as I came in at the Fore-door, ſo I would go out at the Fore-door. When therefore they ſaw they could not bow me to their Will, they brought me out at the Fore-door into the Street, and wiſhed me a good Journey. Yet before I went, calling for the Woman of the Houſe, I paid her for my Supper and Lodging, for I had now got a little Money in my Pocket again.

After

1661. After this I got home (as I thought) very well; but I had not been long at home, before an Ilneſs ſeized on me, which proved to be the *Small-pox*. Of which, ſo ſoon as Friends had Notice, I had a Nurſe ſent me; and in a while *Iſaac Penington*, and his Wife's Daughter *Gulielma Maria Springett* (to whom I had been Play-fellow in our Infancy) came to viſit me, bringing with them our dear Friend *Edward Burrough*, by whoſe Miniſtry I was called to the Knowledge of the Truth.

It pleaſed the Lord to deal favourably with me in this Ilneſs, both inwardly and outwardly. For His ſupporting Preſence was with me, which kept my Spirit near unto Him; and though the Diſtemper was ſtrong upon me, yet I was preſerved through it, and my Countenance was not much altered by it. But after I was got up again, and while I kept my Chamber, wanting ſome Employment for Entertainment-ſake, to ſpend the Time with, and there being at hand a pretty good Library of Books (amongſt which were the Works of *Auguſtine*, and others of thoſe ancient Writers, who were by many called the *Fathers)* I betook myſelf to Reading. And theſe Books being printed in the old Black-letter, with Abbreviations of the Words, difficult to be read, I ſpent too much Time therein, and thereby much impaired my Sight, which was not ſtrong before, and was now weaker than uſual, by reaſon of the Ilneſs I had ſo newly had, which

which proved an Injury to me afterwards; for which Reason I here mention it. 1661.

After I was well enough to go abroad, with respect to my own Health, and the Safety of others, I went up (in the Beginning of the Twelfth Month 1661) to my Friend *Isaac Penington*'s at *Chalfont*, and abode there some Time, for the airing myself more fully, that I might be more fit for Conversation.

I mentioned before, that when I was a Boy, 1662.
I had made some good Progress in Learning, and lost it all again before I came to be a Man; nor was I rightly sensible of my Loss therein, until I came amongst the *Quakers*. But then I both saw my Loss, and lamented it; and applied myself with utmost Diligence, at all leisure Times, to recover it; so false I found that Charge to be, which in those Times was cast, as a Reproach upon the *Quakers*, That *they despised and decried all human Learning*; because they denied it to be essentially necessary to a *Gospel-ministry*, which was one of the Controversies of those Times.

But though I toiled hard and spared no Pains, to regain what once I had been Master of; yet I found it a Matter of so great Difficulty, that I was ready to say as the noble Eunuch to *Philip* in another Case, *How can I, unless I had some Man to guide me?*

This I had formerly complained of to my especial Friend *Isaac Penington*, but now more earnestly; which put him upon considering, and contriving a Means for my Assistance.

He

1662. He had an intimate Acquaintance with Dr. *Paget*, a Phyſician of Note in *London*, and he with *John Milton*, a Gentleman of great Note for Learning throughout the learned World, for the accurate Pieces he had written on various Subjects and Occaſions.

This Perſon, having filled a publick Station in the former Times, lived now a private and retired Life in *London*; and having wholly loſt his Sight, kept always a Man to read to him, which uſually was the Son of ſome Gentleman of his Acquaintance, whom, in Kindneſs, he took to improve in his Learning.

Thus, by the Mediation of my Friend *Iſaac Penington* with Dr. *Paget*, and of Dr. *Paget* with *John Milton*, was I admitted to come to him; not as a Servant to him (which at that Time he needed not) nor to be in the Houſe with him; but only to have the Liberty of coming to his Houſe, at certain Hours, when I would, and to read to him what Books he ſhould appoint me; which was all the Favour I deſired.

But this being a Matter which would require ſome Time to bring it about, I, in the mean while, returned to my Father's Houſe in *Oxfordſhire*.

I had before received Direction, by Letters from my eldeſt Siſter (written by my Father's Command) to put off what Cattle he had left about his Houſe, and to diſcharge his Servants; which I had done at the Time called *Michaelmas* before. So that all that Winter, when I was

at

at Home, I lived like an *Hermit* all alone, having a pretty large House, and no Body in it but myself, a-nights especially; but an elderly Woman, whose Father had been an old Servant to the Family, came every Morning and made my Bed, and did what else I had occasion for her to do, till I fell ill of the *Small-pox*, and then I had her with me, and the Nurse. But now, understanding by Letter from my Sister, that my Father did not intend to return to settle there, I made off those Provisions which were in the House, that they might not be spoiled when I was gone; and because they were what I should have spent, if I had tarried there, I took the Money made of them to myself, for my Support at *London*, if the Project succeeded for my going thither. 1662.

This done, I committed the Care of the House to a Tenant of my Father's, who lived in the Town, and taking my Leave of *Crowell*, went up to my sure Friend *Isaac Penington* again. Where understanding that the Mediation used for my Admittance to *John Milton*, had succeeded so well, that I might come when I would, I hastned to *London*, and in the first Place went to wait upon him.

He received me courteously, as well for the sake of Dr. *Paget* who introduced me, as of *Isaac Penington* who recommended me; to both whom he bore a good Respect. And having enquired divers Things of me, with respect to my former Progression in Learning, he dismist me, to provide myself of such Accommodations

1662. modations as might be most suitable to my future Studies.

I went therefore and took myself a Lodging as near to his House (which was then in *Jewen-street)* as conveniently as I could, and from thenceforward went every Day in the Afternoon, except on the First-days of the Week, and sitting by him in his Dining-room, read to him in such Books in the *Latin* Tongue as he pleased to hear me read.

At my first sitting to read to him, observing that I used the *English* Pronounciation, he told me, *If I would have the Benefit of the* Latin *Tongue, not only to read and understand* Latin *Authors, but to converse with Foreigners, either abroad or at home, I must learn the foreign Pronounciation.* To this I consenting, he instructed me how to sound the Vowels; so different from the common Pronounciation used by the *English*, who speak *Anglice* their *Latin*, that (with some few other Variations in sounding some Consonants, in particular Cases; as *C* before *E* or *I*, like *Ch*. *Sc* before *I*, like *Sh*, &c.) the *Latin* thus spoken, seemed as different from that which was delivered, as the *English* generally speak it, as if it were another Language.

I had before, during my retired Life at my Father's, by unwearied Diligence and Industry, so far recovered the Rules of *Grammar* (in which I had once been very ready) that I could both read a *Latin* Author, and after a Sort hammer out his Meaning. But this Change of Pronounciation proved a new Difficulty to

me.

me. It was now harder to me to read, than it was before to understand when read. But 1662.

——————Labor omnia vincit
Improbus. ——————————

Incessant Pains,
The End obtains.

And so did I. Which made my Reading the more acceptable to my Master. He, on the other hand, perceiving with what earnest Desire I pursued Learning, gave me not only all the Encouragement, but all the Help he could. For, having a curious Ear, he understood by my Tone, when I understood what I read, and when I did not; and accordingly would stop me, examine me, and open the most difficult Passages to me.

Thus went I on for about six Weeks time, reading to him in the Afternoons; and exercising myself with my own Books, in my Chamber in the Forenoons, I was sensible of an Improvement.

But, alas! I had fixed my Studies in a wrong Place. *London* and I could never agree for Health; my Lungs, as I suppose, were too tender to bear the sulphurous Air of that City, so that I soon began to droop; and in less than two Months time, I was fain to leave both my Studies and the City, and return into the Country to preserve Life; and much ado I had to get thither.

I chose

1662. I chose to go down to *Wiccomb*, and to *John Rance*'s House there; both as he was a Physician, and his Wife an honest, hearty, discreet and grave Matron, whom I had a very good Esteem of, and who I knew had a good Regard for me.

There I lay ill a considerable Time, and to that degree of Weakness, that scarce any who saw me, expected my Life. But the Lord was both gracious to me in my Ilness, and was pleased to raise me up again, that I might serve Him in my Generation.

As soon as I had recovered so much Strength as to be fit to travel, I obtained of my Father (who was then at his House in *Crowell* to dispose of some Things he had there, and who in my Ilness had come to see me) so much Money as would clear all Charges in the House, for both Physick, Food and Attendance; and having fully discharged all, I took Leave of my Friends in that Family and in the Town, and returned to my Studies at *London*.

I was very kindly received by my Master, who had conceived so good an Opinion of me, that my Conversation (I found) was acceptable to him, and he seem'd heartily glad of my Recovery and Return; and into our old Method of Study we fell again, I reading to him, and he explaining to me, as Occasion required.

But, as if Learning had been a forbidden Fruit to me, scarce was I well settled in my Work, before I met with another Diversion, which turned me quite out of my Work.

For

For a ſudden Storm ariſing, from I know not what Surmiſe of a Plot, and thereby Danger to the Government; and the Meetings of Diſſenters (ſuch I mean as could be found, which perhaps were not many beſides the *Quakers*) were broken up throughout the City, and the Priſons moſtly filled with our Friends. 1662.

I was that Morning, which was the 26th Day of the eighth Month 1662, at the Meeting at the *Bull* and *Mouth* by *Alderſgate*, when on a ſudden, a Party of Soldiers (of the Trained-bands of the City) ruſhed in with Noiſe and Clamour, being led by one who was called Major *Roſewell*, an *Apothecary* (if I miſremember not) and at that Time under the ill Name of a *Papiſt*.

As ſoon as he was come within the Room, having a File or two of Muſketteers at his Heels, he commanded his Men to preſent their Muſkets at us, which they did; with Intent, I ſuppoſe, to ſtrike a Terror into the People. Then he made a Proclamation that all, who were not *Quakers*, might depart if they would.

It ſo happened, that a young Man, an Apprentice in *London*, whoſe Name was — *Dove*, (the Son of Dr. *Dove* of *Chinner*, near *Crowell* in *Oxfordſhire*) came that Day in Curioſity to ſee the Meeting; and coming early, and finding me there (whom he knew) came and ſate down by me.

As ſoon as he heard the Noiſe of Soldiers, he was much ſtartled, and aſked me ſoftly, *If I would not ſhift for myſelf, and try to get out.*

 I told

1662. I told him, No; I was in my Place, and was willing to suffer if it was my Lot. When he heard the Notice given, that *they who were not* Quakers *might depart*, he solicited me again to be gone. I told him, I could not do so, for that would be to renounce my Profession, which I would by no means do. But as for him, who was not one of us, he might do as he pleased. Whereupon, wishing me well, he turned away, and with Cap in Hand went out. And truly I was glad he was gone, for his Master was a rigid *Presbyterian*, who, in all likelihood, would have led him a wretched Life, had he been taken and imprisoned among the *Quakers*.

The Soldiers came so early, that the Meeting was not fully gathered when they came; and when the mixt Company were gone out, we were so few, and sate so thin in that large Room, that they might take a clear View of us all, and single us out as they pleased.

He that commanded the Party, gave us first a general Charge to come out of the Room. But we, who came thither at God's Requirings, to worship Him (like that good Man of old, who said, *We ought to obey God rather than Men*, Acts v. 29.) stirred not, but kept our Places. Whereupon he sent some of his Soldiers among us, with Command to drag or drive us out; which they did roughly enough.

When we came out into the Street, we were received there by other Soldiers, who with their Pikes holden length-ways from one another, encompassed

encompaſſed us round as Sheep in a Pound; 1662.
and there we ſtood a pretty Time, while they were picking up more to add to our Number.

In this Work none ſeemed ſo eager and active as their Leader, Major *Roſewell.* Which I obſerving, ſtept boldly to him, as he was paſſing by me, and aſked him, If he intended a *Maſſacre?* For of that, in thoſe Times, there was a great Apprehenſion and Talk. The Suddenneſs of the Queſtion, from ſuch a young Man eſpecially, ſomewhat ſtartled him; but recollecting himſelf, he anſwered, *No; but I intend to have you all hanged by the wholſome Laws of the Land.*

When he had gotten as many as he could, or thought fit, which were in Number *Thirty-two*, whereof two were catch'd up in the Street, who had not been at the Meeting, he ordered the Pikes to be opened before us; and giving the Word to March, went himſelf at the Head of us, the Soldiers with their Pikes making a Lane to keep us from ſcattering.

He led us up *Martins*, and ſo turned down to *Newgate*, where I expected he would have lodged us. But, to my Diſappointment, he went on through *Newgate*, and turning through the *Old-Bailey*, brought us into *Fleet-ſtreet.* I was then wholly at a Loſs, to conjecture whither he would lead us, unleſs it were to *Whitehall*, for I knew nothing then of *Old-Bridewell*; but on a ſudden he gave a ſhort Turn, and brought us before the Gate of that Priſon, where knocking, the Wicket was forthwith

1662. opened, and the Maſter with his Porter ready to receive us.

One of thoſe two who were picked up in the Street, being near me, and telling me his Caſe, I ſtept to the Major, and told him, That this Man was not at the Meeting, but was taken up in the Street; and ſhew'd him how hard and unjuſt a Thing it would be, to put him into Priſon.

I had not pleaſed him before in the Queſtion I had put to him about a Maſſacre; and that, I ſuppoſe, made this Solicitation leſs acceptable to him from me, than it might have been from ſome other. For looking ſternly on me, he ſaid, *Who are you, that take ſo much upon you? Seeing you are ſo buſy, you ſhall be the firſt Man that ſhall go into* Bridewell; and taking me by the Shoulders, he thruſt me in.

As ſoon as I was in, the Porter pointing with his Finger, directed me to a fair Pair of Stairs on the further Side of a large Court, and bid me *go up thoſe Stairs, and go on till I could go no further.*

Accordingly I went up the Stairs; the firſt Flight whereof brought me to a fair Chapel on my left Hand, which I could look into through the iron Grates, but could not have gone into if I would.

I knew that was not a Place for me. Wherefore following my Direction, and the winding of the Stairs, I went up a Story higher, which brought me into a Room, which I ſoon perceived to be a *Court-room*, or Place of *Judicature.*

After

After I had ſtood a while there, and taken a View of it, obſerving a Door on the further Side, I went to it and opened it, with Intention to go in; but I quickly drew back, being almoſt affrighted at the Diſmalneſs of the Place. For beſides that the Walls quite round were laid all over, from Top to Bottom in Black, there ſtood in the Middle of it a great Whipping-poſt, which was all the Furniture it had. 1662.

In one of theſe two Rooms Judgment was given, and in the other it was executed on thoſe ill People, who for their Lewdneſs were ſent to this Priſon, and there ſentenced to be whip'd. Which was ſo contrived, that the Court might not only hear, but ſee, if they pleaſed, their Sentence executed.

A Sight ſo unexpected, and withal ſo unpleaſing, gave me no Encouragement either to reſt, or indeed to enter at all there; till looking earneſtly, I ſpy'd on the oppoſite Side a Door, which giving me Hopes of a further Progreſs, I adventured to ſtep haſtily to it, and opened it.

This let me into one of the faireſt Rooms that, ſo far as I remember, I was ever in, and no wonder; for though it was now put to this mean Uſe, it had, for many Ages paſt, been the Royal Seat or Palace of the Kings of *England*, until Cardinal *Woolſey* built *Whitehall*, and offered it as a Peace Offering to King *Henry* the eighth; who until that Time had kept his Court in this Houſe, and had this, as the People in the Houſe reported, for his Dining-room, by which Name it then went.

1662. This Room in Length, for I lived long enough in it to have Time to meaſure it, was Threeſcore Feet; and had Breadth proportionable to it. In it, on the Front-ſide, were very large Bay-windows, in which ſtood a large Table. It had other very large Tables in it, with Benches round; and at that Time the Floor was covered with Ruſhes, againſt ſome ſolemn Feſtival, which I heard it was beſpoken for.

Here was my *Nil ultra*, and here I found I might ſet up my Pillar; for although there was a Door out of it, to a Back-pair of Stairs which led to it, yet that was kept locked. So that finding I had now followed my Keeper's Direction to the utmoſt Point, beyond which I could not go, I ſate down and conſidered that rhetorical Saying, *That the Way to Heaven lay by the Gate of Hell*; the Black-room, through which I paſſed into this, bearing ſome Reſemblance to the latter, as this comparatively and by way of Alluſion, might in ſome ſort be thought to bear to the former.

But I was quickly put out of theſe Thoughts by the flocking in of the other Friends my Fellow-priſoners; amongſt whom yet, when all were come together, there was but one whom I knew ſo much as by Face, and with him I had no Acquaintance. For I having been but a little while in the City, and in that Time kept cloſe to my Studies, I was by that Means known to very few.

Soon after we were all gotten together, came up the Maſter of the Houſe after us, and demanded

manded our Names; which we might reaſon- 1662.
ably have refuſed to give, till we had been legally convened before ſome Civil Magiſtrate, who had Power to examine us and demand our Names. But we, who were neither guilful nor wilful, ſimply gave him our Names, which he took down in Writing.

It was, as I hinted before, a general Storm which fell that Day, but it lighted moſt, and moſt heavy, upon our Meetings; ſo that moſt of our Men-Friends were made Priſoners, and the Priſons generally filled. And great Work had the Women, to run about from Priſon to Priſon to find their Huſbands, their Fathers, their Brothers, or their Servants; for accordingly as they had diſpoſed themſelves to ſeveral Meetings, ſo were they diſperſed to ſeveral Priſons. And no leſs Care and Pains had they, when they had found them, to furniſh them with Proviſions and other neceſſary Accommodations.

But an excellent Order, even in thoſe early Days, was practiſed among the Friends of that City, by which there were certain Friends of either Sex, appointed to have the Overſight of the Priſons in every Quarter, and to take Care of all Friends, the *Poor* eſpecially, that ſhould be committed thither.

This Priſon of *Bridewell* was under the Care of two honeſt, grave, diſcreet and motherly Women, whoſe Names were *Anne Merrick* (afterwards *Vivers*) and *Anne Travers*, both Widows.

1662. They, so soon as they understood that there were Friends brought into that Prison, provided some hot Victuals, Meat and Broth, for the Weather was cold; and ordering their Servants to bring it them, with Bread, Cheese and Beer, came themselves also with it; and having placed it on a Table, gave Notice to us, *That it was provided for all those that had not others to provide for them; or were not able to provide for themselves.* And there wanted not among us a competent Number of such Guests.

As for my part, though I had lived as frugally as possibly I could, that I might draw out the Thread of my little Stock to the utmost Length, yet had I, by this Time, reduced it to Tenpence, which was all the Money I had about me, or any where else at my Command.

This was but a small Estate to enter upon an Imprisonment with, yet was I not at all discouraged at it, nor had I a murmuring Thought. I had known what it was (moderately) to *abound*, and if I should now come to suffer *Want*, I knew I ought to be content; and through the Grace of GOD I was so. I had lived by Providence before (when for a long Time I had no Money at all) and I had always found the LORD a good Provider. I made no doubt therefore that He, who sent the Ravens to feed *Elijah*, and who cloaths the Lilies, would find some Means to sustain me with needful Food and Raiment; and I had learn'd by Experience the Truth of that Saying,

Natura

Natura paucis contenta; i. e. Nature is content 1662.
with few Things, or a little.

Although the Sight and Smell of hot Food, was sufficiently enticing to my empty Stomach, for I had eaten little that Morning, and was hungry; yet considering the Terms of the Invitation, I questioned whether I was included in it; and after some Reasonings, at length concluded, That while I had Ten-pence in my Pocket, I should be but an injurious Intruder to that Mess, which was provided for such as, perhaps, had not Two-pence in theirs.

Being come to this Resolution, I withdrew as far from the Table as I could, and sate down in a quiet Retirement of Mind till the Repast was over, which was not long; for there were Hands enough at it, to make light Work of it.

When Evening came, the Porter came up the Back-stairs, and opening the Door, told us, *If we desired to have any Thing that was to be had in the House, he would bring it us; for there was in the House a* Chandler's *Shop, at which Beer, Bread, Butter, Cheese, Eggs and Bacon might be had for Money.* Upon which many went to him, and spake for what of these Things they had a Mind to, giving him Money to pay for them.

Among the rest went I, and intending to spin out my Ten-pence as far as I could, desired him to bring me a Penny-loaf only. When he returned, we all resorted to him to receive our several Provisions, which he delivered; and

when

1662. when he came to me, he told me, *He could not get a Penny-loaf, but he had brought me two Half-penny-loaves.*

This ſuited me better; wherefore returning to my Place again, I ſate down and eat up one of my Loaves, reſerving the other for the next Day.

This was to me both Dinner and Supper. And ſo well ſatisfied I was with it, that I could willingly then have gone to Bed, if I had had one to go to; but that was not to be expected there, nor had any one any Bedding brought in that Night.

Some of the Company had been ſo conſiderate, as to ſend for a Pound of Candles, that we might not ſit all Night in the Dark, and having lighted divers of them, and placed them in ſeveral Parts of that large Room, we kept walking to keep us warm.

After I had warmed myſelf pretty througly, and the Evening was pretty far ſpent, I bethought myſelf of a Lodging; and caſting mine Eye on the Table which ſtood in the Bay-window, the Frame whereof look'd I thought, ſomewhat like a Bedſtead. Wherefore willing to make ſure of that, I gathered up a good Armful of the Ruſhes wherewith the Floor was covered, and ſpreading them under that Table, crept in upon them in my Cloaths, and keeping on my Hat, laid my Head upon one End of the Table's Frame inſtead of a Bolſter.

My

My Example was followed by the reſt, who gathering up Ruſhes as I had done, made themſelves Beds in other Parts of the Room, and ſo to Reſt we went.

I having a quiet, eaſy Mind, was ſoon a-ſleep, and ſlept till about the Middle of the Night. And then waking, finding my Legs and Feet very cold, I crept out of my Cabbin and began to walk about apace.

This waked and raiſed all the reſt, who finding themſelves cold as well as I, got up and walked about with me, till we had pretty well warmed ourſelves, and then we all lay down again and reſted till Morning.

Next Day, all they who had Families, or belong'd to Families, had Bedding brought in of one Sort or other, which they diſpoſed at the Ends and Sides of the Room, leaving the Middle void to walk in.

But I, who had no Body to look after me, kept to my Ruſhy-pallet under the Table for four Nights together, in which Time I did not put off my Cloaths; yet, through the merciful Goodneſs of GOD unto me, I reſted and ſlept well, and enjoyed Health, without taking Cold.

In this Time divers of our Company, through the Solicitations of ſome of their Relations, or Acquaintance, to Sir *Richard Brown* (who was at that Time a great Maſter of *Miſ-rule* in the City, and over *Bridewell* more eſpecially) were releaſed; and among theſe, one *William Mucklow*, who lay in an Hammock. He, having obſerved

1662. obſerved that I only was unprovided of Lodging, came very courteouſly to me, and kindly offered me the Uſe of his Hammock while I ſhould continue a Priſoner.

This was a providential Accommodation to me, which I received thankfully, both from the LORD and from him; and from thenceforth I thought I lay as well as ever I had done in my Life.

Amongſt thoſe that remained, there were ſeveral young Men who caſt themſelves into a Club, and laying down every one an equal Proportion of Money, put it into the Hand of our Friend *Anne Travers*, deſiring her to lay it out for them in Proviſions, and ſend them in every Day a Meſs of hot Meat; and they kindly invited me to come into their Club with them. Theſe ſaw my Perſon, and judged of me by that; but they ſaw not my Purſe, nor underſtood the Lightneſs of my Pocket. But I, who alone underſtood my own Condition, knew I muſt ſit down with lower Commons. Wherefore not giving them the true Reaſon, I as fairly as I could excuſed myſelf from entring at preſent into their Meſs, and went on, as before, to eat by myſelf, and that very ſparingly, as my Stock would bear. And before my Tenpence was quite ſpent, Providence, on whom I relied, ſent me in a freſh Supply.

For *William Penington* (a Brother of *Iſaac Penington*'s) a Friend and Merchant in *London*, at whoſe Houſe, before I came to live in the City, I was wont to lodge, having been at his Brother's

Brother's that Day upon a Visit, escaped this Storm, and so was at Liberty; and understanding when he came back, what had been done, bethought himself of me, and upon Enquiry hearing where I was, came in Love to see me.

He, in Discourse amongst other Things, asked me, *How it was with me as to Money?* and *how well I was furnished?* I told him, I could not boast of much, and yet I could not say I had none; though what I then had was indeed next to none. Whereupon he put Twenty Shillings into my Hand, and desired me to accept of that for the present. I saw a divine Hand in thus opening his Heart and Hand in this manner to me. And tho' I would willingly have been excused from taking so much, and would have returned one Half of it; yet he pressing it all upon me, I received it with a thankful Acknowledgment, as a Token of Love from the Lord and from him.

On the Seventh-day he went down again, as he usually did, to his Brother's House at *Chalfont*; and in Discourse gave them an Account of my Imprisonment. Whereupon, at his Return on the Second-day of the Week following, my affectionate Friend *Mary Penington* sent me, by him, Forty Shillings, which he soon after brought me; out of which I would have repaid him the Twenty Shillings he had so kindly furnished me with, but he would not admit it, telling me, *I might have Occasion for that and more, before I got my Liberty.*

Not

1662. Not many Days after this, I received Twenty Shillings from my Father, who being then at his House in *Oxfordshire*, and, by Letter from my Sister, understanding that I was a Prisoner in *Bridewell*, sent this Money to me for my Support there; and withal a Letter to my Sister, for her to deliver to one called Mr. *Wray*, who lived near *Bridewell*, and was a Servant to Sir *Richard Brown* in some Wharf of his, requesting him to intercede with his Master, who was one of the Governors of *Bridewell*, for my Deliverance. But that Letter coming to my Hands, I supprest it, and have it yet by me.

Now was my Pocket, from the lowest Ebb risen to a full Tide. I was at the Brink of Want, next Door to nothing, yet my Confidence did not fail, nor my Faith stagger; and now on a sudden I had plentiful Supplies, Shower upon Shower, so that I abounded, yet was not lifted up; but in Humility could say, *This is the* LORD's *doing*. And, without defrauding any of the Instruments of the Acknowledgments due unto them, mine Eye looked over and beyond them to the LORD, who I saw was the Author thereof and prime Agent therein, and with a thankful Heart I returned Thanksgivings and Praises to Him. And this great Goodness of the Lord to me, I thus record, to the End that all into whose Hands this may come, may be encouraged to trust in the Lord, whose Mercy is over all His Works, and

who

who is indeed a God near at hand, to help in the needful Time.

Now I durſt venture myſelf into the Club, to which I had been invited, and accordingly (having by this Time gained an Acquaintance with them) took an Opportunity to caſt myſelf among them; and thenceforward, ſo long as we continued Priſoners there together, I was one of their Meſs.

And now the chief Thing I wanted, was *Imployment*, which ſcarce any wanted but my ſelf; for the reſt of my Company were generally Tradeſmen, of ſuch Trades as could ſet themſelves on work. Of theſe, divers were *Taylors*, ſome Maſters, ſome Journey-men, and with theſe I moſt inclined to ſettle. But becauſe I was too much a Novice in their Art, to be truſted with their Work, leſt I ſhould ſpoil the Garment, I got Work from an *Hoſier* in *Cheap-ſide*; which was to make Night-Waiſtcoats of red and yellow Flannel, for Women and Children. And with this I entred myſelf among the *Taylors*, ſitting Croſs-leg'd as they did, and ſo ſpent thoſe leiſure Hours with Innocency and Pleaſure, which Want of Buſineſs would have made tedious. And indeed that was, in a manner, the only Advantage I had by it; for my Maſter, though a very wealthy Man, and one who profeſſed not only Friendſhip, but particular Kindneſs to me, dealt I thought but hardly with me. For, though he knew not what I had to ſubſiſt by, he never offered me a Penny for my Work, till I had done working

for

1662. for him, and went, after I was releaſed, to give him a Viſit; and then he would not reckon with me neither, *Becauſe* (as he ſmilingly ſaid) *he would not let me ſo far into his Trade, as to acquaint me with the Prices of the Work; but would be ſure to give me enough.* And thereupon he gave me one Crown-piece and no more; tho' I had wrought long for him, and made him many Dozens of Waiſtcoats, and bought the Thread myſelf; which I thought was very poor Pay. But, as Providence had ordered it, I wanted the Work more than the Wages, and therefore took what he gave me without complaining.

About this Time, while we were Priſoners in our fair Chamber, a Friend was brought and put in among us, who had been ſent thither by *Richard Brown* to beat Hemp; whoſe Caſe was thus:

He was a very poor Man who lived by mending Shoes; and on a Seventh-day Night late, a Carman (or ſome other ſuch labouring Man) brought him a Pair of Shoes to mend, deſiring him to mend them that Night, that he might have them in the Morning, for he had no other to wear. The poor Man ſate up at work upon them till after Mid-night, and then finding he could not finiſh them, he went to Bed, intending to do the reſt in the Morning.

Accordingly he got up betimes, and though he wrought as privately as he could in his Chamber, that he might avoid giving Offence

to

to any, yet could he not do it ſo privately, but that an ill-natur'd Neighbour perceived it, who went and informed againſt him for working on the *Sunday*. Whereupon he was had before *Richard Brown*, who committed him to *Bridewell* for a certain Time, to be kept to hard Labour in beating Hemp, which is Labour hard enough. 1662.

It ſo fell out, that at the ſame Time were committed thither (for what Cauſe I do not now remember) two luſty young Men who were called *Baptiſts*, to be kept alſo at the ſame Labour.

The Friend was a poor little Man, of a low Condition and mean Appearance; whereas theſe two *Baptiſts* were topping Blades, that looked high and ſpake big. They ſcorned to beat Hemp, and made a *Piſh* at the Whipping-poſt; but when they had once felt the Smart of it, they ſoon cried *Peccavi*, and ſubmitting to the Puniſhment, ſet their tender Hands to the Beetles.

The Friend, on the other hand acting upon a Principle, as knowing he had done no Evil for which he ſhould undergo that Puniſhment, refuſed to work, and for refuſing was cruelly whipt; which he bore with wonderful Conſtancy and Reſolution of Mind.

The manner of whipping there is, To ſtrip the Party to the Skin from the Waiſt upwards, and having faſtned him to the Whipping-poſt, (ſo that he can neither reſiſt nor ſhun the Strokes) to laſh the naked Body with long,

1662. but ſlender Twigs of Holly, which will bend almoſt like Thongs and lap round the Body; and theſe having little Knots upon them, tear the Skin and Fleſh, and give extream Pain.

With theſe Rods they tormented the Friend moſt barbarouſly; and the more, for that having maſtered the two braving *Baptiſts*, they diſdainded to be maſtered by this poor *Quaker*. Yet were they fain at laſt to yield, when they ſaw their utmoſt Severity could not make him yield. And then, not willing to be troubled longer with him, they turned him up among us.

When we had enquired of him, How it was with him? and he had given us a brief Account of both his Cauſe and Uſage, it came in my Mind, that I had in my Box (which I had ſent for from my Lodging, to keep ſome few Books and other Neceſſaries in) a little Gally-pot with *Lucatellu*'s Balſam in it.

Wherefore cauſing a good Fire to be made, and ſetting the Friend, within a Blanket before the Fire, we ſtripped him to the Waiſt, as if he had been to be whipt again, and found his Skin ſo cut and torn with the knotty Holly-rods, both Back, Side, Arm and Breaſt, that it was a diſmal Sight to look upon. Then melting ſome of the Balſam, I with a Feather anointed all the Sores, and putting a ſofter Cloth between his Skin and his Shirt, helped him on with his Cloaths again. This Dreſſing gave him much Eaſe, and I continued it till he was well. And becauſe he was a

very

very poor Man, we took him into our Mess, 1662.
contriving that there should always be enough for him as well as for ourselves. Thus he lived with us until the Time, he was committed for, was expired, and then he was released.

But we were still continued Prisoners by an arbitrary Power, not being committed by the Civil Authority, nor having seen the Face of any Civil Magistrate, from the Day we were thrust in here by Soldiers, which was the 26th Day of the eighth Month, to the 19th of the tenth Month following.

On that Day we were had to the Sessions at the *Old-bailey*. But not being called there, we were brought back to *Bridewell*, and continued there to the 29th of the same Month, and then we were carried to the Sessions again.

I expected I should have been called the first, because my Name was first taken down; but it proved otherwise, so that I was one of the last that was called; which gave me the Advantage of hearing the Pleas of the other Prisoners, and discovering the Temper of the Court.

The Prisoners complained of the *Illegality* of their Imprisonment, and desired to know, *what they had lain so long in Prison for?* The Court regarded nothing of that, and did not stick to tell them so. *For*, said the Recorder to them, *if you think you have been wrongfully imprisoned, you have your Remedy at Law, and may take it,*

1662. *if you think it worth your while. The Court,* ſaid he, *may ſend for any Man out of the Street, and tender him the Oath: So we take no Notice how you came hither, but finding you here, we tender you the Oath of* Allegiance; *which if you refuſe to take, we ſhall commit you, and at length* Præmunire *you.* Accordingly, as every one refuſed it, he was ſet aſide and another called.

By this I ſaw, it was in vain for me to inſiſt upon falſe Impriſonment, or aſk the Cauſe of my Commitment; though I had before furniſhed myſelf with ſome Authorities and Maxims of Law on that Subject, to have pleaded if Room had been given; and I had the Book, out of which I took them, in my Boſom; for the Weather being cold, I wore a Gown girt about the Middle, and had put the Book within it. But I now reſolved to wave all that, and inſiſt upon another Plea, which juſt then came into my Mind.

As ſoon therefore as I was called, I ſtept nimbly to the Bar, and ſtood up upon the Stepping, that I might the better both hear and be heard, and laying my Hands upon the Bar, ſtood ready, expecting what they would ſay to me.

I ſuppoſe they took me for a confident young Man, for they looked very earneſtly upon me; and we faced each other, without Words, for a while. At length the Recorder, who was called Sir *John Howel,* aſked me, *If I would take the Oath of* Allegiance?

To

To which I anſwered, I conceive this Court hath not Power to tender that Oath to me, in the Condition wherein I ſtand. 1662.

This ſo unexpected Plea ſeemed to ſtartle them, ſo that they looked one upon another, and ſaid ſomewhat low one to another, *What! doth he demur to the Juriſdiction of the Court?* And thereupon the Recorder aſked me, *Do you then demur to the Juriſdiction of the Court?* Not abſolutely, anſwered I, but conditionally, with reſpect to my preſent Condition, and the Circumſtances I am now under.

Why, what is your preſent Condition? ſaid the Recorder. A Priſoner, replied I. *And what is that*, ſaid he, *to your taking, or not taking the Oath?* Enough, ſaid I as I conceive, to exempt me from the Tender thereof, while I am under this Condition. *Pray, what is your Reaſon for that?* ſaid he. This, ſaid I; That if I rightly underſtand the Words of the Statute, I am required to ſay, *That I do take this Oath freely and without Conſtraint*; which I cannot ſay, becauſe I am not a Free-man, but in Bonds, and under Conſtraint. Wherefore I conceive, that if you would tender that Oath to me, ye ought firſt to ſet me free from my preſent Impriſonment.

But, ſaid the Recorder, *will you take the Oath if you be ſet free?* Thou ſhalt ſee that, ſaid I, when I am ſet free. Therefore ſet me free firſt, and then aſk the Queſtion.

But, ſaid he again, *you know your own Mind ſure, and can tell now what you would do, if you were*

1662. *were at Liberty.* Yes, replied I, that I can; but I don't hold myſelf obliged to tell it until I am at Liberty. Therefore ſet me at Liberty, and ye ſhall ſoon hear it.

Thus we fenced a good while, till I was both weary of ſuch trifling, and doubted alſo, leſt ſome of the Standers by ſhould ſuſpect I would take it, if I was ſet at Liberty. Wherefore when the Recorder put it upon me again, I told him plainly, No; though I thought they ought not to tender it me, till I had been ſet at Liberty; yet if I was ſet at Liberty, I could not take that, nor any other Oath, becauſe my Lord and Maſter CHRIST JESUS, had expreſly commanded his Diſciples, *Not to ſwear at all.*

As His Command was enough to me, ſo this Confeſſion of mine was enough to them. *Take him away*, ſaid they; and away I was taken, and thruſt into the Bail-dock to my other Friends, who had been called before me. And as ſoon as the reſt of our Company were called, and had refuſed to *ſwear*, we were all committed to *Newgate*, and thruſt into the common Side.

When we came there, we found that Side of the Priſon very full of Friends, who were Priſoners there before (as indeed were, at that Time, all the other Parts of that Priſon, and moſt of the other Priſons about the Town) and our Addition cauſed a great Throng on that Side. Notwithſtanding which, we were kindly welcomed by our Friends, whom we found there, and

and entertained by them, as well as their Condition would admit, until we could get in our own Accommodations, and provide for ourſelves. 1662.

We had the Liberty of the Hall (which is on the firſt Story over the Gate, and which, in the Day-time, is common to all the Priſoners on that Side, Felons as well as others, to walk in and to beg out of) and we had alſo the Liberty of ſome other Rooms over that Hall, to walk or work in a-Days. But in the Night we all lodged in one Room, which was large and round, having in the Middle of it a great Pillar of oaken Timber, which bore up the Chapel that is over it.

To this Pillar we faſtned our Hammocks at the one End, and to the oppoſite Wall on the other End, quite round the Room, and in three Degrees, or three Stories high, one over the other; ſo that they who lay in the upper and middle Row of Hammocks, were obliged to go to Bed firſt, becauſe they were to climb up to the higher, by getting into the lower. And under the lower Rank of Hammocks, by the Wall-ſides were laid Beds upon the Floor, in which the Sick, and ſuch weak Perſons as could not get into the Hammocks, lay. And indeed, though the Room was large and pretty airy, yet the Breath and Steam that came from ſo many Bodies of different Ages, Conditions and Conſtitutions, packt up ſo cloſe together, was enough to cauſe Sickneſs amongſt us, and I believe did ſo. For there were many ſick, and ſome very weak; though we were not long there, yet in that Time one of our Fellow-priſoners, who lay in one of thoſe Pallet-beds, died.

This cauſed ſome Buſtle in the Houſe. For the Body of the deceaſed being laid out, and put into a Coffin, was carried down and ſet in the Room called the *Lodge*, that the *Coroner* might enquire into the Cauſe and Manner of his Death. And the manner of their doing it is thus: As ſoon as the *Coroner* is come, the Turnkeys run out into the Street under the Gate, and ſeize upon every Man that paſſes by, till they have got enough to make up the *Coroner*'s Inqueſt. And ſo reſolute theſe rude Fellows are, that if any Man reſiſt, or diſpute it with them, they drag him in by main Force, not regarding what Condition he is of. Nay, I have been told, they will not ſtick to ſtop a Coach, and pluck the Men out of it.

It ſo happened, that at this Time they lighted on an ancient Man, a grave Citizen, who was trudging through the Gate in great Haſte, and him they laid hold on, telling him, *He muſt come in, and ſerve upon the* Coroner'*s Inqueſt.* He pleaded hard, beg'd and beſought them to let him go, aſſuring them, *He was going on very urgent Buſineſs, and that the ſtopping him would be greatly to his Prejudice.* But they were deaf to all Intreaties, and hurried him in, the poor Man chaffing without Remedy.

When they had got their Complement, and were ſhut in together, the reſt of them ſaid to this

this ancient Man, *Come, Father, you are the oldest among us, you shall be our Foreman.* And when the *Coroner* had sworn them on the Jury, the Coffin was uncovered, that they might look upon the Body. But the old Man, disturbed in his Mind at the Interruption they had given him, was grown somewhat fretful upon it; said to them, *To what purpose do you shew us a dead Body here? You would not have us think sure, that this Man died in this Room! How then shall we be able to judge how this Man came by his Death, unless we see the Place wherein he died, and wherein he hath been kept Prisoner before he died? How know we, but that the Incommodiousness of the Place wherein he was kept, may have occasioned his Death? Therefore shew us,* said he, *the Place wherein this Man died.* 1662.

This much displeased the Keepers, and they began to banter the old Man, thinking to have beaten him off it. But he stood up titely to them; *Come, come,* said he, *though you have made a Fool of me in bringing me in hither, ye shall not find a Child of me now I am here. Mistake not yourselves; I understand my Place, and your Duty; and I require you to conduct me and my Brethren, to the Place where this Man died: Refuse it at your Peril.*

They now wished they had let the old Man go about his Business, rather than by troubling him, have brought this Trouble on themselves. But when they saw he persisted in his Resolution, and was peremptory, the *Coroner* told them, *They must go shew him the Place?*

It

1662. It was in the Evening when they began this Work; and by this time it was grown Bed-time with us, so that we had taken down our Hammocks (which in the Day were hung up by the Walls) and had made them ready to go into, and were undressing ourselves in Readiness to go into them. When on a sudden we heard a great Noise of Tongues, and of Tramplings of Feet, coming up towards us. And by and by one of the Turnkeys opening our Door, said, *Hold, hold, don't undress yourselves, here's the* Coroner's *Inquest coming to see you.*

As soon as they were come to the Door (for within the Door there was scarce Room for them to come) the Foreman who led them, lifting up his Hand, said, *Lord bless me, what a Sight is here! I did not think there had been so much Cruelty in the Hearts of* Englishmen, *to use* Englishmen *in this manner! We need not now question,* said he to the rest of the Jury, *how this Man came by his Death; we may rather wonder that they are not all dead, for this Place is enough to breed an Infection among them. Well,* added he, *if it please God to lengthen my Life till To-morrow, I will find means to let the King know how his Subjects are dealt with.*

Whether he did so or no, I cannot tell; but I am apt to think that he applied himself to the Mayor, or the Sheriffs of *London.* For the next Day one of the Sheriffs, called Sir *William Turner*, a *Woollen-draper* in *Paul's-yard,* came to the Press-yard, and having ordered the Porter of *Bridewell* to attend him there, sent up a Turnkey

Turnkey amongſt us, to bid all the *Bridewell* 1662.
Priſoners come down to him, for they knew us not, but we knew our own Company.

Being come before him in the Preſs-yard, he looked kindly on us, and ſpake courteouſly to us. *Gentlemen,* ſaid he, *I underſtand the Priſon is very full, and I am ſorry for it. I wiſh it were in my Power to releaſe you, and the reſt of your Friends that are in it. But ſince I cannot do that, I am willing to do what I can for you. And therefore I am come hither to enquire how it is; and I would have all you, who came from* Bridewell, *return thither again, which will be a better Accommodation to you; and your Removal will give the more Room to thoſe that are left behind; and here is the Porter of* Bridewell, *your old Keeper, to attend you thither.*

We duly acknowledged the Favour of the Sheriff to us and our Friends above, in this Removal of us, which would give them more Room, and us a better Air. But before we parted from him, I ſpake particularly to him on another Occaſion; which was this:

When we came into *Newgate,* we found a ſhabby Fellow there among the Friends, who upon Inquiry, we underſtood had thruſt himſelf among our Friends, when they were taken at a Meeting, on purpoſe to be ſent to Priſon with them, in hopes to be maintained by them. They knew nothing of him, till they found him ſhut in with them in the Priſon, and then took no Notice of him, as not knowing how or why he came thither. But he ſoon gave them

1662. them Cauſe to take Notice of him; for whereever he ſaw any Victuals brought forth for them to eat, he would be ſure to thruſt in, with Knife in Hand, and make himſelf his own Carver; and ſo impudent was he, that if he ſaw the Proviſion was ſhort, whoever wanted, he would be ſure to take enough.

Thus lived this lazy Drone upon the Labours of the induſtrious Bees, to his high Content and their no ſmall Trouble, to whom his Company was as offenſive, as his Ravening was oppreſſive; nor could they get any Relief, by their complaining of him to the Keepers.

This Fellow hearing the Notice which was given, for the *Bridewell* Men to go down, in order to be removed to *Bridewell* again, and hoping, no Doubt, that freſh Quarters would produce freſh Commons, and that he ſhould fare better with us than where he was, thruſt himſelf amongſt us, and went down into the Preſs-yard with us. Which I knew not of, till I ſaw him ſtanding there with his Hat on, and looking as demurely as he could, that the Sheriff might take him for a *Quaker*: At Sight of which, my Spirit was much ſtirred.

Wherefore, as ſoon as the Sheriff had done ſpeaking to us, and we had made our Acknowledgment of his Kindneſs, I ſtept a little nearer to him, and pointing to that Fellow, ſaid, That Man is not only none of our Company, for he is no *Quaker*; but is an idle diſſolute Fellow, who hath thruſt himſelf in among our Friends, to be ſent to Priſon with them, that he might live

live upon them; therefore I desire we may not 1662.
be troubled with him at *Bridewell.*

At this the Sheriff smiled; and calling the Fellow forth, said to him, *How came you to be in Prison?* I was taken at a Meeeing, said he. *But what Business had you there?* said the Sheriff. I went to hear, said he. *Aye, you went upon a worse Design, it seems,* replied the Sheriff, *but I'll disappoint you,* said he; *for I'll change your Company, and send you to them that are like your self.* Then calling for the Turnkey, he said, *Take this Fellow, and put him among the Felons; and be sure let him not trouble the* Quakers *any more.*

Hitherto this Fellow had stood with his Hat on, as willing to have passed, if he could, for a *Quaker*; but as soon as he heard this Doom passed on him, off went his Hat, and to bowing and scraping he fell, with *Good your Worship, have Pity upon me, and set me at Liberty. No, no,* said the Sheriff, *I will not so far disappoint you; since you had a Mind to be in Prison, in Prison you shall be for me.* Then bidding the Turnkey take him away, he had him up, and put him among the Felons; and so Friends had a good Deliverance from him.

The Sheriff then bidding us Farewell, the Porter of *Bridewell* came to us, and told us, *We knew our Way to* Bridewell *without him, and he could trust us; therefore he would not stay nor go with us, but left us to take our own Time, so we were in before Bed-time.*

Then

 Then went we up again to our Friends in *Newgate*, and gave them an Account of what had paſſed; and having taken a ſolemn Leave of them, we made up our Packs to be gone. But before I paſs from *Newgate*, I think it not amiſs, to give the Reader ſome little Account of what I obſerved while I was there.

The Common-ſide of *Newgate* is generally accounted, as it really is, the worſt Part of that Priſon; not ſo much from the Place, as the People, it being uſually ſtocked with the verieſt Rogues, and meaneſt Sort of Felons and Pick-pockets, who not being able to pay Chamber-rent on the Maſter's-ſide, are thruſt in there. And if they come in bad, to be ſure they do not go out better; for here they have an Opportunity to inſtruct one another in their Art, and impart each to other what Improvements they have made therein.

The Common-hall (which is the firſt Room over the Gate) is a good Place to walk in, when the Priſoners are out of it, ſaving the Danger of catching ſome Cattle which they may have left in it, and there I uſed to walk in a Morning before they were let up, and ſometimes in the Day-time when they have been there.

They all carried themſelves reſpectfully towards me; which I imputed chiefly to this, That when any of our Women-Friends came there to viſit the Priſoners, if they had not Relations of their own there to take care of them, I, (as being a young Man, and more at leiſure

than

than most others, for I could not play the *Taylor* 1662.
there) was forward to go down with them to the Grate, and see them safe out. And sometimes they have left Money in my Hands for the Felons (who at such Times were very importunate Beggars) which I forthwith distributed among them in Bread, which was to be had in the Place. But so troublesome an Office it was, that I thought one had as good have had a Pack of hungry Hounds about one, as these, when they knew there was a Dole to be given. Yet this I think, made them a little the more observant to me; for they would dispose themselves to one Side of the Room, that they might make Way for me to walk on the other. And when I walked there, I had usually a Book in my Hand, on which I had mine Eye; which made them think I did not heed what they said. By this Means, mine Ear being attentive to them, I heard them relate one to another many of their roguish Pranks.

One Day, as I was thus walking to and fro beside them, I heard them recounting one to another what Feats they had done at Pocket-picking and Shop-lifting. Whereupon, turning short upon them, I asked them, *Which of you all will undertake to pick my Pocket?* They were not very forward to answer, but viewed me round. I wore a long Gown, which was lapt over before and tied about the Middle, and had no Pocket-holes in it. When they had a while considered it, and I, having taken another Turn, was come up again to them,

one

1662. one of them ſaid, *Why, Maſter, if you will promiſe not to proſecute us, we will ſhow you a Piece of our Skill.* Nay, hold there, ſaid I, I won't ſo far encourage you in Evil, as to promiſe not to proſecute; and away I turned again, having mine Eye on my Book, but mine Ears to them. And in a while I heard them contriving how they would have done it. *I,* ſaid one of them, *would give him the Budge, and before he can recover himſelf, you,* ſaid he to another of them, *having your Penknife ready, ſhould ſlit his Gown; and then,* ſaid he, *let* Honeypot *alone for the diving Part.* This *Honeypot* was a little Boy, then in Priſon with them for picking a Pocket, who by his Stature did not ſeem to be above ten, or a dozen Years old; but for his Dexterity at Pocket-picking, was held to be one of the Top of the Trade. As for the *Budge,* I had had it given me often in the Street, but underſtood not the Meaning of it till now; and now I found it was a Joſtle, enough to throw one almoſt upon his Noſe.

I have ſometimes occaſionally been in the Hall in an Evening, and have ſeen the Whores let in unto them, which I take to be a common Practice: Naſty Sluts indeed they were, and in that Reſpect the more ſuitable. And as I have paſſed them, I have heard the Rogues and they making their Bargains, which and which of them ſhould company together that Night. Which abominable Wickedneſs muſt be imputed to the Diſhoneſty of the Turnkeys,

who,

who, for vile Gain to themselves, not only suffer, 1662.
but further this Lewdness.

These are some of the common Evils which make the Common-side of *Newgate*, in measure a Type of *HELL* upon *EARTH*. But there was, at that Time, something of another Nature, more particular and accidental, which was very offensive to me.

When we came first into *Newgate*, there lay in a little By-place like a Closet, near the Room where we were lodged, the quartered Bodies of three Men, who had been executed some Days before, for a real or pretended Plot; which was the Ground, or at least Pretext, for that Storm in the City, which had caused this Imprisonment. The Names of these three Men were *Philips*, *Tongue* and *Gibs*; and the Reason why their Quarters lay so long there was, The Relations were all that while petitioning to have Leave to bury them; which at length with much ado was obtained for the Quarters, but not for the Heads, which were ordered to be set up in some Parts of the City.

I saw the Heads when they were brought up to be boiled. The Hangman fetch'd them in a dirty Dust-basket, out of some By-place, and setting them down amongst the Felons, he and they made Sport with them. They took them by the Hair, flouting, jeering and laughing at them; and then giving them some ill Names, box'd them on the Ears and Cheeks. Which done, the Hangman put them into his Kettle, and parboil'd them with Bay-salt and

1662. Cummin-ſeed; *that* to keep them from Putrefaction, and *this* to keep off the Fowls from ſeizing on them. The whole Sight, as well that of the bloody Quarters firſt, as this of the Heads afterwards, was both frightful and loathſome, and begat an Abhorrence in my Nature. Which as it had rendered my Confinement there by much the more uneaſy, ſo it made our Removal from thence to *Bridewell*, even in that reſpect, the more welcome: Whither we now go.

For having, as I hinted before, made up our Packs, and taken our Leave of our Friends, whom we were to leave behind, we took our Bundles on our Shoulders, and walked, two and two a-breaſt, through the *Old-bailey* into *Fleet-ſtreet*, and ſo to Old *Bridewell*. And it being about the Middle of the Afternoon, and the Streets pretty full of People, both the Shopkeepers at their Doors, and Paſſengers in the Way, would ſtop us, and aſk us what we were, and whither we were going? And when we had told them we were Priſoners, going from one Priſon to another (from *Newgate* to *Bridewell*) *What*, ſaid they, *without a Keeper!* No, ſaid we, for our Word, which we have given, is our Keeper. Some thereupon would adviſe us not to go to Priſon, but to go home. But we told them, we could not do ſo; we could ſuffer for our Teſtimony, but could not fly from it. I do not remember we had any Abuſe offered us, but were generally pitied by the People.

When

When we were come to *Bridewell*, we were 1662.
not put up into the great Room in which we had been before, but into a low Room in another fair Court, which had a Pump in the Middle of it. And here we were not ſhut up as before, but had the Liberty of the Court to walk in, and of the Pump to waſh or drink at. And indeed we might eaſily have gone quite away if we would, there being a Paſſage through the Court into the Street; but we were true and ſteady Priſoners, and looked upon this Liberty, ariſing from their Confidence in us, to be a kind of *Parol* upon us; ſo that both Conſcience and Honour ſtood now engaged for our true Impriſonment.

Adjoining to this Room wherein we were, was ſuch another, both newly fitted up for *Work-houſes*, and accordingly furniſhed with very great Blocks for beating Hemp upon, and a luſty Whipping-poſt there was in each. And it was ſaid, That *Richard Brown* had ordered thoſe Blocks to be provided for the *Quakers* to work on, reſolving to try his Strength with us in that Caſe; but if that was his Purpoſe, it was over-ruled, for we never had any Work offered us, nor were we treated after the Manner of thoſe that are to be ſo uſed. Yet we ſet ourſelves to work on them; for, being very large, they ſerved the *Taylors* for Shop-boards, and others wrought upon them as they had Occaſion; and they ſerved us very well for Tables to eat on.

N 2 We

1662. We had alſo beſides this Room, the Uſe of our former Chamber above, to go into when we thought fit; and thither ſometimes I withdrew, when I found a Deſire for Retirement and Privacy, or had ſomething on my Mind to write, which could not ſo well be done in Company. And indeed, about this Time my Spirit was more than ordinarily exerciſed, tho' on very different Subjects. For, on the one hand, the Senſe of the exceeding LOVE and GOODNESS of the LORD to me, in His gracious and tender Dealings with me, did deeply affect my Heart, and cauſed me to break forth in a SONG of THANKSGIVING and PRAISE to Him: And, on the other hand, a Senſe of the *Prophaneneſs*, *Debaucheries*, *Cruelties*, and other *horrid Impieties* of the AGE, fell heavy on me, and lay as a preſſing Weight upon my Spirit. And this drew from me a cloſe *Exprobration*, which my mournful Muſe vented in the following Lines; to which I gave for a Title,

Speculum

1662.

Speculum SECULI:

OR, A

LOOKING-GLASS

FOR THE

TIMES.

Which began with this *Expostulatory Preface.*

WHY *should my modest* MUSE *forbidden be,*
To speak of that which but too many see?
Why should she, by conniving, seem t' uphold
Mens Wickedness, and thereby make them bold
Still to persist in't? Why should she be shy
To call them Beasts, *who want* Humanity?
Why should she any longer Silence keep,
And lie secure as one that's fast asleep?
Or, how indeed can it expected be,
That she should hold her Tongue, and daily see
Those wicked *and* enormous Crimes *committed,*
Which she in Modesty has pretermitted?

N 3 *Which*

1662. *Which but to name, would with their Filth defile*
Chaſte Ears, and caſt a Blemiſh on her Stile:
Yet, of ſo many, ſhe cannot forbear
To mention ſome, which here detected are.

LOUD were the Cries, which long had pierc'd mine Ear,
Foul the Reports, which I did daily hear.
Unheard of, *new-invented Crimes* were brought,
By *Fame* unto my *Knowledge*, which I thought
Too foul and loathſome to have found a Place
In any Heart, though ne'er ſo *void* of Grace.
This made me take a more obſervant View,
Whether Report ſpake what of Men is true.
But as the celebrated Southern QUEEN,
When ſhe the Court of *Solomon* had ſeen,
And had, with more than uſual Diligence,
Obſerv'd his Splendor and Magnificence,
Conſider'd well his Pomp, his Port, his State,
The great Retinue that on him did wait;
As one with Admiration fill'd (no doubt
Not able longer to contain) burſt out
Into ſuch Words as theſe; *Thrice happy King!*
Whoſe Fame throughout the Univerſe doth ring,

Though

Though of thine Acts I thought Report too bold, 1662.
Yet now I see one Half hath not been told.
Just so did I, though in another kind,
After I had intently fix'd my Mind
Upon Mens Actions, and had duly weigh'd
Not only what they *did*, but what they *said*:
A while I stood, like one that's struck with
Thunder,
Fill'd with Astonishment, and silent Wonder.
At length my Heart, swelling with *Indignation*,
Vented itself in such an *Exclamation*.
O hellish Doings! O infernal Crew!
Of whom, who says the worst he can, says true.
O Herd of lustful *Satyrs, Monsters, Brutes!*
For such a Name to such a Nature sutes;
What Ink is black enough to write! what Pen
Fit to delineate such Beasts, not Men!
Words are too shallow to express the *Rage*,
The *Fury, Madness* of this *frantick AGE*.
Numbers fall short to reckon up the *Crimes*,
Which are the *Recreations* of these Times.
Was *Sodom* ever guilty of a Sin,
Which *England* is not now involved in?
By *Custom, Drunkenness* so common's grown,
That most Men count it a *small Sin*, or *none*.

1662. *Ranting* and *Roaring* they affirm to be,
The true Characters of *Gentility*.
Swearing and *Cursing* is so much in Fashion,
That 'tis esteem'd a Badge of *Reputation*.
What *dreadful Oaths!* what *direful Execrations*
On others! on themselves what *Imprecations*
They tumble out, like roaring Claps of Thunder,
As if they meant to rend the Clouds asunder!
Mockers do so abound in ev'ry Place,
That rare it is to meet a sober Face.
Ambition, *Boasting*, *Vanity* and *Pride*,
With Numbers numberless of Sins beside,
Are grown, thro' Use, so common, that Men call
Them *Peccadillo's*; small, or none at all.
But, Oh! the *Luxury* and *great Excess*
Which by this wanton Age is us'd in *Dress!*
What Pains do Men and Women take, alas!
To make themselves for arrant *Bedlam's* pass!
The Fool's *py'd Coat*, which all wise Men detest,
Is grown a Garment now in great Request;
More *Colours* in one Waistcoat now they wear,
Than in the *Rain-bow* ever did appear,

As

As if they were ambitious to put on
All Colours that they caſt their Eyes upon;
Thereby outſtripping the *Cameleon* quite,
Which cannot change itſelf to red or white.
Each Man, like *Proteus* his Shape doth change,
To whatſoever ſeemeth new or ſtrange,
And he that in a modeſt Garb is dreſt,
Is made the Laughing-ſtock of all the reſt.
Nor are they with their Baubles ſatisfy'd,
But *Sex-Diſtinctions* too are laid aſide;
The Women wear the *Trowſies* and the *Veſt*,
While Men in *Muffs*, *Fans*, *Peticoats* are dreſt.
Some Women (Oh, the Shame!) like ramping Rigs,
Ride flaunting in their powder'd *Perriwigs*;
Aſtride they ſit (and not aſhamed neither)
Dreſt up like Men in *Jacket*, *Cap* and *Feather*.
All Things to *Luſt* and *Wantonneſs* are fitted,
Nothing that tends to Vanity omitted.
To give a Touch on every *antick Faſhion*,
Which hath been worn of late within this Nation,
Might fill a Volume, which would tire, no doubt,
The READER's Patience, if not wear it out.

Come

1662. Come now, ye *ranting Gallants* of the Times,
Who nothing have to boaſt of but your *Crimes*;
Ye *Satan's Hectors*, who diſdain to ſwear
An Oath beneath *God damn me if he dare.*
Blaſphemous Wretches! whoſe *Impieties*,
With rude Aſſaults have ſtorm'd the very Skies,
And dar'd the *God of Heaven*, a dreadful Stroke
Shall ye receive, by which ye ſhall be broke,
And in the fiery Lake thoſe Torments find,
Which for ſuch *Deſperadoes* are aſſign'd.
And ye, who take ſo great Delight to curſe,
As that you think yourſelves a deal the worſe,
Unleſs unto the higheſt Strain ye ſwell,
And wiſh the *Devil* make your Bed in Hell:
This know, the long provoked God is come,
From whom ye muſt receive that dreadful Doom,
Depart ye Curſed, and for ever dwell,
Where Beds of Torment are prepar'd in Hell.
'Twas wonderful to ſee in what a Trice,
This zealous Nation was o'er-run with *Vice.*
As when the boiling Gulf, with furious Gales
Puff't up, o'erflows its Banks and drowns the
Vales;
And when again it ebbs, it leaves (we find)
A loathſome Scum and noiſome Stink behind.

So

So great was, in a Word, the Wickedneſs 1662.
Of that black Day ; ſuch the uncurb'd Exceſs,
As if the fatal Hour had then been come,
For the Deliv'ry of Hell's pregnant Womb,
And that the Devil had a Patent got,
To vend whatever Merchandize he brought ;
Or that *Pandora*'s Box (which POETS feign
Did all *Calamities* in it contain)
Had then been newly op'ned, and from thence
Had flutter'd out this raging Peſtilence ;
Which ſince, the common Body hath o'erſpread
With ſuch a lep'rous Scab from Foot to Head,
That 'tis a lamentable Sight to ſee,
How each Sex, old and young, debauched be.
A Sort of Men have over-run this Nation,
Who are a Burthen to the whole Creation ;
Men ſhall I call them, or the *Viper's Brood?*
Lovers of Evil, *Haters* of all Good.
Theſe, ſwell'd with Envy, in a great Deſpight
To CHRIST, with *Fiſt of Wickedneſs* do ſmite,
(Not their own *Fellow-ſervants* ; for they are
The *Devil's Slaves*, by him bor'd thro' the Ear:
But) *God's Ambaſſadors*, whom He hath ſent
To warn them of their Sins, and cry *Repent* ;

Or

1662. Or to denounce His *Judgments* againſt thoſe,
That ſet themſelves His *Meſſage* to oppoſe.
Theſe perſecute the Innocent, and ſay,
When they are gone, 'twill be a merry Day.
Theſe grind the Poor; the Needy theſe oppreſs;
Widows devour; tread on the Fatherleſs.
Far from themſelves they put the evil Day,
Remove impending Judgments far away;
And yet in vain they ſtrive t'eſcape the Stroke
Of that juſt God whom boldly they provoke.
For they afflict His People; ſlay His Sheep;
Beat thoſe whom He appointed hath to keep
And feed His tender Lambs; rend, tear, devour,
Suppreſs God's Worſhip to their utmoſt Pow'r.
A curſed Generation, who are bent
To ſpare the *Wicked*, ſlay the *Innocent*,
Whoſe Blood doth cry, whoſe Blood doth cry aloud,
As loud as *Abel*'s, pierceth thro' the Cloud,
Preſents itſelf before the Judgment-Seat,
And Juſtice doth of the juſt Judge intreat,
That ſpeedy Vengeance He will take on all,
Who perſecute His *Saints*, and them enthral.
Nor is He deaf; its Cry with Him prevails,
And He hath promiſed (who never fails

In

In the Performance) that He will arife,
And put a Period to their Cruelties;
And that He will, with more than winged
Speed,
Send Comfort to His poor afflicted Seed,
Which under *Pharaoh's heavy Yoke* hath groan'd,
And in *Captivity* itfelf bemoan'd.
O bloody Sin of *Perfecution!*
'Tis thou that pluckeft Judgments down upon
The Heads of *Kings, Princes, Plebeans*, all
That act thee, and by thee the *Saints* enthral.
This is *that Sin, that Sin* which cries aloud,
Louder than all the reft, *The Guilt of Blood*;
Which is the ftrongeft Cord the Devil hath
To draw down on Mankind *God's heavy Wrath.*
Weeping I figh, and fighing weep to fee
The Rod, which God prepared hath for thee,
O *England*, who doft evilly intreat
His *Meffengers*, and doft His *Prophets* beat.
Ah, *England*, ah, poor *England*, I bewail
Thy fad Eftate; O that I might prevail
In my Defires for thee! then fhouldft thou be
As full of Joy, as now of Mifery.
For then fhould Plenty in thy Fields be found,
And all thy *Garners* fhould with Grain abound.

1662. Then Peace, long-lasting Peace should in thee dwell,
For God would all thine Enemies repel;
And He Himself would take Delight in thee,
So thou the Glory of the World wouldst be.
But, ah, alas! small Hope I have to see
Such happy Symptoms of good Health in thee.
No, No, sad Isle, my Reason it doth tell me,
That all the Crosses, which have yet befel thee,
Are but an Earnest of that dreadful Day,
Wherein God will upon thy Head repay
Wrath, Fury, Vengeance and Destruction,
The just Reward of Persecution.
The due Consideration of thy State,
And thine (I fear) inevitable Fate,
Doth move my Heart with *Pity* and *Compassion*,
And leads me to this short *Expostulation*.
Who to the Eye gave Sight? what shall not He
The cruel Sufferings of His People see?
And shall not He that formed hath the Ear,
The mournful Groans of His *dear Children* hear?
Are Men so stupid grown, they think God's blind?
Or that He doth not heed? or cannot find

A Way

A Way to eaſe the Suff'rings of His Seed? 1662.
Whoſe Cry unto Him is, *Father, with Speed*
Ariſe, ariſe; rend Thou the Clouds, deſcend,
Avenge us of our Enemies; defend
Us from their Cruelties, and let them ſee
Thy Care of us, exceeds our Love to Thee.

Nor are theſe Sighs in vain; for He indeed
Is riſing, yea is ris'n, our Cauſe to plead
In *Righteouſneſs*; and henceforth us who kicks,
Shall know *'tis hard to kick againſt the Pricks.*

Be warned then ye *Rulers*, and let all
Of whatſoever Rank, both great and ſmall,
Tremble before the Lord, and ceaſe to rage
Againſt our God's peculiar Heritage;
For, of a Truth, His long-provoked Hand
Is ſtretched out, in Judgment o'er this Land,
And ye muſt feel it; for He hath decreed,
To vindicate His long oppreſſed Seed,
And in His Fury, He will Vengeance take
In our Behalfs, who ſuffer for His Sake:
Then ſhall ye know, that He who ſits on high,
Regards us as the Apple of His Eye.

To

1662. *To this, occasionally I subjoined a POST-SCRIPT, thus.*

SINCE what precedes was written, I have found
An Accusation form'd, but without Ground,
Against me, That *with uncontrouled Pen,*
I too severely lash the Faults of Men ;
And take upon me, in Satyrick Rhimes,
To pass a rigid Censure on the Times.
This drew me on to add another Line,
To shew them that the Fault's their own, not mine.
No Crime can justly to my Charge be laid,
Unless it be a Crime, *That Truth be said.*
Nor can, without Injustice, any blame
My Muse for ecchoing the common Fame.
If any should object, *That wise Men hold,*
That Truth at all Times ought not to be told.
Nor that *whatever comes into one's Head,*
Should straight, because 'tis true, be published.
I readily assent, because I know
Pearls before Swine we are forbid to throw.
Some Truths, I grant, may better be conceal'd,
Than if they out of Season were reveal'd ;

Yet

Yet would I not that any, through Miſtake,
Should of my Words a Miſconſtruction make,
Than that ſhould happen, I had rather be
Taxt by the Reader for Prolixity.
Thus then, in brief, would I be underſtood.
If what I know, concerns my Brother's good,
For him to know; ought I not then unfold
It to him, rather than from him with-hold
A Benefit? So on the other Side,
It is, I think, too plain to be deny'd,
That if I ſee what certainly doth tend
To the Hurt of my Neighbour or my Friend,
I am oblig'd, by *Chriſtian Charity*,
To give them Warning of the Danger nigh;
To ſhew them, that they ſtand upon the Brink
Of certain Ruin; and if then they ſink,
By wilful running on, I ſhall be free
From Guilt, their Blood on their own Heads
will be.
'Tis plain I think; yet if ye can't believe it
Without a Scripture-Proof, lo, here * I give it. *Levit.* 19 17. *Ezek.* 33
This is the very Caſe; which, if well weigh'd,
Will fully juſtify what I have ſaid.
I ſaw Men running to a Precipice,
At Foot of which was ſuch a vaſt Abyſs,

1662. As could have ſwallow'd Nations ſo immenſe,
That 'twas impoſſible to climb out thence.
For if a Man we ſee, but chance to pitch,
O'er Head and Ears into ſome miry Ditch,
How quickly is he ſmothered, unleſs
Some friendly Hand aſſiſt in that Diſtreſs!
And if, with ſtrugling, out at length he get,
Yet how beſmear'd is he with Dirt, and wet!
But into this deep Pit who falls, in vain
Expects an Hand to help him out again.
No, 'tis of Grace that Men forewarned are,
And, e'er their Feet are taken, *ſhew'd the Snare.*
And warned they muſt be. For ſo was I,
While roving in their Paths of *Vanity*;
Toil'd and bewild'red in a diſmal Night
Of thick *Egyptian* Darkneſs, from the Light:
From whence the Lord hath, by His Love me drawn,
And in my Heart hath caus'd his Day to dawn,
His glorious Day, his never-ſetting Sun
To riſe, and Darkneſs to expel begun.
This Love, as it ariſes, warms my Heart,
And fills it with Deſires to impart
To others of its Goodneſs, that none may,
For want of good Direction, miſs their Way.

Know

Know therefore thou, who hitherto hast spent 1662.
Thy Time in *Vanity*, and wholly bent
Thy utmost Strength, thy Lusts to satisfy,
And surfeit with Delights, thy wanton Eye;
The Lord hath in thy *Conscience* plac'd a *Light*,
To teach thee how to guide thy Steps aright.
This checks when into Evil thou hast run,
And gives thee Warning, e'er thou hast begun.
Hast thou not heard, when in thy full Career,
Something within thee say, *What do I here?*
And when thy Mind is cool, another Day,
Doth it not sometimes cause thee thus to say;
O that I had not run into Excess!
O that I had not done this Wickedness!
My Conscience tells me that I have done ill,
In yielding to my own corrupted Will;
And though no Eye did see me, yet my Heart
I feel is full of Torment, Pain and Smart;
Were it to do again I'd have more Care,
And not run wilfully into the Snare.
Consider what that is, which thus doth raise
A Trouble in thee for thy evil Ways;
And what that is, which many Times doth grieve thee,
And often makes thee cry out, *God forgive me.*

1662. When thus it checks thee next, ſtrait call to mind,
That Word, thine Ear ſhall hear a Voice behind
Thee, ſaying *Hither turn, this is the Way,*
When to the right or left, thou go'ſt aſtray.
And having heard, Obedience forthwith give
To its Reproof: *Hear, and thy Soul ſhall live.*
For were Men ſubject to *Chriſt's Light within,*
It certainly would lead Men out of Sin,
And, thro' *Believing*, bring them into Heav'n,
For that's the End, for which by Him 'tis giv'n.
Thus have I faithfully diſcharg'd a Part,
Which long lay as a Weight upon my Heart,
Regardleſs of what Danger may enſue,
For ſeaſonably ſpeaking what is true.
And if ungrateful Men ſhall ill requite
My ſignal Love, with Enmity and Spight,
I let them know, that my undaunted Pen
Scorns the contracted Brows of angry Men.
Prepar'd I am to ſuffer with Content,
The worſt that canc'red Malice can invent;
Which is no more than to my Lord befel,
To *Suffer* evil Things for *doing* well.

Bona

To ſuffer Evil for Well-doing, brings
The Sufferer to ſhare Renown with Kings.

After I had in the foregoing POEM, ſomewhat eaſed my Spirit of that which, for ſome Time, had lain as a Load upon me; I breathed forth the following HYMN to God, in Acknowledgment of His great Goodneſs to me, Profeſſion of my grateful Love to Him, and Supplication to Him, for the Continuance of His Kindneſs to me, in preſerving me from the Snares of the Enemy, and keeping me faithful unto Himſelf.

THEE, Thee alone, O God, I fear,
In Thee do I confide;
Thy Preſence is to me more dear
Than all Things elſe beſide.
Thy Virtue, Power, Life and Light,
Which in my Heart do ſhine,
Above all Things are my Delight,
O make them always mine!
Thy matchleſs Love conſtrains my Life,
Thy Life conſtrains my Love,
To be to Thee as chaſte a Wife,
As is the Turtle-dove

1662. To her elect, eſpouſed Mate,
Whom ſhe will not forſake,
Nor can be brought to violate
The Bond ſhe once did make.
Juſt ſo my Soul doth cleave to Thee,
As to her only Head,
With whom ſhe longs conjoin'd to be
In Bond of Marriage-bed.
But, ah, alas! her little Fort
Is compaſſed about,
Her Foes about her thick reſort,
Within, and eke without.
How numerous are they now grown!
How wicked their Intent!
O let Thy mighty Power be ſhown,
Their Miſchief to prevent!
They make Aſſaults on ev'ry Side,
But Thou ſtand'ſt in the Gap;
Their Batt'ring-Rams make Breaches wide,
But ſtill thou mak'ſt them up.
Sometimes they uſe alluring Wiles,
To draw into their Pow'r;
And ſometimes weep like *Crocodiles*,
But all is to devour.

Thus

Thus they beſet my feeble Heart
With Fraud, Deceit and Guile,
Alluring her from Thee to ſtart,
And Thy pure Reſt defile.
But oh! the Breathing and the Moan,
The Sighings of the Seed,
The Groanings of the grieved One,
Do Sorrows in me breed.
And that immortal, holy Birth,
The Off-ſpring of Thy Breath,
(To whom Thy Love brings Life and Mirth,
As doth thy Abſence, Death;)
That Babe, that Seed, that panting Child,
Which cannot Thee forſake,
In Fear to be again beguil'd,
Doth Supplication make;
O ſuffer not thy choſen One,
Who puts her Truſt in Thee,
And hath made Thee her Choice alone,
Enſnar'd again to be.

Bridewell, London:
1662.

In this Sort did I ſpend ſome leiſure Hours, during my Confinement in *Bridewell*, eſpecially after our Return from *Newgate* thither; when

1662. we had more Liberty, and more Opportunity and Room for Retirement and Thought. For, as the Poet ſaid,

Carmina Scribentes Seceſſum & Otia quærunt.

They who would write in Meaſure,
Retire where they may Stilneſs have and Leiſure.

And this Priviledge we enjoyed by the Indulgence of our Keeper, whoſe Heart God diſpoſed to favour us. So that both the Maſter and his Porter were very civil and kind to us, and had been ſo indeed all along. For when we were ſhut up before, the Porter would readily let ſome of us go home in an Evening, and ſtay at home till next Morning; which was a great Conveniency to Men of Trade and Buſineſs, which I being free from, forbore aſking for myſelf, that I might not hinder others.

This he obſerved, and aſked me *when I meant to aſk to go out?* I told him I had not much Occaſion nor Deſire; yet at ſome time or other, perhaps I might have; but when I had, I would aſk him but once, and if he then denied me, I would aſk him no more.

After we were come back from *Newgate,* I had a Deſire to go thither again, to viſit my Friends who were Priſoners there, more eſpecially my dear Friend, and Father in *Chriſt, Edward Burrough,* who was then a Priſoner, with

with many Friends more, in that Part of 1662.
Newgate which was then called *Justice-hall.*
Whereupon the Porter coming in my Way, I asked him to let me go out for an Hour or two, to see some Friends of mine that Evening.

He to enhanse the Kindness, made it a matter of some Difficulty, and would have me stay till another Night. I told him, I would be at a Word with him; for as I had told him before, that if he denied me, I would ask him no more; so he should find I would keep to it.

He was no sooner gone out of my Sight, but I espied his Master crossing the Court. Wherefore stepping to him, I asked him, If he was willing to let me go out for a little while, to see some Friends of mine that Evening. *Yes,* said he, *very willing*; and thereupon away walked I to *Newgate,* where having spent the Evening among Friends, I returned in good Time.

Under this easy Restraint we lay, till the Court sate at the *Old-Baily* again; and then, whether it was that the Heat of the Storm was somewhat abated, or by what other Means Providence wrought it, I know not; we were called to the Bar, and without further Question discharged.

Whereupon we returned to *Bridewell* again, and having raised some Monies among us, and therewith gratified both the Master and his Porter for their Kindness to us, we spent some Time in a solemn Meeting, to return our thankful Acknowledgment to the LORD, both for His

1662. His Preservation of us in Prison, and Deliverance of us out of it; and then taking a solemn Farewel of each other, we departed with Bag and Baggage. And I took Care to return my Hammock to the Owner, with due Acknowledgment of his great Kindness in lending it me.

Being now at Liberty, I visited more generally my Friends that were still in Prison, and more particularly my Friend and Benefactor, *William Penington*, at his House, and then went to wait upon my Master *Milton*. With whom yet I could not propose to enter upon my intermitted Studies, until I had been in *Buckinghamshire*, to visit my worthy Friends *Isaac Penington*, and his virtuous Wife, with other Friends in that Country.

Thither therefore I betook myself, and the Weather being frosty, and the Ways, by that means, clean and good, I walked it thorow in a Day, and was received by my Friends there, with such Demonstration of hearty Kindness, as made my Journey very easy to me.

I had spent in my Imprisonment that Twenty Shillings which I had received of *William Penington*; and Twenty of the Forty which had been sent me from *Mary Penington*, and had the Remainder then about me. That therefore I now returned to her, with due Acknowledgement of her Husband's and her great Care of me, and Liberality to me in the Time of my Need. She would have had me kept it. But I beg'd her to accept it from me again, since it

was

was the Redundancy of their Kindneſs, and the other Part had anſwered the Occaſion for which it was ſent: And my Importunity prevailed.

I intended only a Viſit hither, not a Continuance; and therefore purpoſed, after I had ſtaid a few Days, to return to my Lodging and former Courſe in *London*; but Providence ordered it otherwiſe.

Iſaac Penington had at that Time two Sons and one Daughter, all then very young; of whom the eldeſt Son *(John Penington)* and the Daughter *(Mary*, the Wife of *Daniel Wharley)* are yet living at the writing of this. And being himſelf both ſkilful and curious in *Pronounciation,* he was very deſirous to have them well grounded in the *Rudiments* of the *Engliſh* Tongue; to which End he had ſent for a Man out of *Lancaſhire*, whom, upon enquiry, he had heard of, who was undoubtedly the moſt accurate *Engliſh* Teacher that ever I met with, or have heard of. His Name was *Richard Bradley.* But as he pretended no higher than the *Engliſh* Tongue, and had led them, by *Grammar* Rules, to the higheſt Improvement they were capable of in that, he had then taken his Leave of them, and was gone up to *London*, to teach an *Engliſh* School of Friends Children there.

This put my Friend to a freſh Strait. He had ſought for a new Teacher to inſtruct his Children in the *Latin* Tongue, as the old had done in the *Engliſh*, but had not yet found one. Wherefore one Evening as we ſate together by

the

1662. the Fire in his Bed-chamber (which, for want of Health, he kept) he asked me, his Wife being by, *If I would be so kind to him, as to stay a while with him, till he could hear of such a Man as he aimed at; and in the mean Time enter his Children in the Rudiments of the* Latin *Tongue.*

This Question was not more unexpected, than surprizing to me; and the more, because it seemed directly to thwart my former Purpose and Undertaking, of endeavouring to improve myself by following my Studies with my Master *Milton*, which this would give at least a present Diversion from, and for how long I could not foresee.

But the Sense I had of the manifold Obligations I lay under to these worthy Friends of mine, shut out all Reasonings, and disposed my Mind to an absolute Resignation to their Desire, that I might testify my Gratitude, by a Willingness to do them any friendly Service, that I could be capable of.

And though I questioned my Ability to carry on that Work, to its due Height and Proportion; yet as that was not proposed, but an Initiation only, by *Accidence* into *Grammar*, I consented to the Proposal, as a present Expedient (till a more qualified Person should be found) without further Treaty or mention of Terms between us, than that of mutual Friendship. And to render this Digression from my own Studies the less uneasy to my Mind,

Mind, I recollected, and often thought of that 1662.
Rule in *Lilly*,

> *Qui docet indoctos, licet indoctiſſimus eſſet,*
> *Ipſe brevi reliquis doctior eſſe queat.*

> He that th' Unlearn'd doth teach, may
> quickly be
> More Learn'd than they, though moſt
> Unlearned he.

With this Conſideration I undertook this Province, and left it not until I married, which was not till the Year 1669, near ſeven Years from the Time I came thither. In which Time, having the Uſe of my Friends Books, as well as of mine own, I ſpent my leiſure Hours much in reading, not without ſome Improvement to myſelf in my private Studies; which (with the good Succeſs of my Labours beſtowed on the Children, and the Agreeableneſs of Converſation which I found in the Family) rendered my Undertaking more ſatisfactory, and my Stay there more eaſy to me.

But, alas! not many Days (not to ſay Weeks) had I been there, e're we were almoſt overwhelmed with Sorrow, for the unexpected Loſs of *Edward Burrough*, who was juſtly very dear to us all.

This not only Good, but Great-good Man, by a long and cloſe Confinement in *Newgate*, through the cruel Malice and malicious Cruelty of *Richard Brown*, was taken away by haſty Death,

1662. Death, to the unutterable Grief of very many, and unſpeakable Loſs to the CHURCH of CHRIST in general.

The particular Obligation I had to him, as the immediate Inſtrument of my Convincement, and high Affection for him reſulting therefrom, did ſo deeply affect my Mind, that it was ſome pretty Time before my Paſſion could prevail to expreſs itſelf in Words; ſo true I found that of the *Tragœdian,*

Curæ leves loquntur,
Ingentes Stupent.

Light Griefs break forth, and eaſily get Vent,
Great Ones are thro' Amazement cloſely pent.

At length my MUSE, not bearing to be any longer mute, brake forth in the following *ACROSTICK*, which ſhe called

A pathetick ELEGY *on the Death of that dear and faithful Servant of GOD,* EDWARD BURROUGH, *who died the* 14*th of the Twelfth Month,* 1662.

And thus ſhe introduceth it.

HOW long ſhall Grief lie ſmother'd! ah, how long,
Shall Sorrow's Signet ſeal my ſilent Tongue!

How

How long ſhall Sighs me ſuffocate! and make
My Lips to quiver, and my Heart to ake!
How long ſhall I, with Pain ſuppreſs my Cries!
And ſeek for Holes to wipe my wat'ry Eyes!
Why may not I, by Sorrow thus oppreſt,
Pour forth my Grief into another's Breaſt!
If that be true which once was ſaid by one,
That * *He mourns truly, who doth mourn alone*:
Then may I truly ſay, My Grief is true,
Since it hath yet been known to very few.
Nor is it now mine Aim to make it known
To thoſe, to whom theſe Verſes may be ſhown;
But to aſſwage my Sorrow-ſwollen Heart,
Which Silence caus'd to taſte ſo deep of Smart.
This is my End, that ſo I may prevent
The Veſſel's burſting, by a timely Vent.

* *Ille dolet vere, qui ſine Teſte dolet.*

——— ——— *Quis talia fando*
Temperet a Lacrymis! ——

Who can forbear, when ſuch Things ſpoke he hears,
His Grave to water with a Flood of Tears.

1662. E cho ye Woods; resound ye hallow Places,
L et Tears and Paleness cover all Mens Faces.
L et Groans like Claps of Thunder, pierce the Air,
W hile I the Cause of my just Grief declare.
O that mine Eyes could, like the Streams of Nile,
O 'erflow their watry Banks; and thou, mean while,
D rink in my trickling Tears, O thirsty Ground,
S o might'st thou henceforth fruitfuller be found.

L ament my Soul, lament, thy Loss is deep,
A nd all that Sion love, sit down and weep.
M ourn O ye Virgins, and let Sorrow be
E ach Damsel's Dowry and (alas, for me!)
N 'er let my Sobs and Sighings have an End,
T ill I again embrace m' ascended Friend;
A nd till I feel the Virtue of his Life
T o consolate me, and repress my Grief:
I nfuse into my Heart the Oil of Gladness
O nce more, and by its Strength remove that Sadness
N ow pressing down my Spirit, and restore

F ully that Joy I had in him before.
O f whom a Word I fain would stammer forth,
R ather to ease my Heart, than shew his Worth:

H is

H *is Worth, my Grief, which Words too shallow are* 1662.
I *n Demonstration fully to declare,*
S *ighs, Sobs, my best Interpreters now are.*

E *nvy be gone. Black* Momus *quit the Place;*
N *'er more,* Zoilus, *shew thy wrinkled Face.*
D *raw near, ye bleeding Hearts, whose Sorrows are,*
E *qual with mine; in him ye had like Share.*
A *dd all your Losses up, and ye shall see,*
R *emainder will be nought but* Woe is me.
E *ndeared Lambs, ye that have the* white Stone,
D *o know full well his Name,* It is your own.

E *ternitiz'd be that right-worthy Name,*
D *eath hath but kill'd his* Body, *not his* Fame,
W *hich in its Brightness shall for ever dwell,*
A *nd, like a Box of Ointment, sweetly smell.*
R *ighteousness was his Robe; bright Majesty*
D *ecked his Brow; his Look was heavenly.*

B *old was he in his Master's Quarrel, and*
U *ndaunted; faithful to his Lord's Command.*
R *equiting Good for Ill; directing all*
R *ight in the Way that leads out of the Fall.*
O *pen and free to ev'ry thirsty Lamb;*
U *nspotted, pure, clean, holy, without Blame.*
G *lory, Light, Splendor, Lustre was his Crown,*
H *appy his Change to him; the Loss our own.*

1662. Unica post Cineres Virtus veneranda beatos
Efficit. ———

Virtue alone (which Rev'rence ought to have)
Doth make Men happy, e'en beyond the Grave.

While I had thus been breathing forth my
Grief,
In hopes thereby to get me some Relief,
I heard, methought, his Voice say, *Cease to*
mourn,
I Live; and though the Vail of Flesh once worn,
Be now stript off, dissolv'd and laid aside,
My Spirit's with thee, and shall so abide.
This satisfy'd me; down I threw my Quill,
Willing to be resign'd to God's pure Will.

1663. Having discharged this Duty to the Memory of my deceased Friend, I went on in my new Province, instructing my little Pupils in the Rudiments of the *Latin* Tongue, to the mutual Satisfaction of both their Parents and myself. As soon as I had gotten a little Money in my Pocket, which as a *Premium* without Compact I received from them, I took the first Opportunity to return to my Friend *William Penington* the Money which he had so kindly furnished me with in my Need, at the Time of my Imprisonment

prisonment in *Bridewell*; with a due Acknowledgement of my Obligation to him for it. He was not at all forward to receive it, so that I was fain to press it upon him. 1663.

While thus I remained in this Family, various Suspicions arose in the Minds of some concerning me, with respect to *Mary Penington*'s fair Daughter *Guli*. For she having now arrived to a marriageable Age, and being in all respects a very desirable Woman (whether regard was had to her outward Person, which wanted nothing to render her compleatly comely; or to the Endowments of her Mind, which were every way extraordinary, and highly obliging; or to her outward Fortune, which was fair; and which with some hath not the last, nor the least Place in Consideration) she was openly and secretly sought, and solicited by many, and some of them almost of every Rank and Condition; Good and Bad, Rich and Poor, Friend and Foe. To whom, in their respective Turns (till he at length came, for whom she was reserved) she carried herself with so much Evenness of Temper, such courteous Freedom, guarded with the strictest Modesty, that as it gave Encouragement, or ground of Hopes to none, so neither did it administer any matter of Offence, or just Cause of Complaint to any.

But such as were thus either engaged for themselves, or desirous to make themselves Advocates for others, could not, I observed, but look upon me with an Eye of Jealousy and

1663. Fear, that I would improve the Opportunities I had, by frequent and familiar Converſation with her, to my own Advantage, in working myſelf into her good Opinion and Favour, to the Ruin of their Pretences.

According therefore, to the ſeveral Kinds and Degrees of their Fears of me, they ſuggeſted to her Parents their ill Surmiſes againſt me.

Some ſtuck not to queſtion the Sincerity of my Intentions, in coming at firſt among the *Quakers*; urging, with a *Why may it not be ſo? That the Deſire and Hopes of obtaining, by that means, ſo fair a Fortune, might be the prime and chief Inducement to me, to thruſt myſelf amongſt that People.* But this Surmiſe could find no place with thoſe worthy Friends of mine (her Father-in-Law and her Mother) who, beſides the clear Senſe and ſound Judgment they had in themſelves, knew very well upon what Terms I came among them, how ſtraight and hard the Paſſage was to me, how contrary to all worldly Intereſt (which lay fair another way) how much I had ſuffered from my Father for it, and how regardleſs I had been of attempting or ſeeking any thing of that Nature, in theſe three or four Years that I had been amongſt them.

Some others, meaſuring me by the Propenſity of their own Inclinations, concluded *I would ſteal her, run away with her, and marry her.* Which they thought I might be the more eaſily induced to do, from the advantageous Opportunities I frequently had of riding and walking

walking abroad with her, by Night as well 1663.
as by Day, without any other Company than her Maid. For ſo great indeed was the Confidence that her Mother had in me, that ſhe thought her Daughter ſafe if I was with her, even from the Plots and Deſigns that others had upon her. And ſo honourable were the Thoughts ſhe entertained concerning me, as would not ſuffer her to admit a Suſpicion, that I could be capable of ſo much Baſeneſs, as to betray the Truſt ſhe, with ſo great Freedom, repoſed in me.

I was not ignorant of the various Fears which filled the jealous Heads of ſome concerning me, neither was I ſo ſtupid, nor ſo diveſted of all Humanity, as not to be ſenſible of the real and innate Worth and Virtue which adorned that excellent Dame, and attracted the Eyes and Hearts of ſo many, with the greateſt Importunity to ſeek and ſolicit her; nor was I ſo devoid of natural Heat, as not to feel ſome Sparklings of Deſire as well as others. But the Force of TRUTH, and Senſe of Honour, ſuppreſt whatever would have riſen beyond the Bounds of fair and virtuous Friendſhip. For I eaſily foreſaw, that if I ſhould have attempted any Thing in a diſhonourable Way, by Force or Fraud upon her, I ſhould have thereby brought a Wound upon mine own Soul, a foul Scandal upon my religious Profeſſion, and an infamous Stain upon mine Honour; either of which was far more dear unto me than my Life. Wherefore having obſerved how ſome others

1663. had befool'd themſelves, by miſconſtruing her common Kindneſs, (expreſſed in an innocent, open, free and familiar Converſation, ſpringing from the abundant Affability, Courteſy and Sweetneſs of her natural Temper) to be the Effect of a ſingular Regard and peculiar Affection to them; I reſolved to ſhun the Rock on which I had ſeen ſo many run and ſplit; and remembring that Saying of the POET,

Fœlix quem faciunt aliena Pericula cautum.

——————— Happy's he,
Whom others Dangers wary make to be.

I governed myſelf in a free, yet reſpectful Carriage towards her, that I thereby both preſerved a fair Reputation with my Friends, and enjoyed as much of her Favour and Kindneſs, in a virtuous and firm Friendſhip, as was fit for her to ſhew, or for me to ſeek.

Thus leading a quiet and contented Life, I had Leiſure ſometimes to write a Copy of Verſes on one Occaſion or another, as the *Poetick Vein* naturally opened, without taking Pains to poliſh them. Such was this which follows, occaſioned by the ſudden Death of ſome luſty People in their full Strength.

Eſt

Eſt VITA caduca.

AS is the fragrant Flower in the Field,
Which in the Spring a pleaſant Smell doth yield,
And lovely Sight; but ſoon is withered:
So's MAN; To-day alive, To-morrow dead.
And as the Silver-dew-beſpangled Graſs,
Which in the Morn bedecks its Mother's Face,
But e're the ſcorching Summer's paſt, looks brown,
Or by the Sythe is ſuddenly cut down.
Juſt ſuch is Man, who vaunts himſelf To-day,
Decking himſelf in all his beſt Array;
But in the midſt of all his Bravery,
Death rounds him in the Ear, *Friend, thou muſt die.*
Or like a Shadow in a Sunny Day,
Which in a Moment vaniſheth away;
Or like a Smile, or Spark; ſuch is the Span
Of Life, allow'd this *Microcoſm*, MAN.
Ceaſe then vain Man to boaſt; for this is true,
Thy brighteſt Glory's as the Morning Dew,

1663. Which disappears when first the rising Sun
Displays his Beams above the Horizon.

As the Consideration of the *Uncertainty of HUMAN LIFE* drew the foregoing Lines from me; so the Sense I had of the *FOLLY of MANKIND*, in mis-spending the little Time allow'd them, in evil Ways and vain Sports; led me more particularly to trace the several Courses, wherein the Generality of Men run, unprofitably at best, if not to their Hurt and Ruin. Which I introduced with that Axiom of the Preacher, *Eccles.* i. 2,

ALL IS VANITY.

See here the State of MAN as in a Glass,
And how the Fashion of this World doth pass.

SOME in a *Tavern* spend the longest Day,
While others *hawk* and *hunt* the Time away.
Here one his *Mistress* courts; another *dances*;
A third incites to *Lust* by wanton *Glances*.
This wastes the Day in *dressing*; th' other seeks
To set fresh Colours on her with'red *Cheeks*,

That,

That, when the Sun declines, ſome *dapper Spark* 1663.
May take her to *Spring-garden*, or the *Park*.
Plays ſome frequent, and *Balls*; others their Prime
Conſume at *Dice*; ſome *bowl* away their *Time*.
With *Cards* ſome wholly captivated are;
From *Tables* others ſcarce an Hour can ſpare.
One to ſoft *Muſick* mancipates his Ear;
At *Shovel-board* another ſpends the Year.
The *Pall-Mall* this accounts the only Sport;
That keeps a *Racket* in the *Tennis-Court*.
Some ſtrain their very Eyes and Throats with *Singing*,
While others ſtrip their Hands and Backs at *Ringing*.
Another Sort with greedy Eyes are waiting
Either at *Cockpit*, or ſome great *Bull-bating*.
This dotes on *Running-horſes*; t'other Fool
Is never well, but in the *Fencing-ſchool*.
Wreſtling and *Football*, *Ninepins*, *Priſon-baſe*,
Among the rural Clowns find each a Place.
Nay *Joan* unwaſh'd will leave her Milking-pail,
To *dance* at *May-pole*, or a *Whitſun-Ale*.
Thus wallow moſt in *ſenſual Delight*,
As if their Day ſhould never have a Night;

Till

1663. Till *Nature*'s pale-fac'd *Serjeant* them surpize,
And as the Tree then falls, just so it lies.
Now look at home, thou who these Lines dost read,
See which of all these Paths thyself dost tread;
And e're it be too late that Path forsake,
Which, follow'd, will thee miserable make.

After I had thus enumerated some of the many Vanities, in which the Generality of Men mis-spent their Time, I sang the following *ODE* in Praise of VIRTUE.

WEALTH, Beauty, Pleasures, Honours, all adieu,
I value *Virtue* far, far more than you.
Y'are all but Toys
For Girls and Boys
To play withal; at best deceitful Joys.
She lives for ever; ye are transitory.
Her Honour is unstained; but your Glory
Is meer Deceit,
A painted Bait,
Hung out for such as sit at Folly's Gate.
True Peace, Content and Joy on her attend;
You (on the contrary) your Forces bend

To

To blear Mens Eyes, 1663.
With Fopperies,
Which Fools embrace, but wiser Men despise.

About this Time my Father, resolving to sell his Estate, and having reserved for his own Use such Parts of his houshold Goods as he thought fit; not willing to take upon himself the Trouble of selling the rest, gave them unto me. Whereupon I went down to *Crowell*, and having before given Notice there and thereabouts, that I intended a Publick Sale of them, I sold them, and thereby put some Money into my Pocket. Yet I sold such Things only as I judged useful; leaving the *Pictures* and *Armour*, of which there was some Store there, unsold. 1664.

Not long after this, my Father sent for me to come to him at *London* about some Business; which, when I came there, I understood was to join with him in the Sale of his Estate, which the Purchaser required for his own Satisfaction and Safety, I being then the next Heir to it in Law. And although I might probably have made some advantageous Terms for myself by standing off; yet when I was satisfied by Counsel, that there was no Entail upon it, or Right of Reversion to me, but that he might lawfully dispose of it as he pleased, I readily joined with him in the Sale, without asking or having the least Gratuity or Compensation; no, not so much as the Fee I had given to Counsel, to secure me from any Danger in doing it.

There

1665. There having been, ſome Time before this, a very ſevere Law made againſt the *Quakers* by Name; and more particularly, prohibiting our Meetings under the ſharpeſt Penalties, of *Five Pounds* for the firſt Offence ſo called, *Ten Pounds* for the ſecond, and *Baniſhment* for the third; under pain of *Felony* for eſcaping or returning without *Licenſe*. Which Law was looked upon to have been procured by the *Biſhops*, in order to bring us to a Conformity to their Way of *Worſhip*: I wrote a few Lines in way of *Dialogue* between a *Biſhop* and a *Quaker*, which I called,

CONFORMITY *Preſt and Repreſt.*

B. W*HAT! You are one of them that do deny*
To yield Obedience by Conformity.
Q. Nay: We deſire conformable to be.
Rom. 8. 29. B. *But unto what?* Q. The Image of the Son.
B. *What's that to us! We'll have Conformity*
Unto our Form. Q. Then we ſhall ne'er have done.
For, if your fickle Minds ſhould alter, we
Should be to ſeek a New Conformity.
Thus who To-day conform to *Prelacy*,
To-morrow may conform to *Popery*.
But take this for an Anſwer, *Biſhop*, we
Cannot conform either to them, or Thee.

For

For while to *Truth* your Forms are opposite,
Whoe'er conforms thereto doth not aright.

B. *We'll make such Knaves as you conform*, or *lie*
Confin'd in Prisons, till ye rot and die.

Q. Well, gentle *Bishop*, I may live to see,
For all thy Threats, a Check to Cruelty,
And thee rewarded, with thy envious Crew,
According as unto your Works is due;
But, in the mean Time, I, for my Defence,
Betake me to my Fortress, PATIENCE.

No sooner was this cruel Law made, but it was put in Execution with great Severity. The Sense whereof working strongly on my Spirit, made me cry earnestly to the Lord, that he would arise and set up His righteous Judgment in the Earth, for the Deliverance of His People from all their Enemies, both inward and outward: And in these Terms I uttered it.

AWake, awake, O Arm o'th' Lord awake,
Thy Sword up take;
Cast what would thine forgetful of Thee make,
Into the Lake.
Awake, I pray, O mighty *Jah*, awake,
Make all the World before Thy Presence quake,
Not only Earth, but Heaven also shake.

Arise,

1665. Ariſe, ariſe, O *Jacob's* God, ariſe,
And hear the Cries
Of ev'ry Soul which in Diſtreſs now lies,
And to Thee flies.
Ariſe, I pray, O *Iſrael's* Hope ariſe,
Set free Thy Seed, oppreſt by Enemies:
Why ſhould they over it ſtill tyrannize!
Make Speed, make Speed, O *Iſrael's* Help, make (Speed,
In time of Need;
For evil Men have wickedly decreed
Againſt Thy Seed.
Make Speed, I pray, O mighty God, make Speed,
Let all Thy *Lambs* from ſavage *Wolves* be freed,
That fearleſs on Thy Mountain they may feed.
Ride on, ride on, Thou valiant Man of Might,
And put to Flight
Thoſe Sons of *Belial*, who do Deſpight
To the Upright.
Ride on, I ſay, Thou Champion, and ſmite
Thine and Thy Peoples En'mies with ſuch Might,
That none may dare 'gainſt Thee, or Thine to Fight.

Although

Although the Storm, raised by the Act for *Banishment*, fell with the greatest Weight and Force upon some other Parts, as at *London*, *Hertford*, &c. yet we were not, in *Buckinghamshire*, wholly exempted therefrom, for a Part of that Shower reached us also. 1665.

For a Friend of *Amersham*, whose Name was *Edward Perot*, or *Parret*, departing this Life, and Notice being given that his Body would be buried there on such a Day, which was the first Day of the fifth Month 1665, the Friends of the adjacent Parts of the Country resorted pretty generally to the Burial; so that there was a fair Appearance of Friends and Neighbours, the Deceased having been well-beloved by both.

After we had spent some Time together in the House, *Morgan Watkins*, who at that Time happen'd to be at *Isaac Penington*'s, being with us, the Body was taken up and borne on Friends Shoulders along the Street, in order to be carried to the Burying-ground, which was at the Town's End, being part of an Orchard belonging to the Deceased, which he in his Life-time had appointed for that Service.

It so happened that one *Ambrose Benett*, a Barrister at Law and a Justice of the Peace for that County, riding through the Town that Morning in his Way to *Aylesbury*, was by some ill-disposed Person or other, informed that there was a *Quaker* to be buried there that Day, and that most of the *Quakers* in the Country were come thither to the Burial.

Upon

1665. Upon this he ſet up his Horſes and ſtaid; and when we, not knowing any Thing of his Deſign againſt us, went innocently forward, to perform our Chriſtian Duty for the Interment of our *Friend*, he ruſhed out of his Inn upon us, with the Conſtables and a Rabble of rude Fellows, whom he had gathered together, and having his drawn Sword in his Hand, ſtruck one of the Foremoſt of the Bearers with it, commanding them to ſet down the Coffin. But the Friend who was ſo ſtricken, whoſe Name was *Thomas Dell*, being more concerned for the Safety of the dead Body than his own, leſt it ſhould fall from his Shoulder, and any Indecency thereupon follow, held the Coffin faſt: Which the Juſtice obſerving, and being enraged that his Word (how unjuſt ſoever) was not forthwith obeyed, ſet his Hand to the Coffin, and with a forcible Thruſt threw it off from the Bearers Shoulders, ſo that it fell to the Ground in the Midſt of the Street, and there we were forced to leave it.

For immediately thereupon the Juſtice giving Command for the apprehending us, the Conſtables with the Rabble fell on us, and drew ſome, and drove others into the Inn, giving thereby an Opportuntiy to the reſt to walk away.

Of thoſe that were thus taken, I was one. And being, with many more, put into a Room under a Guard, we were kept there till another Juſtice (called Sir *Thomas Clayton*, whom Juſtice *Benett* had ſent for to join with him in committing us) was come. And then, being called forth

forth severally before them, they picked out Ten of us, and committed us to *Aylesbury* Jail, for what neither we nor they knew: For we we were not convicted of having either done or said any Thing which the Law could take hold of: For they took us up in the open Street (the King's High-way) not doing any unlawful Act, but peaceably carrying and accompanying the Corpse of our deceased Friend to bury it. Which they would not suffer us to do, but caused the Body to lie in the open Street, and in the Cart-way; so that all the Travellers that passed by, whether Horse-men, Coaches, Carts, or Waggons, were fain to break out of the Way to go by it, that they might not drive over it, until it was almost Night. And then having caused a Grave to be made in the *unconsecrated* Part (as it is accounted) of that which is called the *Church-yard*, they forcibly took the Body from the Widow, whose Right and Property it was, and buried it there.

When the Justices had delivered us Prisoners to the Constable, it being then late in the Day, which was the Seventh-day of the Week, he not willing to go so far as *Aylesbury* (nine long Miles) with us that Night, nor to put the Town to the Charge of keeping us there that Night, and the First-day and Night following, dismist us upon our *Parole* to come to him again at a set Hour on the Second-day Morning: Whereupon we all went home to our respective Habitations; and coming to him punctually

1665. according to Promiſe, were by him, without Guard, conducted to the Priſon.

The Jailer, whoſe Name was *Nathaniel Birch*, had not long before behaved himſelf very wickedly, with great Rudeneſs and Cruelty to ſome of our Friends of the lower Side of the County, whom he, combining with the Clerk of the Peace, whoſe Name was *Henry Wells*, had contrived to get into his Jail; and after they were legally diſcharged in Court, detained them in Priſon, uſing great Violence, and ſhutting them up cloſe in the common Jail among the Felons, becauſe they would not give him his unrighteous Demand of *Fees*; which they were the more ſtraitned in, from his treacherous Dealing with them. And they having, through Suffering, maintained their Freedom, and obtained their Liberty, we were the more concerned to keep what they had ſo hardly gained, and therefore reſolved not to make any Contract or Terms for either *Chamber-rent* or *Fees*, but to demand a Free Priſon; which we did.

When we came in, the Jailer was ridden out to wait on the Judges, who came in that Day to begin the Aſſize, and his Wife was ſomewhat at a Loſs how to deal with us; but being a cunning Woman, ſhe treated us with great Appearance of Courteſy, offering us the Choice of all her Rooms; and when we aſked, *upon what Terms?* ſhe ſtill referr'd us to her Huſband; telling us, ſhe did not doubt but that he would be very reaſonable and civil to us.

Thus

Thus ſhe endeavoured to have drawn us to take Poſſeſſion of ſome of her Chambers at a venture, and truſt to her Huſband's kind Uſage. But we, who at the Coſt of our Friends, had a Proof of his Kindneſs, were too wary to be drawn in by the fair Words of a Woman; and therefore told her, *we would not ſettle any where till her Huſband came Home, and then would have a free Priſon whereſoever he put us.*

Accordingly, walking all together into the Court of the Priſon, in which was a Well of very good Water, and having before-hand ſent to a Friend in the Town, a Widow Woman whoſe Name was *Sarah Lambarn*, to bring us ſome Bread and Cheeſe, we ſate down upon the Ground round about the Well, and when we had eaten, we drank of the Water out of the Well.

Our great Concern was for our Friend *Iſaac Penington*, becauſe of the Tenderneſs of his Conſtitution; but he was ſo lively in his Spirit, and ſo cheerfully given up to ſuffer, that he rather encouraged us, than needed any Encouragement from us.

In this Poſture the Jailer, when he came home, found us; and having before he came to us, conſulted his Wife, and by her underſtood on what Terms we ſtood; when he came to us, he hid his Teeth, and putting on a Shew of Kindneſs, ſeemed much troubled that we ſhould ſit there abroad, eſpecially his old Friend Mr. *Penington*; and thereupon invited us to come in, and take what Rooms in his Houſe we pleased; we asked, *upon what Terms?* letting him know withal, *that we determined to have a free Prison.*

He, like the Sun and Wind in the *Fable*, that strove which of them should take from the Traveller his Cloak; having (like the Wind) tried rough, boisterous, violent Means to our Friends before, but in vain, resolved now to imitate the Sun, and shine as pleasantly as he could upon us. Wherefore he told us, *We should make the Terms ourselves, and be as free as we desired: If we thought fit, when we were released, to give him any Thing, he would thank us for it; and if not, he would demand nothing.*

Upon these Terms we went in and disposed ourselves; some in the Dwelling-house, others in the Malt-house, where they chose to be.

During the Assize we were brought before Judge *Morton*, a sour angry Man, who very rudely reviled us, but would not hear either us or the Cause; but referred the matter to the two Justices who had committed us.

They, when the Assize was ended, sent for us to be brought before them at their Inn, and fined us, as I remember, *Six Shillings and eight Pence* a-piece; which we not consenting to pay, they committed us to Prison again for one Month from that Time, on the Act for *Banishment*.

When we had lain there that Month, I with another went to the Jailer, to demand our Liberty; which he readily granted, telling us, *The Door should be opened when we pleased to go.*

This

This Anſwer of his I reported to the reſt of my Friends there, and thereupon we raiſed among us a ſmall Sum of Money, which they put into my Hand for the Jailer; whereupon I, taking another with me, went to the Jailer with the Money in my Hand, and reminding him of the Terms upon which we accepted the Uſe of his Rooms, I told him, That although we could not pay *Chamber-rent* or *Fees*, yet inaſmuch as he had now been civil to us, we were willing to acknowledge it by a ſmall Token, and thereupon gave him the Money. He putting it into his Pocket, ſaid, *I thank you and your Friends for it; and to let you ſee I take it as a Gift, not a Debt, I will not look on it to ſee how much it is.* 1665.

The Priſon Door being then ſet open for us, we went out, and departed to our reſpective Homes.

But before I left the Priſon, conſidering one Day with myſelf the different Kinds of Liberty and Confinement, Freedom and Bondage, I took my Pen, and wrote the following *Ænigma*, or *Riddle*.

LOE here a Riddle to the Wiſe,
In which a Myſtery there lies;
Read it therefore with that Eye,
Which can diſcern a Myſtery.

The RIDDLE.

Some Men are free, while they in Priſon lie;
Others, who ne'r ſaw Priſon, Captives die.

1665.

CAUTION.

He that can receive it, may ;
He that cannot, let him ſtay,
And not be haſty, but ſuſpend
His Judgment till he ſees the End.

SOLUTION.

He only's free indeed, that's free from Sin,
And he is faſteſt bound, that's bound therein.

CONCLUSION.

This is the Liberty I chiefly prize,
The other, without this, I can deſpiſe.

Some little Time before I went to *Ayleſbury* Priſon, I was deſired by my *quondam* Maſter *Milton*, to take an Houſe for him in the Neighbourhood where I dwelt, that he might go out of the City, for the Safety of himſelf and his Family, the *Peſtilence* then growing hot in *London*. I took a pretty Box for him in *Giles-Chalfont*, a Mile from me, of which I gave him Notice, and intended to have waited on him, and ſeen him well ſettled in it, but was prevented by that Impriſonment.

But now being releaſed and returned home, I ſoon made a Viſit to him, to welcome him into the Country.

After

After some common Discourses had passed between us, he called for a *Manuscript* of his; which being brought he delivered to me, bidding me take it home with me, and read it at my Leisure; and when I had so done, return it to him with my Judgment thereupon. 1665.

When I came home, and had set myself to read it, I found it was that excellent POEM, which he entituled *PARADISE LOST*. After I had, with the best Attention, read it through, I made him another Visit, and returned him his Book, with due Acknowledgement of the Favour he had done me in communicating it to me. He asked me, *how I liked it, and what I thought of it?* which I modestly but freely told him; and after some further Discourse about it, I pleasantly said to him, Thou hast said much here of *Paradise lost*; but what hast thou to say of *Paradise found?* He made me no Answer, but sate some Time in a Muse; then brake off that Discourse, and fell upon another Subject.

After the Sickness was over, and the City well cleansed and become safely habitable again, he returned thither. And when afterwards I went to wait on him there (which I seldom failed of doing, whenever my Occasions drew me to *London*) he shewed me his second POEM, called *PARADISE REGAINED*; and in a pleasant Tone said to me, *This is owing to you; for you put it into my Head by the Question you put to me at* Chalfont; *which before I had*

1665. *not thought of.* But from this Digression I return to the Family I then lived in.

We had not been long at home, about a Month perhaps, before *Isaac Penington* was taken out of his House in an arbitrary manner by military Force, and carried Prisoner to *Aylesbury* Jail again; where he lay three Quarters of a Year, with great Hazard of his Life, it being the *Sickness Year*, and the *Plague* being not only in the Town, but in the Jail.

Mean while his Wife and Family were turned out of his House, called the *Grange* at *Peter's-Chalfont*, by them who had seized upon his Estate; and the Family being by that means broken up, some went one Way, others another. *Mary Penington* herself, with her younger Children, went down to her Husband at *Aylesbury*. *Guli*, with her Maid, went to *Bristol*, to see her former Maid *Anne Hersent*, who was married to a Merchant of that City, whose Name was *Thomas Biss*, and I went to *Aylesbury* with the Children; but not finding the Place agreeable to my Health, I soon left it, and returning to *Chalfont*, took a Lodging, and was dieted in the House of a friendly Man; and after some Time, went to *Bristol* to conduct *Guli* home.

Mean while *Mary Penington* took Lodgings in a Farm-house called *Bottrels*, in the Parish of *Giles-Chalfont*, where, when we returned from *Bristol*, we found her.

We had been there but a very little Time, before I was sent to Prison again upon this

Occasion.

Occasion. There was, in those Times, a Meeting once a Month at the House of *George Salter* a Friend of *Hedgerly*, to which we sometimes went; and *Morgan Watkins* being with us, he and I, with *Guli* and her Maid, and one *Judith Parker*, Wife of Dr. *Parker*, one of the College of *Physicians* at *London*, with a maiden Daughter of theirs (neither of whom were *Quakers*, but as Acquaintance of *Mary Penington* were with her on a Visit) walked over to that Meeting, it being about the Middle of the first Month, and the Weather good.

This Place was about a Mile from the House of *Ambrose Bennett* the Justice, who the Summer before had sent me and some other Friends to *Aylesbury* Prison, from the Burial of *Edward Parret* of *Amersham*; and he, by what Means I know not, getting Notice not only of the Meeting, but (as was supposed) of our being there, came himself to it; and as he came, catched up a Stackwood-stick, big enough to have knock'd any Man down, and brought it with him hidden under his Cloak.

Being come to the House, he stood for a while without the Door, and out of Sight, listning to hear what was said, for *Morgan* was then speaking in the Meeting. But certainly he heard very imperfectly, if it was true which we heard he said afterwards among his Companions, as an Argument that *Morgan* was a *Jesuit*, viz. *That in his Preaching he trolled over his* Latin *as fluently as ever he heard any one*; whereas *Morgan* (good Man!) was better versed

verſed in *Welch* than in *Latin*, which, I ſuppoſe, he had never learned; I am ſure he did not underſtand it.

When this martial Juſtice, who at *Amerſham* had with his drawn Sword ſtruck an unarmed Man, who he knew would not ſtrike again, had now ſtood ſome Time abroad, on a ſudden he ruſhed in among us, with the Stackwood-ſtick held up in his Hand ready to ſtrike, crying out, *Make way there*; and an ancient Woman not getting ſoon enough out of his Way, he ſtruck her with the Stick a ſhrewd Blow over the Breaſt. Then preſſing through the Crowd to the Place where *Morgan* ſtood, he plucked him from thence, and cauſed ſo great a Diſorder in the Room, that it brake the Meeting up; yet would not the People go away or diſperſe themſelves, but tarried to ſee what the Iſſue would be.

Then taking Pen and Paper, he ſate down at the Table among us, and aſked ſeveral of us our Names, which we gave and he ſet down in Writing.

Amongſt others, he aſked *Judith Parker*, the Doctor's Wife, what her Name was? which ſhe readily gave; and thence taking Occaſion to diſcourſe him, ſhe ſo over-maſter'd him by clear Reaſon, delivered in fine Language, that he, glad to be rid of her, ſtruck out her Name and diſmiſt her; yet did not ſhe remove, but kept her Place amongſt us.

When he had taken what Number of Names he thought fit, he ſingled out half a Dozen, whereof

whereof *Morgan* was one, I another, one Man more, and three Women, of which the Woman of the House was one, although her Husband then was, and for divers Years before had been, a Prisoner in the *Fleet* for Tithes, and had no body to take care of his Family and Business but her his Wife. 1665.

Us six he committed to *Aylesbury* Jail. Which when the Doctor's Wife heard him read to the Constable, she attacked him again, and having put him in mind that it was a sickly Time, and that the *Pestilence* was reported to be in that Place, she in handsome Terms, desired him to consider in Time, *how he would answer the Cry of our Blood, if by his sending us to be shut up in an infected Place, we should lose our Lives there?* This made him alter his Purpose, and by a new *Mittimus* sent us to the House of Correction at *Wiccomb*. And altho' he committed us upon the Act for *Banishment*, which limited a certain Time for Imprisonment; yet he, in his *Mittimus*, limited no Time, but ordered us to be kept till we should be delivered by due Course of LAW; so little regardful was he, though a Lawyer, of keeping to the Letter of the LAW.

We were committed on the 13th Day of the Month called *March* 1665, and were kept close Prisoners there till the 7th Day of the Month called *June* 1666, which was some Days above twelve Weeks, and much above what the Act required.

Then

Then were we ſent for to the Juſtice's Houſe, and the reſt being releaſed, *Morgan Watkins* and I were required to find Sureties for our Appearance at the next Aſſize; which we refuſing to do, were committed a-new to our old Priſon, the Houſe of Correction at *Wiccomb*, there to lie until the next Aſſizes: *Morgan* being, in this ſecond *Mittimus*, repreſented as a notorious *Offender in Preaching*, and I, as being upon the *ſecond Conviction, in order to Baniſhment.* There we lay till the 25th Day of the ſame Month; and then, by the Favour of the Earl of *Ancram*, being brought before him at his Houſe, we were diſcharged from the Priſon, upon our Promiſe to appear (if at Liberty and in Health) at the Aſſizes. Which we did, and were there diſcharged by Proclamation.

During my Impriſonment in this Priſon, I betook myſelf for an Imployment, to making of Nets for Kitchen-ſervice, to boil Herbs, &c. in; which Trade I learned of *Morgan Watkins*, and ſelling ſome, and giving others, I pretty well ſtocked the Friends of that Country with them.

Though in that Confinement I was not very well ſuited with Company for Converſation, *Morgan*'s natural Temper not being very agreeable to mine; yet we kept a fair and brotherly Correſpondence, as became Friends, Priſon-fellows and Bed-fellows, which we were. And indeed, it was a good Time, I think, to us all, for I found it ſo to me; the Lord being graciouſly pleaſed to viſit my Soul with the refreſhing

freshing Dews of His divine Life, whereby my Spirit was more and more quickned to Him, and Truth gained ground in me over the Temptations and Snares of the Enemy. Which frequently raised in my Heart Thanksgivings and Praises unto the LORD. And at one Time more especially, the Sense I had of the Prosperity of Truth, and the spreading thereof, filling my Heart with abundant Joy, made my Cup overflow, and the following Lines drop out. 1666.

For Truth *I suffer Bonds, in* Truth *I live,*
And unto Truth this Testimony give,
That TRUTH shall over all exalted be,
And in Dominion reign for evermore;
The Child's already born, that this may see,
Honour, Praise, Glory be to God therefore.

And underneath thus,

Tho' Death and Hell should against Truth *combine,*
It's Glory shall through all their Darkness shine.

This I saw with an Eye of Faith, beyond the Reach of human Sense. For,

As strong Desire,
Draws Objects higher

In

1666. *In Apprehension, than indeed they are;*
I, with an Eye
That pierced high,
Did thus of Truth's *Prosperity declare.*

After we had been discharged at the Assizes, I returned to *Isaac Penington*'s Family at *Bottrel*'s in *Chalfont*, and, as I remember, *Morgan Watkins* with me, leaving *Isaac Penington* a Prisoner in *Aylesbury* Jail.

The Lodgings we had in this Farm-house (*Bottrel*'s) proving too strait and inconvenient for the Family, I took larger and better Lodgings for them in *Berric-house* at *Amersham*, whither we went at the Time called *Michaelmas*, having spent the Summer at the other Place.

1667. Some Time after, was that memorable Meeting appointed to be holden at *London*, through a divine Opening in the Motion of Life, in that eminent Servant and Prophet of God, *George Fox*, for the restoring and bringing in again those who had gone out from Truth, and the holy Unity of Friends therein, by the Means and Ministry of *John Perrot*.

This Man came pretty early amongst Friends, and too early took upon him the ministerial Office; and being, though little in Person, yet great in Opinion of himself, nothing less would serve him than to go and convert the *Pope*: In order whereunto, he having a better Man than himself, *John Luff*, to accompany him, travelled to *Rome*, where they had not been long,

e're

e're they were taken up and clapt into Priſon ; *Luff*, as I remember, was put in the *Inquiſition*, and *Perrot* in their *Bedlam* or Hoſpital for Madmen.

Luff died in Priſon, not without well-grounded Suſpicion of being murthered there, but *Perrot* lay there ſome Time, and now and then ſent over an Epiſtle to be printed here, written in ſuch an affected and fantaſtick Stile, as might have induced an indifferent Reader to believe, they had ſuited the Place of his Confinement to his Condition.

After ſome Time, through the Mediation of Friends (who hoped better of him, than he proved) with ſome Perſon of Note and Intereſt there, he was releaſed and came back for *England*. And the Report of his great Sufferings there (far greater in Report than in Reality) joined with a ſingular Shew of Sanctity, ſo far opened the Hearts of many tender and compaſſionate Friends towards him, that it gave him the Advantage of inſinuating himſelf into their Affections and Eſteem, and made Way for the more ready Propagation of that peculiar Error of his, of *keeping on the Hat in Time of Prayer, as well publick as private, unleſs they had an immediate Motion at that Time to put it off*.

Now although I had not the leaſt Acquaintance with this Man, not having ever exchanged a Word with him, though I knew him by Sight; nor had I any Eſteem of him for either his natural Parts, or miniſterial Gift, but rather a Diſlike of his Aſpect, Preaching and

Way

1667. Way of writing; yet this Error of his being broached in the Time of my Infancy, and Weakneſs of Judgment as to Truth (while I lived privately in *London*, and had little Converſe with Friends.) I, amongſt the many who were catcht in that Snare, was taken with the Notion, as what then ſeemed to my weak Underſtanding, ſuitable to the Doctrine of a ſpiritual Diſpenſation. And the Matter coming to warm Debates, both in Words and Writing, I, in a miſguided Zeal, was ready to have entred the Liſts of Contention about it; not then ſeeing what Spirit it proceeded from, and was managed by, nor forſeeing the Diſorder and Confuſion in Worſhip, which muſt naturally attend it.

But as I had no evil Intention or ſiniſter End in engaging in it, but was ſimply betrayed by the ſpecious Pretence and Shew of greater Spirituality, the Lord, in tender Compaſſion to my Soul, was graciouſly pleaſed to open my Underſtanding, and give me a clear Sight of the Enemy's Deſign in this Work, and drew me off from the Practice of it, and to bear Teſtimony againſt it as Occaſion offered.

But when that ſolemn Meeting was appointed at *London*, for a Travail in Spirit on Behalf of thoſe who had thus gone out, that they might rightly return, and be ſenſibly received into the Unity of the Body again; my Spirit rejoiced, and with Gladneſs of Heart I went to it, as did many more of both City and Country, and with great Simplicity and Humility

of

of Mind, did honestly and openly acknow- 1667.
ledge our Outgoing, and take Condemnation and Shame to ourselves. And some that lived at too remote a Distance, in this Nation as well as beyond the Seas, upon Notice given of that Meeting, and the intended Service of it, did the like by Writing, in Letters directed to and openly read in the Meeting, which for that Purpose was continued many Days.

Thus, in the Motion of Life, were the healing Waters stirred, and many, through the virtuous Power thereof, restored to Soundness, and indeed not many lost. And though most of these who thus returned, were such as with myself had before renounced the Error, and forsaken the Practice; yet did we sensibly find, that Forsaking without Confessing (in Case of publick Scandal) was not sufficient; but that an open Acknowledgment (of open Offences) as well as forsaking them, was necessary to the obtaining compleat Remission.

Not long after this, *George Fox* was moved of the Lord to travel through the Countries, from County to County, to advise and encourage Friends to set up *Monthly* and *Quarterly-meetings*, for the better ordering the Affairs of the Church, in taking Care of the Poor, and exercising a true Gospel-discipline, for a due Dealing with any that might walk disorderly under our Name, and to see that such as should Marry among us, did act fairly and clearly in that Respect.

1668. When he came into this County, I was one of the many Friends that were with him at the Meeting for that Purpoſe. And afterwards I travelled with *Guli* and her Maid, into the Weſt of *England* to meet him there, and to viſit Friends in thoſe Parts; and we went as far as *Topſham* in *Devonſhire* before we found him. He had been in *Cornwall*, and was then returning, and came in unexpectedly at *Topſham*, where we then were providing (if he had not then come thither) to have gone that Day towards *Cornwall*. But after he was come to us, we turned back with him through *Devonſhire*, *Somerſetſhire* and *Dorſetſhire*, having generally very good Meetings where he was; and the Work he was chiefly concerned in, went on very proſperouſly and well, without any Oppoſition or Diſlike; ſave that in the General-meeting of Friends in *Dorſetſhire*, a quarrelſome Man who had gone out from Friends in *John Perrot*'s Buſineſs, and had not come rightly in again (but continued in the Practice of keeping on his Hat in Time of Prayer, to the great Trouble and Offence of Friends) began to cavil and raiſe Diſputes, which occaſioned ſome Interruption and Diſturbance.

Not only *George*, and *Alexander Parker* who was with him, but divers of the ancient Friends of that Country, endeavoured to quiet that troubleſome Man, and make him ſenſible of his Error; but his unruly Spirit would ſtill be oppoſing what was ſaid unto him, and juſtifying himſelf in that Practice. This brought a

great

great Weight and Exerciſe upon me, who 1668.
ſate at a Diſtance in the outward Part of the Meeting; and after I had for ſome Time bore the Burthen thereof, I ſtood up in the conſtraining Power of the LORD, and in great Tenderneſs of Spirit declared unto the Meeting, and to that Perſon more particularly, how it had been with me in that Reſpect; how I had been betrayed into that wrong Practice, how ſtrong I had been therein, and how the LORD had been graciouſly pleaſed to ſhew me the Evil thereof, and recover me out of it.

This coming unexpectedly from me, a young Man, a Stranger, and one who had not intermeddled with the Buſineſs of the Meeting, had that Effect upon the Caviller, that if it did not ſatisfy him, it did at leaſt ſilence him, and made him for the preſent ſink down and be ſtill, without giving any further Diſturbance to the Meeting. And the Friends were well pleaſed with this unlooked for Teſtimony from me, and I was glad that I had that Opportunity to confeſs to the Truth, and to acknowledge once more, in ſo publick a manner, the Mercy and Goodneſs of the Lord to me therein.

By the time we came back from this Journey, the Summer was pretty far gone, and the following Winter I ſpent with the Children of the Family as before, without any remarkable Alteration in my Circumſtances, until the next Spring; when I found in myſelf a Diſpoſition of Mind to change my ſingle Life for a married State.

1669. I had always entertained so high a Regard for Marriage, as it was a divine Institution, that I held it not lawful to make it a Sort of political Trade to rise in the World by. And therefore as I could not but, in my Judgment, blame such as I found made it their Business to hunt after, and endeavour to gain those who were accounted *great Fortunes*; not so much regarding *what she is*, as *what she has*, but making Wealth the chief, if not the only Thing they aimed at; so I resolved to avoid, in my own Practice, that Course; and how much soever my Condition might have prompted me, as well as others, to seek Advantage that Way, never to engage on the Account of *Riches*, nor at all to marry, till judicious Affection drew me to it, which I now began to feel at work in my Breast.

The Object of this Affection was a Friend, whose Name was *Mary Ellis*, whom for divers Years I had had an Acquaintance with, in the way of common Friendship only; and in whom I thought I then saw those fair Prints of Truth and solid Virtue, which I afterwards found in a sublime Degree in her; but what her Condition in the World was, as to Estate, I was wholly a Stranger to, nor desired to know.

I had once, a Year or two before, had an Opportunity to do her a small Piece of Service, which she wanted some Assistance in; wherein I acted with all Sincerity and Freedom of Mind, not expecting or desiring any Advantage by her, or Reward from her, being very well satisfied

in

in the Act itself, that I had served a Friend and helped the Helpless.

That little Intercourse of common Kindness between us, ended without the least Thought (I am verily perswaded, on her Part, well assured on my own) of any other or further Relation than that of free and fair Friendship; nor did it, at that Time, lead us into any closer Conversation, or more intimate Acquaintance one with the other, than had been before.

But some Time (and that a good while) after, I found my Heart secretly drawn and inclining towards her; yet was I not hasty in proposing, but waited to feel a satisfactory Settlement of Mind therein, before I made any Step thereto.

After some Time, I took an Opportunity to open my Mind therein unto my much honoured Friends, *Isaac* and *Mary Penington*, who then stood *Parentum loco*, in the Place or Stead of Parents to me. They having solemnly weighed the Matter, exprest their Unity therewith; and indeed their Approbation thereof was no small Confirmation to me therein. Yet took I further Deliberation, often retiring in Spirit to the Lord, and crying to him for Direction, before I addrest myself to her. At length, as I was setting all alone, waiting upon the Lord for Counsel and Guidance in this (in itself, and) to me so important Affair, I felt a Word sweetly arise in me, as if I had heard a Voice which said, *Go, and prevail.* And Faith springing in my Heart with the Word, I immediately arose and went, nothing doubting.

1669. When I was come to her Lodgings, which were about a Mile from me, her Maid told me ſhe was in her Chamber (for having been under ſome Indiſpoſition of Body, which had obliged her to keep her Chamber, ſhe had not yet left it.) Wherefore I deſired the Maid to acquaint her Miſtreſs, that I was come to give her a Viſit; whereupon I was invited to go up to her. And after ſome little Time ſpent in common Converſation, feeling my Spirit weightily concerned, I ſolemnly opened my Mind unto her, with reſpect to the particular Buſineſs I came about; which I ſoon perceived was a great Surpriſal to her, for ſhe had taken in an Apprehenſion, as others alſo had done, that mine Eye had been fixed elſewhere and nearer home.

I uſed not many Words to her; but I felt a divine Power went along with the Words, and fixed the Matter expreſſed by them ſo faſt in her Breaſt, that (as ſhe afterwards acknowledged to me) ſhe could not ſhut it out.

I made at that Time but a ſhort Viſit. For having told her, I did not expect an Anſwer from her now, but deſired ſhe would, in the moſt ſolemn Manner, weigh the Propoſal made, and in due Time give me ſuch an Anſwer thereunto, as the Lord ſhould give her; I took my Leave of her and departed, leaving the Iſſue to the Lord.

I had a Journey then at hand, which I foreſaw would take me up about two Weeks time. Wherefore, the Day before I was to ſet out,

I went

I went to visit her again, to acquaint her with 1669.
my Journey and excuse my Absence; not yet pressing her for an Answer, but assuring her, that I felt in myself an Increase of Affection to her, and hoped to receive a suitable Return from her in the Lord's Time; to whom, in the mean time, I committed both her, myself, and the Concern between us. And indeed, I found at my Return, that I could not have left it in a better Hand; for the Lord had been my Advocate in my Absence, and had so far answered all her Objections, that when I came to her again, she rather acquainted me with them than urged them.

From that Time forwards we entertained each other with affectionate Kindness in order to Marriage; which yet we did not hasten to, but went on deliberately. Neither did I use those vulgar Ways of Courtship, by making frequent and rich Presents; not only for that my outward Condition would not comport with the Expence, but because I liked not to obtain by such Means; but preferred an unbribed Affection.

While this Affair stood thus with me, I had Occasion to take another Journey into *Kent* and *Sussex*; which yet I would not mention here, but for a particular Accident which befel me on the Way.

The Occasion of this Journey was this. *Mary Penington*'s Daughter *Guli* intending to go to her Uncle *Springett*'s in *Sussex*, and from thence amongst her Tenants, her Mother desired me

1669. to accompany her, and assist her in her Business with her Tenants.

We tarried at *London* the first Night, and set out next Morning on the *Tunbridge* Road, and *Seven-Oak* lying in our Way, we put in there to bait: But truly, we had much ado to get either Provisions or Room for ourselves or our Horses, the House was so filled with Guests, and those not of the better Sort. For the Duke of *York* being, as we were told, on the Road that Day for the *Wells*, divers of his Guards, and the meaner sort of his Retinue, had near filled all the Inns there.

I left *John Gigger*, who waited on *Guli* in this Journey, and was afterwards her menial Servant, to take Care for the Horses, while I did the like, as well as I could for her. I got a little Room to put her into, and having shut her into it, went to see what Relief the Kitchen would afford us; and with much ado, by praying hard and paying dear, I got a small Joint of Meat from the Spit, which served rather to stay than satisfy our Stomachs, for we were all pretty sharp set.

After this short Repast, being weary of our Quarters, we quickly mounted and took the Road again, willing to hasten from a Place where we found nothing but Rudeness; for the *Roysters*, who at that time swarmed there, besides the damning Oaths they belched out at one another, looked very sourly on us, as if they grudged us both the Horses we rode and the Cloaths we wore.

A Knot

A Knot of these soon followed us, designing, 1669.
as we afterwards found, to put an Abuse upon us, and make themselves Sport with us. We had a Spot of fine smooth sandy Way, whereon the Horses trod so softly, that we heard them not till one of them was upon us. I was then riding a-breast with *Guli*, and discoursing with her; when on a sudden hearing a little Noise, and turning mine Eye that Way, I saw an Horseman coming up on the further Side of her Horse, having his left Arm stretched out, just ready to take her about the Waste, and pluck her off backwards from her own Horse, to lay her before him upon his. I had but just Time to thrust forth my Stick between him and her, and bid him stand off; and at the same Time reigning my Horse, to let hers go before me, thrust in between her and him, and being better mounted than he, my Horse run him off. But his Horse being (tho' weaker than mine, yet) nimble, he slipt by me, and got up to her on the near Side, endeavouring to offer Abuse to her: To prevent which, I thrust in upon him again, and in our jostling, we drove her Horse quite out of the Way, and almost into the next Hedge.

While we were thus contending, I heard a Noise of loud Laughter behind us, and turning my Head that Way, I saw three or four Horse-men more, who could scarce sit their Horses for laughing, to see the Sport their Companion made with us. From thence I saw it was a Plot laid, and that this rude Fellow

1669. low was not to be dallied with; wherefore I beſtirr'd myſelf the more to keep him off, admoniſhing him to take Warning in Time, and give over his Abuſiveneſs, leſt he repented too late. He had in his Hand a ſhort thick Truncheon, which he held up at me; on which laying hold with a ſtrong Gripe, I ſuddenly wrenched it out of his Hand, and threw it at as far a Diſtance behind me as I could.

While he rode back to fetch his Truncheon, I called up honeſt *John Gigger*, who was indeed a right honeſt Man, and of a Temper ſo throughly peaceable, that he had not hitherto put in at all. But now I rouzed him, and bid him ride ſo cloſe up to his Miſtreſs's Horſe on the further Side, that no Horſe might thruſt in between, and I would endeavour to guard the near Side. But he, good Man, not thinking it perhaps, decent enough for him to ride ſo near his Miſtreſs, left room enough for another to ride between. And indeed ſo ſoon as our Brute had recovered his Truncheon, he came up directly thither, and had thruſt in again, had not I, by a nimble Turn, chopt in upon him and kept him at a Bay.

I then told him, I had hitherto ſpared him; but wiſh'd him not to provoke me further. This I ſpake with ſuch a Tone, as beſpake an high Reſentment of the Abuſe put upon us, and withal preſſed ſo cloſe upon him with my Horſe, that I ſuffered him not to come up any more to *Guli*.

This

This his Companions, who kept an equal Diſtance behind us, both heard and ſaw, and thereupon two of them advancing, came up to us. I then thought I might likely have my Hands full; but Providence turn'd it otherwiſe. For they, ſeeing the Conteſt riſe ſo high, and probably fearing it would riſe higher, not knowing where it might ſtop, came in to part us; which they did, by taking him away, one of them leading his Horſe by the Bridle, and the other driving him on with his Whip, and ſo carried him off. 1669.

One of their Company ſtaid yet behind. And it ſo happening, that a great Shower juſt then fell, we betook ourſelves for Shelter to a thick and well-ſpread Oak, which ſtood hard by. Thither alſo came that other Perſon, who wore the Duke's Livery, and while we put on our defenſive Garments againſt the Weather, which then ſet in to be wet, he took the Opportunity to diſcourſe with me about the Man that had been ſo rude to us, endeavouring to excuſe him, by alledging that *he had drunk a little too liberally*. I let him know, that one Vice would not excuſe another; that although but one of them was actually concern'd in the Abuſe, yet both he and the reſt of them were Abettors of it, and Acceſſaries to it; that I was not ignorant whoſe Livery they wore, and was well aſſured, their Lord would not maintain them in committing ſuch Outrages upon Travellers on the Road, to our Injury and his Diſhonour; that I underſtood the Duke was coming down, and

1669. and that they might expect to be called to an Account for this rude Action.

He then begg'd hard that we would pass by the Offence, and make no Complaint to their Lord; for he knew, he said, *the* Duke *would be very severe, and it would be the utter Ruin of the young Man.* When he had said what he could, he went off before us, without any ground given him to expect Favour; and when we had fitted ourselves for the Weather, we followed after our own Pace.

When we came to *Tunbridge*, I set *John Gigger* foremost, bidding him lead on briskly through the Town, and placing *Guli* in the Middle, I came close up after her, that I might both observe, and interpose, if any fresh Abuse should have been offered her. We were expected, I perceived; for though it rained very hard, the Street was thronged with Men, who looked very earnestly on us, but did not put any Affront upon us.

We had a good way to ride beyond *Tunbridge*, and beyond the *Wells*, in By-ways among the Woods, and were the later for the Hinderance we had had on the Way. And when, being come to *Harbert Springett*'s House, *Guli* acquainted her Uncle what Danger and Trouble she had gone through on the Way; he resented it so high, that he would have had the Persons been prosecuted for it. But, since Providence had interposed, and so well preserved and delivered her, she chose to pass by the Offence.

When

When *Guli* had finiſhed the Buſineſs ſhe went 1669.
upon, we returned home, and I delivered her ſafe to her glad Mother. From that Time forward, I continued my Viſits to my beſt beloved Friend until we married, which was on the 28th Day of the eighth Month (called *October*) in the Year 1669. We took each other in a ſelect Meeting, of the ancient and grave Friends of that Country, holden in a Friend's Houſe, where in thoſe Times, not only the Monthly-meeting for Buſineſs, but the publick Meeting for Worſhip, was ſometimes kept. A very ſolemn Meeting it was, and in a weighty Frame of Spirit we were, in which we ſenſibly felt the Lord with us and joining us; the Senſe whereof remained with us all our Life-time, and was of good Service, and very comfortable to us on all Occaſions.

My next Care after Marriage, was to ſecure my Wife what Monies ſhe had, and with herſelf beſtowed upon me. For I held it would be an abominable Crime in me, and ſavour of the higheſt Ingratitude, if I, though but through Negligence, ſhould leave room for my Father (in caſe I ſhould be taken away ſuddenly) to break in upon her Eſtate, and deprive her of any Part of that which had been and ought to be her own. Wherefore with the firſt Opportunity (as I remember, the very next Day, and before I knew particularly what ſhe had) I made my *Will*; and thereby ſecured to her whatever I was poſſeſſed of, as well all that which ſhe brought either in Monies, or in Goods,

1669. Goods, as that little which I had before I married her: Which indeed was but little, yet more, [by all that little] than I had ever given her Ground to expect with me.

She had indeed been advised by some of her Relations, to secure before Marriage some Part at least, of what she had, to be at her own disposal. Which, though perhaps not wholly free from some Tincture of Self-Interest in the Proposer, was not in itself the worst of Counsel. But the Worthiness of her Mind, and the Sense of the Ground on which she received me, would not suffer her to entertain any Suspicion of me: And this laid on me the greater Obligation, in point of Gratitude as well as of Justice, to regard and secure her; which I did.

I omitted in its proper Place (because I would not break in upon the Discourse I was then upon) to insert a few Lines, which I writ as a Congratulation to an honoured Friend upon his Marriage, and presented him with the next Morning, thus:

MY Heart's affected with a weighty Sense
Of Yesterday's Proceedings, and from thence,
Desire arises to CONGRATULATE
My happy Friend in his new married State.
Not in that Strain, wherewith some use to cloy
Mens Ears with tedious Peals of giving Joy.

But

But ſhunning all Extreams, I chuſe to tread 1669.
The middle Path, which doth to *Virtue* lead,

This then my Heart deſires for thee, my Friend,
Thy Nuptial Joys may never here have End.
May Happineſs with thee take up her Reſt,
And ſweet Contentment always fill thy Bteaſt.
May GOD thee bleſs with numerous Increaſe,
And may thy utmoſt Off-ſpring reſt in Peace.

Accept this Pledge of Love (tho' but a Part
Of what is treaſur'd for thee in my Heart)
From him, who herein hath no other End,
Than to declare himſelf

Thy faithful Friend,

Stepney, the 9th of the Second Month 1669.

T. E.

I had not been long married, before I was ſolicited by my dear Friends *Iſaac* and *Mary Penington*, and her Daughter *Guli*, to take a Journey into *Kent* and *Suſſex*, to accompt with their Tenants, and overlook their Eſtates in thoſe Counties, which, before I was married, I had had the Care of; and accordingly the Journey I undertook, though in the Depth of Winter.

My Travels into thoſe Parts were the more irkſome to me, from the Solitarineſs I underwent, and Want of ſuitable Society. For my Buſineſs

1669. Business lying among the Tenants, who were a rustick Sort of People, of various Perswasions and Humours, but not Friends, I had little Opportunity of conversing with Friends; though I contrived to be with them as much as I could, especially on the First-day of the Week.

But that which made my present Journey more heavy to me, was a sorrowful Exercise which was newly fallen upon me from my Father, harder to be borne than any I had ever met with before.

He had, upon my first acquainting him with my Inclination to marry, and to whom, not only very much approved the Match, and voluntarily offered, without my either asking or expecting, to give me a handsome Portion at present, with Assurance of an Addition to it hereafter. And he not only made this Offer to me in private, but came down from *London* into the Country on purpose, to be better acquainted with my Friend; and did there make the same Proposal to her; offering also to give Security to any Friend or Relation of hers for the Performance. Which Offer she most generously declined, leaving him as free as she found him. But after we were married, notwithstanding such his Promise, he wholly declined the Performance of it, under Pretence of our not being married by the *Priest* and *Liturgy*. This Usage and evil Treatment of us thereupon, was a great Trouble to me; and when I endeavoured to soften him in the matter, he forbid me speaking

ing to him of it any more, and removed his Lodging that I might not find him. 1669.

The Grief I conceived on this Occaſion, was not for any Diſappointment to myſelf or to my Wife; for neither ſhe nor I had any ſtrict or neceſſary Dependence upon that Promiſe; but my Grief was partly for the Cauſe aſſigned by him, as the Ground of it; which was, *That our Marriage was not by* Prieſt *or* Liturgy; and partly for that his lower Circumſtances in the World, might probably tempt him to find ſome ſuch, though unwarrantable Excuſe, to avoid performing his Promiſe.

And ſurely hard would it have been for my Spirit to have borne up under the Weight of this Exerciſe, had not the Lord been exceeding gracious to me, and ſupported me with the Inflowings of His Love and Life, wherewith He viſited my Soul in my Travel. The Senſe whereof raiſed in my Heart a thankful Remembrance of His manifold Kindneſſes in His former Dealings with me. And in the Evening, when I came to my Inn, while Supper was getting ready, I took my Pen, and put into Words what had in the Day revolved in my Thoughts. And thus it was.

A Song of PRAISE.

THY Love, dear Father, and Thy tender
Care,
Have in my Heart begot a ſtrong Deſire,

1669. To celebrate Thy Name with Praiſes rare,
That others too Thy Goodneſs may admire,
And learn to yield to what Thou doſt require.
Many have been the Trials of my Mind,
My Exerciſes great, great my Diſtreſs;
Full oft my Ruin hath my Foe deſign'd,
My Sorrows then my Pen cannot expreſs,
Nor could the beſt of Men afford Redreſs.
When thus beſet, to Thee I lift mine Eye,
And with a mournful Heart my Moan did make;
How oft with Eyes o'erflowing did I cry,
My God, my God, O do me not forſake!
Regard my Tears! Some Pity on me take!
And, to the Glory of Thy holy Name,
Eternal God, whom I both love and fear,
I hereby do declare, I never came
Before *Thy Throne*, and found Thee *loth to hear*;
But always *ready*, with an open Ear.
And tho' ſometimes Thou ſeem'ſt *Thy Face to hide*,
As one that had *withdrawn Thy Love from me*,
'Tis that my *Faith* may to the full be try'd,

And

And that I thereby may the better see
How weak I am, when not upheld by Thee.
For underneath Thy holy Arm I feel,
Encompassing with *Strength* as with a *Wall*,
That, if the Enemy trip up my Heel,
Thou ready art to save me from a Fall:
To Thee belong *Thanksgivings* over all.
And for Thy tender Love, my God, my King,
My *Heart* shall magnify Thee all my Days,
My *Tongue* of Thy Renown shall daily sing,
My *Pen* shall also grateful Trophies raise,
As *Monuments* to Thy eternal Praise.

Kent, the Eleventh Month 1669. T. E.

Having finished my Business in *Kent*, I struck off into *Sussex*, and finding the Enemy endeavouring still more strongly to beset me, I betook myself to the Lord for Safety, in whom I knew all Help and Strength was; and thus poured forth my Supplication, directed

To the Holy ONE.

ETERNAL God, Preserver of all those
(Without respect of Person or Degree)
Who in Thy Faithfulness their Trust repose,
And place their Confidence alone in Thee;

1669. Be Thou my Succour; for Thou know'st that I
On Thy Protection, LORD, alone rely.
Surround me, Father, with Thy mighty Pow'r,
Support me daily by Thine holy Arm,
Preserve me faithful in the evil Hour,
Stretch forth *Thine Hand*, to save me from all Harm.
Be Thou my *Helmet*, *Breast-plate*, *Sword* and *Shield*,
And make my Foes before Thy Power yield.
Teach me the spirit'al Battel so to fight,
That when the Enemy shall me beset,
Arm'd *Cap-a-pe* with th'Armour of Thy Light,
A perfect Conquest o'er him I may get;
And with Thy *Battle-Axe* may cleave the *Head*
Of him, who bites that Part whereon I tread.
Then being from *domestick* Foes set free,
The *Cruelties* of *Men* I shall not fear;
But in thy Quarrel, LORD, undaunted be,
And, *for Thy Sake*, the Loss of all Things bear.
Yea, tho' in *Dungeon* lock'd, with Joy will sing
An ODE of *Praise* to Thee, my *God*, my *King*.

T. E.

Sussex, the Eleventh
Month 1669.

As

As ſoon as I had diſpatcht the Buſineſs I went 1669. about, I returned home without Delay, and to my great Comfort found my Wife well, and myſelf very welcome to her; both which I eſteemed as great Favours.

Towards the latter Part of the Summer fol- 1670. lowing, I went into *Kent* again, and in my Paſſage through *London*, received the unwelcome News of the Loſs of a very hopeful Youth, who had formerly been under my Care for Education. It was *Iſaac Penington* (the ſecond Son of my worthy Friends *Iſaac* and *Mary Penigton)* a Child of excellent natural Parts, whoſe great Abilities beſpake him likely to be a great Man, had he lived to be a Man. He was deſigned to be bred a Merchant, and before he was thought ripe enough to be entred thereunto, his Parents, at Some-body's Requeſt, gave Leave that he might go a Voyage to *Barbadoes*, only to ſpend a little Time, ſee the Place, and be ſomewhat acquainted with the Sea, under the Care and Conduct of a choice Friend and Sailor, *John Grove* of *London*, who was Maſter of a Veſſel, and traded to that Iſland; and a little Venture he had with him, made up by divers of his Friends, and by me among the reſt. He made the Voyage thither very well, found the wat'ry Element agreeable, had his Health there, liked the Place, was much pleaſed with his Entertainment there, and was returning home with his little Cargo, in Return for the Goods he carried out; when on a ſudden, through Unwarineſs, he dropt over-board, and (the Veſſel being

1669. under Sail with a briſk Gale) was irrecoverably loſt, notwithſtanding the utmoſt Labour, Care and Diligence of the Maſter and Sailors to have ſaved him.

This unhappy Accident took from the afflicted Maſter all the Pleaſure of his Voyage, and he mourn'd for the Loſs of this Youth, as if it had been his own, yea, only Son; for as he was in himſelf a Man of a worthy Mind, ſo the Boy, by his witty and handſome Behaviour in general, and obſequious Carriage towards him in particular, had very much wrought himſelf into his Favour.

As for me, I thought it one of the ſharpeſt Strokes I had met with, for I both loved the Child very well, and had conceived great Hopes of general Good from him; and it pierced me the deeper, to think how deeply it would pierce his afflicted Parents.

Sorrow for this Diſaſter was my Companion in this Journey, and I travelled the Roads under great Exerciſe of Mind, revolving in my Thoughts the manifold Accidents, which the *LIFE of Man* was attended with and ſubject to, and the great *Uncertainty of all human Things*; I could find no Center, no firm Baſis for the *Mind of Man* to fix upon, but the *divine Power* and *Will* of the *Almighty*. This Conſideration wrought in my Spirit a ſort of Contempt of what ſuppoſed *Happineſs* or *Pleaſure* this World, or the Things that are in, and of it, can of themſelves yield, and raiſed my Contemplation higher; which, as it ripened,

and came to ſome degree of Digeſtion, I breath- 1670.
ed forth in mournful Accents, thus:

Solitary Thoughts

On the Uncertainty of human Things,

Occaſioned by the ſudden Loſs of an
Hopeful YOUTH.

Tranſibunt cito, quæ vos manſura putatis.

Thoſe Things ſoon will paſs away,
Which ye think will always ſtay.

WHAT ground, alas! has any Man
To ſet his Heart on Things below,
Which, when they ſeem moſt like to ſtand,
Fly like an Arrow from a Bow!
Things ſubject to exterior Senſe
Are to Mutation moſt propenſe.
If ſtately Houſes we erect,
And therein think to take Delight,
On what a ſudden are we checkt,
And all our Hopes made groundleſs quite!
One little Spark in Aſhes lays
What we were building half our Days.

1670. If on Eſtate an Eye we caſt,
And Pleaſure there expect to find,
A ſecret providential Blaſt
Gives Diſappointment to our Mind.
Who now's on Top, e're long may feel
The circling Motion of the Wheel.
If we our tender Babes embrace,
And Comfort hope in them to have,
Alas, in what a little Space,
Is Hope, with them, laid in the Grave!
Whatever promiſeth Content,
Is in a Moment from us rent.
This World cannot afford a Thing,
Which, to a well-compoſed Mind,
Can any laſting Pleaſure bring,
But in its Womb its Grave will find.
All Things unto their Center tend;
What had * Beginning will have End.
But is there nothing then that's ſure,
For Man to fix his Heart upon?
Nothing that always will endure,
When all theſe tranſient Things are gone?
Sad State! where Man, with Grief oppreſt,
Finds nought whereon his Mind may reſt.

* Underſtand this of Natural Things.

O yes!

O yes! there is a God above,
  Who unto Men is alſo nigh,
On whoſe unalterable Love
  We may with Confidence rely.
    No Diſappointment can befall
    Us, having Him that's *All in All.*
If unto Him we faithful be,
  It is impoſſible to miſs
Of whatſoever He ſhall ſee
  Conducible unto our Bliſs.
    What can of Pleaſure him prevent,
    Who hath the Fountain of Content?
In Him alone if we delight,
  And in His Precepts Pleaſure take,
We ſhall be ſure to do aright,
  'Tis not His Nature to forſake.
    A proper Object's He alone,
    For Man to ſet his Heart upon.

——— *Domino Mens nixa quieta eſt.*

The Mind which upon God is ſtay'd,
Shall with no Trouble be diſmay'd.

Kent, the 4th of the
Seventh Month,
1670.

T. E.

A Copy

1670. A Copy of the foregoing Lines, inclosed in a Letter of *Condolance*, I sent by the first Post into *Buckinghamshire*, to my dear Friends the afflicted Parents; and upon my Return home, going to visit them, we sate down and solemnly mixed our Sorrows and Tears together.

About this Time (as I remember) it was, that some Bickerings happening between some *Baptists*, and some of the People called *Quakers*, in or about *High-Wiccomb* in *Buckinghamshire*, occasioned by some reflecting Words a *Baptist* Preacher had publickly uttered in one of their Meetings there, against the *Quakers* in general, and *William Penn* in particular; it came at length to this Issue, that a Meeting for a publick Dispute was appointed, to be holden at *West-Wiccomb*, between *Jeremy Ives*, who espoused his Brother's Cause, and *William Penn*.

To this Meeting, it being so near me, I went, rather to countenance the Cause, than for any Delight I took in such Work; for indeed, I have rarely found the Advantage equivolent to the Trouble and Danger arising from those Contests. For which Cause I, would not chuse them, as, being justly engaged, I would not refuse them.

The Issue of this proved better than I expected. For *Ives* having undertaken an ill Cause, to argue against the *divine Light* and *universal Grace*, *conferr'd by God on all Men*; when he had spent his Stock of Arguments, which he brought with him on that Subject, finding his Work go on heavily, and the Auditory not well satisfied, stept down from his

Seat

Seat and departed, with purpoſe to have bro- 1670.
ken up the Aſſembly. But, except ſome few of his Party who followed him, the People generally ſtaid, and were the more attentive to what was afterwards delivered amongſt them. Which *Ives* underſtanding came in again, and in an angry railing Manner, expreſſing his Diſlike that we went not all away when he did, gave more Diſguſt to the People.

After the Meeting was ended, I ſent to my Friend *Iſaac Penington* (by his Son and Servant, who returned home, though it was late, that Evening) a ſhort Account of the Buſineſs in the following Diſtich.

Prævaluit VERITAS: *Inimici Terga dedere:*
Nos ſumus in tuto; Laus tribuenda Deo.

Which may be thus *Engliſhed.*

Truth hath prevail'd; the Enemies did fly:
We are in Safety; Praiſe to God on high.

But both they and we had quickly other Work found us; it ſoon became a ſtormy Time. The Clouds had been long gathering and threatned a Tempeſt. The Parliament had ſate ſome Time before, and hatched that unaccountable Law, which was called *The Conventicle Act:* (If that may be allowed to be called a Law, by whomſoever made) which was ſo directly contrary to the Fundamental Laws of *England*, to common

1670. common Juſtice, Equity and right Reaſon, as this manifeſtly was. For,

Firſt, It brake down and over-run the Bounds and Banks, anciently ſet for the Defence and Security of *Engliſhmens* Lives, Liberties and Properties, *viz. Trial by Juries.* Inſtead thereof, directing and authorizing Juſtices of the Peace (and that too privately out of Seſſions) to convict, fine, and by their Warrants diſtrain upon Offenders againſt it; directly contrary to the *Great Charter.*

Secondly, By that Act the Informers, who ſwear for their own Advantage, as being thereby entituled to a third Part of the Fines, were many times concealed, driving on an underhand private Trade; ſo that Men might be, and often were convicted and fined, without having any Notice or Knowledge of it, till the Officers came and took away their Goods, nor even then could they tell by whoſe Evidence they were convicted. Than which, what could be more oppoſite to common Juſtice? which requires that every Man ſhould be openly charged, and have his Accuſer Face to Face, that he might both anſwer for himſelf before he be convicted, and object to the Validity of the Evidence given againſt him.

Thirdly, By that Act, the Innocent were puniſhed for the Offences of the Guilty. If the Wife or Child was convicted of having been at one of thoſe Aſſemblies, which by that Act was adjudged unlawful; the Fire was levied on the Goods of the Huſband or Father of ſuch Wife or

Child,

Child, tho' he was neither preſent at ſuch Aſſem- 1670.
bly, nor was of the ſame religious Perſwaſion that they were of, but perhaps an Enemy to it.

Fourthly, It was left in the arbitrary Pleaſure of the Juſtices, to lay half the Fine for the Houſe or Ground where ſuch Aſſembly was holden, and half the Fine for a pretended unknown Preacher; and the whole Fines of ſuch and ſo many of the Meeters as they ſhould account Poor, upon any other or others of the People, who were preſent at the ſame Meeting (not exceeding a certain limitted Sum;) without any Regard to Equity or Reaſon. And yet, ſuch Blindneſs doth the *Spirit of Perſecution* bring on Men, otherwiſe ſharp ſighted enough, that this unlawful, unjuſt, unequal, unreaſonable and unrighteous Law took place in (almoſt) all Places, and was vigorouſly proſecuted againſt the Meetings of *Diſſenters* in general, though the Brunt of the Storm fell moſt ſharply on the People called *Quakers*; not that it ſeemed to be more particularly levelled at them, but that they ſtood more fair, ſteady and open, as a Butt to receive all the Shot that came, while ſome others found Means and Freedom to retire to Coverts for Shelter.

No ſooner had the Biſhops obtained this Law, for ſuppreſſing all other Meetings but their own, but ſome of the Clergy of moſt Ranks, and ſome others too, who were over-much bigotted to that Party, beſtirr'd themſelves with Might and Main, to find out and encourage the moſt profligate Wretches to turn Informers; and to get

1670. get ſuch Perſons into Parochial Offices, as would be moſt obſequious to their Commands, and ready at their Beck, to put it into the moſt rigorous Execution. Yet it took not alike in all Places; but ſome were forwarder in the Work than others, according as the Agents, intended to be chiefly employed therein, had been prediſpoſed thereunto.

For in ſome Parts of the Nation Care had been timely taken, by ſome not of the loweſt Rank, to chuſe out ſome particular Perſons (Men of ſharp Wit, cloſe Countenances, pliant Tempers and deep Diſſimulation) and ſend them forth among the *Sectaries*, ſo called; with Inſtructions to thruſt themſelves into all Societies, conform to all, or any Sort of religious Profeſſion, *Proteus*-like change their Shapes, and transform themſelves from one religious Appearance to another, as Occaſion ſhould require. In a Word, to be all Things to all; not that they might win ſome, but that they might, if poſſible, ruin all, at leaſt many.

The Drift of this Deſign was, That they who employed them might, by this Means, get a full Account what Number of *Diſſenters* Meetings, of every Sort, there were in each County, and where kept; what Number of Perſons frequented them, and of what Ranks; who amongſt them were Perſons of Eſtate, and where they lived; that when they ſhould afterwards have troubled the Waters, they might the better know where, with moſt Advantage, to caſt their Nets.

He, of theſe Emiſſaries, whoſe Poſt was aſſigned him in this County of *Bucks*, adventured

to

to thruſt himſelf upon a Friend, under the counterfeit Appearance of a *Quaker*; but being by the Friend ſuſpected, and thereupon diſmiſt unentertain'd, he was forced to betake himſelf to an Inn or Alehouſe for Accommodation. Long he had not been there, e're his unruly Nature (not to be long kept under by the Curb of a feigned Sobriety) broke forth into open Profaneneſs; ſo true is that of the POET, 1670.

Naturam expellas furca licet, uſq; recurret.

To Fudling now falls he with thoſe whom he found tippling there before; and who but he amongſt them! In him was then made good the Proverb, *In Vino Veritas*; for in his Cups he out with that which was, no doubt, to have been kept a Secret. 'Twas to his Pot-companions that, after his Head was ſomewhat heated with ſtrong Liquors, he diſcovered that he was ſent forth by Dr. *Mew*, the then Vice-Chancellor of *Oxford*, on the Deſign before related, and under the Protection of Juſtice *Morton*, a Warrant under whoſe Hand and Seal he there produced.

Senſible of his Error too late (when Sleep had reſtored him to ſome degree of Senſe) and diſcouraged with this ill Succeſs of his Attempt upon the *Quakers*, he quickly left that Place, and croſſing through the Country, caſt himſelf among the *Baptiſts*, at a Meeting which they held in a private Place; of which, the over-eaſy Credulity of ſome that went among them,

whom

1670. whom he had craftily insinuated himself into, had given him Notice. The Entertainment he found amongst them, deserved a better Return than he made them. For, having smoothly wrought himself into their good Opinion, and cunningly drawn some of them into an unwary Openness and Freedom of Conversation with him, upon the unpleasing Subject of the Severity of those Times, he most villainously impeached one of them, whose Name was —— *Headach*, a Man well reputed amongst his Neighbours, of having spoken *treasonable Words*; and thereby brought the Man in danger of losing both his Estate and Life, had not a seasonable Discovery of his abominable Practices elsewhere (imprinting Terror, the Effect of Guilt upon him) caused him to fly both out of the Court and Country, at that very Instant of Time, when the honest Man stood at the Bar, ready to be arraigned upon his false Accusation.

This his false Charge against that *Baptist*, left him no further room to play the Hypocrite in those Parts. Off therefore go his Cloak and Vizor. And now he openly appears in his proper Colours, to disturb the Assemblies of God's People; which was indeed the very End, for which the Design at first was laid.

But because the Law provided, *That a Conviction must be grounded upon the Oaths of two Witnesses*, it was needful for him, in order to the carrying on his intended Mischief, to find out an Associate, who might be both sordid

enough

enough for ſuch an Employment, and vicious 1670.
enough to be his Companion.

This was not an eaſy Taſk; yet he found out one, who had already given an Experiment of his Readineſs to take other Mens Goods, being not long before releaſed out of *Aylesbury* Jail, where he very narrowly eſcaped the Gallows for having ſtolen a Cow.

The Names of theſe Fellows being yet unknown in that Part of the Country where they began their Work, the former, by the general Voice of the Country, was called *The Trepan*; the latter, *The Informer*, and, from the Colour of his Hair, *Red-head*. But in a little Time the *Trepan* called himſelf *John Poulter*, adding withal, that Judge *Morton* uſed to call him *John for the King*; and that the Archbiſhop of *Canterbury* had given him a *Deaconry*. That his Name was indeed *John Poulter*, the reputed Son of one —— *Poulter*, a Butcher in *Saliſbury*, and that he had long ſince been there branded for a Fellow egregiouſly wicked and debauched, we were aſſured by the Teſtimony of a young Man then living in *Amerſham*, who both was his Countryman, and had known him in *Saliſbury*; as well as by a Letter from an Inhabitant of that Place, to whom his Courſe of Life had been well known.

His Comrade, who for ſome Time was only called *The Informer*, was named *Ralph Lacy* of *Riſborough*, and ſirnamed the *Cow-ſtealer*.

Theſe agreed between themſelves where to make their firſt Onſet, which was to be, and

1670. was, on the Meeting of the People called *Quakers*, then holden at the House of *William Russell*, called *Jourdan's*, in the Parish of *Giles-Chalfont* in the County of *Bucks*; that which was wanting to their Accommodation, was a Place of Harbour, fit for such Beasts of Prey to lurk in; for Assistance wherein, Recourse was had to Parson *Philips*, none being so ready, none so willing, none so able to help them as he.

A Friend he had in a Corner, a Widow-woman, not long before one of his Parishioners. Her Name was *Anne Dell*, and at that Time she lived at a Farm called *Whites*, a By-place in the Parish of *Beconsfield*, whither she removed from *Hitchindon*. To her these Fellows were recommended by her old Friend the Parson. She with all Readiness received them, her House was at all Times open to them, what she had, was at their Command.

Two Sons she had at home with her, both at Man's Estate; to the eldest of which, her Maid-servant not long before had laid a Bastard, which Infamy to smother up proved expensive to them. The younger Son, whose Name was *John Dell*, hoping by the Pillage of his honest Neighbours, to regain what the Incontinency of his lustful Brother had mis-spent, listed himself in the Service of his Mother's new Guests, to attend on them as their Guide, and to inform them (who were too much Strangers to pretend to know the Names of any of the Persons there) whom they should inform against.

Thus

Thus consorted, thus in a triple League confederated; on the 24th Day of the fifth Month, commonly called *July*, in the Year 1670, they appeared openly, and began to act their intended Tragedy upon the *Quakers* Meeting at the Place aforesaid, to which I belonged, and at which I was present. Here the chief Actor, *Poulter*, behaved himself with such impetuous Violence and brutish Rudeness, as gave Occasion for Enquiry, who or what he was? And being soon discovered to be the *Trepan*, so infamous and abhor'd by all sober People, and afterwards daily detected of gross Impieties, and even capital Crimes, such as *Christ'ning* (so the common Term is) of a Cat, in Contempt of that Practice which is used by many upon Children, naming it *Catharine - Catherina*, in Derision of the then Queen; and the felonious taking of certain Goods from one of *Brainford*, whom also he cheated of Money. These Things raising an Out-cry in the Country upon him, made him consult his own Safety, and leaving his Part to be acted by others, quitted the Country as soon as he could. 1670.

He being gone, Satan soon supplied his Place, by sending one *Richard Aris*, a broken *Ironmonger* of *Wiccomb*, to join with *Lacy* in this Service, prompted thereto, in hopes that he might thereby repair his broken Fortunes.

Of this new Adventurer this single Character may serve, whereby the Reader may make Judgment of him, as of the Lion by his Paw; That at the Sessions holden at *Wiccomb* in

1670. *October* then laſt paſt, he was openly accuſed of having enticed one *Harding* of the ſame Town, to be his Companion and Aſſociate in robbing on the Highway, and Proof offered to be made, that he had made Bullets in order to that Service; which Charge *Harding* himſelf, whom he had endeavoured to draw into that hainous Wickedneſs, was ready in Court to prove upon Oath, had not the Proſecution been diſcountenanced and ſmothered.

Lacy the Cow-ſtealer, having thus got *Aris* the intended Highway-man to be his Comrade, they came on the 21ſt of the Month called *Auguſt* 1670, to the Meeting of the People called *Quakers*, where *Lacy* with *Poulter* had been a Month before; and taking for granted that the ſame who had been there before, were there then, they went to a Juſtice of the Peace called Sir *Thomas Clayton*, and ſwore at all adventure againſt one *Thomas Zachary* and his Wife, whom *Lacy* underſtood to have been there the Month before, that they were then preſent in that Meeting: Whereas neither the ſaid *Thomas Zachary* nor his Wife were at that Meeting, but were both of them at *London* (above twenty Miles diſtant) all that Day, having been there ſome Time before and after. Which notwithſtanding, upon this falſe Oath of theſe falſe Men, the Juſtice laid Fines upon the ſaid *Thomas Zachary* of 10 *l.* for his own Offence, 10 *l.* for his Wife's, and 10 *l.* for the Offence of a pretended Preacher, though indeed there was not any that preached at that Meeting

that

that Day; and issued forth his Warrant to the 1670.
Officers of *Beconsfield*, where *Thomas Zachary* dwelt, for the levying of the same upon his Goods.

I mention these Things thus particularly, tho' not an immediate Suffering of my own, because, in the Consequence thereof, it occasioned no small Trouble and Exercise to me.

For when *Thomas Zachary*, returning home from *London*, understanding what had been done against him, and advising what to do, was informed by a neighbouring Attorney, that his Remedy lay in appealing from the Judgment of the convicting Justice, to the General Quarter Sessions of the Peace: He thereupon ordering the said Attorney to draw up his Appeal in Form of Law, went himself with it and tendered it to the Justice. But the Justice being a Man neither well principled, nor well natured, and uneasy that he should lose the Advantage, both of the present Conviction, and future Service of such (in his Judgment) useful Men, as those two bold Informers were likely to be, fell sharply upon *Thomas Zachary*, charging him that he suffered justly, and that his Suffering was not on a religious Account.

This rough and unjust Dealing engaged the good Man to enter into further Discourse with the Justice, in Defence of his own Innocency. From which Discourse the insidious Justice, taking Offence at some Expression of his, charged him with saying, *The Righteous are oppressed, and the Wicked go unpunished.* Which the Justice

1670. interpreting to be a Reflection on the Government, and calling it an high *Misdemeanour*, required Sureties of the good Man to answer it at the next Quarter Sessions, and in the mean Time to be bound to his good Behaviour. But he, well knowing himself to be innocent of having broken any Law, or done in this Matter any Evil, could not answer the Justice's unjust Demand, and therefore was sent forthwith a Prisoner to the County Jail.

By this Severity it was thought, the Justice designed not only to wreak his Displeasure on this good Man, but to prevent the further Prosecution of his Appeal: Whereby he should at once both oppress the Righteous, by the Levying of the Fines unduly imposed upon him, and secure the Informers from a Conviction of *wilful Perjury*, and the Punishment due therefor, that so they might go on without Controul, in the wicked Work they were engaged in.

But so great Wickedness was not to be suffered to go unpunished, or at least undiscovered. Wherefore, although no Way could be found at present, to get the good Man released from his unjust Imprisonment; yet that his Restraint might not hinder the Prosecution of his Appeal, on which the Detection of the Informers Villany depended, Consideration being had thereof amongst some Friends, the Management of the Prosecution was committed to my Care, who was thought, with respect at least to Leisure, and Disengagement from other Business, most fit to attend it; and very willingly I undertook it.

Wherefore

Wherefore at the next general Quarter-Sessions of the Peace, holden at *High-Wiccomb* in *October* following, I took Care that four substantial Witnesses, Citizens of unquestionable Credit, should come down from *London*, in a Coach and four Horses hired on purpose. 1670.

These gave so punctual and full Evidence, that *Thomas Zachary* and his Wife were in *London* all that Day, whereon the Informers had sworn them to have been at an unlawful Meeting, at a Place more than twenty Miles distant from *London*, that notwithstanding what Endeavours were used to the contrary, the Jury found them *Not Guilty*. Whereupon the Money deposited for the Fines, at the Entring of the Appeal, ought to have been returned, and so was Ten Pounds of it; but the rest of the Money being in the Hand of the Clerk of the Peace, whose Name was *Wells*, could never be got out again.

Thomas Zachary himself was brought from *Aylesbury* Jail to *Wiccomb*, to receive his Trial, and though no Evil could be charged upon him, yet Justice *Clayton*, who at first committed him, displeased to see the Appeal prosecuted, and the Conviction he had made set aside, by Importunity prevailed with the Bench to remand him to Prison again, there to lie until another Sessions.

While this was doing, I got an Indictment drawn up against the Informers *Aris* and *Lacy*, for *wilful Perjury*, and caused it to be delivered to the Grand Jury; who found the Bill. And although the Court adjourned from the Town-

1670. hall to the Chamber at their Inn, in Favour as it was thought to the Informers, on Suppoſition we would not purſue them thither, yet thither they were purſued; and there being too Councils preſent from *Windſor*, the Name of the one was *Starky*, and of the other, as I remember, *Forſter*; the former of which I had before retained upon the Trial of the Appeal, I now retained them both, and ſent them into Court again to proſecute the Informers upon this Indictment; which they did ſo ſmartly, that the Informers being preſent, as not ſuſpecting any ſuch ſudden Danger, were of Neceſſity called to the Bar and arraigned; and having pleaded *Not Guilty*, were forced to enter a Traverſe to avoid a preſent Commitment: All the Favour the Court could ſhew them, being to take them Bail one for the other, though probably both not worth a Groat, elſe they muſt have gone to Jail for want of Bail, which would have put them beſides their Buſineſs, ſpoil'd the informing Trade, and broke the Deſign; whereas now they were turned looſe again, to do what Miſchief they could until the next Seſſions.

Accordingly they did what they could, and yet could make little or no Earnings at it; for this little Step of Proſecution had made them ſo known, and their late apparent Perjury had made them ſo deteſtable, that even the common Sort of bad Men ſhunned them, and would not willingly yield them any Aſſiſtance.

The next Quarter-Seſſions was holden at *Ayleſbury*, whither we were fain to bring down our

our Witnesses again from *London*, in like manner and at like Charge (at the least) as before. 1670.
And though I met with great Discouragements in the Prosecution, yet I followed it so vigorously, that I got a Verdict against the Informers for *wilful Perjury*; and had forthwith taken them up, had not they forthwith fled from Justice and hid themselves. However, I moved by my Attorney for an Order of Court, directed to all Mayors, Bayliffs, High Constables, Petty Constables, and other inferior Officers of the Peace, to arrest and take them up, where-ever they should be found within the County of *Bucks*, and bring them to the County Jail.

The Report of this so terrified them, that of all Things dreading the Misery of lying in a Jail, out of which they could not hope for Deliverance, otherwise than by at least the Loss of their Ears, they hopeless now of carrying on their informing Trade, disjoined, and one of them *(Aris)* fled the Country; so that whatever Gallows caught him, he appeared no more in this Country. The other *(Lacy)* lurked privily for a while in Woods and By-places, 'till Hunger and Want forced him out; and then casting himself upon an hazardous Adventure, which yet was the best, and proved to him the best Course he could have taken, he went directly to the Jail, where he knew the innocent Man suffered Imprisonment by his Means, and for his Sake; where asking for, and being brought to *Thomas Zackary*, he cast himself on his Knees, at his Feet, and with Appearance of

1670. of Sorrow confessing his Fault, did so earnestly beg for Forgiveness, that he wrought upon the tender Nature of that very good Man, not only to put him in hopes of Mercy, but to be his Advocate by Letter to me, to mitigate at least, if not wholly to remit the Prosecution. To which I so far only consented, as to let him know, I would suspend the Execution of the Warrant upon him, according as he behaved himself, or until he gave fresh Provocation. At which Message the Fellow was so overjoyed, that relying with Confidence thereon, he returned openly to his Family and Labour, and applied himself to Business, as his Neighbours observed and reported, with greater Diligence and Industry than he had ever done before.

Thus began and thus ended the informing Trade, in these Parts of the County of *Bucks*; the ill Success that these first Informers found, discouraging all others, how vile soever, from attempting the like Enterprize there ever after. And though it cost some Money to carry on the Prosecution, and some Pains too; yet, for every Shilling so spent, a Pound probably might be saved, of what in all likelihood would have been lost, by the Spoil and Havock that might have been made by Distresses taken on their Informations.

But so angry was the convicting Justice (whatever others of the same Rank were) at this Prosecution, and the Loss thereby of the Service of those *honest Men*, the *perjur'd Informers*. For as I heard an Attorney (one *Hitchcock* of *Aylesbury*,

Aylesbury, who was their Advocate in Court) say, *A great Lord, a Peer of the Realm, called them so in a Letter directed to him; whereby he recommended to him the Care and Defence of them and their Cause*; that he prevailed to have the Oath of Allegiance tendred in Court to *Thomas Zachary*, which he knew he would not take, because he could not take any Oath at all; by which Snare he was kept in Prison a long Time after, and, so far as I remember, until a general Pardon released him.

But though it pleased the divine Providence, which sometimes vochsafeth to bring Good out of Evil, to put a Stop, in a great Measure at least, to the Prosecution here begun; yet in other Parts, both of the City and Country, it was carried on with very great Severity and Rigour; the worst of Men, for the most part, being set up for Informers; the worst of Magistrates encouraging and abetting them; and the worst of the Priests, who first began to blow the Fire, now seeing how it took, spread and blazed, clapping their Hands, and hallowing them on to this evil Work.

The Sense whereof, as it deeply affected my Heart with a sympathizing Pity for the oppressed Sufferers, so it raised in my Spirit an holy Disdain and Contempt of that Spirit and its Agent, by which this ungodly Work was stirred up and carried on. Which at length brake forth in an Expostulatory POEM, under the Title of *GIGANTOMACHIA (the Wars of the Giants against Heaven)* not without some Allusion to the second Psalm, thus:

WHY

1670. WHY do the Heathen in a brutish Rage,
Themselves against the Lord of Hosts engage!
Why do the frantick People entertain
Their Thoughts upon a Thing that is so vain!
Why do the Kings themselves together set!
And why do all the Princes them abet!
Why do the Rulers to each other speak
After this foolish manner, *Let us break*
Their Bonds asunder! Come let us make haste,
With joint Consent, their Cords from us to cast.
Why do they thus join Hands! and Counsel take
Against the Lord's *Anointed!* This will make
Him, doubtless laugh, who doth in Heaven sit,
The Lord will have them in Contempt for it.
His sore Displeasure on them He will wreak,
And in His Wrath will He unto them speak,
For on His holy Hill of *Sion*, He
His King hath set to reign, *Scepters* must be
Cast down before him; *Diadems* must lie
At foot of Him who sits in Majesty
Upon His Throne of Glory; whence He will
Send forth His fiery Ministers to kill
All those His Enemies, who would not be
Subject to His supream Authority.

Where

Where then will ye appear, who are ſo far
From being *Subjects*, that ye *Rebels* are
Againſt His holy Government, and ſtrive
Others from their Allegiance too to drive;
What Earthly Prince ſuch an Affront wou'd bear
From any of his Subjects, ſhou'd they dare
So to encroach on his Prerogative!
Which of them wou'd permit that Man to *live*;
What ſhou'd it be adjudg'd but *Treaſon?* And
Death he muſt ſuffer for it out of hand.
And ſhall the *King* of *Kings* ſuch *Treaſon* ſee
Acted againſt Him, and the Traitors be
Acquitted! No, *Vengeance* is His; and they
That Him provoke, ſhall know He will repay.
And of a Truth, provoked He hath been,
In an high Manner by this daring Sin,
Of Uſurpation, and of Tyranny
Over Mens Conſciences, which ſhould be free
To ſerve the living God as He requires,
And as His holy Spirit them inſpires.
For Conſcience is an inward Thing, and none
Can govern that aright but God alone.
Nor can a well-informed Conſcience low'r
Her Sails to any temporary Pow'r,

1670. Or bow to Mens Decrees; for that wou'd be
Treason in a superlative Degree;
For God alone can Laws to Conscience give,
And that's a Badge of His PREROGATIVE.
This is the Controversy of this Day,
Between the holy God, and sinful Clay.
God hath throughout the Earth, proclaim'd that He
Will over Conscience hold the Sov'raingty,
That He the Kingdom to Himself will take,
And in Man's Heart His Residence will make;
From whence His Subjects shall such Laws receive,
As please His royal Majesty to give.
Man heeds not this; but most audaciously
Says, *Unto me belongs Supremacy:*
And all Mens Consciences within my Land,
Ought to be subject unto my Command.
God by His holy Spirit doth direct
His People how to worship; and expect
Obedience from them. Man says, *I ordain,*
That none shall worship in that Way on pain
Of Prison, Confiscation, Banishment,
Or being to the Stake or Gallows sent.

God

God out of *Babylon* doth People call, 1670.
Commands them to forsake her Ways, and all
Her sev'ral Sorts of Worship, to deny
Her whole Religion as *Idolatry.*
Will Man thus his usurped Pow'r forgo,
And lose his ill-got Government? Oh no:
But out comes his Enacted, be't, *That all*
Who when the Organs play, will not down fall
Before this golden Image, and adore
What I have caus'd to be set up therefore,
Into the fiery Furnace shall be cast,
And be consumed with a flaming Blast.
Or, in the mildest Terms, conform or pay
So much a Month, or so much ev'ry Day,
Which we will levy on you, by Distress,
Sparing nor Widow, nor the Fatherless:
And if you have not what will satisfy,
Y'are like in Prison during Life to lie.
Christ says, *Swear not*; but Man says, *Swear*, [or lie
In Prison, premunir'd, until you die.
Man's Ways are, in a Word, as opposite
To God's, as Midnight-darkness is to Light;
And yet fond Man doth strive with Might and Main
By penal Laws, God's People to constrain

To

1670. To worſhip *What*, *When*, *Where*, *How* he
thinks fit,
And to whatever he injoins, ſubmit.
What will the Iſſue of this Conteſt be!
Which muſt give Place, the Lord's, or Man's
Decree!
Will Man be in the Day of Battle found
Able to keep the Field, maintain his Ground,
Againſt the mighty God! No more than can
The lighteſt Chaff before the winnowing Fan;
No more than Straw cou'd ſtand before the
Flame,
Or ſmalleſt Atoms, when a Whirlwind came.
The LORD (who in Creation, only ſaid,
Let us make Man, and forthwith Man was made)
Can in a Moment by one Blaſt of Breath,
Strike all Mankind with an eternal Death.
How ſoon can God all Man's Devices quaſh,
And, with His iron Rod, in Pieces daſh
Him, like a Potter's Veſſel! None can ſtand
Againſt the mighty Power of His Hand.
Be therefore wiſe ye Kings, inſtructed be,
Ye Rulers of the Earth, and henceforth ſee
Ye ſerve the Lord in Fear, and ſtand in awe
Of ſinning any more againſt His Law,

His

His royal Law of Liberty; to do 1670.
To others as you'd have them do to you.
Oh stoop, ye mighty Monarchs, and let none
Reject His Government, but kiss the Son,
While's Wrath is but a little kindled, lest
His Anger burn, and you that have transgrest
His Law so oft, and wou'd not Him obey,
Eternally shou'd perish from the Way;
The Way of God's Salvation, where the Just
Are bless'd, who in the Lord do put their Trust.

Fœlix quem faciunt aliena Pericula cautum.

——— ——— Happy's he,
Whom others Harms do wary make to be.

As the unreasonable Rage and furious Violence of the Persecutors had drawn the former Expostulation from me; so in a while after, my Heart being deeply affected with a Sense of the great Loving-kindness and tender Goodness of the LORD to his People, in bearing up their Spirits in their greatest Exercises, and preserving them through the sharpest Trials, in a faithful Testimony to his blessed Truth, and opening in due Time a Door of Deliverance to them, I could not forbear to celebrate His Praises in the following Lines, under the Title of 1671.

1671. *A SONG of the Mercies and Deliverances of the LORD.*

HAD not the Lord been on our Side,
May *Iſrael* now ſay,
We were not able to abide
The Trials of that Day.
When Men did up againſt us riſe,
With Fury, Rage and Spight,
Hoping to catch us by Surprize,
Or run us down by Might.
Then had not God for us aroſe,
And ſhewn His mighty Pow'r,
We had been ſwallow'd by our Foes,
Who waited to devour.
When the joint Pow'rs of Death and Hell
Againſt us did combine,
And, with united Forces fell
Upon us, with Deſign
To root us out; then had not God
Appear'd to take our Part,
And them chaſtized with His Rod,
And made them feel the Smart,

We

We then had overwhelmed been,
  And trodden in the Mire,
Our Enemies on us had ſeen
  Their cruel Hearts Deſire.
When ſton'd, when ſtockt, when rudely ſtript,
  Some to the Waiſt have been,
(Without Regard of Sex) and whipt,
  Until the Blood did ſpin;
Yea, when their Skins with Stripes look'd black,
  Their Fleſh to Jelly beat,
Enough to make their Sinews crack,
  The Laſhes were ſo great;
Then had not God been with them to
  Support them, they had dy'd,
His Pow'r it was, that bore them thro',
  Nothing cou'd do't beſide.
When into Priſons we were throng'd
  (Where *Peſtilence* was rife)
By bloody-minded Men, that long'd
  To take away our Life;
Then had not God been with us, we
  Had periſh'd there no doubt,
'Twas He preſerv'd us there, and He
  It was that brought us out.

1670. When ſentenced to Baniſhment
Inhumanly we were,
To be from native Country ſent,
From all that Men call dear ;
Then had not God been pleas'd t' appear,
And take our Cauſe in hand,
And ſtruck them with a pannick Fear,
Which put them to a ſtand :
Nay, had He not great Judgments ſent,
And compaſs'd them about,
They were, at that Time fully bent
To root us wholly out.
Had He not gone with them that went,
The Seas had been their Graves,
Or, when they came where they were ſent,
They had been ſold for Slaves.
But God was pleaſed ſtill to give
Them Favour where they came,
And in His Truth they yet do live,
To praiſe His holy Name.
And now afreſh do Men contrive
Another wicked Way,
Of our Eſtates us to deprive,
And take our Goods away.

But

But will the Lord (who to this Day, 16[illegible]
  Our Part did always take)
Now leave us to be made a Prey,
  And that too for His Sake?
Can any one, who calls to Mind
  Deliverances paſt,
Diſcourag'd be at what's behind,
  And murmur now at laſt!
O that no unbelieving Heart
  Among us may be found,
That from the Lord wou'd now depart,
  And Coward-like, give Ground.
For, without doubt, the God we ſerve
  Will ſtill our Cauſe defend,
If we from Him do never ſwerve,
  But truſt Him to the End.
What if our Goods by Violence,
  From us be torn, and we,
Of all Things but our Innocence,
  Should wholly ſtripped be?
Would this be more than did befal
  Good *Job*? Nay ſure, much leſs;
He loſt Eſtate, Children and all,
  Yet he the Lord did bleſs.

But did not God his Stock augment,
  Double what 'twas before ?
And this was writ to the Intent,
  That we ſhould hope the more.
View but the Lillies of the Field,
  That neither knit nor ſpin,
Who is it that to them doth yield
  The Robes they're decked in ?
Doth not the Lord the Ravens feed,
  And for the Sparrows care ?
And will not He for His own Seed,
  All needful Things prepare ?
The Lions ſhall ſharp Hunger bear,
  And pine for lack of Food,
But who the Lord do truly fear,
  Shall nothing want that's good.
Oh ! which of us can now diffide
  That God will us defend,
Who hath been always on our Side,
  And will be to the End.

Spes confiſa Deo nunquam confuſa recedet.

Hope, which on God is firmly grounded,
Will never fail, nor be confounded.

Scarce

Scarce was the before-mentioned Storm of outward Persecution from the Government blown over, when Satan rais'd another Storm, of another kind, against us on this Occasion. The foregoing Storm of Persecution, as it lasted long, so in many Parts of the Nation, and particularly at *London*, it fell very sharp and violent, especially on the *Quakers*. For they having no Refuge but God alone to fly unto, could not dodge and shift to avoid the Suffering, as others of other Denominations could, and in their worldy Wisdom and Policy did; altering their Meetings, with respect both to Place and Time, and forbearing to meet when forbidden, or kept out of their Meeting-houses. So that of the several Sorts of Dissenters, the *Quakers* only held up a publick Testimony, as a Standard or Ensign of Religion, by keeping their Meeting duly and fully, at the accustomed Times and Places, so long as they were suffered to enjoy the Use of their Meeting-houses; and when they were shut up, and Friends kept out of them by Force, they assembled in the Streets, as near to their Meeting-houses as they could. 1672

This bold and truly Christian Behaviour in the *Quakers*, disturbed and not a little displeased the Persecutors, who fretting complained, *That the stubborn* Quakers *brake their Strength, and bore off the Blow from those other Dissenters, whom as they most feared, so they principally aimed at.* For indeed the *Quakers* they rather despised than feared, as being a People, from whose peaceable both Principles and Practices,

1672. they held themſelves ſecure from Danger; whereas having ſuffered ſeverely, and that lately too, by and under the other Diſſenters, they thought they had juſt Cauſe to be apprehenſive of Danger from them, and good reaſon to ſuppreſs them.

On the other hand, the more ingenious amongſt other Diſſenters of each Denomination, ſenſible of the Eaſe they enjoyed by our bold and ſteady Suffering (which abated the Heat of the Perſecutors, and blunted the Edge of the Sword before it came to them) frankly acknowledged the Benefit received; calling us *The Bulwark that kept off the Force of the Stroke from them*; and praying *that we might be preſerved, and enabled to break the Strength of the Enemy*; nor could ſome of them forbear, thoſe eſpecially who were called *Baptiſts*, to expreſs their kind and favourable Opinion of us, and of the Principles we profeſs'd, which emboldened us to go through that, which but to hear of was a Terror to them.

This their Good-will rais'd Ill-will in ſome of their Teachers againſt us, who tho' willing to reap the Advantage of a Shelter, by a Retreat behind us during the Time that the Storm laſted; yet partly through an evil Emulation, partly through Fear, leſt they ſhould loſe ſome of thoſe Members of their Society, who had diſcovered ſuch favourable Thoughts of our Principles and us, they ſet themſelves, as ſoon as the Storm was over, to repreſent us in as ugly a Dreſs,

Dreſs, and in as frightful Figure to the World, as they could invent and put upon us. 1673.

In order whereunto, one *Thomas Hicks*, a Preacher among the *Baptiſts* at *London*, took upon him to write ſeveral Pamphlets ſucceſſively, under the Title of *A Dialogue between a* Chriſtian *and a* Quaker; which were ſo craftily contrived, that the unwary Reader might conclude them to be not meerly Fictions, but real Diſcourſes, actually held between one of the People called a *Quaker*, and ſome other Perſon. In theſe feigned Dialogues, *Hicks*, having no Regard to Juſtice or common Honeſty, had made his *counterfeit Quaker* ſay whatſoever he thought would render him one while, ſufficiently *erroneous*; another while, *ridiculous* enough; forging in the *Quaker*'s Name, ſome Things ſo abominably falſe, other Things ſo intolerably fooliſh, as could not reaſonably be ſuppoſed to have come into the Conceit, much leſs to have dropped from the Lip or Pen of any that went under the Name of a *Quaker*.

Theſe *Dialogues* (ſhall I call them, or rather *Diabologues*) were anſwered by our Friend *William Penn* in two Books; the firſt being entituled, *Reaſon againſt Railing*; the other, *The Counterfeit* Chriſtian *detected*; in which *Hicks* being charged with manifeſt, as well as manifold *Forgeries*, *Perverſions*, *downright Lyes* and *Slanders* againſt the People called *Quakers* in general, *William Penn*, *George Whitehead*, and divers others by Name; Complaint was made, by

1673. by Way of an *Appeal*, to the *Baptists* in and about *London* for Justice against *Thomas Hicks.*

1674. Those *Baptists*, who it seems were in the Plot with *Hicks* to defame at any Rate, right or wrong, the People called *Quakers*, taking the Advantage of the Absence of *William Penn* and *George Whitehead*, who were the Persons most immediately concerned, and who were then gone a long Journey on the Service of Truth, to be absent from the City, in all probability, for a considerable Time, appointed a publick Meeting in one of their Meeting-houses, under Pretence of calling *Thomas Hicks* to account, and hearing the Charge made good against him; but with Design to give the greater Stroke to the *Quakers*, when they, who should make good the Charge against *Hicks*, could not be present. For upon their sending Notice to the Lodgings of *William Penn* and *George Whitehead* of their intended Meeting, they were told by several Friends, that both *William Penn* and *George Whitehead* were from home, travelling in the Countries uncertain where; and therefore could not be informed of their intended Meeting, either by Letter or Express, within the Time by them limitted; for which Reason they were desired to defer the Meeting till they could have Notice of it, and Time to return, that they might be at it. But these *Baptists*, whose Design was otherwise laid, would not be prevailed with to defer their Meeting; but glad of the Advantage, gave their Brother *Hicks* Opportunity to make a colourable Defence, where

where he had his Party to help him, and none to oppose him; and having made a mock Shew of examining him and his Works of Darkness, they in fine having heard one Side, acquitted him. 1674.

This gave just Occasion for a new Complaint, and Demand of Justice against him and them. For as soon as *William Penn* return'd to *London*, he in Print exhibited his Complaint of this unfair Dealing, and demanded Justice, by a Re-hearing of the Matter in a publick Meeting, to be appointed by joint Agreement. This went hardly down with the *Baptists*, nor could it be obtained from them, without great Importunity and hard pressing. At length, after many Delays and Tricks used to shift it off, constrained by Necessity, they yeilded to have a Meeting at their own Meeting-house in *Barbican*, *London*.

There, amongst other Friends, was I, and undertook to read our Charge there against *Thomas Hicks*, which, not without much Difficulty, I did; they, inasmuch as the House was theirs, putting all the Inconveniences they could upon us.

The particular Passages, and Management of this Meeting (as also of that other, which followed soon after, they refusing to give us any other publick Meeting, we were fain to appoint in our own Meeting-house by *Wheeler-Street* near *Spital-fields*, *London*, and gave them timely Notice of) I forbear here to mention; there being in Print a Narrative of each, to which, for particular Information, I refer the Reader.

But

1674. But to this Meeting *Thomas Hicks* would not come, but lodged himſelf at an Ale-houſe hard by; yet ſent his Brother *Ives*, with ſome others of the Party, by clamorous Noiſes to divert us from the Proſecution of our Charge againſt him; which they ſo effectually performed, that they would not ſuffer the Charge to be heard, though often attempted to be read.

As this rude Behaviour of theirs was a Cauſe of Grief to me; ſo afterwards when I underſtood, that they uſed all evaſive Tricks to avoid another Meeting with us, and refuſed to do us Right, my Spirit was greatly ſtirred at their Injuſtice, and in the Senſe thereof, willing if poſſible, to have provoked them to more fair and manly Dealing, I let fly a Broad-ſide at them, in a ſingle Sheet of Paper, under the Title of *A freſh Purſuit.* In which, having reſtated the Controverſy between them and us, and reinforced our Charge of Forgery, *&c.* againſt *Thomas Hicks* and his Abettors, I offered a fair Challenge to them (not only to *Thomas Hicks* himſelf, but to all thoſe his Compurgators, who had before undertaken to acquit him from our Charge, together with their Companion *Jeremy Ives)* to give me a fair and publick Meeting, in which I would make good our Charge againſt him as *Principal,* and all the reſt of them as *Acceſſaries.* But nothing could provoke them to come fairly forth.

Yet not long after, finding themſelves galled by the Narrative lately publiſhed of what had paſſed in the laſt Meeting near *Wheeler-ſtreet,* they

they to help themſelves, if they could, ſent 1674.
forth a counter Account of that Meeting, and
of the former at *Barbican*, as much to the Advantage of their own Cauſe, as they upon deliberate Conſideration cou'd contrive it. This was publiſhed by *Thomas Plant* a *Baptiſt* Teacher, and one of *Thomas Hicks* his former Compurgators, and bore (but falſly) the Title of *A Conteſt for* Chriſtianity; *or, A faithful Relation of two late Meetings*, &c.

To this I quickly writ and publiſhed an Anſwer. And becauſe I ſaw the Deſign and whole Drift of the *Baptiſts*, was to ſhroud *Thomas Hicks* from our Charge of *Forgery*, under the ſpecious Pretence of his and their *ſtanding up, and contending for* Chriſtianity, I gave my Book this general Title, *Forgery no* Chriſtianity; *or a brief Examen of a late Book*, &c. And having from their own Book, plainly convicted that which they called *A faithful Relation*, to be indeed *a falſe Relation*, I, in an expoſtulatory *Poſtſcript* to the *Baptiſts*, reinforced our Charge and my former Challenge; offering to make it good againſt them before a publick and free Auditory. But they were too wary to appear further, either in Perſon or in Print.

This was the End of that Controverſy, which was obſerved to have this Iſſue; That what thoſe Dialogues were written to prevent, was, by the Dialogues, and their unfair, unmanly, unchriſtian Carriage, in endeavouring to defend them, haſtened and brought to paſs; for not a few of the *Baptiſts* Members, upon this

Occaſion

1674. Occasion left their Meetings and Society, and came over to the *Quakers* Meetings, and were joined in Fellowship with them. Thanks be to God.

Though many of the most eminent among the *Baptists*, in and about *London*, engaged themselves in this Quarrel, to have defended, or, at least, to have brought fairly off, if it had been possible, their Brother *Hicks*, yet the main Service lay upon *Jeremy Ives*. Who having been an unsuccessful Trader in Cheese, and therein failed more than once, had now for some Time given over that Imployment, and, like a mercenary *Switzer*, undertook to be the Champion for the *Baptists*, and to maintain their Quarrels against all Comers.

His Name was up for a topping Disputant; but indeed, on the best Observation I could make of him, both now and formerly, I could not find him a clean and fair Disputant. He seemed, I confess, well read in the *Falacies of Logick*, and was indeed rather ready, than true and sound, in framing *Syllogisms*. But his chief Art lay in tickling the Humours of rude, unlearned and injudicious Hearers, thereby insinuating himself into their good Opinion, and then bantering his Opponent.

1675. He lived not long after this; but the Impression his crafty, false and frothy Carriage (as well at this Time as before) had made upon my Mind, drew from me, when I heard of his Death, something like an *Epitaph*, in a drolling Stile,

Stile, as himself was wont to use. And thus 1675.
it was.

BEneath this Stone depreſt doth lie,
The Mirrour of *Hypocriſy*,
IVES; whoſe mercenary Tongue
Like a Weather-cock was hung,
And did this, or that Way play,
As *Advantage* led the Way.
If well-hir'd, he would diſpute,
Otherwiſe he wou'd be mute;
But he'd baul nigh half a Day,
If he knew, and lik'd his Pay.
For his Perſon, let it paſs;
Only note, his Face was *Braſs*,
His Heart was like a *Pumice* Stone;
And for *Conſcience*, he had none.
Of *Earth* and *Air* he was compos'd,
With *Water* round about encloſs'd,
But *Earth* in him had greateſt Share,
For queſtionleſs, his Life lay there,
And thence his cankred *Envy* ſprung,
Which poyſon'd both his *Heart* and *Tongue*.
Air made him frothy, light and vain,
And puff't him up with proud Diſdain,

Flouting

1675. *Flouting* and *fleering*, more like a *Stage-Player*,
Than an *Anabaptist* Preacher and Prayer;
Fitter to be a *Mountebank*'s Fool,
Than peep into a *Divinity-School*;
More Tricks he had than *Jack Pudding* by half,
To raise the rude *Multitude* into a Laugh.
Into the *Water* oft he went,
And through the *Water* many sent,
That was, ye know his Element:
The greatest Odds that did appear,
Was this (for ought that I can hear)
That he in *Cold* did others dip,
But did himself *hot Waters* sip.
Sip! said I? Nay, more than so,
Sipping wou'd not serve his Turn;
He did unto *Quaffing* go
('Twas much his Guts he did not burn)
For, if Credit may be given
To Report, he'd fuddle, even
Till he reeled to and fro;
And his Cause he'd never doubt,
If well-soak'd o'er Night in *Stout*.

But,

But, mean while, he muſt not lack 1675.
Brandy, or a Draught of *Sack* ;
One Diſpute wou'd ſhrink a Bottle
Of three Pints, if not a Pottle.
One wou'd think he fetch'd from thence,
All his dreaming *Eloquence*,
And his four-leg'd *Syllogiſms*,
Proving *Breakings* are no *Schiſms*.
Wot ye why? Himſelf *brake* twice;
Say no more, the Point is nice.
But let us now bring back the Sot
Unto his *Aqua-vitæ* Pot,
And obſerve, with ſome Content,
How he fram'd his Argument.
That his Whiſtle he might wet,
The Bottle to his Mouth he ſet,
And, being Maſter of that Art,
Thence he drew the *Major* part,
But left the *Minor* ſtill behind,
Good Reaſon why ; he wanted Wind.
If his Breath wou'd have held out,
He had *Concluſion* drawn, no doubt.
But to't again he went, and thence
He fetch'd a luſty *Conſequence*.

1675. Then finding all his Drink was ſpent,
He thus wound up his Argument;
My Sides are not of Iron, neither
Are my Lungs made of Whit-leather;
If therefore you've not, I have done.
Then, leaping down, * away he run.

The Controverſy which had been raiſed by thoſe cavilling *Baptiſts*, had not been long ended, before another was raiſed by an *Epiſcopal* Prieſt in *Lincolnſhire*, who fearing, as it ſeemed, to loſe ſome of his Hearers to the *Quakers*, wrote a Book, which he miſcalled, *A Friendly Conference between a Miniſter and a Pariſhioner of his inclining to* Quakeriſm. In which, he miſ-ſtated and greatly perverted the *Quakers* Principles, that he might thereby beget in his Pariſhioners an Averſion to them; and that he might abuſe us the more ſecurely, he concealed himſelf, ſending forth his Book without a Name.

1676. This Book coming to my Hand, became my Concern (after I had read it, and conſidered the evil Management, and worſe Deſign thereof) to anſwer it; which I did in a Treatiſe called *Truth prevailing, and detecting Error*; publiſhed in the Year 1676.

My

* *From the Diſpute at* Wheeler-ſtreet, London, *the 16th of* October, 1674.

My Anſwer I divided, according to the ſeve- 1676.
ral Subjects handled in the Conference, into
divers diſtinct Chapters, the laſt of which treated of TITHES.

This being the Prieſts *Delilah*; and that
Chapter of mine pinching them it ſeems in a
tender Part, the Belly, they laid their Heads
together, and with what Speed they could, ſent
forth a diſtinct Reply to the laſt Chapter of
Tithes in mine, under the Title of *The Right of
Tithes aſſerted and proved.* This alſo came forth
without a Name, yet pretended to be written
by another Hand.

Before I had finiſhed my Rejoinder to this,
came forth another, called *A Vindication of the
Friendly Conference*; ſaid to be written by the
Author of the feigned Conference, who was not
yet willing to truſt the World with his Name.
So much of it as related to the Subject I was
then upon, *Tithes*, I took into my Rejoinder to
the *Right of Tithes*, which I publiſhed in the 1678.
Year 1678, with this Title, *The Foundation of
Tithes ſhaken*, &c.

After this, it was a pretty while before I 1680.
heard from either of them again. But at length
came forth a Reply to my laſt, ſuppoſed to be
written by the ſame Hand, who had before
written the *Right of Tithes aſſerted*, &c. but ſtill
without a Name. This latter Book had more
of Art than Argument in it. It was indeed a
Haſh of ill-cook'd *Crambe*, ſet off with as much
Flouriſh as the Author was Maſter of, and
ſwell'd into Bulk by many Quotations; but

1680. thoſe ſo wretchedly miſgiven, miſapplied or perverted, that to a judicious and impartial Reader, I durſt oppoſe my *Foundation of Tithes ſhaken*, to the utmoſt Force that Book has in it. Yet it coming forth at a Time when I was pretty well at Leiſure, I intended a full Refutation thereof; and in order thereunto, had written between forty and fifty Sheets; when other Buſineſs more urgent, intervening, took me off, and detained me from it ſo long, that it was then judged out of Seaſon, and ſo it was laid aſide.

Hitherto the War I had been engag'd in, was in a Sort foreign, with People of other religious Perſwaſions, ſuch as were open and avowed Enemies; but now another Sort of War aroſe, an inteſtine War, raiſed by ſome among ourſelves; ſuch as had once been of us, and yet retained the ſame Profeſſion, and would have been thought to be of us ſtill; but having through ill-grounded Jealouſies, let in Diſcontents, and thereupon fallen into Jangling, chiefly about Church-Diſcipline, they at length brake forth into an open Schiſm, headed by two Northern Men of Name and Note, *John Wilkinſon* and *John Story*. The latter of which, as being the moſt active and popular Man, having gained a conſiderable Intereſt in the *Weſt*, carried the Controverſy with him thither, and there ſpreading it, drew many, too many, to abet him therein.

Among thoſe, *William Rogers* a Merchant of *Briſtol* was not the leaſt, nor leaſt accounted of, by

by himſelf and ſome others. He was a bold 1680.
and an active Man, moderately learned, but immoderately conceited of his own Parts and Abilities, which made him forward to engage, as thinking none would dare to take up the Gauntlet he ſhould caſt down. This high Opinion of himſelf, made him rather a troubleſome than formidable Enemy.

That I may here ſtep over the various Steps, by which he advanced to open Hoſtility (as what I was not actually, or perſonally engaged in:) He in a while arrived to that height of Folly and Wickedneſs, that he wrote and publiſhed a large Book in five Parts, to which he maliciouſly gave for a Title [*The* Chriſtian Quaker *diſtinguiſhed from the Apoſtate and Innovator*] thereby arrogating to himſelf, and thoſe who were of his Party, the topping Stile of *Chriſtian Quaker*; and no leſs impiouſly than uncharitably branding and rejecting all others (even the main Body of Friends) for *Apoſtates* and *Innovators*.

When this Book came abroad, it was not a little (and He, for its Sake) cried up by his injudicious Admirers, whoſe Applauſe ſetting his Head afloat, he came up to *London* at the Time of the Yearly-meeting then following, and at 1681.
the Cloſe thereof, gave Notice in writing to this Effect, *viz. That if any were diſſatisfied with his Book, he was there ready to maintain and defend both it and himſelf againſt all Comers.*

This daring Challenge was neither dreaded nor ſlighted; but an Anſwer forthwith returned

1681. in writing, ſigned by a few Friends, amongſt whom I was one, to let him know, That as many were diſſatisfied with his Book and him, he ſhould not fail (God willing) to be met by the ſixth Hour next Morning, at the Meeting-place at *Devonſhire-houſe*.

Accordingly we met, and continued the Meeting till Noon or after; in which Time he, ſurrounded with thoſe of his own Party, as might abet and aſſiſt him, was ſo fairly foiled and baffled, and ſo fully expoſed, that he was glad to quit the Place, and early next Morning the Town alſo; leaving, in Excuſe for his going ſo abruptly off (and thereby refuſing us another Meeting with him, which we had earneſtly provoked him to) this ſlight Shift, That he had before given Earneſt for his Paſſage in the Stage-coach home, and was not willing to loſe it.

I had before this gotten a Sight of his Book, and procured one for my Uſe on this Occaſion, but I had not Time to read it through: But a while after, Providence caſt another of them into my Hands very unexpectedly; for our dear Friend *George Fox*, paſſing through this Country among Friends, and lying in his Journey at my Houſe, had one of them in his Bags, which he had made ſome marginal Notes upon. For that good Man, like *Julius Cæſar*, willing to improve all Parts of his Time, did uſually, even in his Travels, dictate to his *Amanuenſis* what he would have committed to Writing. I knew not that he had this Book with him, for he had not ſaid any Thing to me of it, till going in the

the Morning into his Chamber, while he was dressing himself, I found it lying on the Table by him. And understanding that he was going but for a few Weeks, to visit Friends in the Meetings hereabouts, and the neighbouring Parts of *Oxford* and *Berkshire*, and so return through this County again; I made bold to ask him, if he would favour me so much, as to leave it with me till his Return, that I might have the Opportunity of reading it through. He consented, and as soon almost as he was gone, I set myself to read it over. But I had not gone far in it, e're, observing the many foul Falshoods, malicious Slanders, gross Perversions and false Doctrines, abounding in it, the Sense thereof inflamed my Breast with a just and holy Indignation against the Work, and that devilish Spirit in which it was brought forth. Wherefore, finding my Spirit raised, and my Understanding divinely opened to refute it, I began the Book again, and reading it with Pen in Hand, answered it paragraphically as I went. And so clear were the Openings I received from the Lord therein, that by the Time my Friend came back, I had gone through the greatest Part of it, and was too far engaged in Spirit, to think of giving over the Work: Wherefore, requesting him to continue the Book a little longer with me, I soon after finished the Answer, which, with Friends Approbation, was printed under the Title of *An Antidote against the Infection of* William Rogers *his Book, miscalled, The* Christian Quaker, &c. This was written in the Year 1682.

1682. But no Anſwer was given to it, (either by him or any other of his Party; though many others were concerned therein, and ſome by Name) ſo far as I have ever heard. Perhaps there might be an Hand of Providence over-ruling them therein, to give me Leiſure to attend ſome other Services, which ſoon after fell upon me.

For it being a ſtormy Time, and Perſecution waxing hot, upon the Conventicle-Act, through the buſy Boldneſs of hungry Informers, who for their own Advantage, did not only themſelves hunt after religious and peaceable Meetings, but drove on the Officers, not only the more inferior and ſubordinate, but, in ſome Places, even the Juſtices alſo, for Fear of Penalties, to hunt with them and for them: I found a Preſſure upon my Spirit to write a ſmall Treatiſe, to inform ſuch Officers how they might ſecure and defend themſelves from being ridden by thoſe malepert Informers, and made their Drudges.

This Treatiſe I called, *A Caution to Conſtables, and other inferior Officers, concerned in the Execution of the Conventicle-Act. With ſome Obſervations thereupon, humbly offered by way of Advice, to ſuch well-meaning and moderate Juſtices of the Peace, as would not willingly ruin their peaceable Neighbours,* &c.

This was thought to have ſome good Service where it came, upon ſuch ſober and moderate Officers, as well Juſtices, as Conſtables, *&c.* as acted rather by Conſtraint than Choice; by incouraging them to ſtand their Ground, with

more

more Courage and Resolution, against the Insults of sawcy Informers.

But whatever Ease it brought to others, it brought me some Trouble, and had like to have brought me into more Danger, had not Providence wrought my Deliverance by an unexpected Way.

For as soon as it came forth in print, which was in the Year 1683, one *William Ayrs* of *Watford* in *Hertfordshire*, a Friend and an Acquaintance of mine (who was both an *Apothecary* and *Barber*) being acquainted with divers of the Gentry in those Parts, and going often to some of their Houses to trim them, took one of these Books with him, when he went to trim Sir *Benjamin Titchborn* of *Rickmansworth*, and presented it to him, supposing he would have taken it kindly, as in like Cases he had formerly done. But it fell out otherwise. For he looking it over after *Ayrs* was gone, and taking it by the wrong Handle, entertained an evil Opinion of it, and of me for it, though he knew me not.

He thereupon communicated both the Book, and his Thoughts upon it, to a neighbouring Justice living in *Rickmansworth*, whose Name was *Thomas Fotherly*; who concurring with him in Judgment, they concluded that I should be taken up and prosecuted for it, as a seditious Book: For a Libel they could not call it, my Name being to it at length.

Wherefore sending for *Ayrs* who had brought the Book, Justice *Titchborn* examined him if *he*

knew

1683. *knew me, and where I dwelt.* Who telling him, *he knew me well, and had been often at my House*; he gave him in charge to give me Notice, that *I should appear before him and the other Justice, at* Rickmansworth *on such a Day*; threatning that *if I did not appear, he himself should be prosecuted for spreading the Book.*

This put *William Ayrs* in a Fright. Over he came in haste with this Message to me, troubled that he should be a Means to bring me into Trouble. But I endeavoured to give him Ease, by assuring him I would not fail (with God's Leave) to appear at the Time and Place appointed, and thereby free him from *Trouble* or *Danger.*

In the Interim I received Advice, by an Express out of *Sussex,* that *Guli Penn,* with whom I had had an intimate Acquaintance and firm Friendship from our very Youths, was very dangerously ill, her Husband being then absent in *Pennsylvania,* and that she had a great Desire to see and speak with me.

This put me to a great Straight, and brought a sore Exercise on my Mind. I was divided betwixt Honour and Friendship. I had engaged my Word to appear before the Justices; which to omit, would bring Dishonour on me and my Profession. To stay till that Time was come and past, might probably prove (if I should then be left at Liberty) too late to answer her Desire and satisfy Friendship.

After some little Deliberation, I resolv'd, as the best Expedient to answer both Ends, to go

over

over next Morning to the Juſtices, and lay my 1683.
Straight before them, and try if I could procure from them a Reſpite of my Appearance before them, until I had been in *Suſſex*, and paid the Duty of Friendſhip to my ſick Friend. Which I had the more Hopes to obtain, becauſe I knew thoſe Juſtices had a great Reſpect for *Guli*. For when *William Penn* and ſhe were firſt married, they lived for ſome Years at *Rickmanſworth*, in which Time they contracted a neighbourly Friendſhip with both theſe Juſtices and theirs, who ever after retained a kind Regard for them both.

Early therefore in the Morning I rode over. But being wholly a Stranger to the Juſtices, I went firſt to *Watford*, that I might take *Ayrs* along with me, who ſuppoſed himſelf to have ſome Intereſt in Juſtice *Titchborn*; and when I came there, underſtanding that another Friend of that Town, whoſe Name was *John Wells*, was well acquainted with the other Juſtice *Fotherly*; having imparted to them the Occaſion of my coming, I took them both with me and haſted back to *Rickmanſworth*. Where having put our Horſes up at an Inn, and leaving *William Ayrs* (who was a Stranger to *Fotherly*) there, I went with *John Wells* to *Fotherly*'s Houſe; and being brought into a fair Hall, I tarried there while *Wells* went into the Parlour to him, and having acquainted him that I was there, and deſired to ſpeak with him, brought him to me with Severity in his Countenance.

1683. After he had asked me (in a Tone which spake Displeasure) *what I had to say to him?* I told him, I came to wait on him upon an Intimation given me, that he had something to say to me: He thereupon, plucking my Book out of his Pocket, asked me, *If I owned myself to be the Author of that Book?* I told him, If he pleased to let me look into it, if it were mine, I would not deny it. He thereupon giving it into my Hand, when I had turned over the Leaves, and look'd it through, finding it to be as it came from the Press, I told him, I wrote the Book, and would own it, all but the Errors of the Press. Whereupon he, looking sternly on me, answered, *Your own Errors you should have said.*

Having Innocency on my Side, I was not at all daunted at either his Speech or Looks; but feeling the Lord present with me, I replied, I know there are Errors of the Press in it, and therefore I excepted them; but I do not know there is any Error of mine in it, and therefore cannot except them. But, added I, if thou pleasest to shew me any Error of mine in it, I shall readily both acknowledge and retract it. And thereupon I desired him to give me an Instance, in any one Passage in that Book, wherein he thought I had erred. He said, *he needed not go to Particulars; but charge me with the general Contents of the whole Book.* I replied, that such a Charge would be too general for me to give a particular Answer to; but if he would assign me any particular Passage, or Sentence in the Book, wherein he apprehended the Ground of Offence

Offence to lie; when I should have opened the 1683.
Terms, and explained my Meaning therein, he might perhaps find Cause to change his Mind, and entertain a better Opinion both of the Book and me. And therefore I again intreated him, to let me know what particular Passage or Passages had given him an Offence. He told me, *I needed not to be in so much Haste for that; I might have it timely enough, if not too soon: But this*, said he, *is not the Day appointed for your Hearing, and therefore*, added he, *what, I pray, made you in such Haste to come now?* I told him, I hoped he would not take it for an Argument of Guilt, that I came before I was sent for, and offered myself to my Purgation before the Time appointed. And this I spake with somewhat a brisker Air, which had so much Influence on him, as to bring a somewhat softer Air over his Countenance.

Then going on, I told him I had a particular Occasion which induced me to come now, which was, That I received Advice last Night, by an Express out of *Sussex*, that *William Penn*'s Wife (with whom I had had an intimate Acquaintance, and strict Friendship, *ab ipsis fere Incunabilis*, at least, *a teneris Unguiculis*) lay now there very ill, not without great Danger, in the Apprehension of those about her, of her Life; and that she had exprest her Desire that I would come to her, as soon as I could; the rather, for that her Husband was absent in *America*. That this had brought a great Straight upon me, being divided between

1683. between Friendſhip and Duty, willing to viſit my Friend in her Ilneſs, which the Nature and Law of Friendſhip required; yet unwilling to omit my Duty, by failing of my Appearance before him and the other Juſtice, according to their Command and my Promiſe, leſt I ſhould thereby ſubject, not my own Reputation only, but the Reputation of my religious Profeſſion, to the Suſpicion of Guilt, and Cenſure of willingly ſhunning a Trial. To prevent which I had choſen to anticipate the Time, and come now, to ſee if I could give them Satisfaction, in what they had to object againſt me, and thereupon being diſmiſt, purſue my Journey into *Suſſex*; or if by them detained, to ſubmit to Providence, and by an Expreſs to acquaint my Friend therewith, both to free her from an Expectation of my coming, and myſelf from any Imputation of Neglect.

While I thus delivered myſelf, I obſerved a ſenſible Alteration in the Juſtice; and when I had done ſpeaking, he firſt ſaid, *He was very ſorry for Madam* Penn's *Ilneſs*; of whoſe Virtue and Worth he ſpake very highly, yet not more than was her Due: Then he told me, *That, for her Sake, he would do what he could to further my Viſit to her*; *But,* ſaid he, *I am but one, and of myſelf can do nothing in it*; *therefore you muſt go to Sir* Benjamin Tichborn, *and, if he be at home, ſee if you can prevail with him to meet me, that we may conſider of it.*

But I can aſſure you, added he, *the Matter which will be laid to your Charge concerning your Book,*

Book, is of greater Importance than you ſeem to 1683.
think it. For your Book has been laid before the
KING *and* Council; *and the Earl of* Bridgewater,
who is one of the Council, *hath thereupon given us*
Command to examine you about it, and ſecure you.

I wiſh, ſaid I, I could ſpeak with the Earl myſelf; for I make no Doubt but to acquit myſelf unto him: And, added I, if thou pleaſeſt to give me thy Letter to him, I will wait upon him with it forthwith. For although I know, continued I, that he hath no Favour for any of my Perſwaſion, yet knowing myſelf to be wholly innocent in this matter, I can with Confidence appear before him, or even before the KING in Council.

Well, ſaid he, *I ſee you are confident; but for all that, let me tell you, how good ſoever your Intention was, you timed the publiſhing of your Book very unluckily; for you cannot be ignorant, that there is a very dangerous Plot lately diſcovered, contrived by the* Diſſenters, *againſt the* Government *and* His Majeſty's *Life.* (This was the *Rye-Plot,* then newly broke forth, and laid upon the *Preſbyterians:*) *And for you,* added he, *to publiſh a Book, juſt at that Juncture of Time, to diſcourage the Magiſtrates and other Officers, from putting in Execution thoſe Laws which were made to ſuppreſs their Meetings, looks, I muſt tell you, but with a ſcurvy Countenance upon you.*

If, replied I, with ſomewhat a pleaſanter Air, there was any miſ-timing in the Caſe, it muſt lie on the Part of thoſe Plotters, for timing the breaking forth of their Plot while my Book

was

1683. was a printing; for I can bring very good Proof, that my Book was in the Preſs, and well-nigh wrought off, before any Man talked or knew of a Plot, but thoſe who were in it.

Here our Diſcourſe ended, and I taking, for the Preſent my Leave of him, went to my Horſe, and changing my Companion, rode to Juſtice *Tichborn*'s, having with me *William Ayrs*, who was beſt acquainted with him, and who had caſually brought this Trouble on me.

When he had introduced me to *Titchborn*, I gave him a like Account of the Occaſion of my coming at that Time, as I had before given to the other Juſtice. And both he, and his Lady who was preſent, expreſt much Concern for *Guli Penn*'s Ilneſs.

I found this Man to be of quite another Temper than Juſtice *Fotherly*; for this Man was ſmooth, ſoft and oily, whereas the other was rather rough, ſevere and ſharp. Yet at the winding up, I found *Fotherly* my trueſt Friend.

When I had told Sir *Benjamin Tichborn*, that I came from Juſtice *Fotherly*, and requeſted him to give him a Meeting to conſider of my Buſineſs; he readily, without any Heſitation, told me he would go with me to *Rickmanſworth* (from which his Houſe was diſtant about a Mile) and calling for his Horſes, mounted immediately, and to *Rickmanſworth* we rode.

After they had been a little while together, I was called in before them; and in the firſt place they examined me, *What was my Intention and Deſign in writing that Book?* I told them the

introductory

introductory Part of it gave a plain Account of 1683.
it, *viz.* "That it was to get Eaſe from the Pe-
"nalties of a *ſevere Law*, often executed with "too great a Severity by unſkilful Officers, who "were driven on beyond the Bounds of their "Duty, by the impetuous Threats of a Sort "of inſolent Fellows (as needy as greedy) who, "for their own Advantage, ſought our Ruin." To prevent which, was the Deſign and Drift of that Book, by acquainting ſuch Officers how they might ſafely demean themſelves, in the Execution of their Offices, towards their honeſt and peaceable Neighbours, without ruining either their Neighbours or themſelves, to enrich ſome of the worſt of Men. And that I humbly conceived, it was neither unlawful nor unreaſonable for a Sufferer to do this, ſo long as it was done in a fair, ſober and peaceable Way.

They then put me in mind of the Plot; told me *It was a troubleſome and dangerous Time, and my Book might be conſtrued to import Sedition, in diſcouraging the Officers from putting the Laws in Execution, as by Law and by their Oath they were bound.* And in fine brought it to this Iſſue, *That they were directed to ſecure me, by a Commitment to Priſon until the Aſſize, at which I ſhould receive a further Charge than they were provided now to give me; but becauſe they were deſirous to forward my Viſit to Madam* Penn, *they told me they would admit me to Bail, and therefore if I would enter a Recognizance, with ſufficient Sureties, for my Appearance at the next Aſſize, they would leave me at Liberty to go on my Journey.*

1683. I told them, I could not do it. They ſaid, *They would give me as little Trouble as they could, and therefore they would not put me to ſeek Bail; but would accept thoſe two Friends of mine, who were then preſent, to be bound with me for my Appearance.*

I let them know, my Straight lay not in the Difficulty of procuring Sureties, for I did ſuppoſe myſelf to have ſufficient Acquaintance, and Credit in that Place, if on ſuch an Occaſion I could be free to uſe it; but, as I knew myſelf to be an innocent Man, I had not Satisfaction in myſelf, to deſire others to be bound for me, nor to enter myſelf into a Recognizance; that carrying in it, to my Apprehenſion, a Reflection on my Innocency, and the Reputation of my *Chriſtian* Profeſſion.

Here we ſtuck and ſtruggled about this a pretty while, till at length finding me fixed in my Judgment, and reſolved rather to go to Priſon than give Bail, they aſk'd me, *If I was againſt appearing, or only againſt being bound with Sureties to appear.* I told them I was not againſt appearing; which as I could not avoid, if I would, ſo I would not if I might; but was ready and willing to appear if required, to anſwer whatſoever ſhould be charged againſt me. But in any Caſe of a religious Nature, or wherein my *Chriſtian* Profeſſion was concerned, which I took this Caſe to be, I could not yield to give any other or further Security than my Word, or Promiſe, as a *Chriſtian.*

They,

They, unwilling to commit me, took hold of that, and aſk'd, *If I would promiſe to appear.* I anſwer'd, Yes; with due Limitations. *What do you mean by due Limitations,* ſaid they. I mean, replied I, if I am not diſabled, or prevented by Sickneſs or Impriſonment. For, added I, as you alledge that it is a troubleſome Time, I perhaps may find it ſo. I may, for ought I know, be ſeized and impriſoned elſewhere, on the ſame Account for which I now ſtand here before you, and if I ſhould, how then could I appear at the Aſſize in this County? *Oh,* ſaid they, *theſe are due Limitations indeed! Sickneſs or Impriſonment are lawful Excuſes, and if either of theſe befal you, we ſhall not expect your Appearance here; but then you muſt certify us, that you are ſo diſabled by Sickneſs or Reſtraint.*

But, ſaid I, how ſhall I know when and where I ſhall wait upon you again after my Return from *Suſſex? You need not,* ſaid they, *trouble yourſelf about that; we will take Care to give you Notice of both Time and Place, and till you hear from us, you may diſpoſe yourſelf as you pleaſe.*

Well then, ſaid I, I do promiſe you, that when I ſhall have received from you a freſh Command to appear before you, I will (if the Lord permit me Life, Health and Liberty) appear when and where you ſhall appoint.

It is enough, ſaid they, *we will take your Word:* And, deſiring me to give their hearty Reſpects and Service to Madam *Penn,* they diſ-

1683 mist me with their good Wishes for a good Journey.

I was sensible, that in this they had dealt very favourably and kindly with me, therefore I could not but acknowledge to them the Sense I had thereof. Which done, I took Leave of them, and mounting, returned home with what Haste I could, to let my Wife know how I had sped. And having given her a summary Account of the Business, I took Horse again, and went so far that Evening towards *Worminghurst*, that I got thither pretty early next Morning, and, to my great Satisfaction, found my Friend in an hopeful Way towards a Recovery.

I staid some Days with her; and then finding her Ilness wear daily off, and some other Friends being come from *London* to visit her, I (mindful of my Engagement to the Justices, and unwilling, by too long an Absence, to give them Occasion to suspect I was willing to avoid their Summons) leaving those other Friends to bear her Company longer, took my Leave of her and them, and set my Face homewards, carrying with me the welcome Account of my Friend's Recovery.

Being returned home, I waited in daily Expectation of a Command from the Justices to appear again before them; but none came. I spake with those Friends who had been with me when I was before them, and they said, *They had heard nothing of it from them, although they had since been in Company with them.* At length

length the Aſſize came; but no Notice was given 1683.
to me, that I ſhould appear there; in fine, they never troubled themſelves nor me any further about it.

Thus was a Cloud, that look'd black and threatned a great Storm, blown gently over by a providential Breath, which I could not but, with a thankful Mind, acknowledge to the all-great, all-good, all-wiſe Diſpoſer, in whoſe Hand, and at whoſe Command, the Hearts of all Men, even the greateſt, are, and who turns their Counſels, diſappoints their Purpoſes, and defeats their Deſigns and Contrivances, as He pleaſes. For if my dear Friend *Guli Penn* had not fallen ſick, if I had not thereupon been ſent for to her, I had not prevented the Time of my Appearance, but had appeared on the Day appointed: And, as I afterwards underſtood, that was the Day appointed for the Appearance of a great many Perſons, of the diſſenting Party in that Side of the County, who were to be taken up and ſecured, on the Account of the aforementioned Plot, which had been caſt upon the *Preſbyterians.* So that if I had then appeared, with and amongſt them, I had in all likelihood, been ſent to Jail with them for Company, and that under the Imputation of a Plotter; than which, nothing was more contrary to my Profeſſion and Inclination.

But though I came off ſo eaſy, it fared not ſo well with others; for the Storm increaſing, many Friends in divers Parts, both of City and

 Country,

1683. Country, suffered greatly; the Sense whereof did deeply affect me, and the more, for that I observed the Magistrates, not thinking the Laws, which had been made against us severe enough, perverted the Law in order to punish us. For calling our peaceable Meetings *Riots* (which in the legal Notion of the Word [*Riot*] is a *Contradiction in Terms)* they indicted our Friends as *Rioters* for only sitting in a Meeting, though nothing was there either said or done by them, and then set Fines on them at pleasure.

This I knew to be not only against *Right* and *Justice*, but even against *Law*; and it troubled me to think that we should be made to suffer not only by Laws made directly against us, but even by Laws that did not at all concern us. Nor was it long before I had Occasion offered more throughly to consider this Matter.

For a Justice of the Peace in this County, who was called Sir *Dennis Hampson* of *Taplow*, breaking in with a Party of Horse upon a little Meeting near *Wooburn*, in his Neighbourhood, the 1st of the fifth Month 1683, sent most of the Men, to the Number of twenty three whom he found there, to *Aylesbury* Prison, tho' most of them were poor Men who lived by their Labour; and not going himself to the next Quarter-Sessions at *Buckingham*, on the 12th of the same Month, sent his Clerk with Direction, *That they should be indicted for a Riot.* Whither the Prisoners were carried and indicted accordingly, and being pressed by the Court to traverse

verse and give Bail, they moved to be tried forthwith, but that was denied them. And they, giving in writing the Reason of their refusing Bail and Fees, were remanded to Prison till next Quarter-Sessions; but *William Woodhouse* was again bailed, (as he had been before) and *William Mason* and *John Reeve*, who not being Friends, but casually taken at that Meeting, entred Recognizance as the Court desired, and so were released till next Sessions. Before which Time *Mason* died, and *Reeve* being sick, appeared not, but got himself taken off. And in the eighth Month following, the twenty one Prisoners that remained were brought to Trial, a Jury was found, who brought in a pretended Verdict, that they were *Guilty of a Riot*, for only sitting peaceably together, without Word or Action; and tho' there was no Proclamation made, nor they required to depart: But one of the Jurymen afterwards did confess, *he knew not what a Riot was*; yet the Prisoners were fined a Noble a-piece, and re-committed to Prison *during Life* (a hard Sentence) or the *King's Pleasure*, or until they should *pay the said Fines*. *William Woodhouse* was forthwith discharged, by his Kinsman's paying the Fine and Fees for him. *Thomas Dell* and *Edward Moore* also, by other People of the World paying their Fines and Fees for them; and shortly after *Stephen Pewsey*, by the Town and Parish where he lived, for fear his Wife and Children should become a Charge upon them. The other seven-

1683. teen remained Prisoners till King JAMES's Proclamation of Pardon; whose Names were *Thomas and William Sexton*, *Timothy Child*, *Robert Moor*, *Richard James*, *William* and *Robert Aldridge*, *John Ellis*, *George Salter*, *John Smith*, *William Tanner*, *William Batchelor*, *John Dolbin*, *Andrew Brothers*, *Richard Baldwin*, *John Jennings* and *Robert Austin*.

A SUPPLE-

A

SUPPLEMENT.

BEING

A Continuation of the History of the Life of THOMAS ELLWOOD; *giving Account in particular of his* Books *and* Writings.

OUR dear Friend *Thomas Ellwood*, for whom we cannot but have an honorable Eſteem for his Service in the Church, having written an hiſtorical Account of Part of his Life, well worth the Knowledge of Poſterity, ſo far as it goes, *viz.* to the Year 1683, and there left off. Whether he writ any further, or whether ever he deſigned it, or for what Reaſon he did not proceed, is uncertain; but ſo it is, that no more of it can be found at preſent, which is to be lamented, he being a Man ſo eminent many Ways, that any Part of it ſhould be loſt. In Conſideration whereof, it aroſe in my Heart to write ſomething in Order to ſupply the Deficiency thereof, many Things occurring to my Mind, which it is pity ſhould be omitted. Therefore for the Reſpect I bore him, and owe to his Memory, being acquainted with him for more than the laſt twenty Years of his Life, I ſhall endeavour to make up that Defect as far as I am capable of; tho' far ſhort of what himſelf might

might have done, by giving an Account of ſome of the moſt material Paſſages of the remaining Part of his Life, and ſuch Memorials of him and his Works, as came to my Hands; which I ſhall ſet down with as much Brevity and Plainneſs as I can, in Sincerity to him, and the Truth he profeſſed and adorned. Particularly, of his Labours, Writings, Sufferings and End, from the Time he left off.

But firſt I muſt look back a little, to give ſome additional Account of ſome Paſſages in relation to his Anſwers to the Prieſts about Tithes, for the Reader's Information and Satisfaction, which every Body may not know, to prevent Miſapprehenſions in the Caſe.

In the Year 1676 he anſwered a nameleſs Book, miſcalled, *A friendly Conference between a Miniſter, and a Pariſhioner of his inclining to* Quakeriſm, in a Book intituled *Truth prevailing and detecting Error*; which he divided into nine Chapters, according to the various Subjects treated of (wherein that nameleſs Author had endeavoured to miſrepreſent us) the laſt of which was of Tithes. 'This (*to uſe his own Words*) 'pinching the Prieſts in a tender Part, the *Belly*, '(as *Eraſmus* wittily ſaid *Luther* did the Monks) 'made them beſtir themſelves, and lay their 'Heads together, to conſider what was to be 'done.' After divers Debates, and much Conſultation (as he was informed) about it, it was at laſt reſolved to anſwer that firſt, which tho' the laſt Chapter in his Book, yet having the firſt and chiefeſt Place in the Prieſts Minds and Affections,

Preface to Foundation of Tithes ſhaken, Pag. 1, 2.

fections, the Priests *Delilah*; the *very Darling and Minion of the Clergy* (says *T. Ellwood*) the *Oil by which their Lamp is nourished*; the *Pay by which their Army is maintained* (as the Priest confesses) and to take away Tithes, would be to *stop the Oil that nourishes the Lamp, and force them to disband for want of Pay*. This being, I say, their chiefest Concern, and lying nearest at Heart, obtain'd from them the first and chiefest Defence; which at length came forth by a nameless Author also, in a Book intituled, *The Right of Tithes asserted and proved.* To which *T. Ellwood* reply'd in 1678, in a large Book intituled, *The Foundation of Tithes shaken, and the four principal Posts (of* Divine Institution, Primitive Practice, Voluntary Donation *and* Positive Laws) *on which the nameless Author of the said Book had set his pretended Right to* Tithes, *removed.* Tracing them all along from the *Patriarchs* to the Time of the *Law*; shewing the Design and Use of them under it, and how they were abolished by the Coming and Suffering of Christ in the Flesh; and how they came to be set up again in the Declension of the Church, by *Popish* Kings and Councils, in the Night of Apostacy, for superstitious and idolatrous Ends and Uses, contrary to the Gospel Dispensation, and consequently not obligatory on *Christians*, by any *divine Right*, to pay in this Gospel Day; answering all the Objections and Pretences, which were brought by that Author for them, from the four forementioned Topicks.

Introduction: Page 3. Right of Tithes. p. 13.

To this Book of *T. Ellwood*'s, there was a pretended Anſwer put forth two Years after, ſuppoſed by the Author of the former, but nameleſs ſtill; the Author not daring to own his Work with his Name, (though ſince called *Combers)* intituled, *The Right of* Tithes *re-aſſerted*; wherein the Proofs from the four former Points are ſaid to be further *ſtrengthened and vindicated, eſpecially from the Objections taken out of Mr.* Selden's *Hiſtory of Tithes.* As if it was chiefly deſigned againſt *John Selden*; *T. Ellwood*'s Name, or Book, not being ſo much as mentioned in the Title-page, though often in the Book; as if it was however deſigned as an Anſwer to him: Which therefore *T. Ellwood* (though not intituled to it) took in hand to rejoin to, and had begun and made ſome conſiderable Progreſs in it; but before he had gone through, or finiſhed it, ſome other Occaſions falling in his Way (of which hereafter) it was laid by and never finiſhed; though he had writ, as he told me, near ſixty Sheets (though I find but forty-ſix among his Papers; but theſe, with his Notes and Quotations will make near ſixty) for he had collected a vaſt Number of Materials out of Authors, in order thereto, as appears by his Papers, which I have ſince ſeen. For thus it was; That ſome of the Prieſts Party, vaunting that this ſecond Book of the Prieſts was not anſwered, I took Occaſion once at *London*, in the Year 1692, to ſpeak to him about it; and he told me, *That the Subſtance of the Prieſts Arguments, in this ſecond Book, were anſwered*

answered in his former, [The Foundation of Tithes shaken] *only some new Quotations, which he had brought; and that was what he chiefly designed to deal with the Priest about, to examine and clear, by adding some new ones also; but that he never expected to have the last Word with the Priests about* Tithes, *which their Interest lay so much in, that they would never be satisfied; but always be cavilling about some way or other, how little soever it was to the Purpose; and some other Services taking him off* (as aforesaid) *he laid it by.* Which I mention to satisfy any who may question in their Minds, Why it was never answered, or at least gone through? And this is the Reason why I resumed this Matter.

'In handling the Argument of Tithes (says he, in a Paper found among his *Manuscripts*, as an Introduction to his said intended Answer) 'I write with this Disadvantage; That I encounter a numerous Party and Order of Men, 'with whom Interest is far more prevalent than 'Truth; whose Profit will not permit them to 'yield to Reason; whose Advantage will not 'suffer them to acknowledge the plainest Demonstration; their Gain as apparently lying in 'that which I oppose, as *Demetrius*'s, and his 'Fellow-craftsmen the *Silversmiths* of *Ephesus*, 'did in that which the Apostle preached against, '*Acts* xix. 25, 26. Hence is it that they bend 'all their Strength, and employ their utmost 'Force to maintain this Point, by which they 'are maintained; and like those *Shrine-makers* 'of old, they endeavour to carry it by Noise

'and

'and Clamour, instead of Truth and Reason. 'Nor do they regard what they say, how false 'soever; or whom they bespatter, how unde-'servedly soever, in order to the upholding 'their adored *Diana*, and enjoying their most 'beloved *Delilah*, TITHES. My present 'Adversary is not ashamed to say (pag. 1, 2.) '*That I and my fellow quaking Speakers* (as he 'reproachfully calls us) *have our Gain by railing 'against Tithes.* A Charge so apparently and 'ridiculously false, that it needs no more than 'its own Malice and Folly to detect it. With 'equal Reason might *Demetrius* have charged 'St. *Paul*, that he and his Brethren had their 'Gain by impugning the idolatrous Worship 'of *Diana*.

'*Sacriledge* and *Idolatry*, the Priests say, *are 'Sins near of kin*; but *Covetousness* and the '*Clergy* are perhaps nearer. The great Outcry 'against *Sacriledge* is made for the most part by 'Idolaters and false Ministers, who, as they are 'most greedy and crafty to get, so are they most 'solicitous and careful to keep, most enraged 'and clamorous when they come to lose their 'unjustly acquired Gains. Thus was it with 'the *Popish* Clergy, after they had gull'd the 'People, by a religious Cheat, of a great Part 'of their Substance, they laboured to terrify 'them by the Name of *Sacriledge*, from at-'tempting to recover that which had been so 'fraudulently gotten from them; and doubtless 'the *English* Clergy, as they derive [in chief 'part] the Maintenance they possess from their

'Predecessors

'Predeceſſors the *Popiſh* Clergy, from whom
'they received their Prieſthood, have therewith
'alſo taken up from them their old Cry of *Sa-*
criledge, with which, as a Bugbear, they
'would ſcare all from attempting to diſcover
'the Cheat. But the legal Alienation of a great
'Part of thoſe ſurreptitious Acquiſitions of the
'Clergy, begun in *HENRY* the Eighth's Time,
'carried on in *EDWARD* the Sixth's, and
'compleated in Queen *ELIZABETH*'s,
'(of theſe three, the two laſt were *Proteſtant*
'Princes) hath abated the Edge of that *clerical*
'Weapon, and ſatisfied the diſ-intereſted Part
'of the Nation, that the Word [*Sacriledge*] in
'this Caſe, is but like a Scare-crow, eſpecially
'when uſed by the Prieſts for their own Profit,
'as moſt commonly it is; for though they pre-
'tend the Maintenance of *God's Worſhip*, yet it
'is their own Maintenance they intend. And
'herein *Demetrius* and they moſt patly agree;
'for he alſo urged (as the moſt ſpecious Pre-
'tence, and which was moſt likely to impreſs
'the People) the Danger leſt, by *Paul*'s preach-
'ing, *the Temple of the great Goddeſs* Diana
'*ſhould be deſpiſed, and her Magnificence deſtroyed,*
'Acts xix. 27. Whereas the great Inducement
'to him for ſtirring, was the Danger leſt his
'Craft ſhould be ſet at nought, and he ſhould
'thereby loſe the Gains he made by *Diana*'s
'Temple, Verſ. 25, 27. Do the Prieſts now
'cry out againſt *Sacriledge*? So did *Demetrius*
'and his Craftſmen then. Did they cloak their
'private Intereſt with a ſeeming Regard and
'Care

'Care for the *Temple and Magnificence of their* '*Goddeſs* Diana? So do the Prieſts theirs now, 'with a Pretence of Zeal for the *Worſhip of* '*God.* Did they in their Fury take no Notice 'of the Magiſtrates nor Laws of their Country? 'So neither do many of the Prieſts now, who 'without Regard to Law or Magiſtrates, run fu'riouſly and tumultuouſly into their Neighbours 'Grounds, with their Servants and Teams, and 'forcibly and arbitrarily take and carry away 'their Corn and Hay, when, where, and in 'what Quantity they pleaſe. Will the Prieſts 'alledge, that notwithſtanding theſe irregular 'Practices, yet they have the Laws and Magi'ſtrates on their Sides? So had *Demetrius* and 'his Company too, while the good Apoſtle, not 'backt by Laws, nor countenanced by Magi'ſtracy, was yet enabled by divine Aſſiſtance, 'to ſtand the Shock of all their Rage and Fury, 'and boldly to teſtify againſt that which was 'corrupt and naught, altho' it had the Favour 'and Support of a Law and Magiſtracy too: 'And indeed, ſo apt is the Compariſon in moſt 'Reſpects, between thoſe *Shrine-makers* and 'theſe *Tithe-takers*, that my Adverſary in vain 'labours to retort it; for even the very Parti'culars he inſtances to caſt it upon me, fix it 'the more firmly on the Head of himſelf and 'his own Party.

'Nor is he leſs put to it, to avoid the Force 'of his own unwary Expreſſions of the *Oil for* '*the Lamp*, and *Pay for the Soldier*; whereby 'he hath diſcovered, that he and his Brethren are

'meer

‘ meer mercenary Men; whose Lamp will burn ‘ no longer than it is fed with the *Oil of Tithes.* ‘ This is one of the *Arcana Cleri*, a Secret (it ‘ seems) that should not have been divulged. ‘ But Children, and he knows who besides, are ‘ said to tell true. And he having inconside- ‘ rately blab'd it out, his chief Care and Art is ‘ now how to palliate, extenuate and mince the ‘ Matter, and varnish it over with some kind ‘ of Flourish, that the Ground of it may not be ‘ seen; but this he does so weakly, and lays his ‘ Colour so thin, that even the weakest Eye may ‘ easily see through it. The mention I made ‘ of these Passages in my former Book, he calls ‘ *tedious and nauseous Repetitions*; and tedious ‘ no doubt, and nauseous it is to him and his ‘ Brethren, to see the false Foundation of their ‘ Ministry so openly exposed: But so little do I ‘ fear those Repetitions being nauseous or tedious ‘ to the indifferent Reader, that upon this Oc- ‘ casion I desire him to peruse them again, in ‘ the 6, 7, 8 and 9 Pages of my former Book.

‘ *From Tithes being the Oil to their Lamp,* ‘ *and Pay to their Army*, he says, *I draw (as I* ‘ *imagine) a cutting Consequence*, viz. *That their* ‘ *Lamps will not burn without Oil, nor they fight* ‘ *without Pay.* This *cutting Consequence* (as he ‘ calls it) he touches as tenderly as if he was ‘ afraid it would cut his Fingers, though he ‘ well knew, that in the wording of it, he had ‘ taken off its Edge as much as he could: For ‘ if my Consequence had been only, that their ‘ *Lamps will not burn without Oil*, it would not 'then have been ſo keen. He might then have 'replied, *Whoſe will? Can any Lamp burn without Oil?* No ſure: Every *Lamp* muſt have '*Oil*; but the *Oil* ſhould be ſuitable to the '*Lamp*; an *outward Lamp* ſhould have *outward* '*Oil*, an *inward Lamp*, *inward Oil*. Now they 'pretending their Miniſtry to be a *ſpiritual* '*Lamp*, a *religious Lamp* (as the true Miniſtry 'indeed is, and is and can be nouriſhed only by 'the *ſpiritual heavenly Oil* of the *divine eternal* '*Word*; and yet confeſſing *Tithes to be the* '*Oil that nouriſhes their Miniſterial Lamp, and* '*without which their Lamp will not burn*: This 'plainly ſhews their Lamp is not *ſpiritual*, nor 'their *Miniſtry* what they pretend, &c.'

By this we may judge, *Ex pede Herculem*, of the Prieſts Performance, and *T. Ellwood*'s Anſwer, had he gone through and finiſhed it; which yet I hope, ſo far as he hath gone, may one Time or other ſee the Light, being well worth the Peruſal as it is; and had he finiſhed it, I am ſatisfied it would have been a very ſerviceable Piece; no Hand, in my Judgment, being more capable of ſuch a Performance. But he had, as I ſaid, ſome other Services on his Hands to divert him; of which, his Anſwer to *William Rogers*'s great Book aforeſaid, in 1682, intituled, *An Antidote againſt the Infection of* William Roger'*s Book, miſcalled the* Chriſtian Quaker, in five Parts, ſoon after, no doubt was one, containing above thirty Sheets: In which he anſwered him Chapter by Chapter, and almoſt Paragraph by Paragraph, in Relation to Church

Church Government, and the good Order of Truth eſtabliſhed amongſt us; and alſo as to moſt of the Principles of Truth, which the ſaid *W. Rogers*, in one Part of his Work, had endeavoured to pervert to his own Ends. A laborious Work it was, and difficult Taſk to go through ſo evenly as he hath done; and though it is Controverſy, yet pleaſant to read. As alſo his *Caution to Conſtables, and other inferior Officers, concerning the Execution of the Conventicle-Act. With ſome Obſervations thereupon. Humbly offered, by way of Advice, to ſuch well-meaning and moderate Juſtices of the Peace, as would not willingly ruin their peaceable Nighbours*, &c. Which is mentioned in his own Account.

And now to come to the Time where he 1683. breaks off his own Relation, and to carry it on, in ſome meaſure, though far ſhort and inferior to what his own Hand could have done: For it cannot be expected, that any one can write another Man's Life like himſelf, there being many Paſſages, publick and private, outward and inward, even as to the Frame of his own Mind and Condition between God and his own Soul, which, as *No Man knoweth the Things of a Man, ſave the Spirit of a Man which is in him*; ſo none can relate but himſelf, or like himſelf: For as the Wiſeman ſays, *The Heart knoweth his own Bitterneſs, and the Stranger cannot intermeddle with his Joy.* But what occurs from my own Knowledge, or from his Books and Papers, pertinent to the Caſe in hand, ſhall faithfully be related.

1683. Therefore to resume the Thread of his Discourse, and begin where he leaves off. He intimates at the Close of his own Account, that the Magistrates not thinking the Laws made against us, *viz.* the *Conventicle-Act*, &c. severe enough, perverted the Law by making our peaceable Meetings *Riots*, and indicting our Friends as *Rioters*, that they might fine at Pleasure; which he knew to be contrary to Law and Justice: Nor was it long, says he, before he had Occasion offered more throughly to consider this matter (*viz.* the breaking up of the Meeting near *Wooburn* by Justice *Hampson*; sending Friends to Prison, and indicting them for a *Riot*;) which shews he design'd to write a Book on that Subject, though he doth not mention it; and accordingly did this Year, after the *Caution to Constables*, &c. as aforesaid. This he called *A Discourse concerning* Riots: *Occasioned by some of the People called* Quakers *being indicted for* a Riot, *&c.* Of which he gives, by way of Preface, this further Account. 'The Proceedings of late in City and Country, against some 'of the People called *Quakers* for *Riots*, for only 'meeting peaceably together to serve and worship GOD, first put me upon enquiring into 'the Nature of *Riots*: What upon Enquiry I 'have found, I here present to publick View 'for common Benefit, that none through Ignorance may be the Occasion of bringing an unjust Suffering upon an innocent People, and 'thereby Guilt on themselves. I do not pretend 'much Skill in *Law* (a Study and Profession I

'was

'was never bred to) but having ſpent ſome 1683.
'Hours on this Occaſion, in ſearching what the
'Law-books ſay in this Caſe, I hope I may,
'without incurring the Cenſure of Preſump-
'tion, communicate my Gleaning to ſuch of
'my well-meaning Countrymen, as have not
'Leizure or Opportunity to inform themſelves
'otherwiſe. I ſolemnly declare, I have no other
'End or Aim in this Work, than to *do Good*,
'and *prevent Evil:* Which Conſideration, with
'Men of Candour and Ingenuity, will be, I
'hope, a ſufficient Apology for my ſeeming
'Boldneſs in this Undertaking.' And ſo he proceeds to ſet forth what *Riots* are in the Law and Law-books; of which he cites divers (and Scripture too) to ſhew that our peaceable Meetings, which in thoſe Days they uſed to make *Riots*, that they might impriſon and fine us at pleaſure, could not be *Riots*; though through Ignorance or Envy, they were often ſo rendred, (which ſhewed their Injuſtice) ſaying, 'How
'truly I have ſtated the Caſe on the one hand,
'with reſpect to *Riots*, the many Quotations in
'the foregoing Diſcourſe will ſhew. How true
'an Account, on the other hand, I have given
'of our Meetings, the whole Nation, and all
'Nations where we have Meetings, may judge
'upon the whole. My Requeſt is, *ſays he*, that
'all, both Juſtices and Jurors, who have or
'ſhall be concerned in this or the like Caſe,
'will ſeriouſly weigh the matter, and not ſtrain
'the Law beyond its due Extent: *(adding)*
'To oppreſs any by Colour of Law, is the

1683. 'greatest Abuse of Law.' Concluding with a serious Re-capitulation, and Application of the whole, That none for the future might err ignorantly in that Respect; and if any would wilfully, they might be left without Excuse.

About the same Time, or not long after, he writ also *A seasonable Disswasive from* Persecution, *Humbly and modestly, yet with* Christian *Freedom and Plainness of Speech, offered to the Consideration of all concerned therein; on Behalf generally, of all that suffer for Conscience-sake; particularly the People called* Quakers. In the Beginning of which, he defines what *Persecution* is. '*Persecution* (says he) is a Word of so 'harsh a Sound, and so generally distasteful to '*English* Ears, that scarce any of those who are 'most forward and active in that Work, are 'willing to have their Actions called by that 'Name. That none therefore, who have set an 'Hand to that Work, or whose Minds are any 'whit inclining thereto, may, from the Dislike 'they have to the Word [*Persecution*] reject this '*Disswasive* as a Thing wherein they are not 'concerned; I think it needful here to declare, 'what it is I mean by *Persecution*. By *Persecution* then, I intend *a forcing or compelling any, 'by Pains or Penalties, bodily or pecuniary, to 'relinquish or forsake that Exercise of Religion, 'or Way of Worship, which they believe to be the 'right Way of Worship, and the true and acceptable Exercise of Religion, which God hath 'required of them. And to receive, embrace, 'conform to, and perform some other Exercise of*

'*Religion,*

'*Religion, and Way of Worſhip, which they who* 1683.
'*are ſo compelled, are either firmly perſwaded is*
'*not the right, or at leaſt have no Belief that it*
'*is right*. This (in ſhort) is that which I call
'*Perſecution*; and this is that which I diſſwade
'from, whatever other Name the Actors of it
'may pleaſe themſelves in calling it by.'

I. To begin with the firſt of theſe, *viz.* the *forcing, or compelling any to forſake and leave that Exerciſe of Religion, or Way of Worſhip*, &c. The Reaſons by which he endeavours to diſſwade all Men from ſuch an Undertaking, are theſe. [*i. e.* the Heads of them]

'1. You may, for ought you know, be found '*fighting againſt God*: You are not, you cannot 'be, upon your own Principles infallibly ſure, 'that that Way of Worſhip which you thus 'endeavour to force us from, is not the true 'Worſhip of God.—

'2. By endeavouring to force us from that 'Way of Worſhip, which we believe the Lord 'hath led us into and requireth of us, you 'endeavour to force us to make *Shipwreck of* '*Faith*.—

'3. In endeavouring by Force and Cruelty, 'to reſtrain us from worſhipping God, as we 'are fully perſwaded He hath taught us, and 'doth require us, you go out of the Path of 'the Righteous, and tread in the Steps of the 'wicked and ungodly.—

'4. That Exerciſe of Religion which you 'would force us from, is not ſimply of itſelf 'condemned and diſallowed by that Law, by

1683. 'the Severity of which you would force us 'from it.—

'5. In thus eagerly pursuing us, and disturbing our peaceable Meetings, you give yourselves, as well as us, a great deal of needless 'Trouble. — *Refrain from these Men, and let them alone.*—

'6. And lastly, Be pleased to consider, what 'Sort of Agents and Instruments you are fain 'to make Use of (and not seldom are yourselves 'made use of by) to carry on this Work.' *Concluding this Part thus*: 'O never give Cause 'for this *Epitaph* to be written on your Tombs, '*Here lies a Persecutor of the People of God.*'

II. Now for the other Branch of *Persecution*, viz. *The forcing or compelling of any, by Pains or Penalties, to receive, embrace, conform to, and perform some Exercise of Religion, and Way of Worship*, &c. The Reasons by which he endeavours to disswade all Men from such an Undertaking, are these, (*viz.* the Heads.)

'1. In thus imposing your Way of Worship 'upon others, you act quite contrary to Christ 'and his Apostles.—

'2. In thus imposing your Way of Worship 'upon others, you follow the worst of Patterns, '*Nebuchadnezzar* King of *Babylon*, &c.—

'3. In forcing People to your Way of Worship, who have no Belief that it is the right, 'you cause them to sin; for *whatsoever is not of Faith is Sin.*—

'4. In forcing People to your Way of Worship, who have a firm Perswasion and Belief that 'it

'it is not the right, you make Men *Hypocrites* 1683.
'and *Time-servers.*—

'5. By obtruding and inforcing your Religion upon others, you greatly disparage and undervalue it, and give Men the more Ground to suspect and dislike it.—

'6. You break that great Command, which Christ says is the *Law and the Prophets*, viz. *All Things whatsoever ye would that Men should do to you, do ye even so to them*, Mat. vii. 12.—'

All these Reasons are illustrated and backed with Scripture and Reason, concluding with a very close and seasonable Application to our *Persecutors.* A solid serious Discourse it is, if any Arguments had been sufficient to disswade Men from *Persecution*, (of which there was very great about this Time, particularly in *London*, *Bristol*, and divers other Places) the whole being well worth Perusal; and I should have inclined to insert it at large, but that it hath pleased God to incline the Hearts of our Superiors to ease us in that respect, by granting a Toleration to *Protestant Dissenters*; for which we are thankful. These three, *viz.* the *Caution to Constables*, *Discourse of Riots*, and *Disswasive from Persecution*, were all written, or at least printed this Year 1683.

And he acquitted himself so well on these 1684.
Subjects, that one *William Tournay*, to him unknown, sent him a Letter from *London*, taking Notice of the aforesaid *Tracts*, which he was so well pleased with, that he desired his Judgment

1684. on the 23d, 29th and 35th of Queen *ELIZABETH*, in relation to the Proceedings then upon them: To which our Friend *T. Ellwood* return'd him an Anſwer in a large Letter, which is in his *Decades* of Letters, among many others to divers Perſons, and on various Subjects, well worthy the Peruſal, from the Year 1670 down to his latter Times; and if they were publiſhed, would help to ſupply the Deficiency of his own Account of the latter Part of his Life.

About this Time he writ the following POEM, or HYMN of Praiſe to the Lord; which I think well deſerves to be inſerted in this Place; intituled,

COLLAUDEMUS DOMINUM.

COME, let us praiſe the LORD with one Conſent,
All ye, whoſe Hearts to honour Him are bent;
Come, let us of His gracious Dealings tell,
For with us He hath dealt exceeding well;
When Him we did not ſeek, He did us find,
He gave us Sight, when we were dark and blind;
He brought us home, when we were run aſtray,
And ſet our Feet i'th' new and living Way;
When Hunger-pin'd, He gave us heavenly Bread,
And, with the choiceſt Dainties, hath us fed;

He

1684.

He from miſ-leading Guides deliver'd hath,
And led us forward in the juſt Man's Path;
He hath with Strength and Courage us endu'd,
With Zeal for Truth and *Chriſtian* Fortitude;
He Wiſdom from above doth daily give,
To them that in His Truth ſincerely live.
In Battle He hath us preſerv'd thus far,
And made us Victors in the holy War;
Our Enemies He greatly hath ſubdu'd,
His Sword in Blood o'th' ſlain hath been imbru'd;
He hath preſerved from the roaring Lion,
And brought a little Remnant ſafe to *Sion*,
Where, in His Preſence, they ſit down and ſing
Eternal *Hallelu-jah's* to their KING,
Who lives and reigns, and may His Reign extend
Throughout the Univerſe, and have no End.

T. E.

But to proceed:

William Rogers, whom our Author anſwered in the Year 1682, as aforeſaid, though he did not reply to it, or ever attempted it that I have heard of, putting forth a rhiming *Scourge* for *George Whitehead*, againſt whom he bent his moſt inveterate Spleen, and who had alſo anſwered his great Book, falſly called *The* Chriſtian Quaker, in a Book intituled, *The Accuſer of the Brethren caſt down*, &c. *T. Ellwood* writ an Anſwer

1685. Anſwer to his Scourge in Verſe, intituled, *Rogero-Maſtix, A Rod for* William Rogers, *in Return for his rhiming Scourge:* For which he gives the following Reaſon;

To ſuch as aſk, why I in Verſe have writ?
This Anſwer I return, I held it fit,
Verſe ſhou'd in *Verſe* be anſwer'd, *Proſe* in
Proſe,
My Adverſary his own Weapon choſe.
He choſe before in *Proſe* to write, and then
I anſwer'd him in *Proſe*. So now agen,
Since he his Stile from *Proſe* to Verſe *hath*
chang'd,
And in the Muſes Walks *hath boldly rang'd*,
In his own Method him I choſe to treat,
Leſt he ſhould wiſe be in his own Conceit.

And begins thus:

Prov. 26. 5. The Preacher tells us, that *beneath the Sun*
There's no new Thing; for *that which ſhall be*
done,
Hath been before; and *what is now a doing*,
Shall acted be again in Times enſuing.
Let none be ſhaken therefore in his Mind,
If he God's People now reviled find,
Reproach'd with bitter Words, and vilify'd,
With filthy Slanders loaded, and bely'd

By

By wicked Men. Such was the Churches State 1685.
Of old, as Sacred Story doth relate.

And having recounted the Oppoſition made by *Rabſhaketh*, *Sanballat* and *Tobiah*, &c. to the *Jews*, and *Diotrephes* to the Apoſtles; he proceeds, page 6.

By theſe Examples, plainly it appears,
How Satan play'd his Pranks in former Years;
What Arts he us'd, how craftily he wrought,
What Inſtruments, whereby to work he ſought:
One while profeſſed Enemies, and then
Another while he choſe falſe Brethren;
And though thoſe Agents now are dead and gone,
Satan remains the ſame, the *evil One*.
He Miſchief always to the Church intends,
And, Miſchief to effect, his Agents ſends.
Though *Rabſhaketh* be dead, *Tobiah* rotten,
Sanballat and *Diotrephes* forgotten,
The wicked Spirit, that in them did ſtrive
Againſt God's Truth and Church, is ſtill alive,
And other Inſtruments doth daily raiſe,
To hinder Truth's fair Progreſs in theſe Days.
He Agents has, great Store of ev'ry Size
And Sort. How numerous are Truth's Enemies!

Yet

1685. Yet bleſt be God! a greater Number's thoſe
That ſtand for Truth, than thoſe that it oppoſe,
I liſt not here a Muſter-roll to make
Of all who, from without, in hand did take
To battle againſt Truth, and ſhake their Spears
At *Iſrael's* Camp within theſe twenty Years.
Nor do I purpoſe to enum'rate all,
Who, in that Time, themſelves did *Quakers* call,
That through miſguided Zeal, or Diſcontent,
Their Bows againſt their Brethren have bent.
But ſince ſome few of late, appear to be
With Rage and Envy fill'd, to that Degree,
That with more Bitterneſs than all the reſt,
Their Malice againſt Truth they have expreſt,
My Purpoſe is to ſingle out from theſe,
Him that appears as their *Diotrephes*;
And that is ROGERS: For tho' *Criſp* and *Bug*,
With other ſome, do at the ſame Oar tug,
And toil hard at it too with all their Might,
Yet can they do no more but ſhew their Spight.
And for the reſt, that lie behind the Skreen,
And move the Wheels, but like not to be ſeen,
Although they help to carry on the Work,
I take leſs Notice of them, while they lurk.

Them

Them therefore leaving, I return again, 1685.
To view *Will. Rogers* his poetick Strain,
Who having been too often foil'd in *Prose*,
To try his Fortune now in *Verse* hath chose ;
If *Verse*, without Offence, that may be call'd,
Which is delivered in Rhimes so bald,
So flat, so dull, so rough, so void of Grace,
Where *Symphony* and *Cadence* have no Place ;
So full of *Chasmes*, stuck with prosy Pegs,
Whereon his tired Muse might rest her Legs,
(Not having Wings) and take new Breath, that
then
She might, with much ado, hop on again.
His Words [*to that Effect,—Why so? How so?*
Hence I observe,—Hence I conclude,—] do show,
His pursy *Muse* was often out of Wind,
And glad when she a Perching-place could find.
What drew thee *William*, to this rhiming Fit,
Having no more Propensity to it ?
Couldst think such hobling and unequal Rhimes,
That make a Jangling like disorder'd Chimes,
Could of a POEM e'er deserve the Name,
Or e'er be read without the Author's Shame ?
What Clouds of Darkness in thy Lines appear !
How is thy Stile perplex't ! How far from clear !
Thy

1685. Thy *Muſe* is wrapt in thickeſt Fogs of Night,
Which ſhews thou art departed from the Light.
Nor Sun, nor Moon, nor Star throughout thy Book,
Is to be ſeen. No Spring nor criſtal Brook
Glides thro' thy Margin. No, thy Waters run
Black like the Streams of *Styx*, or *Phlegeton*.

And having gone through, and anſwered this Adverſary's Book, he ſums it up, and concludes as followeth. Page 29.

William, thy Work is weigh'd, thy Spirit try'd,
And both thy Work and Spirit are deny'd.
Thy Spirit is the ſame that wrought of old
In *Sanballat*, *Tobiah*, and the bold
Aſſyrian Railer *Rabſhaketh*, who ſought
God's Work and People to have brought to nought,
As thou haſt done: And what the Prophet cry'd
In that Caſe, may to thee be well apply'd.
The Virgin hath deſpis'd thee, Zion's *Daughter*
Makes thee the Object of her Scorn and Laughter.
The Daughter of Jeruſalem *hath ſhook*
At thee her Head (with a diſdainful Look:)

For,

For, *whom hast thou reproached and blasphem'd,*
And against whom hast thou so loudly scream'd,
And lift thine Eyes on high? Thy Spleen doth swell,
Against the holy One of Israel.
To this Effect the Prophet did declaim
Against the proud *Assyrian*, from whom came
That cursed Railer, who e'en seems to be,
In railing Blasphemies, a Type of thee.
What *Nehemiah* to *Sanballat* said,
(When he foul Slanders to his Charge had laid)
That I to thee, of all thy Slanders, Thus,
There are no such Things acted amongst us,
As thy abusive Pamphlet doth contain,
But out of thine own Heart thou dost them feign.
And where thou carp'st at what we do aright,
We can for Truth's-sake in Reproach delight.
The Lord rebuilding is His holy City,
Which thou and others envy (more's the pity)
And put forth all the Strength and Art you have,
The Work to stop, the Workmen to deprave.
But never be so vain, to think you can
The Work obstruct; *'tis not the Work of Man.*
The God of Heaven, He will prosper us,
And therefore we His Servants, (strengthned thus)

1685. Will riſe and build, as God ſhall us endue
With Courage, Strength and Counſel for't: *But you*
No Portion have, who do the Work condemn,
Right nor Memorial in JERUSALEM.
My Soul laments your State, who once have felt
That tend'ring Pow'r, which ſtony Hearts can melt,
And have been in ſome meaſure, tend'red by it,
But now ſo hard'ned are as to defy it:
All you I mean, who have in Print appear'd
With envious Hearts, and Conſcience doubly ſear'd,
To fight againſt the *Truth*, and to expoſe
God's People to the *Fury* of their *Foes*.
And all you too, who do that *Work* abet,
Although your Names thereto ye have not ſet.
Ah! had ye kept unto the *heav'nly Grace*,
Which in your *inward Parts* the *Lord* did place,
And not, in *diſcontented Humour*, run
After *Lo-heres*, *Lo-theres*, as you have done;
Ye might, in *Truth*, the *Bond of Peace* have known,
And in the *Spirit's Unity* have grown,

Which

Which is the *Churches Girdle*, highly priz'd 1685.
By all the *Faithful*, though by you despis'd;
Whereas (by letting in first *false Surmisings*
Of others, which e're long produc'd Despisings,
And so made Way for *Prejudice* to enter,
Till *cancred Malice* in your *Hearts* did center)
Ye now are broke, and into Pieces shatter'd,
And from the *Body* and the *Head* are scatter'd;
Without the Camp ye stand (Oh dismal State!)
Snarling amongst the Dogs, *without the Gate*;
Belching forth *Slander* and *Calumniation*
'Gainst those that in the *Light* have kept their
Station.

Oh! may the God of Heaven stop your Way,
That ye no more the Simple may betray.

I could not but recite thus much, of the Beginning and End of that Book, which is so excellent, both for the Subject and Composure, that one may sooner transcribe too little than too much; the whole being well worth the reading.

In the second Month 1686, he had a Concern 1686.
upon his Spirit, in a deep Sense of the Enemy's working to sow Divisions, and endeavouring to lay waste the Testimony of Truth, to write an Epistle to Friends; which he did very solidly and weightily, to stir up Friends to Faithful-

1686. ness, and to beware of the Eenmy's Wiles, and avoid that rending dividing Spirit, which was then at work to cause Division and Strife among Friends; which being so seasonable and excellent, both for Matter and Stile, the whole is thought meet to be here inserted at large; and is as followeth:

An EPISTLE to

FRIENDS.

DEAR Friends, unto whom the gathering Arm of the Lord hath reached, and who have known, in your several Measures, a being gathered thereby into the heavenly Life, and are Witnesses of the preserving Power, by which ye have been kept faithful to the Lord, and regardful of His Honour: Unto you, in an especial manner, is the Salutation of my true and tender Love in the Lord; and for you, as for myself, are the Breathings and fervent Desires of my Soul offered up, in the one Spirit, unto Him who is your God and mine, that both you and I may be for ever kept in the fresh Sense of His tender Mercies and great Loving-kindness unto us, that therein our Souls may cleave firmly unto Him, and never depart from Him. For Friends, it is a trying Day, a Day of great Difficulty and Danger, wherein the Enemy

Enemy is at work and very busy, setting his Snares on every Side, and spreading his Temptations on every Hand: And some, alas! have entred thereinto, and are caught and held therein, for whom my Soul in Secret mourns.

And truly Friends, a great Weight hath been upon my Spirit for many Days, and my Mind hath been deeply exercised, in the Sense I have of the Enemy's prevailing, by one Bait or other, to unsettle the Minds of some, whom the Arm of the Lord had reached unto, and in some measure gathered to a resting Place: But not abiding in that pure Light, by which they were at first visited, and to which they were at first turned, the *Understanding* hath been vailed again; the *Eye*, which was once in some measure opened, hath the God of the World insensibly blinded again, and Darkness is again come over, to that degree, that they can now contentedly take up again, what in the Day of their Convincement, and in the Time of their true Tenderness, they cast off as a Burthen too heavy to be borne. O my Friends, this hath been the Enemy's Work; therefore it greatly behoves all to watch against him, for it hath been for want of Watchfulness, that he hath got Entrance into any. For when the Mind hath been from off the true Watch, in a secure and careless State, then hath he secretly wrought, and presented his fair Baits, his Allurements or Enticements by Pleasure or Profit, to catch the unwary Mind. And hence it hath come to pass that some, who have come out fairly, and begun

 well,

1686. well, and have ſeemed in good Earneſt to have ſet their Hands to God's Plow, have looked back, and been weary of the Yoke of Chriſt, and have either *luſted after the Fleſh-pots of* Egypt again, or turned aſide into ſome By-path or crooked Way in the Wilderneſs, and thereby have fallen ſhort of the promiſed good Land.

But you, my dear Friends, in whom the Word of Life abides, and who abide in the Virtue and Savour thereof, ye know the Wiles of the Enemy, and the Power which ſubdues him, and the Rock in which the Preſervation and Safety is. So that I write not theſe Things unto you becauſe ye know them not; but the End of my thus writing is, to ſtir up the pure Mind in all, upon whom the Name of the Lord is called, that we all may be provoked to Watchfulneſs againſt the Workings of the wicked One. Therefore, dear Friends, bear, I beſeech you, the Word of Exhortation, though from one that is little and low (and through Mercy ſenſible of it) and who hath not been accuſtomed to appear after this manner; for *the Wind*, ye know, *bloweth where it liſteth.*

Friends, call to mind the former Times, and remember the Days that are paſt and gone, when the Day of the Lord firſt dawned unto you, and His Power ſeized upon you. Ye know how weighty and retired the Spirits of Friends then were; how grave and ſolid their Deportment and Carriage; how few and ſavoury their Words, tending to edify the Hearers; how great a Fear and Backwardneſs was in them, to enter into Familiarity with the World's People. O Friends, that was a good Day, and that was a safe State; for Fear begets Watchfulness, and Watchfulness is a Means to prevent Danger. Therefore all Friends, keep in the holy Fear, and therein watch against the Enemy, that he entangle you not, nor hurt your Spirits, by a too near Familiarity, and intimate conversing with the People of the World; for therein, I assure you, lies a Snare. For though it be both lawful and necessary, and in some Cases also useful and serviceable to the Truth, to converse with them that are without; yet if any Friend should adventure in a frank and free Mind, *beyond the Limits of the pure Fear*, to entertain Familiarity with the World's People, the Spirit of the World in them will *seek an Entrance*, and, if not diligently watched against, will also *get an Entrance*, and bring a Hurt and a Loss upon him or them into whom it so gets. For being once entred, it will insensibly work and dispose the Mind, into which it is got, to a Condescention to and Compliance with the People of the World it converses with, first in one Thing, then in another, in *Words*, in *Behaviour*, &c. (little Things in Appearance, but great in Consequence) till at length an Indifferency gets up in the Mind, and the Testimony of Truth by degrees is let fall. But while the pure Fear is kept to and dwelt in, the Watch is always set, the Spirit is retired and weighty, and an holy Awfulness rests upon the Mind, which renders

1686. ſuch Converſe both ſafe to the Friends, and more ſerviceable to them they converſe withal.

And, Friends, not only in your converſing with the World's People, but in all your Converſation and Courſe of Life, watch againſt the Spirit of the World, for it lies near to tempt, and to draw out the Mind, and to lead back into the World again. You know, Friends, that at the firſt, when the viſiting Arm of the Lord reached to us, He led us out of the World's *Ways, Manners, Cuſtoms* and *Faſhions*, and a cloſe Teſtimony, both in Word and Practice, was borne againſt them. But how hath this Teſtimony been kept up, and kept to by all, who have ſince made Profeſſion of the Truth? Ah, how hath the Enemy, *for want of Watchfulneſs*, ſtole in upon too too many, and led out their Minds from that which did at firſt convince them, into a Liberty beyond the Croſs of Chriſt Jeſus; and in that Liberty they have run into the World's Faſhions, which the worldly Spirit continually invents to feed the vain and airy Minds withal, that they may not come to Gravity and Solidity?

Thence it hath come to paſs, that there is ſcarce a *new Faſhion* come up, or a *fantaſtick Cut* invented, but ſome one or other that profeſſes Truth, is ready with the foremoſt to run into it. Ah, Friends, the World ſees this and ſmiles, and *points the Finger at it*. And this is both a Hurt to the particular, and a Reproach to the general. Therefore, O let the Lot be caſt, let Search be made by every one,

and

and let every one examine himſelf, that this *Achan*, with his *Babyloniſh* Garment, may be found out and caſt out; for indeed he is a *Troubler* of *Iſrael*. And all Friends, who upon true Search ſhall find yourſelves concerned in this particular, I warn and exhort you all, Return to that which at firſt convinced you; to that keep cloſe, in that abide, that therein ye may know as at the firſt (not only a *Bridle to the Tongue*, but) a *Curb to the roving Mind*, a *Reſtraint to the wandring Deſire*. For aſſuredly, Friends, if Truth be kept to, none will need to learn of the World what to wear, what to put on, or how to ſhape and faſhion their Garments; but Truth will teach all how beſt to anſwer *the End of cloathing*, both for *uſeful Service* and *modeſt Decency*. And the Croſs of Chriſt will be a Yoke to the unruly Will, and a Reſtraint upon the wanton Mind, and will crucify that Nature that delights in *Finery* and in *Bravery of Apparel*, in which the true Adorning doth not ſtand, but *in the hidden Man of the Heart*, 1 Pet. 3.
in that which is not corruptible, even *a meek and* 4.
quiet Spirit. And the Grace of God, which hath appeared to all, and which hath brought Salvation to many, will not only teach *to deny* Tit 2.
all Ungodlineſs and worldly Luſts, and to live 11, 12.
ſoberly, righteouſly and godly in this preſent World, but will alſo lead thoſe that obey it, out of all Exceſs, and out of all Superfluities and worldly Vanities, and will teach them to order their Converſation aright. Therefore to this heavenly Grace let every Mind be turned, and therein

ſtay'd,

1686. ſtay'd, that thereby all who profeſs the Truth may be kept in the holy Limits of it; that in their whole Converſation and Courſe of Life, in eating, in drinking, in putting on Apparel, and in whatſoever elſe we do or take in hand,
1 Cor. 10. 31. that all may be done *to the Glory of God*, that our Moderation in all Things may appear unto all Men.

And let not any deceive and hurt themſelves with a falſe Plea, ſaying, *I will be left to my Liberty*; *I have Freedom to do, go, or wear ſo and ſo*; and *Religion ſtands not in Cloaths*, &c. For that Liberty which the worldly Spirit leads into, is not indeed the true Liberty, but is a falſe and feigned Liberty, which leads into true and real Bondage. And tho' Religion ſtands not ſimply in Cloaths; yet true Religion ſtands in that which ſets a *Bound* and *Limit* to the *Mind* with reſpect to Cloaths, as well as to other Things. So that where there is a running out into *Exceſs* and *Vanity* in Apparel, that is a certain Indication and Token that the *Mind is got looſe*, and hath caſt off the Yoke, and is broke away from its due Subjection to that divine Power, in which the true Religion ſtands.

Great hath been the Hurt which the Enemy hath done in this Day, by leading into a *falſe Freedom*, and crying up a *wrong Liberty*; for under this Pretence have crept in great Diſorders, ſome running out one Way, and ſome another; ſome mixing in Marriages with the World's People, and ſome going to the Prieſt to be married. And many looſe and unclean Spirits have

ſhrouded

shrouded themselves under this plausible Pretence of *being left to their Liberty*, unto whom Truth's Order is irksome and uneasy; and they kick against it, and call it *Imposition*, because it *checks their licentious Liberty*. Therefore all, who join with their Plea, examine and try what Liberty it is ye claim and stand for; for the true Liberty is not inconsistent with the Cross of Christ, nor repugnant to His Yoke, but agrees with it, and is obtained through it, and maintained by it. And none whom the Son hath made free indeed, will or can plead or make Use of that Liberty, in Opposition to any Means which the God of Order hath appointed, or set up in His Church for the keeping out Confusion, Disorder and Looseness. And hereby all may take a right Measure, and may certainly know *what kind of Liberty* that is, which some have so hotly contended for, in Opposition to that necessary and commendable Order which God hath led His People into, and which the Enemy, in his Agents, labours so hard to lead them out of. For the Enemy well knows, that the Tendency and Service thereof, is to detect and discover his secret Workings, and to bring his Deeds to Light and Judgment; and therefore he strives with Might and Main to overturn it, crying out through his Instruments, *Away with your Order*; *let every one be left to his Liberty*. By which seemingly fair and specious Plea, not only the loose, disorderly, factious Spirits have been let up, and encouraged to greater Boldness and Licentiousness, but some

ſome ſimple and well-meaning Friends alſo, not ſeeing the Deſign of Satan therein, have been miſled thereby, and made Uſe of by the Enemy, and the more ſubtle of his Inſtruments, to oppoſe the good Order of Truth. Thus hath the Enemy wrought, and ſought to lay waſte the Work of the Lord. But the Lord, magnified be His holy Name, hath not been wanting to His People, who in Sincerity of Heart have diligently waited on Him, and truſted in Him; for He hath all along raiſed up ſome, whoſe Eye He hath opened to ſee the Deſign and Working of the evil One, and whoſe Spirits He hath engaged to ſtand up in a faithful Teſtimony againſt him, *contending for the Way of Truth.* Which when they, in whom the Enemy wrought, perceived, and found they could not run over the Heads of Friends, and carry Things on as themſelves pleaſed, they ſet themſelves, *in a heady wilful Spirit*, to raiſe Diſturbances in Meetings for Buſineſs, by encouraging and abetting ſuch heady, looſe, contentious and diſorderly Perſons as would join with them; thus hardning themſelves, and provoking the Lord to give them up to Blindneſs and Hardneſs of Heart, till at length the Enemy prevailed ſo far upon them, as to work them, by degrees, from *Diſcontent* to *Prejudice*, then to *Enmity*, and ſo at length, in divers Places, to an open *Defection*, *Apoſtacy* and *Separation.*

Now although I know, my dear Friends, that ye who have *kept your Habitation in the Light of the Lord*, and whoſe *Eye is ſingle* therein, have a clear

clear Sight and Underſtanding, that the Spirit 1686.
which hath thus *wrought* and *fought againſt the Truth*, is not, nor can be of God, but is of the *wicked One*; and although the Fruits it hath brought forth, through the Agents and Inſtruments in and by which it hath wrought, *viz. Making Diſturbances in Meetings, to the Breaking the Churches Peace*; *cauſing Diviſions amongſt Friends*; *publiſhing to the World moſt wicked, malicious, railing and ſcandalous Books againſt Friends*, (an Effect of the greateſt Enmity) *ſhutting and keeping Friends out of their common Meeting-houſes, in which they have a juſt Right and Property, and not ſuffering them to meet therein*, (which is a part of the Perſecution inflicted on Friends by the World) *and at length alſo ſet up ſeparate Meetings, in Oppoſition to the Meetings of God's People.* Although, I ſay, theſe Fruits are ſufficient of themſelves to diſcover and manifeſt, to an *unclouded Mind*, what Spirit that is and muſt needs be, which hath brought them forth; yet inaſmuch as ſome, partly through *Weakneſs of Judgment*, and partly through *perſonal Affection to ſome of thoſe leading* Separatiſts, are yet in danger to be betrayed by their *fair Words and feigned Speeches, wherewith they lie in wait to deceive*; I feel a Concern remain upon my Spirit, in the Love of God to warn all ſuch, that they join not with, nor give Countenance unto that Spirit, that hath thus wrought againſt the Lord, and againſt His People.

For

1686. For Friends, in the holy Fear of the living God, and in the Openings of the Spring of His pure Life in my Soul at this Time, and from the certain Knowledge and clear Demonſtration which I have received from Him therein, I teſtify and declare unto you, That this Spirit, which in this Day hath run out, and hath drawn out ſome into Oppoſition againſt the Way and Work of the Lord, into Diviſion and Separation from the People of the Lord, and from the holy Aſſemblies which the Lord hath gathered, and by His powerful Preſence hath owned and daily doth own: This Spirit I ſay, is the ſame with that which hath formerly wrought, in other Appearances, againſt the Truth in our Time, and is the ſame with that Spirit, that wrought againſt the Work of the Lord in the Days of the holy Apoſtles. This Myſtery of Iniquity then wrought, and cauſed many to turn aſide, and to leave the right Way
Heb. 10. 25. of the Lord, and to *forſake the Aſſemblies of God's People*; yea, and to run into *Separation* too; upon whom the holy Ghoſt hath ſet His
Jude 19. Brand, that they were *Senſual, having not the Spirit.* And many cloſe and ſharp Teſtimonies did the Lord give forth through His Servants in that Day againſt this Spirit, and againſt thoſe that were joined to it, and acted by it, as may be ſeen in the holy Scriptures.

Yea, Friends, this Spirit that hath led ſome now to ſet up their *ſeparate Meetings*, is the ſame that led *Jeroboam* the Son of *Nebat* to ſet up his ſeparate Altar at *Bethel*, of which you

may

muy read, 1 *Kings* 12 and 13 Chapters. He was 1686.
afraid, that if the People ſhould continue to go up to the Houſe of the Lord, to do Sacrifice there, as they had been accuſtomed to do, and as the Lord had required, they would then forſake him, and return to the Lord again. And this Spirit now is afraid, that if they whom he hath ſeduced and drawn aſide, ſhould ſtill frequent the Aſſemblies of God's People, and continue to meet with Friends as before; that heavenly Power which is eminently manifeſt in the Meetings of God's People, might at one Time or other reach unto them, touch their Hearts, open the right Eye in them, and give them to ſee the Miſchief and Miſery he is leading them into. And therefore to prevent this, and to keep his Captives cloſe unto him, he hath contrived to ſet up *ſeparate Meetings*, in Oppoſition to the Meetings of God's Appointment, as *Jeroboam* ſet up his ſeparate Altar, in Oppoſition to the Altar which God hath commanded to be ſet up; and to keep the People from going thereto. And ſo ſubtilly did this Spirit work then, as well as now, that *Jeroboam* contrived to have his falſe Worſhip bear ſome Reſemblance to the true, that he might the more eaſily beguile the People; for he ordained a *Feaſt like unto the Feaſt that was in* Judah, 1 Kings xii. 32; but it was *in the Month which he had deviſed of his own Heart*, Verſ. 33. Mark that, there is a Blot upon it. How fair or ſpecious ſoever the Worſhip he ſet up appeared, or ſeemed to be, yet it was but the *Device of his own Heart*;

it

1686. it was neither appointed by God, nor accepted of God. For you may read in the 13th Chapter, that the Lord ſent a Prophet, a Man of God, out of *Judah* to *Bethel*, and he cried againſt the Altar in the Word of the Lord, and propheſied the Deſtruction thereof by *Joſiah*; which was afterwards outwardly fulfilled, as you may read, 2 *Kings* xxiii. 15, *&c.* Now *Joſiah* ſignifies *the Fire*, or *Burning of the Lord*. And, in the holy Dread of the living, eternal God, I declare, the Fire of the Lord is kindled, and kindling againſt this accurſed ſeparating Spirit, and againſt its Work, and againſt all thoſe that join with it therein. Therefore all fear before the mighty God, and ſtand ſtill and conſider your Ways, and let none reſiſt or reject the Warning of the Lord, leſt ſuch be hardned to Deſtruction. For *Jeroboam*, you may read, ſtood by his ſeparate Altar, Verſ. 1. *And when he heard the Saying of the Man of God, which he cried againſt the Altar in* Bethel, *he put forth his Hand, ſaying*, Lay hold on him. But *his Hand which he put forth againſt him, dried up, ſo that he could not pull it in again to him*, Verſ. 4. O Friends, conſider, How hath Drineſs and Withering come upon many a great and ſtout One in this Day, who have lifted up themſelves againſt the Lord, and have ſought, by the *Devices of their own Hearts*, to eſtabliſh themſelves in their own Way, againſt the Way of the Lord, ſo that the Hand they have put forth in that Work, they could not pull in again. Now mind I pray you, Friends, and obſerve the Way

of

of the Working of this Spirit in that Day. 1686.
Here was the Enmity, the rough Nature of *Cain* and *Esau*, the Spirit of *Persecution*, got up first in *Jeroboam*, to dismay the Man of God: *Lay hold of him*, says he. But when he saw that would not do, then the subtle Serpent, the crafty Fox, the fair Speeches, the smooth Words, the seeming Friendship and Shew of Kindness to betray him. *Come home with me*, says he to the Man of God, *and refresh thyself, and I will give thee a Reward*, Vers. 7. O Friends, stand in the Fear and Counsel of the Lord, and in the Dominion of His Power, over this wicked Spirit in all its Twistings and Twinings. Let neither the Frowns nor the Fawnings, the Threats nor the Flatteries, the hard Speeches nor the oily Words, the Pharisaical Friendship, the dissembling Love, the seeming Kindness, the familiar Carriage, the free Entertainment, the fine Bit, the Offer of Advantages, &c. have any Influence upon you, to draw you in the least measure to join or touch with God's Enemy; with him that sets up a separate Altar, a separate Meeting in Opposition to, and to draw or keep from the right Way of the Lord: Mind well the Answer, which the Man of God gave to *Jeroboam*'s tempting Invitation. *If*, said he, *thou wilt give me half thine House, I will not go in with thee; neither will I eat Bread, nor drink Water in this Place*, Vers. 8. This was where the separate Altar was set up. And he gives a forcible Reason for it: *For so it was charged me by the Word of the Lord*, Vers. 9.

1686. Here now you ſee both the Charge of the Lord, and the good Reſolution of the Man of God: *I will not go in with thee, who haſt revolted from God; neither will I eat or drink in this Place, where an Enſign of Separation and Oppoſition to the Way of God is ſet up.* Conſider this well, I warn you All, in whom there is yet any true Breathings after the living God, who retain any Tenderneſs, and in whom there is any Simplicity left: Conſider this well, I ſay, when thy pretended Friend or Friends, in a great deal of ſeeming Love and Kindneſs, ſhall invite thee to partake with them at their ſeparate Altar, to ſit down with them in their ſeparate Meeting. Thou canſt not be a Man of God, and go in with them, or eat or drink in that Place. Thou canſt not ſit down there to wait for the Bread of Life, or the Water of Life to be given thee there: No, the Word of the LORD, if thou giveſt heed unto it, will charge thee otherwiſe. Therefore to that pure living Word let every Mind be turned, and thereto kept, in a diligent waiting to receive Wiſdom, Strength and Power from the Lord therein, that none may be betrayed by the Subtilty of the Enemy, with whatſoever fair Pretences he may come. For remember how the Man of God, that was enticed by another to eat and drink outwardly at *Bethel*, the Place where the ſeparate Altar was ſet up, loſt his outward Life therefor, Verſ. 18. and 24. And if thou ſhalt perſume to go in, to eat or to drink ſpiritually; that is, to join in Worſhip with

with the Sons of *Nebat* at this Day, in the ſe- 1686.
parate Meetings, which any of them have ſet up, in Oppoſition to the Aſſemblies of God's People, and to the bleſſed Way and Work of the Lord; how knoweſt thou, but thou mayſt for ever loſe thy ſpiritual Life, and never know a Day of Quickning more?

Therefore all Friends, watch againſt every Temptation thereunto, as you love your Lives, as you regard the Good and eternal Welfare of your Souls; and let not the Name, nor Perſon of any Man, have Power over you, to draw you aſide, neither let *Numbers* ſway with you; in which, I know, theſe Adverſaries of Truth do not a little boaſt (though bleſſed be God, with little Reaſon) but remember that *Jeroboam* of old had ten Tribes out of twelve to cry up his ſeparate Altar; notwithnanding which, he is branded to Poſterity in the holy Record with this Brand, Jeroboam *the Son of* Nebat, WHO MADE *ISRAEL* TO SIN, 2 Kings xiv. 24. Therefore let not any follow a Multitude to do *Evil*, Exod. xxiii. 2. But all *follow that which is good, both among yourſelves and to all Men*, 1 *Theſſ.* v. 15. For Friends, you know whither the *Broad-way* leads, and what it is the *Wide-gate* opens into, which the *many* go in at; but keep ye to the *ſtraight Gate*, and walk ye on in the *narrow Way*, for in it is Safety, and at the End of it everlaſting Happineſs.

But Friends, becauſe of the Straightneſs of this Gate, and the Narrowneſs of this Way,

1686. some that have attempted to walk in it, are grown weary of it, and have sought out another Way, a Way which (*Jeroboam* like) they have devised of their own Hearts, wherein they may have more Room, more Scope, more Company, Ease in the Flesh, Liberty to the Flesh, and all without Controul. And this I am satisfied, hath not been the least Motive to the Separation in this Day, as it was the greatest in Days past; though some that have been drawn into it, may not perhaps see the Ground upon which it was undertaken. But the Lord hath opened an Eye in many, which sees the Rise and Ground, Entrance and End of this libertine Spirit and its Work. And this Eye will the Lord daily open more and more in all, that diligently and in Sincerity wait upon Him. Therefore all Friends every where, who have not yet a clear Sight, and a thorough Understanding of the Nature and Work, Design and Drift of this dividing Spirit, wait, I beseech you, in Simplicity of Heart, and Lowliness of Mind upon the Lord, and keep to the Measure of the Grace you have received from Him; and suffer not your Minds to be swayed or byassed by any personal Kindness, natural Affection, Relation, Kindred or Acquaintance, but stand single and open to the Lord, not joining to, nor any way countenancing that which the Testimony of Truth, in the Arisings of the heavenly Life, and Breakings forth of the divine Power through any, goes forth against. So will your present Standing be safe, and you be preserved out of

the

the Snares of this insinuating and treacherous 1686
Spirit: And the Lord, in His appointed Time, as ye abide with Him, will open your Understandings further, and give you a clearer Sight of that, which at present you do not fully see, and thereby bring you to that Certainty and Assurance, which, blessed be His Name, He hath brought many unto.

And you, my dear Friends, whose Spirits the Lord hath stirred up, and whose Hearts he hath engaged in an holy Zeal, to stand up for His blessed Name and Truth, and to bear a faithful Testimony against this wicked rending Spirit; go on in the Strength and Power of the Lord, in the Might of the God of *Jacob*, for you are assuredly on the Lord's Side, and the Lord *Jehovah*, the Strength of *Israel*, is on your Side. Therefore, Friends, be encouraged in the Lord, to stand stedfast in your Testimony, not giving Way to the Enemy, no not for a Moment. And take heed, I beseech you in the Love of God, how ye enter into any Treaty of Peace, or Terms of Agreement with this ungodly treacherous Spirit, which is out of the Truth, and draws out of the Truth, and fights against the Truth; for there is no Peace unto it, saith my God. And they who have joined themselves unto it, and have wickedly given themselves up to be acted by it, and to act for it, must pass through the River of Judgment, if ever they be redeemed from under its Power. Friends, Condemnation must first be felt and owned, before Reconciliation can be

1686. known; and the Fire of the Lord muſt paſs upon the Tranſgreſſor, to conſume the Works of Darkneſs, the ungodly Deeds, the envious reviling Speeches, the wicked, malicious, ſlanderous Books and Pamphlets, &c. and to burn up the Ground from whence they ſprang. For a flaming Sword hath the Lord God ſet in His *Eden*, which turneth every Way; and none that are gone out can ever come in again, but they muſt paſs under the flaming Edge thereof. Therefore, my dear Friends, ſtand your Ground, in the Authority of the heavenly Life, and tamper not with God's Enemies: Remember

Jer. 15. 19, 20. the Word of the Lord to the Prophet, *Let them return unto thee, but return not thou unto them.* And then what follows? *I will make thee unto this People a fenced brazen Wall, and they ſhall fight againſt thee, but they ſhall not prevail againſt thee, for I am with thee, to ſave thee, and to deliver thee, ſaith the Lord.* So the God of Life fill your Hearts daily more and more with a *Phineas* Zeal for the Honour of His Name, and furniſh you abundantly with Wiſdom and Counſel, with Boldneſs and Courage, with Strength and Power, to encounter and overcome the Enemy; and make every one more watchful againſt the Spirit of the World, to withſtand it in all its Allurements to Vanity, of whatſoever kind; that whatſoever would defile the Camp of the Lord, may be purged out, and kept out, that the Lord may more and more delight in His People, and ſhower down His

His Bleſſings upon them; which is the fervent Deſire of, 1686.

Your faithful Friend in the Love and Service of the unchangeable Truth,

The 24th of the ſecond Month, 1686.

THOMAS ELLWOOD,

After this, I do not find he writ any Thing (only ſome private Letters in his *Decades)* but lived retired till the Year 1688. In which Time of Privacy (as fitteſt for it) he began a Work which he did not finiſh till many Years after, and that was, *The Life of* David *King of* Iſrael, in Verſe; which he began for his own Diverſion, not thinking then of printing it, and carried it on to the End of the third Book. But then the Prince of *Orange* landing, and the Revolution following, the Nation being in Arms againſt King *James*; the Noiſe of Guns, and Sound of Drums, &c. ſo diſturbed his Meditation and gentle Muſe (which like the *Halcion*, breeds in calm Weather) that his poetical Genius left him for a Time, and he thereupon left his Work, for above twenty Years; of which more hereafter in its Place. 1688.

And here he retired again for two Years; ſo that I find nothing to remark of him, either publick or private, but ſome private Letters, till the Year 1690. When *John Raunce* and *Charles Harris* of *Wiccomb* in that County, publiſhing *A Memorial* (as they call'd it) *for the preſent Generation, and alſo for that which is to come*;

1690. *being an Account from* Wiccomb *concerning the Difference*, &c. This, *Thomas Ellwood* anſwered in a Book intituled, *The Account from* Wiccomb *(lately publiſhed by* John Raunce *and* Charles Harris) *examined, and found falſe. And a Warning thereof given, to all ſuch well-meaning Perſons among the People called* Quakers, *as through perſonal Affection, Want of Conſideration, or Weakneſs of Judgment, have been betrayed, or may be in Danger to be betrayed by them, or any other in the ſame dividing Spirit with them; and led aſide from the Way of Truth, into a Separation from the People of God: For whoſe Recovery and Preſervation this is written.* Which begins thus:

'For your Sakes it is, O ye much pitied 'Ones, more than for any Weight in the Account itſelf, or Worth in the Authors of it, 'that I have thus taken Notice of it. For indeed, as ſoon as I had peruſed it, I felt a 'compaſſionate Concern ſpring in my Heart on 'your Behalfs, and a Direction in Spirit to open 'ſome Paſſages therein, and relating thereto, 'to you, that ye might be preſerved from being 'taken; or, if in any meaſure taken, might 'be reſcued and delivered from the Snare, 'which the Enemy of your Souls, and of all 'Righteouſneſs, hath made Uſe of theſe Men 'to ſet, to entangle, entrap and catch you by. 'And to the true Witneſs of the holy God, in 'every one of your Conſciences, who retain 'any honeſt Breathings after the Lord, and 'the Way of Holineſs, do I recommend this 'my Undertaking, and the Sincerity of my

'Intention herein.' Wherein he discovered their Deceit, as to their Separation; and that it was not for Conscience, but from a libertine Spirit, to lay waste the good Order in the Church, as their Actions manifested: Of which he gave some Instances, not to their Advantage. But their Works have made them manifest. 1691.

The next Book he published, was in 1691, viz. *A Reply to an Answer, lately published, to a Book long since written by* W. Penn, *Intituled, A brief Examination and State of Liberty spiritual; both with respect to Persons in their private Capacity, and in their Church Society and Conversation.* Which Book was written, or at least published by *W. Penn*, in the Year 1681, to distinguish between true and false Liberty, little understood by some, and too frequently abused by others: *Liberty from Sin, not to sin; to do His* (God's) *Will, and not our own*; as *W. Penn* expresses it. Which true spiritual Liberty, being abused by some in the Profession of the Truth, (as our Friend *T. Ellwood* observes in his Preface) 'Who under Pretence of being left to that 'Liberty in themselves, and to their own Free-'dom therein, both took Liberty to do such 'Things as were inconsistent with that true Li-'berty, and with the Principle of Truth which 'they professed; and despising those useful, 'good and necessary Helps and Means which 'the Lord hath provided, and furnished His 'Church and People with, for the preventing 'and keeping out such Disorders, Evils and 'Scandals, as the unruly Nature of Man, thro'

'such

1691. 'ſuch a Miſtake of true Liberty, might and 'would bring in; did reject the Counſel, Admonition or Reproof of their Brethren, with '*What haſt thou to do with me? Leave me to my own Freedom.* To reclaim, if it might be, 'thoſe who are thus deceived, and prevent 'others from being ſo, the Author being preſſed 'in Spirit for *Zion*'s Sake, and for the Peace 'of *Jeruſalem*; and having a deep Senſe *(as himſelf expreſſes)* of the working of the Enemy 'of *Zion*'s Peace, to rend and divide the Heritage of God, did write the forementioned 'Treatiſe for the Eſtabliſhment of the Faithful, Information of the Simple-hearted, and 'Reproof of the arrogant and high-minded.' Which ſtriking at the falſe Liberty and Pretences of the ſeparate Party, it ſeems it had lain on their Stomachs undigeſted theſe ten Years, and then came forth an Anſwer to it by *J. H.* (ſuppoſed to be *John Hog*, one of the Separates about *Hull.*) This Anſwer our Friend *T. Ellwood* undertakes, and replies to in a pretty large Book; in which he ſhews what is meant by true ſpiritual Liberty, in *W. Penn*'s own Definition, which he defends; ſhews their Abuſe of it, anſwers their Arguments, or rather Cavils againſt it, in Behalf of their falſe libertine Spirit and Practices, which too many ran into to their own Hurt, and Separation from the Church, the Body of Chriſt, whereof He is Head; ſaying, in the *Preface*, 'The God of 'Truth knows, I have no other End in this 'Reply, than to defend Truth and the Children 'of

'of it, against the slanderous Suggestions, false 1691.
'Charges, and wicked Insinuation of the Adversaries; to lay open their deceitful Dealing, and to remove (as the Lord shall enable me) the Stumbling-blocks which they have laid in the Way of the Weak, whereby they have caused some to fall into Misapprehensions and hard Thoughts of Friends, without Cause. And I beseech the God of Mercy to open the Understandings, and clear the Sight of all those, whose Simplicity has been betrayed by the others Subtilty, that they may see and escape the Enemy's Snares, and return to the true Fold, from which they have been led astray.' To which I never heard of any Rejoinder; only some private Letters past between *J. Hog* and *T. Ellwood* about some Passages in it.

His next were two Broadsides, the first (in 1692) *viz.* T. Ellwood's *Answer to so much of* Leonard Key's *late printed Sheet as relates to him.* Which Paper of *L. Key*'s was intended mostly to excuse their shutting Friends out of their Meeting-house at *Reading*. But therein taking Occasion to slant at some Passages in *T. Ellwood*'s Answer to the Account from *Wiccomb*, gave our Friend *Thomas* an Occasion, not only to open that Matter further, but also to lay open their Deceit in Relation to that Affair, as well as *L. Key*'s and his Party at *Reading*. To which I refer the Reader.

The Second was in 1693, *viz. Deceit discovered, and Malice manifested, in* L. Key's *late Paper*

1693. *Paper from* Reading. *Thomas* being then at *London* at the Yearly-meeting, met with Benjamin Coal's *Expedients, for a true Reconciliation among the People of God called* Quakers: Which *L. Key* it ſeems promoted. But when *T. Ellwood* came home, he found a Letter at his Houſe directed to him, from *L. Key* with a printed Sheet incloſed, ſo different in Terms and Tendency from the other, ſign'd by *B. C.* and *C. H.* (that propoſing Expedients for Peace, this renewing the Difference;) and yet but one Day different in the Dates, this being dated the 3d, the other the 4th of the fourth Month 1693, that he could not but admire at it; which therefore he compares, and ſhews the Difference of, and diſcovers their Deceit in; and not only in that, but alſo in Relation to the Difference at *Wiccomb*, which they were not yet eaſy under, and yet would not confeſs the Truth; but inſtead thereof, *J. Raunce* endeavours to fix a Slander on *T. Ellwood* about his Father's Burial, pretending he was not buried in the right Ground, but among Strangers; he and his Party riding twenty Miles or more about the Country; and *J. Raunce* going himſelf to the Place where he was buried at *Holton*, to pick up a Stone at the Father's Grave to throw at the Son, above ſeven Years after is Death; enquiring, examining, yea, provoking ſome, to pretend as if *T. Ellwood* had been unkind to his Father, and that they had ſhewed him Kindneſs, to bring *Thomas* under Obligation of Requital, or upbraid him for Ingratitude if he did not. In all which

J. Raunce's

J. Raunce's Malice was manifest more than any thing else; for as to the Ground he was buried in, *T. Ellwood* confesses he was not so well acquainted with the Grave-yard, as to know the Difference of Places in it, or whether some Parts of it be more holy than others; which he thinks, considering their former Principles, they should not have quarrel'd with him about. However the Place was not of his appointing; for he was prevented of being at the Burial, by a Message his Father received in his Sickness, that his Sister (but which of them he doth not say) lay then sick in *London* near unto Death. After he had waited on his Father until he had finished his Life, and given Direction for his Interment, he hastened up to his Sister at *London*, thinking he might be more serviceable to the Living than to the Dead, and knew not in what Part of the Ground his Father was buried, till after his Return from *London*, he went thither to defray the Charges of his Sickness and Funeral, as some of them knew; and and therefore the more Shame to raise such a Story. And as to the other of *Unkindness*, they could prove nothing, but shew their Envy against him; which we shall have Occasion to take further Notice of e're we have done.

The next and last Book he writ in Relation to this Controversy with the Separates, was, *A fair Examination of a foul Paper, called* Observations and Reflections, *&c. lately published by* John Raunce *and* Leonard Key; who after their separate Bickerings, come now to join their Forces together

1693. together in this Paper, which ſeems to be Reflections on *T. Ellwood*'s laſt mentioned Paper; and which Paper of theirs our Friend anſwers in this Examination, wherein *their Envy is rebuked, and their Folly and Falſhood laid open*, in endeavouring to excuſe *L. Key's* former Paper of Revival of the Difference, at the ſame Time when *B. Coale*'s Expedient for Reconciliation was for having it all forgotten and buried; which *T. Ellwood* expoſes in its proper Colours, beginning thus; 'We read among the Proverbs of

Prov. 4. 19. '*Solomon*, that *the Way of the Wicked is as Darkneſs, they know not at what they ſtumble*. This is 'verified in *J. Raunce* and *L. Key*, and others of 'their ſeparate Party. Since their turning againſt 'the Truth, their Way is become as Darkneſs, 'they ſtumble and know not at what. They fall 'into many idle Abſurdities, many groſs Follies and Errors, and into many hurtful Evils, 'and labour to draw others (better than themſelves) after them; for whoſe Sake chiefly the 'following Lines are written, that the Deceit 'and Hypocriſy of theſe Men, their Falſhood 'and Envy being further and further laid open, 'the more Simple and well-meaning Ones 'amongſt them, may ſee them as they are, 'and be no longer beguiled by them.' So he goes on to anſwer their Cavils, confirming by Certificate his former Charge of their ſcandalous Practice at *Wiccomb*; then anſwers their new Slander (the old proving falſe) *That he ſuffered his Father to want*; raking into his Aſhes when he had been dead above ten Years, to caſt ſomething

ſomething at his Son (ſo reſtleſs is Envy) as if he had been ſhort in his Duty to his Father; which *T. Ellwood* fairly and clearly wipes off, vindicating himſelf as to his not being at his Father's Burial (which *J. Raunce* throws at him) though *Thomas* in his laſt had fairly related the Occaſion, which was his Siſter's Ilneſs at *London* (though ſhe recovered;) and which one would think might have ſatisfied any one not overgrown with Envy; which yet *J. Raunce* revives again, and alſo about his Burial, *&c.* All which appears to be nothing but *J. Raunce*'s Rancour; which ſeeing he has made ſo much a-do about, out of his inveterate Malice to *T. Ellwood*, under Pretence of Friendſhip to his Father, but to be ſure Hatred to the Son; and as *T. Ellwood* ſays, *If this be the Effect of his Friendſhip, he ſhould not deſire to be numbred among his Friends.* To ſet which in a clear Light, I ſhall here ſet down his Vindication in his own Words, becauſe it bears ſome Analogy to his Relation of the former Part of his Life; *viz.* Pag. 20. of the *Fair Examination.* ' 'Tis well known to many, that my ' Father was poſſeſt of a good Eſtate, and they ' that knew him well, knew alſo that he had ' the ſpending of it himſelf. How he ſpent it ' becomes not me to ſpeak; he was my Father, ' to whom I ow'd and always paid Reſpect and ' Honour while living, and whoſe Frailty, being ' dead, I deſire to cover. It is enough for me to ' ſay, I did not help him to ſpend his Eſtate, ' nor was I much chargeable to him after I was ' capable of ſhifting for myſelf. And when it ' pleaſed 1693.

1693. ‘pleaſed the Lord to viſit me with the ſaving ‘Knowledge of His Truth, and bring me under ‘the viſible Characters of the Profeſſion thereof, ‘(which was about the twentieth Year of my ‘Age) my Father expreſſing a Diſlike to me on ‘that Account, by degrees withdrew his Care of ‘me, not making any Proviſion for my Main‘tenance, ſave the giving me ſuch of his houſ‘hold Goods as he could ſpare, upon his giving ‘over Houſe-keeping, though he had then a ‘plentiful Eſtate remaining. When afterwards ‘he ſold his Eſtate, I had no Part at all of the ‘Money.’ — [Though upon his Marriage, he promiſed both him and his intended Wife to do ſomething conſiderable for them, yet after they were married he refuſed to give them any Thing (as aforeſaid, pag. 238) and ſo far withdrew himſelf, that he would not let him know where he lodged. —] ‘Notwithſtanding this, ‘ſays *T. Ellwood*, he would ſometimes come to ‘my Houſe, which was always open and free to ‘him, to come when he pleaſed, and to tarry ‘as long as he pleaſed. Whenever he came, he ‘was well habited both for Linen and Woollen, ‘and made no Appearance of Want, other ‘than ſuch as may befal any Man, to have his ‘Money fall ſhort in a Journey; upon which ‘Occaſion (when he had, as he ſaid, been ‘longer from home than he expected, or when, ‘being here, he had a mind to go further than ‘at his coming forth he intended) he has divers ‘Times aſked me to lend him Money, which ‘I always did, and never aſked him for it again.

‘And,

'And, to the best of my Remembrance, it was 1686.
'not above two Weeks time before his last
'Sickness, that he had been at my House, and
'had Money of me on that Account. As soon
'as I heard of his Ilness, I hastened to him,
'and took the best Care of him I could during
'his Life; and after his Death defrayed the
'Charge of his Sickness and Burial, and repaid
'to my Sister that Money she had sent him,
'before I knew of his Ilness. I could say more
'on this Subject than I intend, or at present
'think fit, but I forbear, and commit my inno-
'cent Cause to the Lord, not doubting but that,
'as I am clear in His Sight from any Undutiful-
'ness or Unkindness towards my Father, so He
'will clear mine Innocency in the Hearts of
'His People, and of all unprejudiced Persons.'

This I hope will satisfy the Reader of *T. Ellwood*'s Carriage towards his Father, which we are beholding to *J. Raunce* for, or else perhaps might never have had this Account, which one would think Envy itself should not be able to cavil at. Yet after this *J. Raunce* being restless, trumpt up another Story, answered by *T. Ellwood* in his Postscript to that Book, which we shall meet with again hereafter on another Occasion, and therefore I shall say no more of it here.

Here ends his Controversy with the *Separates*: In which I must needs say, he acquitted himself as an ingenuous Man, a *Christian*, and a fair Opponent. And now to come to something more pleasant: Our dear Friend *George Fox* dying in

1693. the Eleventh Month 1690, and leaving behind him an excellent Journal of his Travels and Sufferings, our Friend *T. Ellwood*, (as no body fitter) about this Time was at the Pains of transcribing it, and fitting it for the Press; (a laborious Work) which was printed next Year in a large Folio: To which *T. Ellwood* prefixed a notable Account concerning him, which is the only single Testimony printed with it, except his Wife *M. Fox*'s, and an excellent *Preface* by *W. Penn.*

1694. But now a new Scene opens. For *George Keith*, who had known better Things than most Opposers that ever rose up against Truth and Friends, having been a *Quaker*, and a Preacher among them near thirty Years, and had writ many Books in Vindication of Truth and Friends; but now falling out, and differing with some of his Brethren in *Pennsylvania* (whither he went some Years before) because he could not have his own Way in every Thing, came over with some of his Party, full fraught with Contention, against the Yearly-meeting in 1694. Which Difference coming before the Meeting by some Letters from beyond Sea, which were read in Course in the Meeting, whereupon *G. Keith* desired to be heard; which, after the other Business of the Meeting was over, Friends condescended to for several Days, to hear him and his Party; and *Samuel Jennings*, &c. on the other Side; in Hopes to have reconciled the Difference before it went any
Hos 7.1. further: But as the Prophet said, *When I would have*

have healed Iſrael, *then the Iniquity of* Ephraim 1694.
was diſcover'd, &c. which may be applied to him; for the more Endeavours were uſed to reconcile him to his Brethren, the more his Deceit appear'd; and the more Tenderneſs any ſhewed towards him, the more perverſe he was in turning it to a wrong Uſe, and ſtrengthening himſelf in his Oppoſition. There was no holding *what would away* (as the Proverb is) reſolved he was for a Breach, by oppoſing Friends more and more, till he ran himſelf quite out from among them. Which our Friend *T. Ellwood* obſerving the Bent and Tendency of, not only in the Yearly-meeting, but after; and how he endeavoured to make Diviſions among Friends, to divide the Heritage of God, he took up his Pen again, and writ an excellent *Epiſtle to Friends; briefly commemorating the gracious Dealings of the Lord with them, and warning them to beware of that Spirit of Contention and Diviſion which hath appeared of late in* George Keith, *&c.* which he addreſſes to Friends thus:

'Dear Friends, whom the Lord hath called 'with an holy Calling, and who, through 'Faithfulneſs to the heavenly Call, are become 'the Choſen of the Lord. It is in my Heart, 'in the Openings of the Love of God, to ſend 'theſe few Lines amongſt you, as a Salutation 'of true and hearty Love unto you; and in the 'tendering Senſe of the Lord's unſpeakable 'Goodneſs unto us, which at this Time reſts 'with an affecting Weight upon my Spirit, 'briefly to commemorate the gracious Dealings

 'of

1694. 'of the Lord with us since we have been a 'People.' ' *Which he commemorates as follows.*

'Great and manifold have been the Mercies 'of our God unto His People, in this His Day, 'and His loving Kindnesses are beyond expressing: When we were young and little, His 'fatherly Care was over us, He preserved us 'and nourished us, and caused us to grow up 'before Him. How did He carry His Lambs 'in His Bosom, when the Beasts of Prey roar'd 'on every Side, seeking to devour! Who can 'rehearse the many Deliverances He hath 'wrought for His People, in their Passage from 'spiritual *Egypt!* How hath He girded their 'Loins with Strength, and covered their Heads 'in the Day of Battle! How hath he subdued 'their Enemies before them, and put to flight 'the Armies of Aliens! How hath he fed them 'with Bread from Heaven, and made them to 'suck Honey out of the Rock! Yea, He hath 'caused the Rock to give forth Water abundantly, and hath been to His People as a 'Brook in the Way [and *the Shadow of a mighty* '*Rock in a weary Land.*] So that from a sensible 'Experience we can say, to His Praise, Our 'Bread hath been sure, and our Water hath not 'failed, as we have singly relied on Him. Oh! 'His Goodness is unutterable, and His Faithfulness hath never failed them that have trusted 'in Him. When have we ever been in Prison 'for His Sake, and He hath not visited and 'comforted us there? What Sufferings have any 'undergone on His Account, and He hath not

'abundantly

'abundatly recompensed the Loss? Nay, hath 1694.
'He not often stopped the Mouths of Lions, and
'reproved Rulers for the Sake of His People,
'saying, *Touch not mine Anointed, and do my*
'*Prophets no Harm.* In all our Exercises He
'hath been with us, and He hath stood by us in
'our sorest Trials; yea, He hath caused His
'Angel to encamp round about us, so that no
'Weapon formed against us hath prospered; but
'every Tongue that hath risen up against us,
'the Lord hath given us Power to condemn:
'Blessed be His holy Name, and exalted and
'magnified be His glorious Power for ever.

'These Things and much more than I can
'write, I doubt not but ye, my dear Friends,
'are Witnesses of; ye especially, my elder Bre-
'thren, who were called early in the Morning
'of this Day, and have stood faithful in your
'Testimony for God until now, who from your
'own both early and late Experiences can set
'your Seals to the Truth hereof; and unto you
'I do believe this brief Commemoration of the
'Goodness and loving Kindness of the Lord to
'His People, will be pleasing and delightful, as
'I hope it may prove useful and profitable unto
'us all, in the stirring up of the *pure Mind*,
'and putting us in fresh Remembrance of the
'Lord's manifold Favours towards us, and gra-
'cious Dealings with us; which should be as
'a renewed Engagement upon us to cleave fast
'unto the Lord, and in Humility of Heart, to
'walk closely with Him, both that we may, as
'far as in us lies, answer His great loving Kind-

1694. ' neſs to us-ward, and receive from Him ſtill ' daily Strength and Ability to ſtand, and with- ' ſtand the Aſſaults and Temptations of the Ene- ' my, and eſcape his Snares, wherewith he is, ' at this Time, as buſy and induſtrious to betray, ' and draw aſide from the Simplicity of the ' Truth, as ever he was.

' For Friends, ye know we have a reſtleſs ' Adverſary to watch againſt, and to war with ; ' one that ſometimes walks about as a *roaring* ' *Lion*, ſeeking whom he may devour ; and ' ſometimes creeps about as a *ſubtil Serpent*, ſeek- ' ing whom he may betray ; whom, in each ' Appearance, it is our Duty and Intereſt to reſiſt, ' ſtedfaſt in the Faith which overcomes. I need ' not recount unto you, my Friends, the many ' Winds and Floods, Storms and Tempeſts, of ' open and cruel *Perſecutions*, which this roaring ' Adverſary hath often raiſed, and cauſed to beat ' upon us, to have driven us, if poſſible, from ' off our Foundation ; ye cannot have forgotten ' it, nor that noble *Arm of the Lord*, which was ' made bare for our Preſervation, and by pre- ' ſerving us againſt the moſt furious Shocks, ' gave Evidence even to the World, that we are ' that People whoſe Houſe is founded and built ' upon the immoveable Rock *Chriſt Jeſus*. At ' this Sort of fighting the Enemy hath been ' foiled ; which hath made him ſhift his Hand, ' and like a cunning Hunter *ſpread his Nets*, ſet ' his *Snares*, lay his *Baits*, to catch the ſimple ' and unwary Ones. Thus wrought this ſubtil ' Enemy in the early Times of *Chriſtianity*,

' ſometimes

'sometimes stirring up the Rulers, both *Jews* 1694.
'and *Gentiles*, to fall with violent and bloody
'Hands upon the little Flock of Christ; and
'sometimes in the Intermissions of those Storms,
'covering his Hooks with the taking Baits of
'*Pleasure*, *Profit* and *Preferment*, catch some
'(perhaps of those that had withstood the
'strongest Storm of outward Persecution) and
'made them Instruments for himself to work
'by, to betray others. Such was *Diotrephes* of 3 John
'old, whose aspiring Mind, loving and seeking 9. 10.
'*Pre-eminence*, laboured to make a *Schism* in
'the Church, prating against even the Elders
'thereof *with malicious Words*, &c. What Mis-
'chief the wicked One hath wrought in our
'Day by such *ambitious Spirits*, I need not re-
'count, nor is it pleasing to me to remember;
'ye know it, to your Grief, as well as I. But
'this in all such Cases is observable, that such
'as have made *Disturbances* in the Church, and
'have run into *Divisions* and *Separations* from
'Friends, have framed to themselves some spe-
'cious Pretence or other, as the Inducement to
'their Undertaking, which they have industri-
'ously spread abroad, and varnished over with
'the fairest Colours they could, to allure and
'draw others to join with them, *&c.*'

This, with much more to the same purpose, which might be cited, I thought meet to mention of the Mercies of the Lord to His People, and Preservation of them from the Beginning, well worth the reading. Then recounting the Wiles and Workings of the Enemy, in drawing

1694. some aside from the Simplicity of the Truth, and stirring them up to make Divisions (on one Pretence or other) to disturb the Peace of the Church, and hinder the Work of the Lord in the Earth; as lately in the *Separates*. So now being disappointed in that, he hath formed a new Design in *G. Keith*; yet to shew the Difference between the former and this, and consequently the Confusion of their Pretences, *Theirs* relating to *Discipline*, *This* to *Doctrine*; They alledged *That Friends were gone too much from the inward to the outward*; This, *That Friends were gone too much from the outward to the inward*, &c. for our Adversaries seldom agree in their Charges. And so he goes on to examine and compare his Books, published beyond Sea, with those he writ here, as to the Ground of the Difference and Separation; which he lays at his Door, manifesting his deceitful Pretences, Falacies and Self-contradictions. Answering his Cavils, and consulting his Calumnies, that none might be deceived by him. Concluding by way of Application and Warning to Friends, to beware of the Enemy's Wiles; which I doubt not had a good Effect as to many, in preserving them out of the Enemy's Snare, who were in Danger of being stagger'd by him.

When our Friend *T. Ellwood* had written this Epistle, he went up to *London* with it, and presented it to the *Second-day's Morning-meeting*, where such Books and Writings of Friends, as are intended for the Press, use to be read and consider'd, and read it through in that Meeting, and

and not one Friend (though the Meeting was pretty full) ſhewed any Diſ-unity therewith, but approved it, and left it to him to publiſh it. And yet *G. Keith* pretended that it was printed in great Diſ-unity, and againſt the Mind of many Friends, as though it was only approved and promoted by a Party, *&c.* Which I mention, to ſhew he ſtuck at nothing to make good his Part. 1694.

Againſt this Book of *T. Ellwood's*, *G. Keith* made a heavy Complaint to Friends to have it called in, as very injurious to him (to his Cauſe to be ſure) poor Man! who had writ ſo many Books againſt Friends, after he had writ ſo many for them, and would not take Friends Advice himſelf; and how then could he expect they ſhould anſwer him? So that his Complaint and Clamour not prevailing to ſtifle it, he takes another Way, firſt putting out a Sheet againſt it, called a *Loving Epiſtle*, but envious enough: In which he charged *T. Ellwood* with *fifty Perverſions*, &c. which he ſaid he had noted in his Book, but left his Proofs behind to come after (*The firſt by* Poſt, as the Proverb is, *the ſecond by* Tom Long *the Carrier)* in another Book which he threatned to publiſh, if *T. Ellwood*'s was not called in and diſowned: Which not prevailing neither, ſome Weeks after he ſent forth his threatned Book, miſcalled *A ſeaſonable Information*, &c. but very unſeaſonable for himſelf, as to his Reconciliation with Friends; which he pretended he had rather lay down his natural Life, or have his right Hand cut off, than

1694. than be dis-united or dis-jointed from them. This Book he pretended to be an Answer to *T. Ellwood*'s Epistle, and to contain his Proofs (such as they were) of the Charge he had published before. To both these our Friend *T. Ellwood* replied this Year (1694) in a Book intituled, *A further Discovery of that Spirit of Contention and Division, which hath appeared of late in* George Keith, *&c. wherein his Cavils are answered, his Falshood is laid open, and the Guilt and Blame of the Breach and Separation in* America, *&c. are fixed faster on him; written by way of Epistle* (as the former was) *and recommended as a farther Warning to Friends.* Which begins thus:

'Dear Friends, who have received the Truth 'in the Love of it, and have kept your Habi-'tation therein, unto whom the Truth is ex-'ceeding precious, and who desire the Prospe-'rity thereof above all Things; unto you is the 'Salutation of my endeared Love, in this bles-'sed Truth, in which the Fellowship of the 'Faithful stands. In this it is I desire to know 'you, to be known by you, and to have Fellow-'ship with you; earnestly breathing to the 'God of Truth, the Father of Spirits, that He 'would be pleased to pour forth more abundant-'ly of His good Spirit into all our Hearts, and 'fill us with the blessed Fruits thereof, that 'there may be no room for the Enemy to enter, 'to break this holy Fellowship; but that all, 'who profess to believe in the Light, may so 'walk therein, that a clear Sight they may

'have

'have thereby, and a true Discerning between 'Things that differ, and may be able to make a 'right Judgment what is of God, and what is 'not; that so the Design of that Spirit (by 'whatsoever Instrument it works) which would 'break or disturb the Churches Peace, and cast 'Reproach upon the Heritage of God, may be 'so discovered and laid open, that all may see 'and shun it. As this is the Exercise and Tra-'vail of my Spirit, so it is the Service I have been 'of late, and am at present engaged in. For 'Friends, 'tis not many Months since I saluted 'you with an Epistle, wherein my Spirit was 'drawn forth, *briefly to commemorate the gracious* '*Dealings of the Lord with His People*; and, as in 'a general way, to remind you of the many 'Attempts the Enemy hath made by Force 'and Fraud, to hinder the Work of God from 'going on; so more particularly to warn you *to* '*beware of that Spirit of Contention and Division,* '*which hath appeared of late in* George Keith, '*and some few others that join with him, who have* '*made a Separation from Friends in some Parts* '*of* America. In writing that Epistle I did not 'consult Flesh and Blood, neither had I an Eye 'to my own Ease and Quiet, as outwardly, (for 'I had no Reason to expect Rest from so restless 'a Man, nor fair Treatment from one, who in 'his late Writings and personal Debates hath so 'notoriously let loose his Pen and Tongue, to 'an *unbridled Liberty* of railing and reviling) 'but I clear'd my Conscience, in discharging 'my Duty to God and to His Church, and

'therein

1694. 'therein have that Peace, which all his Abuſes 'cannot diſturb.'

And ſo he proceeds to clear himſelf of the Perverſions, &c. which G. *Keith* charged him with, and anſwers all his Cavils againſt his Book; manifeſting his Deceit, Evaſions and Sophiſtry ſo effectually, that I do not find that G. *Keith* ever replied to it, being anſwered home, and having his Belly full, I ſuppoſe of the Controverſy with *T. Ellwood*; for though our Friend *Thomas* anſwered ſeveral other of G. *Keith*'s Books afterwards (of which hereafter) he never replied to any of them; which ſhews he had enough of it.

At the End of this Book of G. *Keith*'s, *J. Raunce* came forth again, with a new Slander againſt *T. Ellwood*, (all his old ones being baffled) as if his Father had not been buried decently; which however falſe, G. *Keith*'s mean Mind, it ſeems, could not reſiſt *J. Raunce*'s ſlight Offer, to take off an Hundred of his Books; but rather glad of any Help to run down his Opponent, if he could with Slander, which he found he could not do with Arguments. 'But had G. *Keith* 'been a Man of any Worthineſs (ſays *T. Ellwood*) 'or his Cauſe defenſible, he would not (though 'an Adverſary) have ſuffer'd *J. Raunce* to have 'clapt on his abuſive Piece at the End of his 'Book, to throw Dirt at his Opponent. And 'had *J. Raunce* been a manly Adverſary, he 'would have ſcorn'd to have crept in at the Tail 'of another's Book, to renew his Slander, no 'way relating to the Subject of the Book, when

' *T. Ellwood*'s

'*T. Ellwood*'s *fair Examination* had lain a 1694.
'Twelve-month at his Door unanſwered.' But
to creep behind ſuch a mickle Man as *G. Keith*
was taken to be, *J. Raunce* perhaps might count
it no Diſgrace to repeat his Slander, which *T.
Ellwood* had anſwered in his Poſtſcript to the
fair Examination: And for a final Stroke to it,
he produces Certificates from thoſe who were
concerned about his Father at the Time of his
Death and Interment, that he was decently
buried as uſual; which may be ſeen at the End
of this Book, in Reply to *G. Keith.* And there's
an End of all thoſe lying Stories raiſed concerning the Dead, to aſperſe the Living, to the
Shame and Confuſion of all the Inventors and
Fomentors of them; the Man was dead and in
his Grave, and there ſhould have reſted without
Envy or Detraction; and I am only ſorry he
ſeemed to retain his Averſion to his Son for the
Truth's-ſake, which he received in his early
Days. To the Honour of which I attribute it,
that he was preſerved and carried through, and
over all Oppoſition, and lived in Reputation and
Renown to his dying Day.

His next Book is in 1695, intituled *Truth de-* 1695.
*fended, and the Friends thereof cleared from the
falſe Charges, foul Reproaches, and envious Cavils
caſt upon it and them by* George Keith *(an Apoſtate from them) in two Books by him lately publiſhed; one called* A true Copy of a Paper delivered into the Yearly-meeting, &c. *The other*,
The pretended Yearly-meeting's nameleſs Bull
of Excommunication, &c. In which laſt, *G.
Keith*

1695. *Keith* gives an Account of his coming to the Yearly-meeting (1695) and of his Entertainment in it (when admitted) as if he had never been there before, *viz. That he was allowed to ſit at the great ſquare Table among the Miniſters and Commiſſioners* (as he calls them) *that could hold about it, either fully, or near double, to the Number of twenty-four; whether by Alluſion to the twenty-four Seats and Elders, mentioned* Rev. iv. *but doubling the Number he doth not determine*; adding, *I think it ſuits not their crying out ſo much as they were wont againſt chief Seats in the Synagogues, to erect ſuch a ſtately Fabrick in their Meeting-houſe at that Time, little differing from the manner of a Throne, but that it is low upon the Floor, covered with green Cloth.* All which only ſerves to ſhew his own *Pageantry*, and which our Friend *T. Ellwood* corrects him for according to his Deſerts. For the Table will hold few more than twenty-four or twenty-eight at moſt, and only neceſſary to lay Books and Papers on to write.

In the Beginning of this Book, our Friend *T. Ellwood* reſumes the Controverſy from the Beginning, ſhews the Riſe of the Difference, and Proceedings thereupon, in relation to *George Keith*, particularly after his coming into *England* in the Beginning of 1694, and how he came to be diſowned by the Yearly-meeting in 1695, for his rejecting the Advice of the former, and oppoſite Carriage thereunto; which being ſo excellent to the Matter in hand, and ſetting the

Controverſy

Controversy in a clear Light, I shall here insert 1695.
it; which begins thus:

'It is an old Observation, That none prove
'more angry and implacable Enemies to any
'Society of People, than those that for their
'Disorders and unruly Behaviour, have been
'disowned by the Society they once were of; a
'certain vindictive Enmity usually getting up
'in such, and stirring them up to load that
'Society, by which they were denied, with all
'the Reproach and Infamy they can, thereby
'both gratifying a revengeful Spirit in them-
'selves, and thinking also by recriminating
'others, to extenuate at least their own Crimes.
'That thus it was in the early Times of *Christi-*
'*anity*, may be gathered from the Writings
'of the Apostles, particularly 2 *Tim.* iv. 14.
'2 *Pet.* ii. 1 *John* ii. 18, *&c.* 3 *John* 9, *&c.*
'*Jude*, vers. 4. Among those in this Age, whom
'Satan hath drawn to this degree of Malice and
'Madness, *George Keith* a *Scotchman* is the
'latest, but not the least, whether with respect
'to his Anger or his Envy. He having been
'bred a Scholar before he came amongst the
'People called *Quakers*, and having acquired
'more of School-learning than most (it may
'be, in his own Opinion, than any) of that
'People have, hath given in himself a demon-
'strative Proof of the Apostle's Proposition,
'*Knowledge puffeth up, where edifying Charity* 1 Cor.
'*is not joined with it.* For *human Knowledge* 8 1.
'is apt of itself to lift up Mens Minds that
'have, or think they have it, in any degree of
'Eminency,

'Eminency, and makes them think better of 'themselves than of others, or than themselves 'deserve; whereas true Charity useth Know-'ledge to instruct, and therereby builds up; not 'to puzzle and confound, and thereby destroy 'others: But that Charity this Man not having, 'but being vainly puffed up in his fleshly 'Mind, from a proud Conceit of his own Abi-'lities, and being gotten into *America* among 'a plain People, who better understood the 'the plain and simple Truth than the nice 'Distinctions and Subtilties of the Schools, and 'there advanced to the Office of a School-'master, with a standing Sallary, as I have been 'informed, of an hundred and twenty Pounds 'by the Year, he soon began, like *Diotrephes*
3 John 9, 10. 'of old, to affect *Pre-eminence in the Church*; 'and nothing less would serve his Turn, than 'to rule and over-rule all. And that he might 'not want Matter to work upon, and some 'Pretence to begin on, he not only found fault 'with Friends Ministry and Discipline there; 'but having, in private Discourses, put some 'captious and ensnaring Questions to some par-'ticular Persons there, whose Simplicity he 'thought he might most easily betray, he (by 'wresting their Answers to a wrong Sense) took 'Advantage to complain against them, *for hold-'ing*, as he said, *gross and vile Errors*, and with 'impetuous Heat prosecuted his Charge; and 'not being so fully nor speedily answered as he 'expected, by those Friends to whom he com-'plained, who seeing the Innocency of the

'accused,

'accused, and his evil Design in accusing, could 1695.
'not countenance him therein, he involved
'them also in the like Charge of *cloaking or*
'*covering gross and vile Errors, damnable Heresies*
'*and Doctrines of Devils*, &c. Nor gave he
'over, till by continual Clamours and frequent
'Disturbances, he had filled Friends Meetings
'with Strife and Contention; and at length
'having leavened a Party to himself, made an
'open Division and Separation from Friends,
'setting up separate Meetings for himself and
'his Party, in Opposition to the Meetings of
'Friends before settled there. And having got
'the Printer to his Party (and thereby the only
'Press there at his Command) he maliciously
'put the Difference into Print, and thereby
'spread it not only in those Parts of *America*,
'but in these of *Europe* also. These Things
'drew Friends there, after much Patience and
'long Forbearance, to deal with him in a
'Church-way, and to give forth at length a
'Testimony against him; which proving uneasy
'to him, he came over from thence to *England*,
'about the Beginning of the Year 1694, of
'which some Friends of *Pennsylvania* having
'Notice, came over also; and at the Yearly-
'meeting of the People called *Quakers*, holden
'at *London* in the fourth Month that Year, the
'Matters relating to that Difference being fully
'heard and considered, the Sense of that Meet-
'ing was, *That the Separation lay at* G. Keith's
'*door*; *and that he had done ill, in printing and*
'*publishing those Differences as he had done.* And

1695. ‘ the Advice of the Meeting to him thereupon ‘ was, *To call in those Books of his, or publish* ‘ *something innocently and effectually to clear the* ‘ *Body of the People called* Quakers *and their* ‘ *Ministers, from those gross Errors charged on* ‘ *some few in* America ; *and retract the bitter* ‘ *Language in them, so far as he was concerned ;* ‘ *and sincerely to use his utmost Endeavours with* ‘ *his Friends concerned, to remove the Separa-* ‘ *tion*, &c. Which Sense and Advice being ‘ drawn up at large in writing, was then in ‘ that Meeting delivered to him, and soon after ‘ printed by one of his Party with very envious ‘ Reflections upon it, as may be seen in a small ‘ Pamphlet, called *A true Account*, &c. to ‘ which I refer. But so far was *G. Keith* from ‘ regarding the Sense, or following the Advice ‘ of that Yearly-meeting, that in several printed ‘ Books by him soon after published, he rejected ‘ it, denying it to be the Sense or Advice of the ‘ Yearly-meeting, or that to be the Yearly-‘ meeting that gave it. Which Abuse this last ‘ Yearly-meeting (in the third Month past) ‘ taking Notice of, and upon further dealing ‘ with him, finding him instead of being hum-‘ bled and sorry for the Evil he had done, more ‘ hardned therein, justifying himself both by ‘ Word and Writing, and rejecting the Meet-‘ ing's Advice. That Meeting (after it had heard ‘ him patiently, till he of his own Accord ‘ withdrew) gave forth a Testimony against ‘ him ; which he hath since printed, with his ‘ Answer thereunto. As he hath also (in another Pamphlet)

‘ Pamphlet) a Copy of his Paper which he read 1695.
‘ in the Meeting; together with a Narrative
‘ (of his own making) of the Proceedings of
‘ the Meeting with him, and a Liſt of Errors
‘ charged by him on ſome particular Perſons.
‘ To each of theſe I intend to ſpeak, now that
‘ I have premiſed this ſhort Introduction; which
‘ I thought needful for the Information of any
‘ ſuch Reader as had not before heard the Riſe
‘ of the Difference, nor the Courſe of Proceed-
‘ ings thereupon.’

This I thought fit to inſert, being ſo material as to the Ground of the Controverſy with *G. Keith*; after which *T. Ellwood* proceeds to anſwer all his Cavils in his ſaid two Books or Papers. And ſhews that by his diſorderly Practices he had excluded himſelf from our Society, before Friends diſowned him. So leaving him without Excuſe, and the Weight of his Iniquity upon his own Head, which he could never get from under, but waxed worſe and worſe, as evil Men and Seducers uſe to do, ſo that Truth was ſet over his Head, and Friends were clear of him.

But now another Occaſion offer'd, and that was, one *Gerard Croeſe* a *Dutchman*, publiſhing *A general Hiſtory* (ſo called) *of the* Quakers, *containing the Lives, Tenets, Sufferings, Trials, Speeches* and *Letters* (as pretended) *of the moſt eminent of them*, firſt in *Latin*; which was tranſlated and printed in *Engliſh* in the Year 1696. Wherein, though he had repreſented ſome Things pretty fairly; yet in others, through

1696. Inadvertency or Ignorance (I hope not wilfully) he had misrepresented us, and our Principles and Practices; whereupon our Friend *T. Ellwood*, according to an Advertisement at the End of the said History in *English*, that *some Remarks on it would be published*, he writ some Remarks on it in *Latin* (perhaps before the *English* came out, which would no doubt have been turn'd into *English*) intending doubtless to publish them; but in the mean Time before they were finished, a Book of the same Nature and to the same Purpose, in *Latin*, was published in *Holland*, by way of Remarks or Observations on the said *History*; which seemed again to circumvent him in his intended Remarks on it, so that he laid them by, and never finished them, and so the World was deprived of this Piece also.

But now *G. Keith* being gone out from the Fellowship of the Faithful, and hardned in his Enmity against Friends, he arrived to the Top or Height of Opposition; he had been playing small Stakes hitherto, but now came to throw all at once. In order to which he erected a Stage of Contention at *Turners-hall* in *Philpot-lane*, *London* (where he had held separate Meetings for some Time before) to oppose Friends in general, under Pretence of discovering divers Errors out of the *Quakers* Books (that were never in them) and published an Advertisement of a Meeting he intended to hold there, in the fourth Month 1696, to discover the *Quakers* Errors (though he had been one so long himself, and

and vindicated them, as to all that any could 1696.
object against, and yet now came to accuse them himself;) but Friends slighted him, not thinking it worth their while to follow him, or dance after his Pipe to *Turners-hall.* Of which contentious Meeting he afterwards published a Narrative; which our Friend *T. Ellwood* answered this Year, in a Book intituled, *An Answer to* George Keith's *Narrative of his Proceedings at* Turners-hall, *&c. wherein his Charges against divers of the People called* Quakers *(in that and another Book of his, called* Gross Errors, *&c.) are fairly considered, examined and refuted.* And he made his Title good in a close Answer, and entire Confutation of all his Cavils against our Friends Books; which, because I have given the Preambles or Introductions of his former, to illustrate the matter, I shall also, in like manner, introduce this with his general Account of the Controversy, by Way of Introduction to his Answer, being so pertinent to the Case in hand, for the Reader's better Information and Satisfaction, which follows, beginning thus:

'It is not surely without good Reason, that 'the Church of Christ here on Earth, is called 'the *Church-militant:* For, besides the inward 'and spiritual Enemies, which her several Mem-'bers have to encounter with, in their Pilgri-'mage through this troublesome World, such 'hath been and is her Lot and Portion, that she 'hath rarely been free from outward Enemies 'of one kind or other, her great Adversary 'Satan, continually raising up some evil Instru-

1696. 'ments or other to fall upon her; all aiming
'at her Ruin, though after divers Ways and
'Manners. Sometimes the Civil Powers under
'which ſhe hath lived, have been ſtirred up to
'proclaim as it were open War againſt her, and
'to inflict ſevere and heavy Penalties upon her,
'for her faithful Adherence to her Lord and
'Maſter, Chriſt Jeſus. When through Faith
'and Patience ſhe hath overcome, and the
'Wrath and Fury of Men hath been aſſwaged,
'ſo that ſhe hath had ſome Reſpite from thoſe
'outward Sufferings; then hath her old Adver-
'ſary (the common Enemy of Mankind) be-
'ſtirr'd himſelf in another Way, to raiſe up
'*Perſecution* againſt her of another kind, by
'inſtigating ſome or other (either ſuch as were
'always avowed Enemies to her, or ſuch as for
'ſome time appeared to be of her, but by the
'Sweep of his Tail had been ſtruck off from her)
'to ſpeak or write againſt her, falſly to accuſe
'her, and load her with the fouleſt Reproaches,
'and moſt infamous Slanders and Scandals, that
'by ſo miſrepreſenting her, they might hinder
'others from joining to or favouring her, and ſtir
'up the Civil Magiſtrate again to perſecute her
'afreſh. This hath been the Lot, this the Con-
'dition of the little Flock of Chriſt in former
'Ages, as *Eccleſiaſtical Hiſtories* declare. As for
'the preſent Age, and with reſpect to the People
'called *Quakers*, whom God by an inviſible Arm
'of Power hath raiſed up, and held up, and
'made a peculiar People to himſelf, Experience
'gives ſufficient Proof, the Matter being yet freſh
'in

'in Memory. For, not to look back ſo far as
'that which was called the *Common-wealth*'s
'Time, wherein many of the leading Men in
'moſt Profeſſions, put forth their utmoſt Strength
'againſt us, both in preaching and printing,
'raiſing thoſe falſe Reports concerning us, and
'charging many falſe Accuſations upon us, with
'reſpect both to *Doctrine* and *Practice*, which
'others of our Adverſaries that followed after,
'have taken up upon Truſt from them; no
'ſooner was that great Perſecution a little abated
'(which ſoon after the Reſtoration of King
'*Charles* the Second, through the Fault of ſome
'*Diſſenters* fell upon *all*, but moſt heavily upon
'*us)* and that a little Calm and Quiet enſued,
'but out came ſeveral Books againſt us, written
'by ſome of thoſe Profeſſors, who either in
'ſome meaſure did ſuffer, or (if they had been
'faithful to their own Principle) ſhould have
'ſuffered in the ſame Storm with us. By that
'time the Duſt, which thoſe Books had raiſed,
'was laid by our Anſwers thereunto, a freſh
'Perſecution from the Government aroſe upon
'the *Informing Act*, the main Weight of which
'it is well known fell upon us; they who
'before and afterwards aſſaulted us in Print,
'finding Ways then to hide and ſave themſelves
'from Suffering. But when that Storm was a
'little over, out they came again, and in divers
'Books written by *Faldo*, *Hicks*, and others,
'heaped up many wrong Charges, Defama-
'tions, Slanders and falſe Accuſations againſt us;
'all which were refuted and wiped off in our

1696. 'Books, printed in Anſwer thereunto: Nor 'have thoſe of other Profeſſions been ſo forward 'to attack us ſince. But now that Liberty of 'Conſcience, in the free Exerciſe of religious 'Worſhip, is by Authority granted, and there-'by outward Sufferings, in a great meaſure 'abated, our old Enemy envying us ſo great a 'Benefit, though but in common with others, 'hath contrived Ways and Means to raiſe a '*new War* againſt us, by ſtirring up ſome who 'have formerly walked with us, and for ſome 'Time profeſſed to be of us (but upon ſome 'peeviſh Diſcontent or other, have turned aſide 'and left us) to turn now againſt us and oppoſe 'us, and to pour forth Floods of Reproach, 'Slanders and falſe Accuſations upon us. His 'chief Agent, at preſent in this Work, is *George* '*Keith* a *Scotchman*, whoſe *ambitious Aims* not 'being anſwered, nor his *abſurd* and *fantaſtical* '*Notions* received by and amongſt the People 'called *Quakers*, he is now become, of a *ſeem-*'*ing Friend*, a *real Enemy*. He having pub-'liſhed many Books againſt us, and in Defence 'of thoſe Books wrangled with us for a while 'in Print, till he found himſelf too cloſely 'pinched, to be able to give an Anſwer fit to be 'ſeen in Print, hath at length bethought him-'ſelf of a *Wile* to excuſe himſelf from anſwer-'ing; which was to ſet up a kind of *Judicial* '*Court*, of his *own Head* and by his *own Autho-*'*rity*, in a Place at his *own Command*, on a 'Day of his *own Appointing*, there to charge 'and try divers of us who are called *Quakers*,

'whether

'whether present or absent, concerning Matters 1696.
'of *Faith* and *Doctrine*; and that the rude
'Multitude might not be wanting to his Assist-
'ance there, he gave publick Notice of it some
'Time before, by an Advertisement in Print,
'and therein a Sort of *Summons* to some of us
'by Name, to others by Designation, to be pre-
'sent. This *arbitrary* Proceeding, and *usurped*
'Authority, as we judged it unreasonable in
'him to impose, so we did not think fit to
'submit to, or own, and therefore forbore to
'appear at the Time and Place by him appoint-
'ed. Yet lest any whom he should draw
'thither, might mistake the Cause of our not
'appearing, the Reasons thereof drawn up in
'short Heads, were sent thither to be read, and
'given among the People; which they were.
'However, according to his before declared In-
'tention, to proceed whether any of us were
'there or no, he being *Judge in his own Court*,
'over-ruled our Reasons, and went on to arraign
'and convict us absent. The *Pageantry* of
'which Day's Work, as acted there by himself,
'he hath since published with his Name to it,
'under the Title of *An exact Narrative of the
'Proceedings at* Turner's-hall, *&c. Together with
'the Disputes and Speeches there, between* G. Keith
'*and other* Quakers, *differing from him in some
'religious Principles.* How idle is this in him,
'to pretend in his Title to give an Account of
'Disputes and Speeches between him and other
'*Quakers*, whenas his *Narrative* itself gives no
'Account of any Dispute there, nor any thing
'like

1696. 'like it; and of that little that was said by any 'of those few *Quakers* that were present, most 'was to the People (tending to shew them the 'Unreasonableness of his Undertaking, and de'siring them to reserve one Ear for the other 'Side) very little of it to him.'

Then he goes on to shew *G. Keith*'s Falshood, in calling it *An exact Narrative*; and yet not inserting the Reasons why our Friends did not appear, which he confesses were read; and his Fallacies in evading them, which theretore *T. Ellwood* sets down, obviates *G. Keith*'s Quibbles on them: So proceeds to answer his *Narrative*, clearing the Quotations he brought out of our Friends Books, from his Perversions (being either unfairly or falsly quoted, or perverted in their Sense to what they never intended, according to his carping and cavilling Way.) Vindicating the Soundness of their Doctrine, shewing *G. Keith*'s Self-contradictions (in opposing what he had so often vindicated as Orthodox; and yet pretending to hold the same Doctrines and Principles still) and laying open his Deceit, Falshood and Prevarications so plainly and effectually, that *G. Keith* never replied to it; and good reason why, because he could not to the Purpose, being answered home and defeated in all his vile Pretences, envious Cavils, and false Accusations.

But being pinch'd and driven to a Nonplus, by Quotations out of his own Books in Favour of what he opposed, which he could not answer; wherein he had asserted or defended the same Doctrines and Principles, in as plain or higher

higher Words, which he now blamed Friends for as groſs Errors, *&c.* Which yet he would not allow to be ſo in himſelf, but paliated them under the ſoft Term of *Miſtakes*; ſaying, *Narrative*, pag. 15. *I know not any fundamental Principle, nor indeed any one Principle of* Chriſtian *Faith, that I have varied from to this Day, ever ſince I came among the* Quakers, *which is about Thirty-three Years ago.* —— And in his Preface to his *Narrative*, pag. 6. he ſays, *The Things* (he does not call them *Errors*, nor hardly ever uſes the Word *Error* with reſpect to himſelf and his own Writings.—) *that need Correction in my Books, compared with the vile Errors in theirs, are but as my Motes to their Beams: —Nor are they ſuch Things as oppoſe any* Chriſtian *Principles of Faith; but of an inferior Nature.* [and yet they were as full in the Points, as any he could cite out of ours.] And in *The true Copy of a Paper*, printed 1694, where, in pag. 17. he faintly intimates a Purpoſe to publiſh ſome *ſhort Explication*, &c. — *of ſome Words and Paſſages in his former Books.* He adds, *For upon a Review of my fomer Books,—I freely acknowledge, I have found ſome Paſſages and Words, that not only need ſome farther Explanation; but even in ſome Part, an Emendation and Correction.* ‘ How gently ‘ doth he touch himſelf? (ſays *T. Ellwood)* How ‘ ſoftly doth he handle his own Sores? Not a ‘ Syllable of *Errors* or *Hereſy* there; no, the ‘ hardeſt Word he can afford to give them, is, ‘ his *former Miſtakes.*’ And leſt the Reader ſhould extend them too far, he explains it in the

1696. the next Page, ſaying, *Upon the moſt impartial Search I have made, I find not any Cauſe to correct either my Judgment or Books, as touching any of the great Doctrines and Principles of the* Chriſtian *Religion; nor do I know that I am of another Faith in any one Principle of* Chriſtian *Doctrine, contrary to what I believed, ever ſince I went under the Profeſſion of a* Quaker, *ſo called.* With much more to the ſame Purpoſe.

Thus partial was he as to himſelf, notwithſtanding his loud Clamours and Outcries of *vile Errors* againſt the *Quakers*, for the ſame Things he had held himſelf, which yet were no *Errors* in him; ſuch a Hypocrite was he to diſſemble with God and Man. So that when he found his Doctrines compared with what he accuſed Friends of, and ſaw they were the ſame or parallel; 'twas to no purpoſe for him to go to vindicate or clear himſelf of what was ſo notorious: And therefore procured another, or at leaſt he undertook it for him, under Diſguiſe of the *Snake in the Graſs*: And ſo to ſlide by the Quotations out of his Books, that lay in his Way; which would have been a Shame for *G. Keith* to do (a *Snake in the Graſs* indeed) pretending in his Preface, that *it was not meant as a Defence of* George Keith, *any further than he defended the Truth of the* Chriſtian *Faith; for which Reaſon* (ſays he) *I have wholly omitted all the perſonal Reflections caſt upon him, and the Contradictions which* Thomas Ellwood *pretends to find in his former Books (while he was a* Quaker *of their Communion) to the Doctrine he*

now

now sets up in Opposition to them. And so gave 1696.
the go-by to whatever pincht him, which was the Design, as *T. Ellwood* observes, to help *G. Keith* off at a dead Lift, from his manifold and manifest Self-contradictions, which it was impossible for him to reconcile or defend; and because it had been as absurd for him to have undertaken a Reply to *T. Ellwood*'s Answer, and not have attempted to acquit himself of those Contradictions charged upon him therein, as it would have been impossible for him to have clear'd himself of them. Therefore this Contrivance was found out, that another (or perhaps he in a Mask, under the Disguise of another, for Satan, though disrob'd from his Disguise of Light, has many black Robes and dark Disguises to put on) should undertake the Task of replying (for a Task it seems it was) upon such a Foot, and under such Circumstances, as might give him some colourable Pretence to wave the Contradictions, and wholly to omit them, and with them, whatsoever else he found too hard to meddle with.

So that any one might plainly see this was a Contrivance (as our Friend *T. Ellwood* observes) to help *G. Keith* out at a dead Lift. To which Book of the *Snake*'s, *T. Ellwood* writ an Answer, though he did not quite finish it, or publish it: Of which, and that Controversy, he gives the following Account.

'This Crontroversy begun by *George Keith* '(upon a Pick he took against the People called '*Quakers*'; because they could not answer his 'ambitious

'ambitious Desire of Rule, nor receive some 'wild and fantastical Notions of his) has been 'carried on by him in his own Name, 'till he 'could go no further. The Doctrines he con-'demns us for as erroneous and heritical, have 'been either so clearly cast off by us as Slan-'ders, or so rivetted on himself by undeniable 'Instances and Proofs taken out of his own 'Books, that (having fore-closed his Way to a 'Retraction of them, as shall be shewed anon) 'he had no Way left, but as his last Shift, to 'shift the Cause into another's Hand; to carry 'it on under the Disguise of another Person; 'which brought to my Mind the Fable of '*Achelous*, who being too weak for his Anta-'gonist in fair Force, was fain to shift from 'one Shape to another; first to that of a *Snake*, 'then to that of a *Bull*; and is thereupon 'brought in by the Poet; saying,

Inferior Virtute, meas divertor ad Artes
Elaborque Viro, Longum formatus in Anguem, &c.
Metam. lib. 9. Fab. 1.

In Strength too weak, I to my Wiles betake,
And slide from Man into a twining Snake.

'Somewhat a like crafty Course has *G. Keith* 'taken; who finding himself over prest the last 'Year with Books, which he knew not how to 'answer, got, as was supposed, an Adjutant 'of his to publish a Book against us under Dis-'guise, without a Name to it, and with the

very

‘ very Title of *the Snake in the Graſs* ; thereby 1697.
‘ to have diverted us from purſuing the Contro-
‘ verſy (then, and ſtill in hand) with him: But
‘ when he found that would not do (for the
‘ Deſign was ſeen) he roar'd againſt us like a
‘ Bull at *Turners-hall*, in the Month called
‘ *June* 1696, and afterwards in his *Narrative*
‘ thereof: The Anſwer to that, which ſoon
‘ followed, has it ſeems involv'd him in ſuch
‘ Difficulties, that he hath not thought fit to
‘ appear againſt it in his own Shape; but either
‘ aſſuming another Perſon, or turning over his
‘ broken Forces (with the united Forces of the
‘ whole Party) to the hiſſing Author of the
‘ *Snake*, they have amongſt them lately thruſt
‘ forth another Book, as a Reply to that Anſwer
‘ of mine to *G. Keith*'s Narrative: This (with-
‘ out a Name too, and ſaid to be written *by the*
‘ *Author of the Snake in the Graſs)* is called
‘ *Satan Diſ-rob'd from his Diſguiſe of Light.*
‘ But the obſervant Reader will find Cauſe
‘ enough I think, to conclude that whoever
‘ writ it, was fully inrob'd in *Satan*'s Over-guiſe
‘ and proper Dreſs of *Darkneſs*, from the many
‘ bitter and ſcornful Invectives therein uſed
‘ againſt the *Light*.

And for the Controverſy itſelf, he remarks,

‘ 1. That the Matters therein charged upon us,
‘ are generally the ſame that have been charged
‘ on us heretofore, by *Faldo*, *Hicks*, and other
‘ Adverſaries; and always refuted over and over,
‘ both formerly and of late.

'2. That the Things they charge on us as 'Errors and Heresy, are not pretended to be 'proved by any plain express Positions or Assertions of ours; but from our Adversaries own 'perverse Meanings, and wrested Constructions 'of our Words; always denied and rejected 'by us.

'3. That the Words and Passages brought 'by our Adversaries for Proof of their Charges 'against us, are not taken out of our Doctrinal 'Treatises, or Declarations of Faith and Prin'ciples; but (for the most part) out of Con'troversial Books; wherein, oft-times, the Scope 'and Aim of the Author is not so much to 'assert or express his own Principles or Doc'trines, as to impugn and expose his Adversary's, 'by shewing the Contradictions, Absurdities, and 'ill Consequences of his Adversary's Opinions; 'from whence, positively to conclude the Au'thor's own Judgment, is neither safe nor fair.

'4. That however any of our former Adver'saries might have been misled in their Judg'ments concerning us, *G. Keith* who hath now 'moved this Controversy against us, knows full 'well, that we do not hold those Things either 'generally as a People, or as particular Persons, 'which he has charged on us as Errors. As a 'People he has clearly acquitted us from them, 'in his *Preface* to his *Narrative*, pag. 6. where 'he says, *I charge them not, either upon the 'Generality, far less upon the Universality of all 'them called* Quakers. For particular Persons, 'hear what he says of *George Whitehead*, one

'of

‘ of the principal Butts he ſhoots at, *Narrative* 1697.
‘ pag. 16. where having charged him with *deny-*
‘ *ing that Chriſt in Heaven has any bodily Exiſt-*
‘ *ence without us*, being conſcious that *G. White-*
‘ *head* did not ſo hold, but that he had therein
‘ abuſed him, he immediately adds, *If he* (G.
‘ Whitehead) *has ſaid otherwiſe in any of his*
‘ *late printed Books, I am glad of it.* And a
‘ Line lower, *There is a* G. Whitehead *orthodox,*
‘ *and a* G. Whitehead *not orthodox. He is — in*
‘ *this and ſome other Things, orthodox and not*
‘ *orthodox :* And a little further, *I own it, that*
‘ *I have cited divers Paſſages out of his later*
‘ *Books that are orthodox, to prove him ſound.*
‘ What can be made of all this, but that *G.*
‘ *Whitehead* was orthodox and ſound in his own
‘ both Intentions and Expreſſions; not orthodox
‘ in *G. Keith*'s perverſe and falſe Conſtructions?
‘ And whereas he harps upon the Word *later*
‘ *Books*, thereby to inſinuate as if *G. Whitehead*
‘ had of late altered his Judgment; he has cut
‘ off that alſo in his *Narrative*, pag. 38. where
‘ he gives an Account, That *in the Year* 1678
‘ (which is eighteen Years ago) *ſome*, whom he
‘ would not name, *queſtioning him about ſome*
‘ *Principles in a Book of his*, both *G. Whitehead*
‘ and *W. Penn* took part with him againſt them,
‘ tho' thoſe Principles (as he calls them) which
‘ he ſays he was then *queſtioned about*, were of
‘ the ſame Nature with ſome of thoſe he now
‘ charges upon them as Errors. From whence
‘ it appears, that he found them then, as well as
‘ now, *ſound* and *orthodox* in thoſe Principles.

1697. ‘ 5. That as this Controverſy lies properly ‘ and directly between *G. Keith* and us, and ‘ that he being baffled in it, and driven to a *Ne* ‘ *plus ultra* on his own Part, hath contrived to ‘ carry it on under Diſguiſe, by the Aſſiſtance ‘ of another, (yet without a Name) who under ‘ Pretence of *Indifferency, and being unconcerned* ‘ *with or for* G. Keith, ſhould drop the Quota- ‘ tions I had loaded him with, out of his own ‘ Books againſt himſelf, and thereby free him, ‘ if he could, from thoſe pinching *Dilemma's* ‘ which lay againſt him, and *draw* Dun (as the ‘ Proverb ſpeaks) *out of the Mire* he was plung'd ‘ into; ſo to obviate and diſappoint the Deſign. ‘ That I may not ſuffer myſelf to be bubbled ‘ by ſuch artificial Shams, but that the Con- ‘ troverſy may be kept, as much as may be, ‘ upon its firſt Bottom, I have thought fit in ‘ this Rejoinder. ſo to order the Matter, as not ‘ to let *G. Keith* ſlip away (which I perceive he ‘ would fain do) while I am contending with I ‘ know not whom in this Quarrel. Therefore ‘ as I paſs through the ſeveral Heads of the ‘ Controverſy, I purpoſe not only to anſwer the ‘ moſt material Cavils of the preſent Adverſary, ‘ but withal to repeat (ſome at leaſt of) thoſe ‘ Paſſages that lay ſo heavy upon *G. Keith*, and ‘ ſettle (not to uſe his own ſmithing Metaphors ‘ of *clinching* and *rivetting*) them faſter on him; ‘ to the End that both the Reader may more ‘ plainly ſee the true Reaſon why *G. Keith* did ‘ not himſelf reply in his own Name, to my ‘ Anſwer to his Narrative, and *G. Keith* may

‘ know

'know that I expect it from him, and in the 1697.
'mean time look upon him but as a baffled
'shifting Adversary.

'He begins his Epistle with telling his Rea-
'der, that *his Reply is short in comparison of the
'Answer.* Therein he and I agree, but in *Words*
'rather than in *Meaning*; for he means in
'Number of Pages, I mean in Truth and fair
'Dealing, in which I am confident the indif-
'ferent Reader will find his Reply *short* indeed:
'And even as to Bulk, upon due Consideration,
'the Disproportion is not so great as he would
'represent it, for his Book is rather more than
'half as big as mine, though he replies not to
'the tenth Part of the Matter contained in
'mine. He makes nothing of skipping over
'ten or fifteen Pages at a time, so nimble
'heel'd he is.' [And yet this is the Man that caution'd the *Quakers*, that *if they answer'd his Book* (Snake, third Edit. pag. 344.) *that they would reply distinctly,— and not answer a Book as Rats do, by nibbling at some Corners of the Leaves, stealing through it like Moths, to no other Purpose than to deface some Words at a venture*; who yet could reply thus slightly himself] 'Nay, in
'his first Page he throws off no less than twenty
'five Pages at once, and barely mentioning, in
'less than nine Lines, a few Words contained
'in some of them, without a Syllable of Reply
'thereto, sets in his Margin, *Reply to the first
'twenty three Pages*; and yet he hath the Con-
'fidence to miscal his Book, and that even in
'the same Page, *A full Reply* (he might better

1697. 'have called it a *foul* and *false Reply) to* T. Ell-
'wood's *Answer*. And in his Epistle says, *he 'has omitted nothing that is material.* I suppose 'he means, that he has omitted nothing which 'he thought might tend to abuse and defame 'the *Quakers* and me; for that he has omitted 'the most material Parts of my Book, and thrust 'in many Passages, idle, impertinent, false and 'wholly foreign to the Subject, only that he 'might misrepresent, ridicule and slander us, I 'shall have Occasion hereafter, by plenty of In-'stances to shew.'

I might cite a great deal more, to explicate this Controversy, and shew their Dis-ingenuity in it; but by this we may judge what a Reply this of the *Snake*'s was, and by this Taste (to use his own Words at the End of the *Snake*) *the Reader may guess what a plentiful Meal we might have had*, if *T. Ellwood* had published his *Rejoinder*, but that, as I said, he did not; for what Reason I cannot justly assign: For though our Friend *George Whitehead* (in his Answer to the *Snake in the Grass*) writ also *A brief Examination of some Passages in the said Book of the Snake's, stiled* Satan disrob'd, *&c.* as being concerned therein; yet he refer'd to a further Answer by *T. Ellwood*, pag. 186. judging it 'No fair Reply 'to *T. Ellwood*'s Answer; and so it appears (says 'he) and I expect will be made further appear, 'if *T. Ellwood* deems it worth the while to un-'dertake it:' Which he did, and writ twenty seven Sheets in order thereto; and why he should be prevented from publishing it, by *G. Whitehead's*

Whitehead's brief Examination, I do not ſee, 1697.
being much larger and fuller; but perceive he
was ſo modeſt, that he was apt to be put by of his Work, if any other put in before him, as will further appear on another Occaſion hereafter. And ſo I ſhall leave it, hoping however one Time or other, to ſee this and ſome other of his Poſthumous Works publiſhed by themſelves, as they well deſerve.

And here our Friend drop'd his Pen, till another Occaſion offer'd.

And that was next (or at leaſt the next he laid hold on) after a Vacancy of two or three Years, on this Occaſion:

Some angry Prieſts in *Norfolk*, on our Friends having a Meeting near one of them, and Truth ſpreading to their Regret, they challenged a Diſpute with ſome of our Friends at *Weſt-Deerham* in that County, the 8th of the tenth Month 1698, where ſome of our Friends appearing and anſwering them, ſo diſappointed the Prieſts in their envious Deſigns in the ſaid Diſpute, that they afterwards promoted two Petitions againſt our Friends to the Parliament (one from *Norfolk*, the other from *Suffolk)* to ſtir up Perſecution againſt them, that what they could not do by Arguments, they might by Force. To which two Petitions, our Friend *T. Ellwood* (having obtained Copies of them) writ *A ſober Reply on Behalf of the People called* Quakers, *to two Petitions againſt them (the one out of* Norfolk, *and the other from* Bury *in* Suffolk) *being ſome brief Obſervations upon them*, &c.

 printed

1698. printed 1699, manifesting their mischievous Machinations against the Truth and Friends; which, with some other Discouragements, through the Labour and Industry of Friends at *London*, in attending the Parliament, and delivering printed Papers, particularly, *A few Considerations humbly offered to the Members of Parliament, to obviate some evil Jealousies and Designs against the People called* Quakers, so quashed their malicious Purposes, that their Petitions were never delivered to, or received by the Parliament; but fell and came to nothing, and their evil Designs were frustrated, Friends were preserved, and Truth prospered over their Heads.

1699. About this Time also, our Friend *William Penn* being gone to *Pennsylvania* (in the seventh Month this Year) and *G. Keith* continuing his Opposition against Truth and Friends, sometimes more general at *Turners-hall*, where, as the Course of his *delirious Distemper* returned (as *Joseph Wyeth* observes, in his Answer to his Advertisement this Year) he held his contentious Meetings once a Year, to pick Passages out of our Friends Books to cavil at (though he could not answer nor clear himself of *T. Ellwood's*, or others that were writ against him) and sometimes more particularly against single Persons, especially *William Penn*, against whom he chose to vent his Malice above most others, especially now in his Absence, making him the Butt of his Indignation; and published two Books against him, one called *The Deism of* William Penn

Penn *and his Brethren*, &c. This our Friend T. *Ellwood* undertook to anſwer, and made a conſiderable Progreſs in it, in a large Book of between thirty and forty Sheets, which I ſhall cite ſome of, beginning thus:

'We read of one in former Times, who be-'cauſe he had given up himſelf to do Evil, 'was ſaid to have *ſold himſelf to work Wickedneſs* '*in the Sight of the Lord*, 1 Kings xxi. 20, and '25. Whether *George Keith* hath directly ſold 'himſelf, or only let himſelf out to hire, I will 'not undertake to determine; but evident it is, 'that ſince he crept into the Intereſt of that 'which is called the *Church of England*, and 'become a mercenary Hackney to ſome of the 'Clergy, he hath laid out himſelf, with his 'utmoſt Vigour, to *work Wickedneſs*, not only *in* '*the Sight of the Lord*, but *in the Sight of the* '*Sun*; aſſerting, defending, maintaining and 'upholding divers both *Doctrines* and *Practices* 'in Religion, which upon a declared full Con-'viction, and from a profeſſed Aſſurance of di-'vine Openings, and immediate Guidance of 'the *holy Spirit*, he had before not only re-'nounced, but declared and written againſt as '*falſe*, *ſuperſtitious* (if not *idolatrous*) and *anti*-'*chriſtian*; and to fill up his Meaſure of *Iniquity*, 'and heap it up that it might run over, he hath 'not only (to gratify his Supporters) ſhot his 'unadviſed Bolts at the ſeveral other Bodies of '*Proteſtant* Diſſenters, but in an eſpecial manner '(and in a moſt virulent, and to him peculiar 'Stile) hath evomitted Floods, not of *Reproach*

1699. 'only and *bitter Revilings*, but of the most 'malicious Slanders and Falshoods, that ever perhaps were poured from the Pulpit, or squeezed 'through the Press against the People called '*Quakers*, whom once he owned for his Brethren, and with whom he professed to hold 'Communion for more than thirty Years. 'Herein he hath exceeded good *Joseph* of old in 'his Liberality, but in another kind: That 'good Man bestowed a *Fivefold-mess* of his *good* '*Things* on his Brother *Benjamin*, as a Token 'of his peculiar and abundant Love to him. 'This bad Man has bestowed *double* and *treble* 'that Proportion of his *evil Things* on us: The 'Effect of his peculiar and superabundant 'Hatred to us, to say nothing here of his railing Rhetorick and bitter Invectives against us, 'wherewith he hath prophaned the Pulpit, 'which lie under the just Censure of the more 'discreet and well-minded of his Auditors. An 'Instance of his Malice and Injustice from the 'Press, is a late Book of his now lying before 'me, called *The Deism of* William Penn *and his* '*Brethren, destructive to the* Christian *Religion,* '*exposed*, &c. The Word [*Deism*] being somewhat an uncommon Term, may not perhaps be readily understood by every Reader. 'As it has been opposed to *Atheism*, it has been 'taken in a good Sense; but as it is now used, it 'is taken in an ill Sense, as importing an Acknowledgement or owning of God *only*, or of 'the *Godhead*; but not of Christ, with respect 'to his Incarnation, or being manifest in the

Flesh

' Flesh for the Redemption of Man: So that to 1699.
' charge any one now with *Deism*, is to charge
' him with denying that Christ is come, and
' hath suffered in the Flesh. Now herein *G.*
' *Keith*'s both Injustice and Malice is the greater,
' in charging *W. Penn*, and his Brethren the
' *Quakers*, with *Deism*; inasmuch as he assuredly
' knows (which some other Adversaries have
' not had the like Opportunity to know, as
' he hath had) by certaian Experience, drawn
' by so many Years intimate Conversation with
' *W. Penn* and the *Quakers*, in free and familiar
' Conferences, and in reading their Books, that
' *W. Penn* and the *Quakers*, both in Word and
' Writing, publickly and privately, have always,
' and on all Occasions confest, acknowledged,
' owned as well as believed, the Incarnation of
' Christ, according to the holy Scriptures, *viz.*
' That *the Word was made Fesh.* That *when the* John 1. 14.
' *Fulness of Time was come, God sent forth his Son* Gal. 4. 4, 5.
' *made of a Woman, made under the Law, to*
' *redeem them that were under the Law.* That
' *Christ Jesus being in the Form of God, and* Phil. 2. 5, 6, 7, 8.
' *thinking it no Robbery to be equal with God;*
' *made Himself of no Reputation, and took upon*
' *Him the Form of a Servant, and was made in*
' *the Likeness of Men; and being found in Fashion*
' *as a Man, He humbled Himself, and became*
' *obedient unto Death, even the Death of the Cross.*
' *Christ died for our Sins, according to the Scrip-* 1 Cor. 15. 3, 4.
' *tures, and that He was buried, and that He*
' *rose again the third Day, according to the Scrip-*
' *tures.* That *He was delivered for our Offences,* Rom. 4. 25.

' *and*

1699. ' *and was raised again for our Justification.* ' That *He is the Propitiation for our Sins; and*
1 John 2. 2. ' *not for ours only, but for the Sins of the whole*
Ephes. 4. 10. ' *World.* That *He ascended up far above all* ' *Heavens, that He might fill all Things.* That
1 Tim. 2. 5. ' *He is one Mediator between God and Men.* That
Rom. 8. 34. ' *He is at the right Hand of God, and maketh* ' *Intercession for us.* And is *our Advocate with*
1 John 2. 1. ' *the Father.* And *that it is He which was or-* ' *dained of God, to be the Judge of Quick and*
Acts 10. 42. ' *Dead.* These Things, I say, *G. Keith* certain-' ly knows have been constantly held, believed, ' professed and owned by *W. Penn* and his ' Brethren the *Quakers* in general, both privately ' and publickly, in Word and Writing. These ' Things are so often testified of in our Meetings, ' and have been so fully and plainly asserted and ' held forth in our Books, that we might call ' in almost as many Witnesses thereof, as have ' frequented our Meetings, or attentively read ' our Books.

' The Book of *W. Penn*'s, called *A Discourse* ' *of the general Rule of Faith and Life.* (To ' which *G. Keith*'s *Deism* is an Answer) *G.* ' *Keith* tells us in his Preface, *was first printed* ' *in the Year* 1673, as an Appendix to *W. Penn*'s ' Part of the *Christian Quaker.* (A folio Book ' in two Parts; the former written by *W. Penn,* ' the latter by *G. Whitehead)* In that former ' Part of the *Christian Quaker*, written by *W.* ' *Penn*, though the Tendency of it is to assert ' and defend the Divinity of Christ, and His ' spiritual Appearance by His divine Light in

' the

'the Hearts of Men; yet there is enough ſaid 1699.
'concerning His Manhood, His outward Ap-
'pearance, and Sufferings in the Fleſh, to free
'*W. Penn* from the Imputation or Suſpicion
'of *Deiſm*.—In pag. 101. *W. Penn* ſays, Not-
'withſtanding the ſame Light and Life, with
'that which afterwards cloathed itſelf with that
'outward Body, did in meaſure inwardly ap-
'pear for the Salvation of the Souls of Men;
'yet, as I have often ſaid, never did that Life
'ſo eminently put forth itſelf to that End, as in
'that ſanctified and prepared Body; ſo that
'what He then ſuffered and did, in that tran-
'ſcendent Manifeſtation, may, by Way of Emi-
'nency, aſſume the whole Work unto itſelf, that
'He ever did before, or might do afterwards.—
'Pag. 102. His righteous Life, with reſpect to
'its Appearance in that Body, was grieved by
'Sin, and the Weight of the Iniquity of the
'whole World, with the Concernment of its
'eternal Well-being, lay hard upon Him; nor
'was His *Manhood* inſenſible of it, under the
'Load of this did he travel: *He alone trod the*
'*Wine-preſs*, &c.—*Not that we would irreve-*
'*rently rob the holy Body of whatſoever Acknow-*
'*ledgement is juſtly due; nor yet ſeparate what*
'*God joined*.—Pag. 104. Chap. 21. A Confeſ-
'ſion in particular to Chriſt's Redemption, Re-
'miſſion, Juſtification and Salvation.—which
'was actually to the Salvation of ſome, and in-
'tentionally of the whole World.—As there was
'a Neceſſity that *one ſhould die for the People*,
'ſo whoever then, or ſince believed in Him,
'had

1699. 'had and have Seal, or Confirmation of the 'Remission of their Sins, in His Blood. — This 'grand Assurance of Remission do all receive, 'in the ratifying Blood of Christ, who repenting 'of their Sins, believe and obey the holy Light, 'with which he hath illuminated them. — Pag. '107. But there is yet a further Benefit that 'accrueth by the Blood of Christ, *viz.* That '*Christ is a Propitiation and Redemption, to such* '*as have Faith in it:* For though I still place 'the Stress of particular Benefit upon the Light, 'Life and Spirit revealed and witnessed in every 'particular; yet in that general Appearance, 'there was a general Benefit, justly to be attri-'buted to the Blood of that very Body of Christ; '*to wit*, That it did propitiate: For however it 'might draw stupendious Judgments upon the 'Heads of those who were Authors of that dis-'mal Tragedy, and died impenitent, yet doubt-'less, it thus far turned to very great Account, 'in that it was a most precious Offering in the 'Sight of the Lord, and drew God's Love the 'more eminently to Mankind; at least, such as 'should believe in his Name. — Pag. 108. Doubt-'less it did greatly influence to some singular 'Tenderness and peculiar Regard unto all such, 'as should believe in his Name, among other 'his weighty Performances: For the Sake of 'that last, and greatest of all His external Acts, 'the *resisting unto Blood*, for the spiritual Good 'of the World, thereby offering His Life upon 'the Cross, through the Power of the eternal 'Spirit, that Remission of Sin, God's Bounty to

'the

'the World, might be preached in His Name, 'and in His very Blood too, as that which was 'the most ratifying of all His bodily Sufferings. 'And indeed, therefore might it seem meet to 'the holy Ghost, that Redemption, Propitia-'tion and Remission should be declared, and 'held forth in the Blood of Christ, unto all that 'have a right Faith therein; as saith the Apo-'stle to the *Romans*; — because it implies a firm 'Belief, that *Christ was come in the Flesh*, and 'that none could then have Him as their *Propi-'tiation* and *Redemption*, who withstood the Ac-'knowledgement of, and Belief in His *visible 'Appearance*. — Pag. 110. Faith in His Blood 'was requisite, that they might confess Him, 'whose Body and Blood it was, to be Christ. 'To conclude, we confess, He who then ap-'peared, was and is the Propitiation, &c. and in 'Him was Redemption obtained by all those, 'who had such true Faith in His Blood.

1699.

'Thus much (and much more which I have 'omitted) against *Deism*, in that very Treatise 'of *W. Penn*'s, to which the Book out of which '*G. Keith*, by his Art of counterfeit *Chymistry* 'would extract *Deism*, was an Appendix; and 'yet this was not the direct Subject of that 'Treatise, but only toucht on occasionally or 'by the by: Should I gather up all Quotations 'on this Argument out of our other Books, 'such especially as have more directly handled 'this Subject, I might therewith fill a large Vo-'lume: To prevent which, I refer the Reader 'to my *Answer to* G. Keith's *first Narrative of*

'*his*

'*his Proceedings at* Turners-hall, from pag. 33.
'to 63, where he may find this Cavil fully con-
'futed. Which Anſwer to his firſt *Narrative*,
'may ſerve for an Anſwer to his other following
'*Narratives* alſo, they for the moſt part being
'but the Scraps of his firſt heated again, and
'ſerved up afreſh with ſome new Garniſh.

'It is obſervable that that Book, called *A
'Diſcourſe of the general Rule of Faith and Life*,
'was firſt printed (as *G. Keith* in his Preface to
'his *Deiſm* takes Notice) in the Year 1673,
'which is twenty ſeven Years ago, and about
'twenty Years before he quite left us; it appears
'he had read it in the firſt Impreſſion; for
'making as if when he ſaw the laſt Impreſſion,
'he did not know but that it was a new Book,
'— *So little had I read or conſidered the Contents
'of it.* Both read it then it ſeems he had, and
'conſidered the Contents of it, and though
'here he would ſuggeſt he had but ſlightly read
'it, yet he would not be taken for an heedleſs
'Reader, or a ſuperficial Conſiderer of what he
'reads. Now ſince he held the ſame Doctrine,
'with reſpect to the *General Rule of Faith and
'Life*, which is laid down by *W. Penn* in that
'Diſcourſe, during the Time he was amongſt
'us, and profeſſed himſelf one of us, as well
'after the publiſhing of that Book in the Year
'1673, as before; and did not only openly de-
'fend and maintain that Doctrine in publick
'Diſputations, both in *England* and in *Scotland*,
'after the Year 1673. But no longer ago than
'in the Year 1692, nineteen Years after that
'Book

'Book of *W. Penn*'s (called *A Discourse of the General Rule of Faith and Life)* was in Print, 'G. Keith in his *Serious Appeal*, pag. 7. says, '*According to the best Knowledge I have of the 'People called* Quakers, *and those most generally 'owned by them, as Preachers and Publishers of 'their Faith, of unquestioned Esteem among them, 'and worthy of double Honour (as many such 'there are) I know none that are guilty of any 'one such Heresies and Blasphemies as thou ac-'cusest them: And I think I should know, and 'do know these called* Quakers, *better than* C. 'Mather (against whom he then writ) *or any 'of his Brethren; having been conversant with 'them, in publick Meetings as well as in private 'Discourse, with the most noted and esteemed 'among them, for above Twenty-eight Years past, 'and that in many Places of the World, in* Europe, '*and for these divers Years in* America. I say, 'all this considered, how will *G. Keith* (upon 'the Charges he now makes against *W. Penn*) 'acquit himself from having been a profest *Deist*, 'all the while he was among the *Quakers*? Yet 'he himself well knows, that neither he, nor '*W. Penn*, nor any of the *Quakers*, ever were '*Deists*; ever did deny, disown, or disbelieve 'the Coming, Incarnation, Sufferings and Death 'of Christ, as Man outwardly in the Flesh, His 'Resurrection, Ascention and Mediatorship; 'and he himself has undesignedly acquitted *W. 'Penn* from his present Charge of *Deism*, by a 'Story he told in his first *Narrative*, pag. 38. That 'upon some urging him to give an Instance of

'one

1699. ‘ of one *English Quaker* that he ever heard pray
‘ to Christ: *W. Penn* being present, said, *I am*
‘ *an* Englishman, *and a* Quaker, *and I own I*
‘ *I have oft prayed to Christ Jesus*; *even Him that*
‘ *was crucified.* This, he says, was in the Year
‘ 1678. Which was five Years after the Pub-
‘ lishing of that Book, from which he attempts
‘ to prove him a *Deist*; that is, a Denier of the
‘ Man Christ Jesus, who was crucified. Judge
‘ now, Reader, how rank the Malice of *G.*
‘ *Keith* must needs be against *W. Penn*, and his
‘ Brethren the *Quakers*, who would choose to
‘ subject himself with them, to the foul Imputa-
‘ tion of *Deism* (though in his own Conscience,
‘ he knows the Charge is false on them, as well
‘ as on himself) rather than not gratify his Envy
‘ and Revenge upon them: In this resembling
‘ the envious Man in the *Apologue*, who desired
‘ that he might lose one of his Eyes, on Con-
‘ dition his Neighbour might lose both his.’

Whence th' Observation rose, a wicked Will
Would wound itself, to work another's Ill.

1700. But before he had finished this Answer (tho' he had gone about two-thirds through it) *Benjamin Coole* of *Bristol*, published a Book there, intituled, *Honesty the truest Policy*; *shewing the Sophistry, Envy and Perversion of* George Keith, *in his three Books*, (viz.) *His* Bristol *Quakerism*, Bristol *Narrative*, and his *Deism*. On Perusal of which, *viz.* his Answer to *G. Keith's Deism*, &c. *T. Ellwood* writ the following Verses.

INDEED

INDEED, is then the Work by me begun, 1700.
And which I labour'd at with ſuch good Will,
Already, by a readier Workman done,
Who Nimbleneſs hath added to his Skill!
Well may it thrive, ſucceſsful may it prove,
Truth's Way to clear, and Stumbling-blocks remove!

I never was ambitious to appear
In Print, nor to myſelf Applauſe have ſought,
With Satisfaction therefore, I can bear
What thou deſign'ſt, another Hand hath wrought;
This ſuperceeds my Work. I'm glad to ſee
Such Help come in, that there's no need of me.

This is the third Time, I have thus been put
Beſides my Work, which makes me think (my Friend)
The controverſial Door to me is ſhut,
And of my ſcribling Service there's an End.
If ſo, content, I can with Pleaſure ſee
The Work well done, altho' not done by me.

The 17th of the Eleventh Month, 1700. T. ELLWOOD.

1700. The three Times he was put besides his Work, of which, he says, this was the third; the other two I suppose, were his *Remarks on* Gerrard Croese's *History of the* Quakers, and his Answer to *the Snake in the Grass* his Book called *Satan disrob'd.* Both before mentioned.

However, this of *B. Coole's* anticipating his Answer to the *Deism,* he laid it by and never finished it, thinking perhaps the other (tho' far short of his) might suffice at present for an Answer thereto; and so we were deprived of his Labour in this respect also: Which yet I hope, one Time or other may be published for the Service of Truth, which it is pity the World should be deprived of.

1701. His next Service, upon a general Foot, which I find any Footsteps of, was on this Occasion: One *John Shockling,* a Priest of *Ash* near *Sandwich* in *Kent,* having got some of the *Snake's* Books, set up for an Opposer or Disputant about *Water-baptism,* and sends a Paper to *John Love,* called, *A Question upon those Words in* Matthew xxviii. 19. *Go ye therefore and teach all Nations, baptizing them in the Name of the Father, and of the Son, and of the Holy Ghost. Whether the Apostles were not commanded by them to baptize with Water?* This Paper and Question our Friend *T. Ellwood* answered in the fourth Month 1701, very much to the Purpose. To which the Priest being unwilling to take an Answer, and let it drop so, replying (I might say to little purpose) *T. Ellwood* writ a Rejoinder, in the fourth Month 1702. Both which,

Answer

Anſwer and Rejoinder, being very pertinent to 1702.
the Purpoſe, and notable on that Subject, I ſhould inſert ſome Part of it, but that it was only private, and never publiſhed that I know of; and therefore I would not begin to be the firſt Publiſher thereof.

But now we come to his great Work of the 1703.
Hiſtory of the Old Teſtament, which, at his Leiſure, he had in hand for ſome Years; and both he and we had this Advantage of his being put by his Work in anſwering Adverſaries, particularly that of the *Snake*, and *G. Keith*'s *Deiſm*, (having now ſeem'd to have done with Controverſy) that he had the more Time and Leiſure to proſecute this more excellent Work; which having finiſhed in 1704, he brought it up to 1704.
London to ſhew it to Friends, for their Peruſal and Approbation. Which being done, it was publiſhed in Folio the next Year 1705, under 1705.
the Title of *Sacred Hiſtory; or the hiſtorical Part of the holy Scriptures of the Old Teſtament. Gathered out from the other Parts thereof, and digeſted (as near as well could be) into due Method, with reſpect to Order of Time and Place: With ſome Obſervations here and there, tending to illuſtrate ſome Paſſages therein.* In his Preface to which, having mentioned the Praiſe of Hiſtory out of *Cicero*, viz. That it is *The Witneſs of Times, the Light of Truth, the Life of Memory*, &c. which he thinks cannot be ſo well verified of any particular Hiſtory, as of that which, being written by divinely-inſpired Penmen, is contained in the Books of the Old and New Teſta-

1705. ment. Then ſpeaking of the Motive or Inducement to the Undertaking, two Things (he ſays) more eſpecially led him to it: One, That the divine Providence, the Wiſdom, Power, Goodneſs and Favour of God, in ordering, diſpoſing, providing for, preſerving, defending, and wonderfully delivering his Servants and People out of the greateſt Straits, Difficulties, Hardſhips, Dangers and Sufferings, being more directly, and in a continued Series and Courſe of Actions ſet before the Reader's Eye, he might be thereby the more ſtirred up, and engaged to admire and magnify, to love, reverence and fear the Lord, and be the more careful not to offend Him. The other Motive was, That all, the Youth eſpecially of either Sex, under whatſoever religious Denomination they go, might be furniſhed with ſuch an Entertainment, to ſpend (at leaſt) their leiſure Hours upon, as might yield them at once both Profit and Delight. After which he proceeds to ſpeak of the Manner of Performance under eight Heads; the Subſtance of which are,

1. That in digeſting the following Hiſtory, he hath not ſtrictly tied himſelf to the Letter and very Syllables of the Text; but with all due Circumſpection and Care to retain the Matter and Senſe, hath ſometimes varied the Expreſſions, *&c.*

2. Where he hath left the laſt *Engliſh* Tranſlation of the BIBLE, he hath followed for the moſt part ſome other *Engliſh* or *Latin*; or the Judgment of ſome eminently learned *Expoſitors.*

3. As

3. As to the Chronology (espically with respect to the Times of the Judges and Kings of *Israel* and *Judah)* he found so much Incertainty, and so little Certainty or Agreement amongst Interpreters about it, that he had a mind to have it left out; but at the Desire of some he added it in the Margin; wherein for the most part he followed *R. Blome*'s History of the Old and New Testament. 1705.

4. The few Helps (he says) he had, were chiefly from Dr. *Gell*'s Essay towards an Amendment of the last *English* Translation of the Bible. *Hugh Broughton*'s Consent of Scripture. *Godwin*'s Moses *and* Aaron. The Annotations of *Tremelius* and *Junius*. And for Names of Persons and Places, the Tables of *Robert F. Herry*.

5. The whole Work is divided into three Parts, without any particular Regard had to the *seven Periods of Time*, into which Chronologers and Historiographers, out of a Desire to reduce them to some Sort of Proportion with the *six Days Work* and *seventh Day's Rest*, in the first Week of the Creation, have generally divided the Ages of the World, from *Adam* until now.

6. Of these three Parts, the first reaches from the Creation to the Death of *Moses*, when the Children of *Israel* being come to the Borders of the promised Land (the second Time) were ready to enter in; and contains the Remarkables in the five Books of *Moses*, taking in *Job* between *Genesis* and *Exodus*.

1705. 7. The ſecond Part beginning with the Book of *Joſhua*, goes through that and the Book of *Judges*, with the firſt Book of *Samuel*, and carries on the Hiſtory from the Death of *Moſes* to the Death of *Saul*, and the Account that was brought to *David* of it. In which are recounted the Tranſactions of chief Note under all the *Judges* and *Saul*, the firſt anointed King of *Iſrael*.

8. The third Part (by much the largeſt) goes on with the ſecond Book of *Samuel*, thro' the reſt of the canonical Scripture, ſets forth the Reigns of the Kings of *Iſrael* and *Judah* throughout the *Jewiſh* Monarchy, with the moſt remarkable Acts and Occurrences therein, from *David* to the Return of the laſt *Babyloniſh* Captivity, and Re-building of the Temple, taking in the Prophets as near as may be, in their ſeveral Times.

Then he gives Account who hath writ on this Subject; particularly a Treatiſe called, *The General View of the holy Scriptures*, ſuppoſed to be the learned *Broughton*'s; which *T. Ellwood* commends as a uſeful Diſcourſe in its kind. And of late Years *Chr. Neſs* his *Hiſtory and Myſtery of the Old and New Teſtament*, in four Volumes; a Book (ſays he) well fraught with Variety of uſeful Matter; but (wittily obſerves) the Myſtery is not only interwoven with the Hiſtory, but hath alſo ſo much overgrown it, that the Reader who deſires to peruſe the Hiſtory by itſelf, will be at ſome Loſs in that reſpect. And that which promiſes moſt to anſwer his End,

he

he ſays, is *R. Blome*'s Hiſtory of the Old and New Teſtament. A Work indeed (ſays he) not only inſtructive and delightful, but pompous and magnificent. A Character that may juſtly be apply'd to his own (except the Word *pompous.)* A Work indeed it is both pleaſant and profitable; ſuch judicious Obſervations, and witty (though grave) Turns on Paſſages and Things, as make it, as well as his other Writings, not only pleaſant to read, but profitable to the Reader. A Work that will remain a Monument of his Worth and Ingenuity to Generations to come. 1705.

I would only add, that there is a Book of *Sulpitius Severus*, intituled, *Sacred Hiſtory*; but as that is in *Latin*, and far ſhort of this of *T. Ellwood*'s, ſo this cannot interfere with that, or be juſtly thought to be in Imitation of it.

About this Time we entred into a more particular Correſpondence by Letters on ſeveral Occaſions, which we continued, at Times, almoſt till his Death. So that I uſually imparted to him the moſt remarkable Occurrences that paſſed here, and often adviſed with him in the moſt important Affairs, as I had Oacaſion: And he, in Requital, was always ready to anſwer me, in a very obliging manner, in any Thing I deſired. And I muſt acknowledge, he was very helpful to me by his Advice, in ſome Controverſies I had with ſome late Adverſaries, which I ſhall not now name, ſome of them being gone to their Graves; and his friendly Correſpondence was always very acceptable, and inſtruc-

1705. tive as well as grateful to me, in his agreeable Letters; of which I have many by me. Some of which he hath inserted in his *Decades*.

1706. The next Year, *viz.* 1706, there followed an Intercourse of some Letters between him and *William Sewell* of *Holland*, upon some particular Points; which led into a friendly Correspondence between them, in some other Matters not unpleasant to read. Several of which Letters of *T. Ellwood*'s, are in his *Decades*, with many others to divers Persons, Friends and others, on various Subjects; which, if ever it should be thought meet to publish them, or any of them, they would, I doubt not, be very instructive as well as diverting.

His next publick Work was on this Occasion. About this Time a Book was published by a nameless Author, called *A divine Treatise, written by way of Essay*, (pretending) *to demonstrate, according to the* Mosaical Philosophy, *Water-baptism, Imposition of Hands, and the Commemoration of the Death and Passion of our ever blessed Lord and Saviour, under the Species of Bread and Wine*, &c. This Treatise coming accidentally or providentially to our Friend *Thomas Ellwood*'s Hands (as he says in his Preface) he observed that the Design of the Author therein was, To re-introduce and set up again those *typical Representations* therein treated of, among those who have been led by the Lord out of the Use thereof, into a more spiritual Dispensation. And finding his Understanding in some measure opened, to see the Danger and Mischief

Mischief of that Undertaking, and his Spirit 1706. withal stirred in him against it, he felt a Concern upon his Mind to publish his *Observations* which he had made thereon, that others might the more clearly see and readily escape the Snare therein laid to entangle them, and draw them into Bondage to outward Ceremonies, and elementary Shadows again. This he did in a Book printed 1707, intituled, *The glorious Brightness* 1707. *of the Gospel Day, dispelling the Shadows of the legal Dispensation, and whatsoever else of human Invention hath been super-added thereunto.* And hoped to make it evident, that they are not of the Nature of the Gospel Dispensation; nor have by any divine Institution a continued Place or Service in the Church of Christ, without taking Notice who or what he was that writ it. 'Since the Author of the Treatise, (says *T. Ellwood*) under my Observation, hath thought 'fit to conceal his Name, I shall not pry behind 'the Curtain which himself hath thereby drawn 'before him, or concern myself to enquire either 'who or what he is, or has been; but without 'any Regard to that, shall directly apply myself 'to give a plain Answer to the most material 'Parts of his Treatise:' Which he did to the Purpose, in a close and nervous Answer; it being indeed an excellent Treatise, well worth the Perusal of every impartial Reader: To whom therefore I recommend it.

And now I must say something of him under another Consideration as well as writing. He had writ several Books against Tithes, as before

1707. fore hinted, to ſhew the Unſuitableneſs of them to the Goſpel Diſpenſation, being *Jewiſh* in their Original, and *Popiſh* in their Revival, and that the Obligation of paying them was ceaſed under the Goſpel, as to any *Divine Right* from Scripture. And now it fell to his Lot to ſuffer alſo in his Turn for his Teſtimony againſt the Payment of them; *for to him it was given, in the Behalf of Chriſt, not only to believe in Him* (and bear witneſs to His coming in the Fleſh, and offering up Himſelf, to put an End to the Law and Prieſthood, Tithes and Offerings) *but alſo to ſuffer for His Sake*, being proſecuted, with three Friends more, *viz. John Penington*, *Abraham Butterfield* and *William Catch*, in the *Exchequer* for Tithes, at the Suit of *Joſhua Leaper*, Tithe-farmer of *Amerſham* in the County of *Bucks*, under *Humphry Drake*, Clerk, Rector and Parſon (ſo called) of the Rectory and Pariſh-Church of *Agmondeſham*, alias, *Amerſham*, aforeſaid. *Thomas Ellwood*, with the reſt, were *Subpœna'd* to appear at *Weſtminſter* in *Trinity-Term* 1707, which they did by an Attorney to prevent being in Contempt of the Court, and took a Copy of the Complainant's Bill. But for not anſwering, Attachments were iſſued out in *Michaelmas-Term* to take them up; on which they were taken into Cuſtody in the eleventh Month, and afterwards an *Habeas Corpus* ſent down to the Sheriff of *Bucks*, to bring them up to the *Exchequer-bar* in *Trinity-Term* 1708, on which they came up. And to prevent the Plantiff's going on to a Sequeſtration

by

by Default, they put in their Anſwers; ſetting 1708.
forth the Value of the Tithes, according to the beſt of their Knowledge. Yet ſo vexatious was the Adverſary, that he would not be ſatisfied with their Anſwer, but got a Commiſſion of *Enquiry* to examine Witneſſes in the Country, as to the Value of the Tithes; which they did at *Amerſham* in the tenth Month. The firſt Witneſs they examined, was one *E*——. *G*——. of the Pariſh of *Cheſſam*, aged (as they ſay) forty four Years or threabouts, who depoſed, *That he knew the Complainant and Defendants; and had known the Complainant about ſixty Years* (which was about ſixteen Years before he was born.) Whereby we may judge of the reſt of his Evidence: The Charge of which Commiſſion, and executing it, came to between thirty and forty Pounds, though ſome of it was abated on taxing the Coſt; and yet they proved little, if any thing more than the Defendants had ſet down in their Anſwers, yet went on to a Hearing on it, and obtain'd a Decree for the Tithes and Coſt. For not performing which, Attachments were iſſued out afreſh againſt them in *Trinity-Term* 1709, to the Sheriff of *Hert-* 1709.
fordſhire (*T. Ellwood*, *A. Butterfield* and *W. Catch* living in that County, but *John Penington* living in *Bucks*, was dropt, becauſe the Attachments to the Sheriff of *Hertfordſhire* would not reach him) and then a Proclamation; but the Sheriff living remote, did not endeavour to take them, and the Proſecutor ſeemed rather to aim at a *Sequeſtration* on their Goods and

Eſtates,

1709. Eſtates, than their Bodies; ſo that ſeeing them reſolved to go on, the Defendants, to prevent it, offer'd to ſurrender themſelves to the Sheriff; but he return'd them each, *Non eſt inventus*, and they got a Commiſſion of *Rebellion* antedated, and moved for a Serjeant at Arms the ſame Day, to run them to a Sequeſtration in all haſte, (*Leaper* being ſick and bad, like to die) leaſt he ſhould not live till it was accompliſh'd; but being ſo *illegal*, at leaſt in point of Time, for that there ought to be eight Days between the *Teſt* and *Return of the Writ*, in thirty Miles off *London*, and fourteen beyond, on our appearing againſt it, they could not obtain it till *Hillary-Term*. In which Time *Leaper* recovered, and one might have hoped that he might have repented; but inſtead thereof, then got a *Sequeſtration* againſt them and their Eſtates, both real and perſonal, for Tithes of *Thomas Ellwood*, which

was but ——— ———	—	12	—
And *Abraham Butterfield*'s ———	15	15	6
And *William Catch*'s ———	16	7	4
And Coſt as tax'd by the Deputy	71	17	8
In all for Tithes and Coſt	104	12	6

For which they ſeized and took from *T. Ellwood* in houſhold Goods, Bedding, Pewter, *&c.* (throwing out the Meat to take the Diſhes) to the Value of 19*l.* and a Horſe he uſed to ride on, which he would not have took five Guineas for. In all about ——— 24 10 — which they ſold (working and hobbling about the

the Horse, till they had almost spoil'd him) for about ——— ———	14	15	—
And from *Abraham Butterfield*, Cattle, Corn, Hay, *&c.* to the Value of ——— ———	86	17	—
which they sold by their own Account for so much. ———	———		
And from *William Catch* they took, by their Account, Grass, *&c.*	8	14	8
and a Year's Rent of his House, (deducting for Taxes, 11 Shillings	2	9	—
being about 3*l.* *per Annum*, which they seized, and kept till paid; which for four Years, since the Time called *Michaelmas* 1709, when they gave in their Account, came to	9	16	—
In all from *W. Catch* about	20	19	8
Seized & taken in the whole about	132	6	8
For Tithes and Cost	104	12	6
More than demanded	27	14	2

all 1709.

And yet, what by Charge of *Sequestration* making out, and selling the Corn; selling underhand, *&c.* they brought in the Defendants in Debt, and wanted more.

I have been the larger in this Account, to shew the Proceeding of the *Exchequer*, and the Fruit of Tithes, to ruin the QUEEN's Subjects for small Matters, when they might recover by Justices Warrants to the Value of 10*l.* with the hundredth Part of the Charge.

Now

1709. Now we come to the ſecond Volume of his great Work, the *Hiſtory of the New Teſtament*; which he had had in hand at Times, for the moſt part ſince he finiſhed his former; and when he had finiſhed this, he brought it up to *London* for Friends Peruſal and Approbation; where it was read, and afterwards publiſhed this Year 1709 in Folio, under the ſame Title with the former, only as that was of the Old Teſtament, this was of the New, *viz. Sacred Hiſtory, or the hiſtorical Part of the holy Scriptures of the New Teſtament*, &c. (as in the Title of the former) which as I gave ſome Account of, ſo it behoves I ſhould of this. The former Treatiſe (ſays he in his Preface) having found a favourable Reception, he was thence encouraged to reſume his Pen (which at the Cloſe of that Volume he had let fall) and proceed to the Methodizing of the hiſtorical Part of the New Teſtament in two Parts. In the firſt Part whereof the Reader will find an Account of the Conception, Birth, Life, Travels, Doctrines, Diſcourſes, Miracles, Sufferings, Death, Burial, Reſurrection and Aſcention of our bleſſed Lord and Saviour JESUS CHRIST (the Author of the true *Chriſtian* Religion) plainly, fairly and ſuccinctly given; uſhered in with a brief Account of the Conception, Birth, Manner of Life, Miniſtry and Death of his Forerunner, *John*, ſirnamed the *Baptiſt*: And attended (in the ſecond Part) with a like hiſtorical Account of the Acts and Travels of the Apoſtles of our Lord, in the Propagation of His bleſſed Goſpel, after

after the Ascention of our blessed Saviour; so 1709.
far, at least, as the Evangelist *Luke*, in the Acts of the Apostles, hath recorded, or the Clue or Thread of the holy Text leads him; beyond which (he says) he was not willing to adventure, *&c.*

In this Undertaking, he says, he aimed at the same End as in the former, *viz.* That all the Youth especially of either Sex, under whatsoever religious Denomination they go, might be further furnished with such an Entertainment, to spend, at least, their leisure Hours upon, as might yield them at once both Profit and Delight; and might be thereby drawn off from mis-pending their precious Time upon other, either hurtful, or (at best) unprofitable Subjects. Then he gives Account why he hath, with the Matter of Fact, delivered the Discourses, Speeches, Sermons and Doctrines delivered by our blessed Lord to his Disciples, *&c.* viz. That the Nature of the History required it, and that without it the Discourse would have been less profitable and pleasant to the Reader, and by that Means less conducive to the End he proposed, which is to allure him to read the holy Scriptures with Delight, *&c.* according to the Poet,

Omnia tulit punctum, qui miscuit utile dulci.

He certainly doth hit the White,
Who mingleth Profit with Delight.

After

1709. After which he gives an Account of his going from Place to Place in the Evangeliſts, to reduce the ſeveral Parts and Paſſages of the Hiſtory (in the firſt Part) to their due and proper Times and Places, which he endeavoured to do, (tho' difficult) as near as he could. But the ſecond Part (the *Acts*) being all written by one Hand, the Method (he ſays) is more regular, and the Courſe of the Hiſtory more clear. Yet the Apoſtolical Epiſtles being without Date, are hardly, he conceives, to be reduced with indubitable Certainty to exact Order; which yet he hath endeavour'd to place them right, according to the beſt of his Underſtanding. Then owning the Helps he had in compiling this Hiſtory, had been chiefly from the Criticks, and *Cradock's Harmony of the four Evangeliſts*, and his *Apoſtolical Hiſtory*, with a few Words of the Performance; which if not done as it ſhould (nor as he would) yet as well as he could; and therefore, in all Humility, recommending and committing it to the divine Diſpoſal, he concludes his Preface.

Next to the Preface is an Introduction, concerning the Penmen of the New Teſtament, and in what Language originally written, and in what Order of Time; particularly of the four Evangeliſts, *Matthew*, *Mark*, *Luke* and *John*, what they were, the Time of their writing, and ſome particular Circumſtances concerning them and their Ends; well worth the Readers peruſal, for the better underſtanding the Hiſtory, both of the Evangeliſts and Apoſtles. So proceeds to the

the Hiſtory; which he deduces from the *Promiſed Seed* after the Fall, for Man's Reſtoration, which the Prophets foretold the Coming of, and which he pleaſantly draws out at large in Order of Time; and explains with the like judicious Obſervations as in the former, taking in the Epiſtles of St. *Paul*, &c. (in the ſecond Part) in their proper Places (as near as could be) and gives an Account of them, the Occaſion why, the Manner how, and Time when they were written; ending with the Revelations, which he renders as a Revelation unrevealed; with ſome brief Notes on it. The whole, as I ſaid of the former, being both pleaſant and profitable. Both which will remain a laſting Monument of him in Time to come. 1709.

This Year 1710, our Friend *Oliver Sanſom*, formerly of *Faringdon*, ſince of *Abington* in *Berkſhire*, who had long War with the Prieſts about Tithes, dying in the ſecond Month, and leaving behind him *An Account of ſome remarkable Paſſages of his Life*, which he communicated in his Life-time to our Friend *T. Ellwood* to peruſe, who being always ready to be helpful and ſerviceable to all; eſpecially his Friends, he tranſcribed the ſame, and fitted it for the Preſs, which was printed this Year; to which *T. Ellwood* prefixed a Teſtimony concerning him, pertinent to the Occaſion, 1710.

There is one Book more of his, which he publiſhed in his Life-time, which it ſeems he had had by him, for the moſt part, a long Time, and after he had finiſhed his *Sacred Hiſtory of the New*

1710. *Testament*, he took in hand to finish, and compleated; and that is *The Life of* DAVID *in Verse*; first begun (for his own Diversion, not then thinking of the Press) and carried on, by degrees, to the End of the third Book, in the Year 1688, as hinted before in that Year, when the Prince of *Orange* landing, and the Nation being in Arms, the Noise of Guns, and Sounds of Drums and Trumpets so affrighted and disturbed his peaceful Muse (as he says in his Preface) that both she for a while forsook him, and he thereupon the Work, for above twenty Years; save that on a Review, observing how abruptly *David* was brought in, he added the first Chapter of the first Book, to introduce his Hero from the Beginning of his Story. Where it rested again, without any Prospect of its ever
1711. going further, until the last Winter, (1711) when having (as he says) less Health and more Leisure, than at some Times before, he took it up for an Entertainment, to make some uneasy Hours pass somewhat less uneasily over. And after he had read it through, considering that if, after his Death, it should be found among his Papers and committed to the Press, it would be but an imperfect Piece; he found an Inclination to carry on the Story to the End of *David*'s Life, (I wish he had done so by his own) and giving a kind Invitation to his gentle Muse to return (which by some short Visits on particular Occasions in the Interval, had given him some Ground to hope she had not quite forsook him) he entred again upon the Subject where he had

left

left off, and by degrees went through it, till he 1711.
had brought his *warlike Hero* to his *peaceful* ⁓
Grave.

After it was finiſhed, deliberating whether to publiſh it himſelf, or leave it as a *Poſthume*, to be publiſhed by ſome kind Hand after his Death; for ſome Reaſons particularly, That if any ſhould *carp* at it, he might be capable to anſwer for himſelf, he thought beſt to publiſh it in his Life-time; and accordingly brought it up with him, when he came to the Yearly-meeting
1712, but not having then an Opportunity to 1712.
have it read, he came up again with it ſome ⁓
Time after (which I think was the laſt Time he was at *London*) and after reading, committed it to the Preſs this Year, under the Title of *DAVIDEIS*. *The Life of* David, *King of* Iſrael. *A ſacred Poem, in five Books in* Octavo. Tho', as he obſerves, *Abraham Cowley* writ a Poem called *Davideis*, he had not read it till after he had finiſhed his; and beſides, their different way of writing, *A. Cowley*'s was but of the Troubles of *David* in his Youth, and that not half finiſhed. And that he had the ſame Aim in this, as in that of his *Sacred Hiſtory* aforeſaid. Which Book begins thus:

I ſing the Life of *David*, *Iſrael*'s King,
Aſſiſt, Thou ſacred Pow'r who didſt him bring
From the Sheepfold, and ſet him on the Throne,
Thee I invoke, on Thee rely alone.

1712. Breathe on my Muſe, and fill her ſlender Quill
With Thy refreſhing Dews from *Hermon-hill*;
That what ſhe ſings may turn unto Thy Praiſe,
And to Thy Name may laſting Trophies raiſe.

But I would not anticipate the Reader, but leave him to read and judge for himſelf, as it deſerves.

I ſhall conclude his Works and Writings, with a Copy of Verſes he formerly writ; which though out of Courſe as to Time, is ſo well worth the inſerting, that I hope they will make amends for being miſ-placed, *viz.*

O That mine Eye might cloſed be,
To what becomes me not to ſee!
That Deafneſs might poſſeſs mine Ear,
To what concerns me not to hear!
That *Truth* my Tongue might always tie,
From ever ſpeaking fooliſhly!
That no vain Thought might ever reſt,
Or be conceived in my Breaſt!
That by each Word, each Deed, each
Thought,
Glory may to my God be brought!
But what are Wiſhes? Lord! mine Eye
On Thee is fixt, to Thee I cry:
O purge out all my Droſs, my Tin,
Make me more white than Snow within;

Waſh,

Waſh, Lord, and purify my Heart,
And make it clean in every Part,
And when 'tis clean, Lord keep it too,
For that is more than I can do.

T. E.

Thus having gone through his printed Books and Papers, which I have endeavoured to give a plain and ſuccinct Account of, and of him out of them, as far as I could, and with as much Brevity as well might be, I ſhall now ſpeak ſomewhat of him in his private Capacity, and other Services and Station in the Church, with his Death and Character; and ſo conclude the whole.

He lived many Years, if not moſt of his Time, eſpecially after he was married, at *Hunger-hill* in the Pariſh of *Agmondeſham*, alias, *Amerſham* in *Buckinghamſhire*, though his Houſe ſtood in *Hertfordſhire* as aforeſaid; where the Monthly-meetings of Men and Women were conſtantly kept, for that Part of the County of *Bucks*: Wherein he was very ſerviceable in writing, adviſing, and exhorting to keep all Things well and in good Order, according to Truth and the Teſtimony thereof; and had a peculiar Gift for Government in the Church, and ordering Things in Monthly and Quarterly-meetings, and uſed to come up conſtantly to the Yearly-meeting at *London*, and was very ſerviceable therein; not only by his grave

 Counſel

1712. Counsel and Advice, but also in reading and writing on Occasion, especially in difficult Matters. He had a singular Talent in indicting and composing of Things, Epistles and Papers, beyond many; so that I must needs say, he was an Ornament to the Meeting, and will be much missed therein, and many other ways. His Wife died about five Years before him, being a solid weighty Woman, who had a publick Testimony for the Lord and His Truth in Meetings; and therefore the greater Loss to him and Friends: And for himself, he lived a private retired Life, not concerning himself with much Business in the World, but gave himself much to reading and writing, and lived in good Repute among Friends, and all Sorts of People, as far as ever I heard of, to a pretty good Age; but bore his Age very well, being of a regular Life and healthy Constitution; only in his latter Years was somewhat troubled at times with an *Asthma*; and at last he was taken ill of a *Palsy*,
1713. the 23d of the second Month 1713, which he bore with great Patience and Resignation; an Account of which, and his dying Words, I leave to them who were with him in the Time of his Sickness, the eighth Day of which he departed this Life, being the 1st of the third Month, in the seventy fourth Year of his Age, *having served his Generation according to the Will of God, he fell asleep*, and was honourably buried the Second-day following, being the 4th of the third Month, at *Jordans*; being accompanied from his own House by a great many Friends and others, to

the

the Meeting-houſe there (the Meeting he belong'd to) and interr'd in the Burying-ground belonging thereto, where was a very large Meeting, and great Appearance of Friends and others, ſeveral publick Friends being there from *London*, and other Parts; and divers living Teſtimonies borne to the Truth he lived and died in, in a living Remembrance of him, and his Services in the Church. A Man of a comely Aſpect, of a free and generous Diſpoſition, of a courteous and affable Temper, and pleaſant Converſation; a Gentleman born and bred, a Scholar, a true *Chriſtian*, an eminent Author, a good Neighbour, and kind Friend; whoſe Loſs is much lamented, and will be much miſſed at home and abroad. The Lord, if it be His Will, raiſe up many more ſuch Pillars, Elders and Overſeers of His Flock and Family, as Watchmen upon *Sion*'s Walls, for His Honour and the Benefit of His Church and People, ſaith my Soul, *Amen*.

London, *the 30th of the ninth Month*, 1713.

J. WYETH.

POSTSCRIPT.

SINCE the writing of the foregoing *Supplement*, I have underſtood that our Friend *Thomas Ellwood*, after he had finiſhed and publiſhed his *Davideis*, ſignified, *That he had but one Thing more that lay upon his Mind*; and that was, *to add ſomething to his* Journal, *or Account of his* Life; *which was chiefly to give an Account*

 of

of his Books *and* Writings: Which, as it ſhews he had not done it, or finiſhed it before, and 'tis to be doubted he did not after (not living long after that) and ſo no more to be expected (more's the Pity) from his own Hand. So it ſhews what his Deſign was, as to what he intended to have added to it, had he lived to perform it, or had not Death prevented him. So that the foreſaid *Supplement* ſeems (in ſome Sort at leaſt) to anſwer his own Intention, though far ſhort, as was ſaid, of what his own Hand could have done; yet ſo far as it does any Way anſwer his Mind, I am therein glad that I have done any Service to his Memory, or the Truth in that reſpect, having endeavoured to repreſent Things according to his own Mind, and to ſpeak of him and Things as probably he would have done if he had been living, and hope the Reader will accept it the better. To whom therefore I recommend it, as giving at leaſt, a fair Character of the Books he writ, and Controverſies he managed, both publiſhed and unpubliſhed; which I hope will be no Diſſervice (but Service) to the *Truth*, as it is intended in the Fear of God: To whoſe Honour, and the Service of His *Truth*, I deſire with great Sincerity, to dedicate the Remainder of my Days, and reſt

A Friend to all Men.

J. WYETH.

A Catalogue of his printed Books before mentioned.

About 464 Sheets.

A LIST of the MANUSCRIPTS he left behind him.

1. AN *Answer to a Paper directed to the Members of the Society of* Quakers, *especially to those that frequent the Town of* Feversham (*in* Kent) 1672. To which the Priest replying, *T. Ellwood* writ a *Rejoinder*, very notable, and worth the Publishing. The whole about 15 Sheets, in 1672, or 1673.
2. *His Reply, or Rejoinder to the Priests second Book, called* The Right of Tythes Re-asserted, 46 Sheets. About 1681.
3. *Some Remarks on* Gerard Croese's *General History of the* Quakers, *in* Latin, 3 or 4 Sheets. About 1995, or 1696.
4. *A Rejoinder to the* Snake in the Grass, *his Book called* Satan disrob'd, *in Reply to* T. Ellwood's *Answer to* G. Keith's Narrative, 27 Sheets. 1696.
5. *Some Instructions for Children.* About 2 Sheets.
6. *An Answer to* G. Keith's *Deism of* W. Penn *and his Brethren.* 37 Sheets. 1700.
7. *An Answer to* John Shockling, *Priest of* Ash *near* Sandwich *in* Kent, *concerning Baptism*, 1701, and a *Rejoinder to his Reply*, 1702, both about 3 Sheets.
8. *The Tithe Dialogue improved, for the better explaining the present State of Tithes, by the same Method of a Dialogue, supposed to be holden between a Titheman and a* Quaker. 6 Sheets. 1707.
9. *A Volume of Miscellany* Poems, about 20 Sheets.
10. *Several Decades of Letters to particular Persons*, about 35 Sheets.
11. *To* Robert Snow, *in Answer to his Objections.*
12. *An Account of Tithes in general.*

An INDEX *of the Names of* Persons *and* Places, *and some particular Things.*

Canterbury

Married

Hersent

Moor

Predestination

Toleration

Papers in this Book.

F I N I S.

AN Account of the Life and Travels of *Samuel Bownas*. The ſecond Edition, price 2*s*.

The Life of *Deborah Bell*, price 9*d*.

The Life of *Richard Claridge*; together with a Collection of his Poſthumous Works, price 5*s*.

The Life of *John Crook*, price 4*d*.

The Life of *William Crouch*, price 1*s*. 6*d*.

The Life of *Joſeph Coale*, price 1*s*.

The Life of *Richard Davies*. The ſecond Edition, price 1*s*.

The Life of *William Edmundſon*, price 3*s*.

The Life and Works of *Benjamin Holmes*, pr. 2*s*.

The Life and Works of *David Hall*, price 2*s*.

The Life of *Alice Hays*. The ſecond Edition, price 6*d*.

The Life of *Roger Haydock*, price 2*s*.

The Life of *Luke Howard*, price 1*s*. 6*d*.

The Life of *Gilbert Latey* price 1*s*.

The Life of *John Peters*, price 9*d*.

The Life of *Ambroſe Rigg*, price 3*s*.

The Life of *John Richardſon*. The ſecond Edition, price 2*s*. 6*d*.

The Life of *Oliver Sanſom*, price 3*s*.

The Life of *Chriſtopher Story*, price 1*s*.

The Life of *Elizabeth Stirridge*. The Second Edition, price 1*s*.

The Life of *Thomas Taylor*, price 4*s*.

The Life of *John Taylor* of *York*, price 6*d*.

The Life of *George Whitehead*, price 5*s*. 6*d*.

The Life of *Samuel Watſon*, price 1*s*. 6*d*.

Sacred Hiſtory: Or the hiſtorical Part of the holy Scriptures of the Old and New Teſtament, digeſted into due Method, with Reſpect to Order of Time and Place, with ſome Obſervations tending to illuſtrate the ſame; in one Volume folio, large Paper, by *Thomas Ellwood*. The ſecond Edition, pr. 1*l*. 5*s*.

Davidies, the Life of *David* King of *Israel*: A sacred Poem; by *Thomas Ellwood*. The fourth Edition, price 2*s*. 6*d*.

A Collection of Poems on various Subjects, (never before printed) by *Thomas Ellwood*, price 6*d*.

Counsel to the Christian Traveller, by *William Shewen*. The second Edition, price 1*s*.

Useful Instruction for Children, by way of Question and Answer, by *Abiah Darby*. The second Edition, price 4*d*.

The History of the Rise, Increase, and Progress of the People called *Quakers*; intermixed with several remarkable Occurrences, by *William Sewell*. The second Edition, price 14*s*.

No Cross, no Crown: a Discourse shewing the Nature and Discipline of the holy Cross of Christ; and that the Denial of Self, and daily bearing of Christ's Cross, is the alone Way to the Rest and Kingdom of God. To which are added, the living and dying Testimonies of many Persons of Fame and Learning, both of Ancient and Modern Times, in Favour of this Treatise. By *William Penn*. The tenth Edition, price 3*s*. 6*d*.

Reflections and Maxims, relating to the Conduct of human Life, by *W. Penn*. The seventh Edition, price, 1*s*. 6*d*.

Fruits of a Father's Love; being the Advice of *William Penn* to his Children. The second Edition, price 6*d*.

A brief Account of the Rise and Progess of the People called *Quakers*, in which their Fundamental Principle, Doctrines, Worship, Ministry, and Discipline, are plainly declared. By *W. Penn*. The sixth Edition, price 1*s*.

The *Christian-Quaker*, and his divine Testimony, stated and vindicated from Scripture, Reason and Authority, by *W. Penn*, price 2*s*.

Primitive

Primitive Christianity revived, in the Faith and Practice of the People called *Quakers*, by *W. Penn*, price 8*d*.

A Key; opening the Way to every Capacity, how to distinguish the Religion professed by the *Quakers*, from the Perversions and Misrepresentations of their Adversaries; by *W. Penn*. The fifteenth Edition, price 4*d*. in *English* or *French*.

Solomon's Recantation, intituled *Ecclesiastees*, paraphrased; with a Meditation on every Chapter. A Poem, by *Francis Quarles*, price 6*d*.

An Essay concerning the Restoration of primitive Christianity, by *Thomas Beaven*. The second Edition, price 1*s*.

Scripture Truths demonstrated, in 32 Sermons, or Declarations of *Stephen Crisp*, price 3*s*.

The Harmony of Divine and Heavenly Doctrines, demonstrated in sundry Declarations on Variety of Subjects, preached at the *Quakers* Meetings in *London*, by *William Penn*, *George Whitehead*, *Samuel Waldenfield*, and *Benjamin Coole*, price 1*s*. 6*d*.

The Grounds of a holy Life; or the Way by which many who were Heathens came to be renowned Christians, by *Hugh Turford*. The eigth Edition, price 9*d*.

The Spirit of the Martyrs revived, in a brief compendious Collection of the most remarkable Passages, and living Testimonies of the faithful Martyrs in all Ages, price 5*s*.

An Abridgement of *Eusebius Pamphilius*'s Ecclesiastical History, by *William Caton*, price 1*s*. 6*d*.

The enormous Sin of Covetousness detected; with its Branches, Fraud, Oppression, Lying and Ingratitude. By *William Crouch*, price 2*s*.

Some Considerations relating to the present State of the Christian Religion, in three Parts, by *Alexander Arscott*. The second Edition, price 2*s*. 6*d*.

A Letter

A Letter from *Josiah Martin* to *Francis de Voltaire*, occasioned by his Remarks on the *Quakers*, in his Letters concerning the *English* Nation. The second Edition, price 6*d*.

The Trial of Spirits, both in Teachers and Hearers. By *William Dell*, late Master of *Convil* and *Caius* College in *Cambridge*. The second Edition, pr. 1*s*. 6*d*.

The Doctrine of Baptisms, reduced from its ancient and modern Corruptions, and restored to its primitive Soundness and Integrity, by *W. Dell*. The seventh Edition, price 6*d*.

The spiritual Worship and Service of God exalted, and acceptably performed only in the Spirit of Christ. By *George Myers*, price 9*d*.

The Archbishop of *Cambray*'s Desertation on pure Love; with an Account of the Life and Writings of the Lady *Guion*, for whose sake he was banished from Court; and the grievous Persecutions she suffered in *France* for her Religion. The third Edition, price 3*s*.

Memoirs of the Life and Convincement of *John Whiting*; together with the Characters of many eminent Friends, price 2*s*.

Christ's Spirit a Christian's Strength, by *W. Dell*, price 6*d*.

God's Protecting Providence, Man's surest Help and Defence in Times of greatest Danger, evidenced in the remarkable Deliverance of several Persons who suffered Shipwreck in the Gulph of Florida; faithfully related by one concerned therein. *J. Dickenson*. The fourth Edition, price 1*s*.

The Foundation of Tithes shaken; and the four principal Posts, *viz.* Divine Institution, primitive Practice, voluntary Donations, and positive Laws, are removed; by *T. Ellwood*. The second Edition, price 4*s*.

The glorious Brightness of the Gospel-day, dispelling the Shadows of the legal Dispensation. By *T. Ellwood*, price 1*s*.

A brief

A brief Hiſtory of the cruel Sufferings of *Katherine Evans* and *Sarah Chevers*, in the Inquiſition on the Iſle of *Malta*, price 1*s*.

A Collection of Epiſtles, writ by *George Fox*, price 10*s*. in folio.

A Collection of his doctrinal Books, in folio, price 18*s*.

The Works of *Margaret Fox*, Wife of *G. Fox*, price 4*s*.

A Treatiſe concerning the Fear of God, ſcripturally recommended, from the Example of the Patriarchs, Prophets, Kings and Judges, by *John Field*, price 1*s*.

Piety Promoted; being a Collection of the dying Sayings of many of the People called *Quakers*, in ſeven Parts, price 1*s*. each.

A Treatiſe concerning Tithes, by *John Gratton*, price 6*d*.

A Treatiſe concerning Baptiſm and the Lord's Supper, by *J. Gratton*, price 9*d*.

Chriſt the only Sacrifice and Altar, by *C. Goad*, price 4*d*.

An Exortation to the Inhabitants of South *Carolina*, by *Sophia Hume*; in which is inſerted, an Account of the Author's Experience in the important Buſineſs of Religion. price 1*s*.

A ſecond Epiſtle to the Inhabitants of S. *Carolina*, by *S. Hume*, price 9*d*.

A ſerious Addreſs to the People of the Church of *England*, in ſome Obſervations upon their own Catechiſm, by *John Jeffrys*; to which is added an Account of his Life; price 3*d*.

Miſcellaneous Poems, moral and divine, by *Mary Mollineaux*, the fifth Edition, price 1*s*. 6*d*.

A Collection of the Works and Life of *Charles Marſhall*, price 2*s*.

A Collection of the Works of *James Nailer*, with an Account of the moſt remarkable Paſſages of his Life. price 6*s*.

A Light

A Light ſhining out of Darkneſs; being Diſcourſes concerning the Miniſtry, Inſpiration, the Scriptures, Oaths, Tithes, *&c.* By an indifferent, but learned Hand; the third Edition, price 1*s.* 6*d.*

Chriſtian Epiſtles, on ſundry Occaſions, in Verſe; by *William Maſſey*. The ſecond Edition, price 6*d.*

A comprehenſive Diſcourſe of the Faith and Practice of a true Chriſtian, by *W. Penn*, price 1*s.*

William Penn's Reflections and Maxims, relating to the Conduct of human Life, turn'd into Verſe, by another Hand, price 1*s.*

A Defence of a Paper intituled *Goſpel Truths*, againſt the Exceptions of the Biſhop of *Cork*'s Teſtimony; by *W. Penn*, price 1*s.*

Tender Counſel and Advice, by way of Epiſtle, to all thoſe who are ſenſible of their Day of Viſitation; by *W. Penn*, the fourth Edition, price 4*d.*

A Collection of Teſtimonies, concerning ſeveral Miniſters of the Goſpel amongſt the People called *Quakers*, deceaſed: With ſome of their laſt Expreſſions and Exhortations; price 3*s.*

New-England judg'd; containing a Relation of the cruel Sufferings of the People call'd *Quakers* in *New-England*, from their firſt Arrival there in 1656, to the Year 1665. By *George Biſhop*. To which is added, An Anſwer to *Cotton Mather*'s Abuſes of the ſaid People, in his Hiſtory of *New-England*. price 5*s.*

A Treatiſe concerning Baptiſm, and the Supper; ſhewing that the one Baptiſm of the Spirit, and ſpiritual Supper of the Lord, are only and alone eſſential and neceſſary to Salvation By *Joſeph Pike*, price 1*s.* 6*d.*

Truth's Vindication: Or, a gentle Stroke to wipe off the foul Aſperſions, falſe Accuſations, and Miſrepreſentations, caſt upon the People called *Quakers*, both with reſpect to their Principles, and their proſelyting People over to them. By *Elizabeth Bathurſt*, price 1*s.*

www.ingramcontent.com/pod-product-compliance
Lightning Source LLC
Chambersburg PA
CBHW052337110726
47901CB00005B/1267
9783337775254